The Professionalization of Coaching

Astrid Schreyögg
Christoph Schmidt-Lellek
Editors

The Professionalization of Coaching

A Reader for the Coach

Springer

Editors
Astrid Schreyögg
Berlin, Germany

Christoph Schmidt-Lellek
Oberursel, Germany

ISBN 978-3-658-16804-9 ISBN 978-3-658-16805-6 (eBook)
DOI 10.1007/978-3-658-16805-6

Library of Congress Control Number: 2017930615

This book was advertised with a copyright holder in the name of the author(s) in error, whereas the publisher holds the copyright.
Previously published in German under the title "Die Professionalisierung von Coaching". Please note that the German original features some chapters not included in the English edition.

Printed on acid-free paper

This Springer imprint is published by Springer Nature
The registered company is Springer Fachmedien Wiesbaden GmbH
The registered company address is: Abraham-Lincoln-Str. 46, 65189 Wiesbaden, Germany

Contents

Contributors

Dr. Thomas Bachmann Dipl.-Psych., artop, Humboldt-Universität, Berlin, Germany

Gabriele Bollhöfer Dipl.-Psych., Cologne, Germany

Prof. Dr. Ferdinand Buer Münster, Germany

Thomas Dallüge Dipl.-Phys., Dipl.-Psych., Trinfactory GmbH, Berlin, Germany

Dr. Beate Fietze Dipl.-Soz., Dipl.-Psych., Berlin, Germany

Prof. Dr. Harald Geißler Helmut-Schmidt-Universität, Hamburg, Germany

Prof. Dr. Siegfried Greif Dipl.-Psych., Osnabrück, Germany

Denise Elisabeth Hinn M.Sc., Universität Kassel, Kassel, Germany

Stella Kanatouri Helmut-Schmidt-Universität, Hamburg, Germany

Dr. Silja Kotte Dipl.-Psych., Universität Kassel, Kassel, Germany

Prof. Dr. Heidi Möller Dipl.-Psych., Universität Kassel, Kassel, Germany

Katrin Oellerich Dipl.-Psych., Universität Kassel, Kassel, Germany

Dr. Christoph Schmidt-Lellek Oberursel, Germany

Dr. Astrid Schreyögg Dipl.-Psych., Berlin, Germany

Prof. Dr. Ulrich Schueler Dipl.-Psych., Dipl.-Inform., Hoisdorf b. Hamburg, Germany

Dr. Cornelia Seewald Düsseldorf, Germany

Ingo Steinke Dipl.-Psych., COATRAIN, Hamburg, Germany

Dr. Beate West-Leuer Neuss, Germany

Introduction

The Professionalization of Coaching as a Continuous Process

The developments in the fields of coaching continue to progress. It has become all but impossible to keep track of the number and variety of offerings, areas of application, concepts, and themes related to coaching, or the attempts at structuring the field, e.g., via the founding of professional associations. Efforts at providing a scientific basis, e.g., in the form of effectiveness studies, have also grown significantly. In all this, it has become even more important to reflect on the conceptual fundamentals of coaching: What exactly are we talking about when we speak of coaching? How does it differ from other forms of professional consultation? What basic concepts and competencies should we expect—or even require—a professional coach to have? How can professional coaching be described and be distinguished from "charlatanry" (i.e., from apparent quality without any actual professional content; cf. Kühl 2006, p. 88)? Because there are no generally binding statutory definitions and quality standards as there are for other professions such as in the medical professions and psychotherapy, we as coaches are faced with the challenge of coming up with these regulations ourselves, and to provide options that practicing coaches and academics—but also potential users of coaching services—can use as a basis of orientation.

This is what the German Federal Association of Executive Coaching (DBVC) has dedicated itself to since being founded in 2004. In this book, we aim to continue to honor the high requirements placed on the professionalism of coaches as represented by the DBVC. These requirements have already been formulated in the "DBVC Compendium" ("Coaching as a Profession," 1st ed., 2007, now in its 4th, expanded edition, 2012; the English edition can be accessed online for free:

www.dbvc.de/publikationen). The compilation of the Compendium was commissioned by the DBVC board in the "Fachausschuss Profession" (FAP) expert committee. This was decided in a complex voting procedure at the members' meeting of the DBVC. In this manner, it was able to acquire a relatively high degree of authority with regard to its definitional and qualitative standards, as it can now be viewed as being binding for all DBVC members. Furthermore, it also enjoys a certain degree of recognition in the entire coaching world, as it has been cited in a large number of academic publications. Despite its success, the Compendium is not to be seen as a final standard. This is because developments in coaching continue to progress; new issues and problem complexes emerge all the time, which require new answers and new concepts. This book serves as yet another milestone in an ongoing process.

Hence, the contributions published here are a continuation and an in-depth analysis of the discussions which were initiated by the Compendium. This book, too, owes its existence to the "Fachausschuss Profession" expert committee, which currently comprises the following members: Dr. Thomas Bachmann, Gabriele Bollhöfer, Thomas Dallüge, Dr. Beate Fietze, Dr. Christoph Schmidt-Lellek, Dr. Astrid Schreyögg, Ingo Steinke, and Dr. Thomas Stölzel. However, this volume follows a different format: While the Compendium follows a strict system, this book offers a collection of contributions that are independent in nature, even if there are many common threads and references between the individual chapters. This is because all chapters were read by FAP members and discussed in depth at the working meetings in Berlin. In this respect, this book is a collaborative effort by the FAP.

Our overarching topic of "Coaching as a Profession" will be outlined here with preliminary information. Our use of the term "profession" makes us part of a powerful tradition, as the sociologist Beate Fietze points out (Chap. 1). However, coaching is not a profession in the strict sense of the word, as there are no regulated access pathways to this practice; i.e., there is no state-approved license and mandate, nor a market monopoly defined by them. Despite this, there is a clear trend toward the professionalization of coaching. This can be "seen in the growth in the subject-specific generation of knowledge and the academization of professional and further qualifications, as well as the expansion and intensification of the degree of organization of all involved parties" (Fietze, Chap. 1, p. 8). It is precisely these developments that all chapters of this book aim to describe, support, and substantially enrich.

However, the fact that coaching does not consist of a profession in the full sense of the word (cf. Kühl 2008) also results in a valuable advantage. Namely, this facilitates a greater openness toward novel approaches without resulting in a loss of "standards for ethics, qualifications, basic dialogical attitudes, the use of concepts and methods, and quality assurance" (DBVC 2012, p. 11). This also clearly shows that professionalization is not a process with a defined end. This can also be seen as a particular characteristic of coaching: As a business-oriented form of counseling, it is in a unique position to serve as a seismograph for developments—both innovations and deformations—in the economy and society. This is because, in the free space that coaching sessions offer, these developments—in addition to individual, personal issues—can come to light and be discussed. But new problem complexes sometimes also require new or advanced concepts to be able to support the appropriate perception, understanding, and acting in coaching processes in each case. Yet this does not mean that there is no continued development in other professions; this is because the orientation toward science and research, as well as the resulting updates to the corresponding fields of expert knowledge, is one of the characteristics that defines professions per se. However, coaching—which is understood as an open space for discussion between equals—has particularly challenging requirements when it comes to a professionally informed self-reflection with regard to the concepts, methods, and in particular value orientations, which need to be questioned anew all the time. It is this professional self-reflection that the contributions in this book aim to stimulate. The aim of this lies not only in the professional advancement of the coach, but also equally in the cultivation of the reflection space that is coaching. As Greif (2008) described, coaching can above all be understood as a manual for a "results-oriented self-reflection."

A few remarks about terminology: With the translation of this book, we enter the English-speaking world, where some terms are used differently than in German. To bring the understanding of "coaching," which informs the German discussion, to bear on the English translation, it is first of all necessary to reflect on the central term "consultation" (*Beratung*). In German, there is a difference between a "transitive" and a "reflexive" form of consultation (cf. Fietze, Chap. 1 in this book). Transitive consultation deals with the imparting of expertise by experts and is usually translated as "consulting." With "reflexive" consultation, which comes nearest to our understanding of coaching (cf. Greif 2008), the effort consists in the development of expertise in the process of consultation itself; that is, the reflexive self-reference of the client is systematically encouraged and becomes the real source from which a solution for the particular problems is developed in dialogue with the counselor—this can be translated as "counseling." But since these two forms of the coaching practice inevitably overlap and since the authors of this book think and act from different contexts, this terminological differentiation could not be maintained consistently. And frequently, the more general term "consultation" is used.

This book is subdivided into four parts. In Part I, the articles discuss issues that are constitutive for professions, particularly the—rather disputed—relationship between the sciences and the "translation" of general expert knowledge for application in individual case scenarios. This takes place in the context of the unique relationship between the involved persons (cf. DBVC 2012, p. 13). In Part II, the specific characteristics of coaching are illustrated by discussing delineations and overlaps with regard to other formats of consultation (cf. DBVC 2012, p. 26 ff.). Part III comprises contributions that discuss the issue of "Knowledge and competences in coaching" (cf. DBVC 2012, p. 33 ff.). This mainly consists of meta-theoretical standpoints that have only very seldom been discussed for coaching thus far, but which offer a great deal of material for the professional reflection on coaching processes. In the final part, "Conceptual Variations of Coaching" will be introduced; i.e., new approaches and working modes of coaching, which have only rarely been reflected on and examined.

We would like to take this opportunity to express our heartfelt thanks to all colleagues who collaborated in the "Fachausschuss Profession" expert committee, as well as all others who contributed to this book. We hope that this book will stimulate further discussion, and look forward to feedback, critique and supplemental contributions that will enable the continued professionalization of coaching.

Astrid Schreyögg
Christoph Schmidt-Lellek

References

DBVC—Deutscher Bundesverband Coaching e.V. (Hrsg.) (2012). *Leitlinien und Empfehlungen für die Entwicklung von Coaching als Profession. Kompendium mit den Professionsstandards des DBVC* (4., erw. Aufl.). Osnabrück: DBVC Geschäftsstelle; Engl. Version http://www.dbvc.de/publikationen

Greif, S. (2008). *Coaching und ergebnisorientierte Selbstreflexion*. Göttingen: Hogrefe.

Kühl, S. (2006). Coaching zwischen Qualitätsproblemen und Professionalisierungsbemühungen. Thesen zur Entwicklung des Coaching. *Organisationsberatung, Supervision, Coaching, 13*(1), 86–96.

Kühl, S. (2008). *Coaching und Supervision. Zur personenorientierten Beratung in Organisationen*. Wiesbaden: VS Verlag.

Part I
Coaching as Profession

Is Coaching on Its Way to Becoming a Profession? A Profession-Centric Sociological Assessment

1

Beate Fietze

Abstract

Following a historical and sociological introduction to the special organizational forms of professions, the classical profession model will serve as the background against which the professionalization of coaching is discussed. While the development of expertise and degree of organization are showing significant progress, the definition of the specific scope of activities involved in coaching remains unclear. A look at the emergence of coaching in the context of the new capitalism shows a relationship between the deprofessionalization in many occupational fields and a complementary differentiation and professionalization of extrafunctional competencies. The professionalization of coaching as well as of other, new forms of reflexive process consultation, is a continuation of this development. This article argues that, despite the relativization of the classical profession model, the clarification of responsibilities and autonomy in order to ensure the quality of professional work continue to remain crucial challenges even today. The article offers an outlook for both aspects.

Since the 1990s, the visibility of coaching has increased in the public eye, and since then it has established itself as a form of personalized consultation which is primarily concerned with work-related issues. Coaches see their consultation services not only as a commercial service offering, but show increasing confidence in representing themselves as professionals, and do so in the tradition of the classical professions (Buchinger and Klinkhammer 2007, p. 9; cf. Chap. 4 in this book).

B. Fietze (✉)
Düsseldorfer Str. 4, 10719 Berlin, Germany
e-mail: beate.fietze@sowi.hu-berlin.de

A. Schreyögg and C. Schmidt-Lellek (eds.), *The Professionalization of Coaching*, DOI 10.1007/978-3-658-16805-6_1

Coaching originated in sports and in the tutor system at American universities, and from the very beginning it was linked with the idea of improving individual performance and with a focus on success (Abbott 1988, p. 203; Böning 2005). In the 1990s, coaching was applied to management counseling and practiced in the form of a discrete reflection space in confidence (Looss 1997). Since then, coaching has enjoyed increasing acceptance. Today, coaching is used in various areas and in various ways, and the genuine efforts towards develop quality standards are immense.

Coaching has undergone visible professionalization—but does this also make coaching a profession? What does this claim entail? What distinguishes professions from other occupational categories? Due to the radical changes in the general social conditions of professional occupations over the past three decades, the question is also: What do modern organizational forms which serve as the benchmark against coaching's claim to be a profession look like? In the following, this issue will be reflected upon in the context of the profession-centric sociological discussion.

1.1 The Historical Constitution of Professions

Professions look back on a "venerable history" (Oevermann 1996; cf. Pfadenhauer and Sander 2010, p. 364). They arose as a special form of the institutionalization of expertise in the transition to a modern society, and have their origins in the universities of the modern age (Stichweh 1994). They represent field-specific groups of experts who develop and administer special science-based resources of knowledge and contribute to "practical life problems", the importance of which is acknowledged by society (Oevermann 1996). Within the system of the societal division of labor, the professions represent an independent organizational form of work whose exclusive and autonomous status sets them apart from other forms of gainful employment. In the heyday of the professions in the 19th century, professionals no longer saw themselves exclusively as being "the educated", but instead defined themselves primarily via their *practical professional activities* (Wehler 1995, p. 736). In this case, classic representatives of such professionals are pastors, doctors, and lawyers. However, up till the late 19th century, the general populace seldom had contact with academic specialists who were experts in their field. If they fell ill, for example, most turned to trusted healers, and it was only upon the creation of the state health insurance system in the 1880s in Germany that the people were able to consult a licensed physician on a relatively regular basis (Wehler 1995, p. 738).

Due to the different initial conditions in Europe and in the Anglo-American regions, the historical process of professionalization followed different paths of development. Particularly in Germany and France, the state played a significant role in the emergence of professions via the regulation of vocational qualification systems and professional codes. Over the course of the 19th century, the control over professional occupations increasingly shifted from state-managed controlling bodies to self-regulation among colleagues via professional associations. From then on, professions managed and sanctioned their own members; in return, the state assured professionals a market monopoly for their range of products and services (Kämmerer 2010). In contrast to this form of professionalization "from above" which took place in continental Europe, there was no comparable influence from the state during the constitution phase in England and the USA. In these areas, the professions asserted their special societal position "from below" (Mieg 2005, p. 342).

Despite the different emphasis in various societies around the world, the relationship between the state and the market remains characteristic for professions till today. In certain respects, the professions follow a "third logic" (Freidson 1988). This is because professional logic differs both from the logic of the market as well as from the logic of hierarchical management; professions follow neither the single-minded profit-oriented mentality of the market, nor the purely bureaucratic mentality of hierarchical organizations (Parsons 1964). Professionals organize their work according to their own standards: They define their own areas of responsibility and define the content and forms of vocational training, they evaluate the products and services that characterize their professions via internal professional review processes, and regulate access to the market. The principle of collegiality underlines the fact that professionals treat each other as equals with regard to their professional competencies. Evaluation and assessment are based exclusively on professional ethical standards and the quality of their professional work. Performance evaluations are strictly separate from the remuneration for products and services rendered and the social status of the person (Mieg 2005).

Members of a profession are bound to its professional and ethical standards as part of a collective self-obligation. In return, the protection of the professional collective provides the individual representative of a profession with a foundation for his or her autonomy when dealing with clients and also when dealing with hierarchical structures within organizations. The self-obligation to follow professional and ethical standards not only limits competition on the market against suppliers who are not part of the profession, but also against competing colleagues, who are also bound by the same standards, at the risk being excluded from the professional *community* if they do not adhere to them. Hence, the professional can e.g. turn down assignments that are professionally and ethically questionable without having the fear of suffering from economic disadvantages, as competing professional colleagues are also bound by the same ethical standards (*client autonomy*). Similarly, within an organization, the obligatory standards of the professional community also form the basis for autonomy when making decisions or following courses of action when faced with persons or collectives authorized to issue orders in internal organizational hierarchies (*organizational autonomy*), as a professionally appropriate review of a "case" cannot be ordered; instead, it can only be developed as part of expert rationality. This relative autonomy is a characteristic specific to professions.

1.2 Profession-Centric Sociological Aspects

In the context of the historical development of the professions, sociology has increasingly concerned itself with the social functions and developmental mechanisms—i.e. the constitution—of professions in controversial debates since the 1960s. As part of the structural and functional approach, the "professional complex" was seen as being of crucial systemic importance for the development and stability of modern societies (cf. Parsons 1964). According to Talcott Parsons, they represented the rationality of modern society, handle central societal issues, and administer central societal values "in trust". This view of professions was sharply criticized in the 1970s/1980s from the perspective of a Marxist-inspired theory of power as being an idealistic and ideological misinterpretation (Larsons 1977; Collins 1987). Professions in no way guarantee the rational and charitable handling of the existential problems of individuals. Instead, professionals secure their privileges through the control they exert over vocational training and the monopolization over how occupations are practiced. Furthermore, they use this to consolidate their power as experts and utilize this power to exclude the lower social classes from their occupational position. "Professionalization projects" (Larsons 1977) are to be understood primarily as promising strategies for members of the middle class to rise up the ranks and gain power.

In the 1980s/90s, the power-critical perspective was expanded via hermeneutic, interactionist, and knowledge-based sociological approaches for the analysis of professions (Schützeichel 2007; Pfadenhauer and Sander 2010). Picking up on the classical Parsons profession model, the professions' entitlement to autonomy can be derived from the "inherent principles" of the *issue of which course of action to take* in a revised version of the structural and functional approach (Oevermann 1996). Professionals can by no means derive their professional actions from academic knowledge; instead, they need to reconcile the "theory" with the complexity of individual *real-life situations and experiences*. Hence, professional practice never utilizes standardized one-size-fits-all knowledge. Instead, it relies on individual evaluation and discretionary decisions, and the artistry of each individual practitioner. Professional intervention is always used when the congruency between the individual life situations and experiences and structural societal requirements is derailed, and the individuals are thrown into a crisis. Professionals are tasked with conducting "vicarious crisis management" (Oevermann 1996), and it is with this assistance that the individuals are to be empowered to manage their own real-life situations and experiences autonomously once again.

The interactionist approach, which was formulated according to American pragmatism, focuses particularly on the relationship between professionals and clients and shows how "the case" only takes shape in the course of the dialog in a negotiation process between professionals and the client (Schütze 1984, 1992; cf. Chap. 4 in this book). The knowledge-based sociological approach interprets the specialist problem definitions as "social constructions of reality", not only in each individual "case", but also for the definition of the professional issues at the macro-social level (Berger and Luckman 1998). The formulation of professional issues that need to be dealt with is always an examination of the interpretative sovereignty over societal problem perception and their relevance as well as the group-specific interests of professionals, who claim exclusive competence for their problem-solving expertise over other providers of goods and services. Both at an individual and at a societal level, professions develop via complex processes of negotiation (Schützeichel 2007, p. 553).

This relationship between societally negotiated issues and the group-specific interests of professionals can be described most clearly with Andrew Abbott's (1988) concept of the "system of professions". Abbott views the individual professions not as isolated collective forms of mutualization, but instead of interrelated groups which compete for professional areas of competence and exclusive market access. The influence of professionals on the preservation, the change, or their commitment for the enforcement of new problem definitions and areas of competence—as is the case for coaching today—is always simultaneously a dispute for appropriate views on societal issues and for one's own market opportunities (Fietze 2011a). This view of the conflict dynamics between the claimed areas of competence of competing professions highlights the procedural character of the "professionalization project" and its open outcome: Certain professionalization projects remain, without achieving the typical autonomy for the professions, stuck halfway, as one might say (Etzioni 1969; Rueschmeyer Rüschemeyer 1983; Schütze 1992; Kühl 2001).

1.3 The Current Degree of Professionalization in Coaching

In order to be able to assess the degree of professionalization coaching has currently achieved, the development of coaching thus far is to be seen against the backdrop of the *classical profession model* as part of research *heuristics*; keeping in mind, however, that this model represents an ideal type whose category is not to be found in any real—not even in classical—profession in its entirety, neither currently nor historically (cf. Wehler 1987, p. 222). The following characteristics of professions will be illustrated in general in the profession-centric sociological discussion: (1) The development of professional expertise with recourse to scientific findings, (2) the clear definition of the scope of activities, (3) the assertion of an exclusive area of competence for the defined scope of activities in the form of a monopoly, which is usually safeguarded formally and legally by a protected title, (4) the formation of professional associations and a corporatist self-administration of their own bodies of knowledge, their orientation towards ethics and standards, and their profession-specific practices (cf. Pfadenhauer and Sander 2010, p. 362). But what would the most effective steps toward the formation of a profession in coaching look like?

1.3.1 Professional Expertise in Coaching

The initial attention coaching received due to its popularization, which was strongly influenced by the media, has long given way to interest in a serious academic discussion, in which many participants from a wide range of occupational fields are involved. Currently, the comprehensive generation of knowledge on the issue of coaching has emerged for an increasing number of distinct fields of practice (Birgmeier 2009; Busse and Ehmer 2010). The initial fixation on methods and the close following of individual approaches have taken a back seat, the reference to academic fields has been established, and the orientation towards overarching issues and the focus on multiple disciplines and the plurality of methods show a developed maturity of the expert discourse in coaching (Körner 2013; Schreyögg and Schmidt-Lellek 2007; Schreyögg 2009, 2012). Coaching is developing into an independent field of research (Möller and Kotte 2011, 2012; cf. Chap. 2 in this book). The number of academic monographs, anthologies, and specialist journals continues to grow, and international academic coaching congresses have also established themselves (Fietze 2011b). The influence of the scientific world is underlined by an increasing academization, including that of further education offerings (cf. Chap. 12 in this book).

1.3.2 Constructing a New Area of Competence

Despite the increasing practical and academic expertise in coaching, the increasing number of practitioners who are entering the field by acquiring further education qualifications as part of their career, and despite the increasing commitment in the field of research, the definition of an exclusive area of competence for coaching remains unclear. The term "coaching" still functions as a container term which can be filled with content as the user pleases (Schwertfeger 2009). Although there currently exist proposed definitions of coaching written by the associations, they only have a weak degree of penetration and a weak binding character (cf. DBVC 2012). The individual providers of coaching services continue to see themselves as needing to explain their own understanding of coaching to clients on their personal websites. This lack of clarity concerning the competence profile of coaching affects a core requirement of the classical profession model.

The lack of definitional strength of the term "coaching" manifests itself primarily in the difficulty faced in distinguishing it from neighboring forms of consultation in the "system of professions" (Abbott 1988), in which the competition for coaching's societally legitimate claim for exclusive representation is settled. Abbott localizes the constitution process of the professions at the *abstract level of semantic claims of competency* for the handling of certain *issues*. However, this does not mean that such claims of competency can be developed on the drawing board. Without the relevant acceptance in society, it will not be possible to realize even the most brilliantly formulated claims. But the claim of competency forms the reference point for quality development in professional practice, as well as further targeted developments, refinements, and further improvements to the methods, the setting, and the role of the counselor. In the *actual execution of professional practice*, it will never be possible to completely distinguish it from the practices of competing professions. In professional work—at the workplace—the lines are crossed all the time—sometimes unavoidably and unnoticed by the parties involved, and sometimes in a targeted manner and intentionally. The tangible allocation disputes take place in day-to-day business. Hence, the professional identity will need to be repeatedly reinforced at this level. It is particularly because of this that a clear concept of one's own professional area of competence is required, according to which one's professional identity and professional practices can be oriented (Fietze 2013).

In contrast to *psychotherapy*, *expert consultation*, and *training*, coaching's claimed area of competence can be defined relatively clearly. The most marked distinction is that between coaching and *psychotherapy*: For one, due to the psychotherapy law (Psychotherapeutengesetz), which has legally regulated the area of competence of psychotherapy as a healing profession in Germany since 1999. For another, due to the need of coaches to distinguish themselves as being not a representative of a healing profession, but instead counselors for "health persons" in occupation-oriented contexts (cf. Chap. 6 in this book). The distinction between coaching and *specialist and expert consultation* is also clear: For many, expert consultation is *the* term that demarcates where coaching ends. Ideally, a coach does not pass on any information to his clients. In a coach's self-conception, the client is instead the expert of his own "case", while the coach's task lies in unleashing the potential that lies within the coachee in a maieutic process. Similarly, *training* can also be clearly distinguished from coaching. In direct contrast to the procedure used in coaching, which encourages the client to independently develop new perspectives and orientations, training integrates prescribed behavioral expectations and patterns into the client's routinized behavioral repertoire through repeated practice (cf. DBVC 2012, p. 26–29).

However, it is much more difficult to clearly draw the line between the claimed areas of competence of the consultation forms *coaching, mentoring, supervision, mediation, moderation, organizational development*, and *facilitation*. The respective definitions are interlinked or overlap each other in many areas, and many of the differences are also disputed. For example, coaching also encompasses advanced forms of team coaching and organizational coaching (cf. Chap. 5 in this book), and in doing so reproduces the expansion movement of supervision, which it has already exceeded (Fietze 2011a; Buchinger and Klinkhammer 2007). Is coaching a special case of supervision, or is it the other way round? Is team supervision a method of organizational development? For coaching, but also for directly related forms of consultation, the formation of the professions is not developed enough that schools and "approaches", methods, settings, and processes can be differentiated from the corresponding superordinate, abstract areas of competence and subordinated to them (cf. Birgmeier 2006). Although some coaching representatives utilize consistent systematization proposals for the various consultation formats (Bachmann 2012), these concepts lack a social anchoring in a consensus among colleagues, which would be binding for all coaches in the carrying out of their practical work. At the level of professional practice, the definitional distinctions between the claimed areas of competence are often ignored and arbitrarily defined according to market opportunities (Fietze 2013). The distinction—and definition-related disputes not only serve the expert and objectively justified profile formation of a separate form of consultation, but also simultaneously that of a (self-)positioning in the competition on the market and for status.

1.3.3 The Market Monopoly of a Defined Area of Competence

For as long as coaching's claimed area of competence is not defined, the issue of a societally sanctioned market monopoly and a formal and legally protected title according to the classical profession model remains pointless. Coaches still have not defined the *societally relevant issues* for which they want to be the exclusive and competent experts, and for which they are able to provide the relevant expertise and problem-solving competencies.

Nevertheless, despite the weakness in the profile of coaching, clear signs for strategies of social consolidation and the regulation of market access can be recognized: The development of standards, the tendency towards the academization of further education for coaching qualifications, the awarding of certificates and the process of their recognition by specialist and occupational associations as well as the emergence of (self-proclaimed) accreditation institutions and the observation of the quality development of coaching by consumer rights protection organizations and the public media continue to intensify.

1.3.4 Corporatist Self-administration

Around the turn of the century, coaches in the German-speaking countries began to organize themselves into professional associations. This signaled the end of the phase of the pioneers and charismatic personalities. An increasing degree of organization among coaches is currently being observed—both with regard to the number of members as well as the increasingly varied association structures in which the establishment of occupational ethical principles, of rules of behavior, as well as the formation of expert committees, arbitration bodies, areas of competence administered by volunteers, and full-time agencies are being advanced. The increasing inclusion and networking of various involved parties such as the providers, the coaches themselves, the users of coaching, the companies and organizations, the providers of further education courses and academics, coaches take the control of their work into their own hands. One inter-associational communication platform is the *Roundtable of German-Speaking Coaching Associations (RTC)*, which has convened regularly since 2005, but which up till now still does not have much of a binding character.

In the context of the characteristic criteria of the classical profession model, the professional development of coaching results in a dilemma that is as disturbing as it is interesting: *On the one hand*, a rapidly progressing professionalization can be seen in the growth in the subject-specific generation of knowledge and the academization of professional and further qualifications, as well as the expansion and intensification of the degree of organization of all involved parties. *On the other*, however, there is still a lack of a clear definition of the scope of activities and a legally regulated market monopoly. Hence, although the professionalization of coaching has made remarkable progress, coaching does not yet live up to the list of ideal criteria that define the classical profession model, because a specifically tailored problem type and a clearly defined claimed area of competence are lacking.

1.4 The Professionalization of Reflexive Forms of Process Consultation

The unsatisfactory definition of coaching stems mainly from the difficulty of distinguishing coaching from other forms of consultation such as supervision and organizational development, mediation and mentoring, which, just like coaching, represent relatively new forms of consultation and which in addition can also be interpreted as special forms of reflexive process consultation (Nestmann et al. 2007a, b; Seel 2013). In contrast to the classic understanding of consultation as a transitive advisory process by experts, its consultation service does not consist of the passing on of information or the application of knowledge acquired from an external source, but in the development of expertise over the course of the consultation itself. This takes place by systematically stimulating and giving consideration to the client's reflexive self-referencing—to his intentions, perceptions, or actions (Moldaschl 2001, 2010; Greif 2008). The special expertise it brings into the consultation process is process expertise (Schein 2000). However, what is common to the aforementioned forms of consultation is that they address the personal, interactional communication processes in the working world in one way or another (cf. Kühl 2008).

1.4.1 The Professionalization of Extrafunctional Competencies

The increasing demand for various forms of *reflexive process consultation* is due to the accelerated societal processes of change associated with the "new capitalism" (Sennett 1998; Lessenich 2008). In the globalized networked society, communicative processes are gaining a great degree of importance (Castells 2001). This increase in significance not only applies to communication via electronic media and the internet, but has also long crossed over to the area of personal communication in organizations. The fields of organization-internal communication processes and human resources management, which previously were only rarely professionalized, have been under strong pressure to economize and streamline themselves for over thirty years now, and are confronted with growing expectations of professionalization (Kühl 2008). Parallel to this development, we are observing a subtle process of *deprofessionalization* in many fields, in which the core competencies of employees are increasingly being displaced in favor of new communications and coordination tasks (Dostal 2002). *Extrafunctional competencies* continue to grow in importance for employees (Mikl-Horke 2008). In order to be able to sustain the performance of coordinative efforts in increasingly complex and continually changing organizational and networking structures through communicative agreement processes, the relevance of self- and process observation, reflexive self-monitoring and the willingness to learn and develop oneself continues to increase. There is clearly a relationship between deprofessionalization and a complementary differentiation of extrafunctional competencies as an independent scope of activities, which itself is experiencing a professionalization boost (Kurtz 2000). One aspect of this development are the new forms of *reflexive process consultation*, which are experiencing increased demand. Coaching is only the most prominent current example.

1.4.2 "Mixed Methods"

The significance of reflexive process consultation has now achieved a degree of recognition that has allowed it to spread to the classic forms of expert consultation, resulting in a new mix of methods.[1] On the one hand, this development is a

[1]Rolf Wimmer describes newly emerging combinations of process and expert consultation as "The 3rd Mode" (cf. osb international: Beratung im 3. Modus: http://www.youtube.com/watch?v=8Jk_0MCG4Sk); link in German).

reaction to the increased competition for classic expert consultation, and on the other, a resonance for the newly-emerged expectations clients have with regard to consultations. Furthermore, a cautious integration of transitive expertise elements into process consultation is also being observed (Königswieser et al. 2006). In coaching too, the tolerance towards the inclusion of information transmission or training components is also increasing, provided that the related change in roles is made apparent to the client (Schreyögg 2010; cf. Chap. 11 in this book).

1.5 Professionalization Today

Overall, the professionalization of coaching takes place via general societal conditions, which are characterized by digitalization and deregulation in the context of the "new capitalism". For coaching—as is the case in other professions—the question is whether the standard of professional autonomy, i.e. the independence of specialist work and professional self-organization, can be lived up to under the current conditions.

1.5.1 Between Managerization and Commercialization

The bureaucratization (managerization) and commercialization (deregulation) of professional practice, which are referred to in sociology as "deprofessionalization", undermine professional self-regulation. The trend towards increasing standardization and the inclusion of the execution of work in organizational structures and towards external, sometimes legally regulated quality controls of such work is a direct intervention in the core area of professional activities.

Standardized diagnostic processes restrict the influencing factors that are considered for the diagnosis. In turn, a diagnosis made in such a manner only affords a small degree of freedom for making the decisions regarding the remedial measures to be taken. The discretionary freedom and the discretionary inference in light of the complexity of each special case, which forms the very foundation of professional activities, are reduced to a minimum. The conclusion then represents a documentary procedure that is prescribed in detail, which makes the entire treatment process visible and regulatable for third parties. In addition, by promoting deregulation, the privileged market access the professions enjoy will be weakened, and opportunities are given to providers who are not subject to the standards of the professions (Münch and Guenther 2005). In this manner, the products and services of the professions approach those of the general industry (cf. Kämmerer 2010).

1.5.2 A Change in Positions in the Relationship Between Professionals and the Client

In addition, the increasing market orientation of professions directly affects the relationship between the professional and his clients: The client is slowly being transformed into a customer. The diagnosis of the assignment and the appropriate measures required to solve the problem are not performed by the professional; instead, the customer determines what service(s) he wishes to receive and the level of quality he is willing to accept. Due to this, the client autonomy of the classic profession model is undermined, and the asymmetry in the relationship between professionals and clients due to the imbalance in the amount of knowledge—and therefore power—possessed is equalized. This new type of relationship between professionals and clients as equals is best served by the new forms of reflexive process consultation. This particularly applies in coaching. In most coaches' self-conception, the coach does not possess more knowledge than the coachee, but instead assists the client with utilizing his own expertise as a resource. Professional activities according to the model of "vicarious crisis management" (Oevermann 1996) may continue to be an appropriate course of action today in classical professions such as for doctors and lawyers, but this is not the case for reflexive process consultation, and in particular for coaching.

1.5.3 "Professionalism" Instead of "Profession"

The changed general conditions of the professions have pushed the term *professionalism* to the foreground even in Europe. This term is established in Anglo-American discourses, but weaker in comparison to the idea of a "profession" in continental Europe (Evetts 2003). "Professionalism" does not describe a specific status group, but instead takes into consideration the actual execution and the performance of professional activities (Muzo et al. 2010; cf. DBVC 2012, p. 15 ff.). The evaluation of *professional performance* circumvents the permanent assignment of a professional's status based on his certified qualification, the acquisition of which is a one-time event. Instead, he is required to prove his competencies repeatedly and convincingly via his professional activities (Pfadenhauer 2003). The definition of professionalism and the orientation towards professional performance shows a great proximity to the definition of competence (cf. Chap. 12 in this book), and appears to be compatible with the current discussion in the context of the Bologna process on the future of education and occupations, as they are understood by the terms "knowledge society", "lifelong learning", and "competence acquisition" (cf. Pfadenhauer and Sander 2010, p. 369; Lenbet 2007). The general focus on competence shifts the assessment of competence directly to the quality-approved outcome, which ultimately needs to satisfy the customer and "end consumer" (cf. Chap. 3 in this book).

1.5.4 New Mechanisms of Self-regulation

Due to the mutual convergence of the industry and professions, the continued and necessary legitimization of professions grew increasingly difficult, even earlier on; today, the state no longer exerts its influence as a regulating authority (cf. Kämmerer 2010). Instead, political processes at the European level can be identified which strive towards a (self-)monitoring of professional work, and which show compatibility as a platform for mechanisms of professional self-regulation. The European Services Directive serves as such a platform. It is intended to create and ensure the freedom of trade and services in the domestic European market.[2] Because the freedom of movement of qualified specialists on the European market requires transparency and comparability, over the past few years the European Commission has pushed for the adoption of the European Professional Card (EPC).[3] As part of this effort, the various interest groups have been called upon to contribute to the definition of their occupational profiles, their competence profiles, and the defining standards of their qualification requirements. Particularly for the professional standards of occupational profiles which are *just only emerging*, the Europeanization process can provide a context in which they can profile their own occupations as they themselves understand it and assert their own standards of quality. Integration into the *European Professional Card* system may serve as a functional equivalent for an assurance of autonomy from the nation states for professionals. Some parties involved in the "professionalization project" that is coaching have already started taking this path. The international coaching associations, the *European Mentoring* and *Coaching Council* (EMCC), the

[2]cf. http://ec.europa.eu/internal_market/top_layer/services/index_de.htm: "The objective of the Services Directive is to release the untapped growth potential of services markets in Europe by removing legal and administrative barriers to trade in the services sector."

[3]cf. http://ec.europa.eu/internal_market/qualifications/policy_developments/european_professional_card/index_de.htm. "The European professional card is a project aimed to facilitate the free movement of professionals in the EU under the modernized Professional Qualifications Directive. The card should simplify the administrative procedure for recognition, make it more transparent for citizens and increase trust among the competent authorities of EU Member States."

International Coach Federation (ICF) and the international umbrella organization *Supervision Association of National Organisations for Supervision in Europe* (ANSE) are already active at the European level. However, the definition of the competence profile of coaching will not be facilitated by the various different national definitional traditions, nor by the varying traditions of the understanding of what constitutes a profession (van Hees and Geißler-Piltz 2010).

1.6 Professional Areas of Competence and Autonomy as a Challenge

Despite the visible advances where professionalization is concerned, coaching does not correspond to the classical profession model. Coaching is not a profession in the classical sense. In the light of changed general societal conditions for the professions as a whole, it remains questionable if coaching will achieve the status of a classical profession, or if it will continue to consolidate its position as a legally "unregulated occupation" in the contexts of self-organization in associations, both in the light of state-mandated requirements as well as the influence of the market. There too, there is still a lot of "development potential" for collaborating on various efforts towards creating a clear occupational profile as part of a more binding association structure (cf. DBVC 2012, p. 14 ff.). The extent to which the European Union will play the role of a catalyst in this case remains to be seen.

Even if a state-licensed monopoly position does not remain a prospect, the standards associated with the classical concept of a profession remain an important orientation for the further professional development of coaching. Both the formulation of a clearly defined claimed area of competence (occupational profile) as well as the development and consolidation of professional autonomy remain the decisive challenges of the further professionalization of coaching.

The problematic consequences of the insufficient independence of a coach on the market can be explained e.g. using the highly ambivalent role of large companies for the professional development of coaching: On the one hand, they promote the practice and acceptance of coaching simply by the demand they represent, and provide an important economic foundation upon which coaching can be further developed and improved. On the other hand, they undermine the autonomy of coaching when human resources management has a company-specific requirements profile for the practice of coaching or even develops internal company programs for the further education of coaches which are not closely connected to the independent association structures of the profession. This results in the market-determining customer exerting active influence on the profile and shaping of the form of consultation that is coaching in coaching's formative phase (cf. Chap. 15 in this book).

The issue of coaching's claimed area of competence is the core issue of the professionalization project that is coaching. It is inextricably linked to the issue of differentiation and the social construction of a societal issue. Coaching captures the zeitgeist like no other form of consultation can. Evidently, the consultation format we call coaching is emerging amidst the interaction of accelerated processes of individualization, the social increase in complexity, and an overarching increase in the significance of extrafunctional, personal competences in the working world. Due to the general societal conditions, the requirements placed on an individual's self-organization and self-management have increased to such an extent that a societally *generalized crisis expectation* now appears to be emerging in the light of the latent crisis potential therein for the working ability and autonomous lifestyle of individuals. Hence, in order to deal with this crisis potential, a *generalized management strategy* in the form of new professional, personalized, and process-oriented consultation services has developed over the past three decades. It appears that coaching is being assigned a recognized professional area of competence for this issue that enjoys increasing societal acceptance—this may not be the case de jure, but it is currently the situation in practice.

References

Abbott, A. (1988). *The System of Professions. An Essay on the Division of Expert Labor.* Chicago, London: The University of Chicago Press.

Bachmann, T. (2012). Coaching? Training? Organisationsentwicklung? Chaos der Begriffe. *Wirtschaft + Weiterbildung*. 3/2012, S. 38–40.

Berger, P. L., & Luckmann, T. (1998). *Die gesellschaftliche Konstruktion der Wirklichkeit. Eine Theorie der Wissenssoziologie*. Frankfurt/M.: Fischer Taschenbuch Verlag.

Birgmeier, B. (2006). Coaching als Methode und/oder Profession? *OSC, 13*(1), 19–30.

Birgmeier, B. (Ed.). (2009). *Coachingwissen. Denn sie wissen nicht, was sie tun?*. Wiesbaden: VS Verlag.

Böning, U. (2005). Der Siegeszug eines Personalentwicklungsinstruments. Eine 10-Jahres-Bilanz. In C. Rauen (Hg.), *Handbuch Coaching* (3. Aufl.). Göttingen: Hogrefe.

Buchinger, K., & Klinkhammer, M. (2007). *Beratungskompetenz*. Supervision, Coaching, Organisationsberatung: Stuttgart. Kohlhammer.

Busse, S., & Ehmer, S. (Eds.). (2010). *Wissen wir, was wir tun? Beraterisches Handeln in Supervision und Coaching*. Göttingen: Vandenhoeck & Ruprecht.

Castells, M. (2001). *Das Informationszeitalter: Wirtschaft, Gesellschaft, Kultur. Bd. 1. Der Aufstieg der Netzwerkgesellschaft*. Opladen: Leske + Budrich.

Collins, R. (1987). Schließungsprozesse und die Konflikttheorie der Professionen. *Österreichische Zeitschrift für Soziologie, 12,* 46–60.

DBVC—Deutscher Bundesverband Coaching e.V. (Hrsg.) (2012). *Leitlinien und Empfehlungen für die Entwicklung von Coaching als Profession. Kompendium mit den Professionsstandards des DBVC* (4., erw. Aufl.). Osnabrück: DBVC Geschäftsstelle; Engl. version available under: www.dbvc.de/publikationen.

Dostal, W. (2002). Der Berufsbegriff in der Berufsforschung des IAB. In G. Kleinhenz (Hg.), *IAB-Kompendium Arbeitsmarkt- und Berufsforschung. Beiträge zur Arbeitsmarkt- und Berufsforschung*, BeitrAB 250, S. 463–474. Berlin: Institut für Arbeitsmarkt- und Berufsforschung der Bundesanstalt für Arbeit.

Etzioni, A. (Ed.). (1969). *The Semi-Professions and Their Organization*. New York: Free Press.

Evetts, J. (2003). The Sociological Analysis of Professionalism: Occupational Change in the Modern World. *International Sociology, 18*(2), 395–415.

Fietze, B. (2011a). Profilbildung und Statuskonkurrenz. Zur Bedeutung der Distinktionsstrategien im Professionalisierungsprozess von Supervision und Coaching. In E.-M. Graf, S. Rettinger, I. Pick & Y. Aksu (Hrsg.), *Beratung, Coaching, Supervision. Multidisziplinäre Perspektiven vernetzt* (S. 23–36). Wiesbaden: VS Verlag.

Fietze, B. (2011b). Chancen und Risiken der Coachingforschung—eine professionssoziologische Perspektive. In R. Wegener, A. Fritze, & M. Loebbert (Eds.), *Coaching entwickeln—Forschung und Praxis im Dialog* (pp. 24–33). Wiesbaden: VS Verlag.

Fietze, B. (2013). *Friedliche Handelsbeziehungen im kleinen Grenzverkehr oder Grenzstreitigkeiten?*. Manuskript: Ein Einhegungsversuch unterschiedlicher Beratungsformen. Unveröff.

Freidson, E. (1988). *Professional Powers. A Study of the Institutionalisation of Formal Knowledge*. Chicago: The University of Chicago Press.

Greif, S. (2008). *Coaching und ergebnisorientierte Selbstreflexion*. Göttingen: Hogrefe.

Kämmerer, J. (2010). *Die Zukunft der Freien Berufe zwischen De-Professionalisierung und Neuordnung*. München: Beck.

Königswieser, R., Sonuc, E., & Gebhardt, J. (2006). *Komplementärberatung. Das Zusammenspiel von Fach- und Prozess-Know-how*. Stuttgart: Klett-Cotta.

Körner, J. (2013). Plädoyer für eine Direktausbildung zum Psychotherapeuten. Entwurf eines Studienganges „von der Profession her". *Forum Psychoanal, 29,* 235–257.

Kühl, S. (2001). Professionalität ohne Profession. Das Ende des Traums von der Organisationsentwicklung als eigenständiger Profession und die Konsequenzen für die soziologische Beratungsdiskussion. In N. Degele et al. (Hg.) (2001), *Soziologische Beratungsforschung. Perspektiven für Theorie und Praxis der Organisationsberatung* (S. 209–238). Opladen: Leske und Budrich.

Kühl, S. (2008). *Coaching und Supervision. Zur personenorientierten Beratung in Organisationen*. Wiesbaden: VS Verlag.

Kurtz, T. (2000). Moderne Professionen und Gesellschaftliche Kommunikation. *Soziale Systeme, 6,* 169–194.

Larson, S. M. (1977). *The Rise of Professionalism. A Sociological Analysis*. Berkeley Los Angeles, London: University of California Press.

Lenbet, A. (2007). Zur Aktualität des Kompetenzbegriffs und zur Bedeutung der Kompetenzentwicklung für das Coaching. In A. Schreyögg & C. Schmidt-Lellek (Eds.), *Konzepte des Coaching* (pp. 46–58). Wiesbaden: VS Verlag.

Lessenich, S. (2008). *Die Neuerfindung des Sozialen. Der Sozialstaat im flexiblen Kapitalismus*. Bielefeld: Transcript.

Looss, W. (1997). *Unter vier Augen. Coaching für Manager*. Landsberg: Moderne Industrie.

Mieg, H. A. (2005). Professionalisierung. In F. Rauner (Ed.), *Handbuch der Bildungsforschung* (pp. 324–349). Bielefeld: Bertelsmann.

Mikl-Horke, G. (2008). Beruf. In S. Farzi & S. Jordan (Hg.), *Lexikon Soziologie und Sozialtheorie. Hundert Grundbegriffe* (S. 35–37). Stuttgart: Philipp Reclam jun.

Moldaschl, M. (2001). Reflexive Beratung. Eine Alternative zu strategischen und systemischen Ansätze. In N. Degele, T. Münch, H. Pongratz & N. Saam (Hg.), *Soziologische Beratungsforschung* (S. 133–157). Opladen: Leske + Budrich.

Moldaschl, M. (2010). *Was ist Reflexivität?* Papers and Preprints of the Department of Innovation Research and Sustainable Resource Management (BWL IX), Chemnitz University of Technology (Fassung 24.2.2011); http://www.tu-chemnitz.de/wirtschaft/bwl9/publikationen/lehrstuhlpapiere/WP_2010_11_Reflexivitaet.pdf#.

Möller, H., & Kotte, S. (2011). *Die Zukunft der Coachingforschung. OSC, 18*(4), 445–456.

Möller, H., & Kotte, S. (2012). Aktueller Forschungsstand und Implikationen für die Zukunft der Coachingforschung. In Deutscher Bundesverband Coaching e.V. (Hrsg.), *Leitlinien und Empfehlungen für die Entwicklung von Coaching als Profession: Kompendium mit den Professionsstandards des DBVC* (4., erw. Aufl., S. 129–138). Osnabrück: DBVC Geschäftsstelle.

Münch, R., & Guenther, T. (2005). Der Markt in der Organisation. Von der Hegemonie der Fachspezialisten zur Hegemonie des Finanzmanagements. In P. Windolf (Hg.), *Finanzmarkt-Kapitalismus. Analysen zum Wandel von Produktionsregimen* (Sonderheft 45 der *Kölner Zeitschrift für Soziologie und Sozialpsychologie,* S. 394–417.). Wiesbaden: VS Verlag.

Muzo, D., Kirkpatrick, I., & Kipping, M. (2010). *Professionalism without professions: the case of management consultancy in the UK*. Working Paper.

Nestmann, F., Engel, F., & Sickendiek, U. (Eds.). (2007a). *Das Handbuch der Beratung. Disziplinen und Zugänge* (2nd ed.). Tübingen: DGVT.

Nestmann, F., Engel, F., & Sickendiek, U. (Eds.). (2007b). *Das Handbuch der Beratung. Ansätze, Methoden und Felder* (2nd ed.). Tübingen: DGVT.

Oevermann, U. (1996). Theoretische Skizze einer revidierten Theorie professionalisierten Handelns. In A. Combe & W. Helsper (Hg.), *Pädagogische Professionalität. Untersuchungen zum Typus pädagogischen Handelns* (S. 70–182). Frankfurt/M.: Suhrkamp.

Parsons, T. (1964). Die akademischen Berufe und die Sozialstruktur. In Ders., *Beiträge zur soziologischen Theorie* (S. 160–179). Neuwied: Luchterhand.

Pfadenhauer, M. (2003). *Professionalität. Eine wissenssoziologische Rekonstruktion institutionalisierter Kompetenzdarstellungskompetenz*. Opladen: Leske + Budrich.

Pfadenhauer, M., & Sander T. (2010). Professionssoziologie. In G. Kneer & M. Schroer (Hrsg.), *Handbuch spezielle Soziologie* (S. 361–378). Wiesbanden. VS Verlag.

Rüschemeyer, D. (1983). Professional Autonmy and the social Control of Expertise. In R. Dingwall (Hg.), *The sociology of the professions. Lawyers, doctors and others* (S. 38–58). London: Macmillan (Oxford socio-legal studies).

Schein, E. (2000). *Prozessberatung für die Organisation der Zukunft*. Köln: Edition Humanistische Psychologie.

Schreyögg, A. (2009). Die Wissensstrukturen im Coaching. In B. Birgmeier (Hg.), *Coachingwissen. Denn sie wissen nicht, was sie tun?* (S. 47–60). Wiesbaden: VS Verlag.
Schreyögg, A. (2010). Ist Coaching reine Prozessberatung oder sind hier auch andere Beratungsmodell relevant? *OSC, 17*(2), 119–132.
Schreyögg, A. (2012). *Coaching. Eine Einführung für Praxis und Ausbildung* (7. Aufl.). Frankfurt/M., New York: Campus.
Schreyögg, A., & Schmidt-Lellek, C. (Eds.). (2007). *Konzepte des Coaching. OSC Sonderheft 1*. Wiesbaden: VS Verlag.
Schütze, F. (1984). professionelles Handeln, wissenschaftliche Forschung und Supervision. In N. Lippmeier (Ed.), *Beiträge zur Supervision* (Vol. 3, pp. 262–389). Kassel: Kassel Univ. Press.
Schütze, F. (1992). Sozialarbeit als bescheidene Profession. In B. Dewe, W. Ferchhoff, & F. O. Radtke (Eds.), *Erziehen als Profession* (pp. 131–171). Opladen: Leske + Budrich.
Schützeichel, R. (2007). Laien, Experten, Professionen. In R. Schützeichel (Ed.), *Handbuch Wissenssoziologie und Wissensforschung* (pp. 546–578). Konstanz: UVK.
Schwertfeger, B. (2009). *Psychologie heute*. November 2009, S. 34–37.
Seel, H. -J. (2013). Aufgaben und Probleme der Professionalisierung von Beratung. In F. Nestmann, F. Engel & U. Sickendiek, U. (Hg.), *Das Handbuch der Beratung, Bd. 3: Neue Beratungswelten* (S. 1645–1661). Tübingen: DGVT.
Sennett, R. (1998). *Der flexible Mensch. Die Kultur des neuen Kapitalismus*. Berlin: Berlin Verlag.
Stichweh, R. (1994). *Wissenschaft, Universität*. Suhrkamp: Professionen. Soziologische Analysen. Frankfurt/M.
van Hees, G., & Geissler-Piltz, B. (2010). *Supervision meets Education: supervision in the Bachelor Social Work in Europe*. Maastricht: CESRT/Zuyd University.
Wehler, H. -U. (1987). *Deutsche Gesellschaftsgeschichte, Bd. 2: Von der Reformära bis zur industriellen und politischen „Deutschen Doppelrevolution"* 1815–1845/49. München: Beck.
Wehler, H. -U. (1995). *Deutsche Gesellschaftsgeschichte, Bd. 3: Von der „Deutschen Doppelrevolution" bis zum Beginn des Ersten Weltkriegs* 1849–1914. München: Beck.

Author Biography

Dr. phil. Beate Fietze Dipl.-Soz., Dipl.-Psych., taught at various universities as a research fellow and conducts research on the professionalization of new forms of consulting at the Humboldt Center for Social and Political Research at the Institute of Sociology of the Humboldt University of Berlin. Coordinator of the research group "Profession and Consulting" of the profession sociology section of the German Society for Supervision (DGSv), since 2013 a fellow in research and further education at the DGSv.

The Ambivalent Relationship Between Coaching Research and Coaching Practice: Discreetly Ignoring, Critically Observing or Beneficially Cooperating?

2

Silja Kotte, Katrin Oellerich, Denise Elisabeth Hinn and Heidi Möller

Abstract

The article argues that it is necessary to take seriously the inherent logic of the two systems "research" and "practice" in the area of coaching in order to come to a realistic assessment of the ambivalent relationship between these two "worlds" and to identify concrete steps for moving towards a more sustainable working alliance between coaching practice and coaching research. For this purpose, we first elaborate on characteristics of both systems. In the main part, we provide an overview of the scientific publication landscape and of the current state of coaching research. We then deduce key challenges concerning the relationship between research and practice and conclude with an appeal to action for both researchers and practitioners.

S. Kotte (✉) · K. Oellerich · D.E. Hinn · H. Möller
Universität Kassel, Holländische Straße 36-38, 34127 Kassel, Germany
e-mail: silja.kotte@uni-kassel.de

K. Oellerich
e-mail: katrin.oellerich@uni-kassel.de

D.E. Hinn
e-mail: denise.hinn@uni-kassel.de

H. Möller
e-mail: heidi.moeller@uni-kassel.de

A. Schreyögg and C. Schmidt-Lellek (eds.), *The Professionalization of Coaching*, DOI 10.1007/978-3-658-16805-6_2

2.1 Introduction

Both coaching researchers and coaching practitioners constantly reassure themselves of their mutual significance and relevance. While the coaching literature for practitioners has been greatly increasing since the mid-1990s, the research literature only started gathering steam since the early- and mid-2000s. Admittedly, the theoretical and methodical foundations of many empirical studies are still built upon shaky ground (Ely et al. 2010; Grant 2013a; Möller and Kotte 2011) but nonetheless, reviews and meta-analyses offer a positive summary of the general increase in empirical studies and the effectiveness of coaching (e.g. De Meuse et al. 2009; Ely et al. 2010; Künzli 2009; Theeboom et al. 2014).

However, do the practitioners pay much attention to this growing body of knowledge, or do they view the research and the resulting publications as uninspiring, uninformative and uninstructive (Möller et al. 2013; Padberg 2012)? And conversely, what do researchers have to say about this? Do they shake their heads in disbelief at what is transacted in coaching practice with neither empirical verification nor empirical proof of effectiveness (Kieser 2005)? Are scientists not primarily interested in practitioners because they want to acquire them as samples for their surveys and studies rather than viewing them as genuine dialog partners?

This chapter contends that it is necessary that the inherent logic of the two coaching systems, the "scientific" and the "practice", be taken seriously in order to come to a realistic evaluation of the ambivalent relationship between these two "spheres" and to identify specific opportunities for facilitating a more sustainable working relationship between coaching practice and research.

This chapter will determine the characteristics of both the "coaching science" and "coaching practice" systems. An overview of the landscape of scientific publications and the state of coaching research will then be given and the core challenges for the research-practice relationship will be derived. It will conclude with an evaluation of the actions required on the part of both the practitioners and the researchers.

2.2 Coaching: The Inherent Logic of the "Scientific" and "Practice" Systems

Coaching practice and coaching science emphasize their complementary relationship at conferences, in journal publications and in their respective presentations. Practitioners openly agree with the importance not just of ensuring a scientific basis for the methods employed by coaches but also of establishing professional standards and contributing to coaching's quality assurance. For their part, the scientists emphasize that dialog with expert practitioners is both valuable and indispensable. Nonetheless, one still encounters the above-mentioned grievances from representatives of both systems. The practitioners criticize the science for not supporting the coaching practice (Möller et al. 2013). According to the scientists, the coaching practitioners present themselves as offering "consultation concepts that brim with unambiguous clarity" (Scherf 2010, p. 11) despite a lack of empirical foundation, they show reluctance to participate in the research, especially in anything that goes beyond the scope of post hoc surveys, and are not truly interested in or receptive to the research results except when it legitimizes their own actions and behavior (Haubl 2009). These criticisms are also presumably rooted in the two fields' different primary tasks. This article will clarify the differences that have arisen when dealing with complexity, with the intimacy of the consultation process and the specific mechanisms of knowledge generation and the relevant types of knowledge (also cf. Möller and Hausinger 2009).

2.2.1 Reducing Versus Increasing Complexity

While the goal of coaching is to make the coachee capable of acting, "organized skepticism" (Kieser 2005) is an essential feature of a scientific approach. Uncertainty must be absorbed in coaching, sometimes by resorting to very simple models. Expanding the complexity, or opening the view up to different perspectives, is generally only a temporary stage that allows, within a comprehensive look into a coaching situation or issue, the selection of a reflected and conscious course of action and its implementation. One function of coaches is to act as the "absorbers of uncertainty", which can also imply that "consultants must present their advice with conviction" (Kieser 2005, p. 12). The task of scientists however is to remain in a state of not knowing, or one of criticism, scrutiny and doubt in regard to ostensibly established facts. They must continually pose new and more specific questions and thereby increase differentiation and complexity. And it is through their respective means of dealing with complexity that these two fields earn their money: by retaining and acquiring clients (practitioners) versus attracting research funding (researchers).

2.2.2 Closed Shop Versus Observation and Measuring

More than other forms of consultation, coaching is a "closed shop", particularly in an individual setting. Confidentiality is a cornerstone and building a sustainable working relationship is essential for successful coaching (cf. Sect. 2.3). Unlike other consulting and development interventions such as training or team-development workshops, clients value the intimate and protected space in which they can talk about their issues and problems "in total privacy" (Looss 2006) without the presence of third parties. Coaching research however requires the most direct access possible to the coaching processes. In addition to questionnaires, video and audio recordings are the medium of choice for obtaining the least obstructed access to what takes place in "black-box" coaching (Ianiro and Kauffeld 2011)—particularly in view of the fact that self-reports made by clients and coaches on the effects of coaching tend to be more positive than the assessment of third parties such as HR managers (Böning and Fritschle 2005; De Meuse et al. 2009; Kotte and Möller 2013). Research unavoidably intrudes upon the intimate environment between coach and coachee and creates a potential disturbance—many coaches identify their concern about this as the reason why they object to participating in coaching research.

2.2.3 Specific Mechanisms for Generating Knowledge, and Types of Knowledge

In the "community of practice" within coaching, knowledge is generated from the realities of daily coaching and the training institutions, while within the scientific community, knowledge derives from university-based research. Within these contexts, different types of knowledge are viewed as valid and relevant.

2.2.3.1 Knowledge Generation in the Scientific Community

For scientists, knowledge must have a scientific foundation; it "consists of statements that have been subjected to methodical doubt as to their claim to validity and have so far withstood it." (Haubl 2009, p. 180) The process of scientific knowledge generation can be described in four stages that ideally take place one after the other in a continuous cycle (Haubl 2009): Individual researchers and research groups act scientifically—they formulate assumptions and hypotheses, develop designs and methods that can test these, then analyze and interpret the results. They present their scientific research at conferences and submit manuscripts to peer-reviewed journals, thereby exposing them to scientific critique from colleagues. Over time the scientific findings that have gained acceptance will be integrated into a "stock of knowledge" or body of knowledge, often in the form of reviews and meta-analyses (descriptive and/or quantifiable overviews of the state of the research, cf. Sect. 2.3). Scientific debate challenges the established approach of scientific conduct and thereby affects the scientific actions of individual researchers and research groups.

As "dwarves standing on the shoulders of giants" (Hall 1991), young generations of researchers build upon the body of knowledge which previous generations of researchers have developed over time, challenge this and further differentiate it. A research frontier is described as "a place where innovative research pushes the boundaries of science or knowledge. It may also be an outpost, a remote or isolated place" (Kelly-Irving 2014). In this context, knowledge generation means systematically redrawing this frontier so that the unknown "region" is gradually mapped out and then making this newly obtained knowledge available to the scientific community.

2.2.3.2 Knowledge Generation in the "Community of Practice"

Within the "community of practice", knowledge generation takes place by means of knowledge transmission within a "matrix of master-novice relationships" (Haubl 2009, p. 203) that ideally, in order to reduce the uncritical transfer of false empirical knowledge, is housed within specialist and professional associations and within training institutions that implement its standards. Haubl's description of supervision (2009) can also be transferred to the coaching field: The principle sources of knowledge generation are one's personal experience as a coachee, one's own coaching practice, supervision by experienced (teaching) coaches and/or intervision among colleagues.

More than anything, this is done in several stages by making implicit knowledge explicit. Firstly, one's own case-specific consultation-related actions are continually reflected upon *during* the coaching where there is a sense of urgency. *Subsequent* to individual coaching sessions, the coach retrospectively reflects upon how it went and, where appropriate, take notes in session journals. By presenting (narrating) one's own actions as a coach within the context of training supervision, intervision or Balint groups, this will be incorporated into a narrative community which acts as a resonance chamber, deepens insight into the case and provides stimuli for further interventions. One step that goes beyond pure narrative yet is seldom encountered in practice would be casuistic seminars, in which coaching cases are not merely incorporated into narrative form but also debated, the interventions and their effects are discussed and the results are documented.

The ultimate goal of this is to compile a range of coachings that have been analyzed and compared with each other [as per Jüttemann's "comparative casuistics" (1990)] through which empirical knowledge is condensed.

However, the learning process and the transfer of knowledge within master-novice relationships cannot necessarily be made explicit—"inexplicable" things can still be learned from the master by observation. If we follow Dreyfus and Dreyfus (1987) and their phenomenological investigations of skill acquisition (from novice to master in a five-stage model) as exhibited by chess grandmasters, pilots, business managers, surgeons, nurses and teachers, it can be established that a more or less internalized set of rules is a guiding basis for beginners only. Experts act according to the situation, "holistically and intuitively" and in a state of "level-headed rationality"; they do not deconstruct different situations into context-free elements, it is rather that they attempt to understand the overall interrelationship. They often cannot describe the approach they took (cf. Möller 2012). And even "novices" can learn by observation without being able to explain what it is that they have just learned (Eagleman 2011).

2.2.3.3 Different Types of Knowledge

Various types of knowledge also arise from the specific knowledge-generation mechanisms mentioned above: Scientific knowledge is explicit and general while coaches' practice-based knowledge is predominantly implicit and case-specific (Haubl 2009). Scientific knowledge is causal, verbal knowledge that, in accordance with scientific standards, can be published in peer-reviewed journals, reproduced and translated into manuals and best practices. The implicit practice-based knowledge however has a great deal to do with "having a feel for it", intuition and Gestalt analysis processes. Subjectivity is quite unavoidably a main factor because the knowledge comes from a person. Due to the specificity of the individual case, the application of a general model cannot provide a concrete solution. According to Haubl (2009), this results in two potential failures: a type I error arises when coaches continue to build on false implicit knowledge instead of allowing this to be corrected (e.g. by means of explicit knowledge), in the case of a type II error, the explication of the implicit knowledge impacts negatively upon the ability to act.

Alongside these various knowledge-generation mechanisms and the determination as to which of these types of knowledge will be accepted as valid, the field boundaries (Bourdieu 1988) between coaching knowledge and coaching practice can be established. Both of these knowledge-generation fields are closed and virtually inaccessible to outsiders: Science due to its highly institutionalized, ritualized and differentiated mechanisms of knowledge generation and knowledge transfer via conferences and journals, and coaching practice because of its rigidly personalized knowledge transfer within master-novice relationships.

2.3 Current State of Coaching Research

What follows is our attempt to provide an insight into the field of "coaching science", initially with a brief overview of the development of the landscape of scientific publications and then with a summary of the "stock of knowledge" of coaching research. We will conclude by pointing out some implications for the relationship between science and practice.

2.3.1 Development of Coaching Research: The Landscape of Scientific Publications in Coaching

This new research field is on the rise. Increasing numbers of university-based "pockets" are being established which investigate coaching both within Germany and internationally. The number of scientific articles that have appeared on the topic of coaching has rapidly increased in recent years (cf. Table 2.1).

A database search using the key word "coaching" in the Kassel Research, Literature and Information Portal of the University of Kassel resulted in 7838 hits in peer-reviewed journals. These figures must however be treated with caution as the term "coaching" is an umbrella term which is not exclusive to psychology and is used in various fields such as sport and in the consultation context. When one considers the publications in the consultation context, one can see that even here it has a broad scope of use (weight-loss coaching, driver training vs. work-related coaching). Using the term "executive coaching" reduces the number of hits in the database to 384. A further search in two established databases in the fields of psychology and business gave the following results: We found more than 600 publications on "executive coaching" in the Business Source Premier database (1984-present) and 327 in PsycINFO (1887-present). However, only three articles could be identified which were published in "top-ranked" journals[1] (Psychology and Management) (Bono et al. 2009; Feldman and Lankau 2005; Smither et al. 2003). This raises the question, which international journals publish these articles?

[1]Scientific magazines that are relevant to work-related and organizational psychology, scaled as per average citation rate during last 5 years.

Table 2.1 Database search on the Kassel Research, Literature and Information Portal of the University of Kassel

Time period	Number of hits for "title: coaching"	Number of hits for "title: executive coaching"
<1980	76	/
1981–1990	243	2
1991–1995	271	5
1996–2000	525	19
2001–2005	1150	101
2006–2010	2634	148
2010–2014	2939	109
Total	7838	384

Table 2.2 shows the results of a search on PsycINFO. It is conspicuous that most of these articles are published in coaching-related journals rather than in general (psychology) journals.

Joo's (2005) review on the coaching literature shows that 71% of the published articles on executive coaching appeared in practitioner journals, 15% in academic journals and 14% in other publications. For this reason, the authors summarized that coaching receives more attention in the practitioner sphere than in the world of science. We cannot disagree with this assessment at the present time. However, an exhaustive and comprehensive search of the literature on the current databases proves to be very difficult as these databases do not encompass all of the significant journals (in particular not the coaching-specific journals). With this in mind, it appears practically impossible for practitioners to access the research literature in scientific journals. And even if such access were possible, the question remains as

Table 2.2 Who's publishing these articles? Search on PsycINFO (1887-present)

Journal	Hits for "executive coaching"
Consulting psychology journal: practice and research	38
Industrial and commercial training	21
International coaching psychology review	17
International journal of evidence based coaching and mentoring	13
Journal of management development	12
The coaching psychologist	12

to what extent these often compartmentalized research results are comprehensible and usable in daily practice. "Bridging journals", located content-wise between research and practice, are helpful for the transfer between science and practice. In Germany, the publication with the broadest spectrum is "Organisationsberatung, Supervision, Coaching" (OSC). It features articles on both research as well as practice with a focus on coaching.

Articles relating to coaching do not figure prominently in those important international scientific journals (A-grade) in the field of psychology that have a high impact factor (i.e. journals whose articles are much cited). The majority of coaching studies were published in B- or C-grade journals (Grant 2013a). This could be because coaching research is still a relatively recent field and it needs to further establish itself before it "graduates" onto the more important journals. Another aspect could be the "gold standard" that is frequently set for high-ranking publications. "Gold standard" studies are those with randomized controlled trials (RCTs) wherein the study participants are randomly allocated into a treatment group or a control group and their results compared. The goal of this study design is to ensure that the observed effects can only be attributed to the intervention, and therefore these studies demonstrate a high level of internal validity (Leichsenring 2004). Within coaching research it is extraordinarily difficult to carry out tests under controlled conditions. Business coaching by definition takes place within the work context. This poses particular challenges to research procedures. Competing political views, organizational structures and the priorities held by various actors within the organization can influence the coaching and these factors can change in the course of the coaching process (Grant 2013a). There are also many factors that exert an influence on a coaching process and its effect. Controlling these is extremely complex if not quite impossible.

In addition to individual studies, general overview articles are also published. These include reviews that collate the research results in a more descriptive form and outline and evaluate the available studies (Carey et al. 2011; De Haan and Duckworth 2012; Ely et al. 2010; Grant et al. 2010b; Greif 2013). To the best of our knowledge there are only two existing meta-analyses on the effectiveness of coaching (De Meuse et al. 2009; Theeboom et al. 2014). Meta-analyses synthesize several studies quantitatively into metadata. These two meta-analyses used the availability of longitudinal research design as the selection criterion. Other studies had to be excluded due to the insufficient quality of the data. The result of this was that in the first meta-analysis by De Meuse et al. (2009), only 6 studies remained out of the original 22, and in the second meta-analysis by Theeboom et al. (2014), only 18 remained out of 107 studies. The situation which is depicted by the selection of studies admitted into the meta-analyses reflects the research field and its development during the last few years; the number of studies increases while their quality is still heterogeneous.

2.3.2 The "Stock of Knowledge" in Coaching: The Current State of Coaching Research

We will present the research results by dividing them into (1) conclusions on the effectiveness or outcome (summative evaluation) and (2) conclusions on input and process factors (formative evaluation) based upon the systematizations of Ely et al. (2010) and Greif (2008, 2013; cf. Möller and Kotte 2011). In doing so, both quantitative as well as qualitative studies will be presented.

2.3.2.1 Research Results on the Effectiveness of Coaching (Outcome)

Greif (2013) distinguishes here between general and specific effects. These will be shown below in relation to the client and the organization. A majority of the studies report high values for the general effects of coaching upon the clients such as the general assessment of success and satisfaction with the coaching as well as goal attainment (Grafe and Kronig 2011; Linley et al. 2010). Möller and Kotte (2011) summarize that a wide range of studies are however based upon self-assessment by the client (cf. De Meuse et al. 2009). Similar to participant surveys relating to training, these consist mostly of positive feedback; a "friendly thank-you" (Greif 2008, p. 219; Kauffeld 2010). Meta-analyses in the training context show that positive assessments of satisfaction and success do not necessarily correlate with learning outcomes (Arthur et al. 2003; Ely and Zaccaro 2011). The results of one qualitative study (Geißler et al. 2013) also show that the degree of goal attainment is relatively low compared to the client's level of satisfaction with the coaching results and his or her the assessment of overall satisfaction.

Other studies on the general results of coaching report a reduction in negative affect such as stress levels and an increase in general wellbeing due to coaching (Grant et al. 2010a; Theeboom et al. 2014) as well as significant positive changes in resilience and self-efficacy (Sherlock-Storey et al. 2013) and career satisfaction (Bozer and Sarros 2012). A study by Leonard-Cross (2010) for instance showed that coaching participants in a two-year coaching course exhibited higher levels of confidence in their self-efficacy compared to the control group.

Positive effects relating to specific, concrete and observable changes in the behavior or performance of the clients that are linked to coaching goals have been observed in various studies including more effective leadership, improvements in interpersonal relationships, cooperation and communication skills, finding other strategies for dealing with conflict, self-reflection, self-acceptance and personality development (Curtis and Kelly 2013; De Haan et al. 2013; De Meuse et al. 2009; Ellam-Dyson and Palmer 2011; Kines et al. 2010; Kochanowski et al. 2010; Theeboom et al. 2014). The results of qualitative studies show that, in addition to an improvement in leadership, coaching is regarded as being effective when it comes to individual self-reflection and conflict resolution (Cerni et al. 2010; Kühl 2014). Coaching also increases the client's awareness of his or her own counter-productive work habits and this positively influences individual motivation and work performance (Cox and Patrick 2012).

First studies now also look into the negative effect of coaching and its causes from the perspective of clients and coaches (Schermuly et al. 2014; Seiger and Künzli 2011). The study results indeed show that coaching can also have negative effects both for the client as well as for the coach.

A large number of evaluations on the effectiveness of leadership development programs with integrated coaching components show that combined training and coaching are more effective than training by itself (Ladyshewsky 2007; Kochanowski et al. 2010; Kotte and Möller 2013; Wallis 2010). Moreover, some qualitative studies clarify the specific added benefits of coaching, for instance a more realistic self-perception and increased self-efficacy (e.g. Spencer 2011; Riedelbauch 2011).

One way of including the organizational context in the examination of coaching outcomes consists of implementing 360-degree feedback as a measuring tool for assessing effectiveness. Various studies show that coaching processes and the associated changes undergone by the clients are evaluated as positive and successful by their supervisors and subordinates (Kaufel et al. 2006; Scherm and Scherer 2011). In most of these studies however, the question remains open as to what extent the effects can actually be attributed to coaching.

When it comes to the long-term effects of coaching on coaching clients, there are currently very few quantitative studies available. They are however able to show positive further developments (Cavanagh 2010; Finn et al. 2006). In one qualitative singe-case study, for example, Libri and Kemp (2006) report that coaching can have lasting effects; even after 18 months, the client's sales performance, self-reported performance and the core self-evaluation were higher than at the start. At present, few studies exist on the distal (i.e. long-term) effects of coaching upon the organization such as changes in organizational climate, productivity and effectiveness (Ely et al. 2010; Greif 2013; Möller and Kotte 2011). By contrast, there are various studies on the economic effects—return on investment (ROI)—that attempt to show that coaching can make a financial profit for the company (Anderson 2011; McGovern et al. 2001); however, their evaluation methods must be viewed with some skepticism. The focus on a purely monetary ROI (being evaluated subjectively) appears to be a narrow view of the potential benefit of coaching. Attention should thus instead be directed towards indirect and long-term effects such as the increase in commitment, improvements in leadership style or the reduction of the cost of conflict within change management (Ely et al. 2010; Grant 2012).

2.3.2.2 Research Results on Common Factors: Input and Process Variables (Process)

The number of studies on common factors in coaching is much more limited than of those on effectiveness (Möller and Kotte 2011). In our article, "input variables" denote the prerequisites relating to the coach (e.g. process competence), to the client (e.g. motivation to change, perseverance) and to the organization (e.g. the time-frame of the coaching, selection of coaches) (Greif 2013; Möller and Kotte 2011). The process variables in coaching are generally subdivided into the following components: coach and client behavior, coach-client relationship and structural variables (Ely et al. 2010; Greif 2013).

In relation to the input variables on the part of the client, positive effects were shown for the relationship between the client's conscientiousness, openness, emotional stability as well as self-efficacy on the one hand and the perceived quality of the coaching results on the other (De Haan et al. 2013; Stewart et al. 2008). Ely et al. (2010) also identified the willingness to engage with the coaching as a significant factor. In a study, Ellam-Dyson and Palmer (2011) compared a coaching and a non-coaching group. The participants were able to decide for themselves whether to take part in the coaching. The non-coaching group evinced significantly lower values in regard to unconditional self-acceptance. The authors assume that those who most needed the coaching avoided it in order to preserve their self-esteem. The motivation to change, reflexivity and perseverance can also be viewed as other pertinent input and process variables on the part of the client. So far however these have only been postulated on a theoretical basis (Greif 2013; Möller and Kotte 2011).

On the part of the coach, aspects such as methodical competence, a sound training background and the ability to professionally clarify goals with the client and the organization emerge as important prerequisites for the effectiveness of coaching (Greif 2013). This is because, according to a qualitative study by Freitag

(2011), companies and clients expect "a coach who acts in a discreet, situative and flexible manner, is goal- and results-oriented, has a wide range of life experiences and shows empathy in their work" (p. 229, own translation). The results from Bono et al. (2009) present a similar picture. In their study, 428 coaches were asked which skills they consider to be essential for effective coaching. The results can be divided into four categories: diagnostic and planning-related skills; intervention and problem-solving skills (e.g. building relationships, giving feedback); knowledge (e.g. personality psychology, industry expertise), and other personal characteristics (e.g. authenticity, sense of humor). In addition, in their study, De Haan et al. (2011) asked the clients which skills they deemed to be most helpful in their coach. The top three responses were: insight into and awareness of the client's problems, the coach's knowledge and experience, and offering support to the client during the process. When it came to the process variables on the part of the coaches, De Haan et al. (2013) found that the range of techniques employed by coaches has a positive influence on the outcome quality as perceived by the clients. On the other hand, the coaches' self-efficacy exerted no influence.

Most of the studies relating to common factors focus on the relationship between client and coach. The quality of the working relationship proves to be a significant predictor of the perceived quality of the results of the coaching process (Baron and Morin 2009, 2012; Boyce et al. 2010; De Haan et al. 2013). Grant (2013b) emphasizes that a goal-oriented relationship can significantly increase the likelihood of coaching success whereas satisfaction with the working alliance is no reliable predictor. A high level of similarity between coach and client in relation to the manifestation of verbal and non-verbal affiliation (friendliness) and to social dominance traits predicts a positive assessment, both of the quality of the relationship and of the goal-attainment by the client (Ianiro et al. 2012). In a mixed-methods study by Van Oorsouw et al. (2013), they also concluded that a similar level of dominance in the coach and client is associated with a high level of satisfaction on the part of the client. Numerous qualitative studies also describe relationship-building as a key factor for a successful coaching process (Alvey and Barclay 2007; Blattner 2005; Jowett et al. 2012; Neukom et al. 2011). Jowett et al. (2012) clarify the significance of proximity (mutual trust and respect), commitment (the development of a lasting relationship in which both parties are willing and motivated to work with each other) and complementarity (beneficial cooperation in view of the differing roles). From the results of 30 semi-structured interviews with HR managers responsible for coaching, Neukom et al. (2011) show that half of the surveyed experts hold the view that a good working relationship is the crucial (efficacy) factor in coaching. A third consider a functioning working relationship as an important prerequisite for the success of a coaching process. As for the characteristics and skills needed by a coach when it comes to building a working relationship, those most frequently mentioned by the coaching conveners were: good listening skills, empathy, appreciation, trustworthiness, interest and openness. For their part, Alvey and Barclay (2007) examine the development of trust in coaching and describe factors that could be considered as prerequisites for the building of trust, for instance clear expectations on both sides or a positive attitude on the part of the organization towards coaching.

Other significant process variables that contribute to positive coaching effects appear to be the initial defining of goals, the fostering the client's goal commitment and the steady progress made towards goal attainment (Behrendt 2004; De Meuse et al. 2009; Möller and Kotte 2011). Some of the studies included in the meta-analysis by De Meuse et al. (2009) showed that coaching produces the best results when it has a direct connection to the coaching goals. Even the study by Schermuly et al. (2014) can be interpreted as indicating that a lack of goal-focusing can compromise coaching success. They found a positive relationship between the amount of topics dealt with and the amount of negative effects from the coaching.

On top of this, attention is now being paid to "critical incidents" in the process. De Haan and Nieß (2012), in a coaching case study, show that coach and clients reported one or more critical incidents in each coaching session. In almost half of the cases both coach and client describe the same incidents as meaningful. The coach however focuses mainly on incidents of self-doubt while the client selects incidents when something new is learned and when a positive change takes place within the coaching relationship. Milner et al. (2013) examine critical incidents in cross-cultural coaching. Coaches were asked in interviews to describe critical incidents. The results show that these occurred in four areas: communication (uncommunicative coachees, inability to take criticism); coach-coachee relationship (problems with building trust, idealizing the coach); coaching setting (location) and understanding of one's role (different role expectations).

The prerequisites on the part of the organization, such as the available budget, the planned number of coaching sessions, notification and acceptance of the measures or the selection of coach and its influence upon the outcome have so far only been postulated on a theoretical basis. This equally holds true for potential common factors such as the organizational culture and the transfer climate (Greif 2013; Möller and Kotte 2011). In one single-case study, good internal marketing, transparency about the coaching process and the emphasis upon free choice when it comes to participation were described as success factors for the sustainable establishment of coaching as a human resources development tool (Kurz 2013). In an interview study with 31 coaches from Asia and Europe, cultural awareness on the part of the coach towards the clients also emerged as best practice for successful coaching. Coaches must therefore familiarize themselves with the client's background and culture and acknowledge these in order to lay the groundwork for successful coaching (Gentry et al. 2013).

2.3.3 Summary of the Current State of Research

In conclusion, the most important points and their implications for the relationship between coaching science and coaching practice can be summarized in view of the development and current state of coaching research:

- Even for university-based researchers, finding coaching studies proves to be difficult and time-consuming despite their extensive access to various databases. Since the research results are published in various journals that are not all included in a single database, even the scientists cannot be certain that they have compiled all of the relevant studies and thus obtained a complete overview of the research landscape. This state of affairs makes it practically impossible for practitioners to keep up-to-date with the current state of research and is far from constructive.
- Both quantitative and qualitative studies are represented in international coaching-research journals. Upon appraisal of the purely qualitative studies it became apparent that these studies seldom tie in with other studies or preliminary work in any systematic way; instead they cover single and often highly specific topics. It is not uncommon for the coach him- or herself to act as the case supplier and thus also as the researcher. The majority of quantitative studies examine the effectiveness of coaching. More recent research frequently focuses on the influence of the relationship between coach and client as a predictor of coaching effectiveness. The complexity of the study designs differs enormously, from basic cross-sectional measurements to longitudinal studies with several measurement points using a variety of psychometric scales. The combination of qualitative and quantitative approaches, in other words mixed methods, is relatively commonplace within coaching research. So for instance, in the study by De Haan et al. (2013), they use both quantitative items,

sometimes from standardized psychometric scales, as well as comments boxes for open answers. Other studies combine quantitative questionnaires with qualitative interviews (Curtis and Kelly 2013).

2.4 Conclusion and Outlook for the Future

The differences between the two systems that were indicated in Sect. 2.2 must be treated seriously if one wishes to engage oneself with the development of a cooperative working relationship between science and practice. Section 2.3 also demonstrated not only how relatively inaccessible the field of coaching research is, even for those involved in it, i.e. scientists, but also that the "stock of knowledge" is growing and offers worthwhile insights for practitioners as well. Therefore, both willingness and pragmatic solutions are required in order to work towards a mutually profitable working relationship that goes beyond selective "openings" between the two systems.

Both communities must be prepared to leave the comfort zone of their own fields and deal with potential disappointments and grievances. After all, one cannot discover new territories without bidding farewell to familiar shores and facing unexpected challenges. For practitioners, this could mean letting go of cherished reference theories—in other words, the recognition that they can be prone to type I errors –, while for researchers, this could mean questioning the belief that their findings, now gradually being made available, are impatiently awaited. Both sides require bridge-builders and go-betweens—researching coaches and coaching scientists—as well as sustainable collaborations in tangible research-practice projects. "The more that supervisors (or coaches) learn about supervision research (or coaching research), then the sooner that they will become more skilled partners within practice-based research that serves to optimize supervisory (coaching) conduct… The hierarchy between science and the profession will however only be dismantled when it achieves a true synthesis in which practitioners are integrated not merely as data providers but as full-fledged members within research groups." (Haubl 2009, p. 202, own translation) Also required is a commitment to creating suitable integration nodes where dialog and debate can be fostered as well as the bundling of the literature. This includes both the published literature (from A-ranked journals to practitioner publications) as well as the coaching research's grey literature that is available on a much wider scale, i.e. the countless unpublished academic theses. With all this in mind, we propose that coaching researchers and practitioners commit to the following specific undertakings:

2.4.1 What Researchers Should Undertake to Do

Researchers must be prepared to balance two demands:

- On the one hand they must promote recognition of the coaching research field within the scientific community where it has yet to properly take root. Among other things, this means seeking out viable solutions such as how scientifically valid research designs and research methods can be linked with approaches that appeal to practitioners (cf. the article by Greif in this book). It is also imperative that systematic research programs that build upon each other be developed and implemented on a long-term basis instead of continuing to only let a range of isolated Bachelor's and Master's theses be produced. This however cannot happen without a more intensive discussion on the topic by established researchers, keeping in mind that experienced practitioners expect to interact with scientists on an equal footing, something which Bachelor and Master's students cannot achieve.
- When it comes to how the "opposing side" is viewed, a rethink of the self-definition is necessary: Researchers are also service providers for the practitioners, i.e. they must be committed to identifying the latter's needs and reacting to these. On the one hand, practitioners must be asked systematically about what is genuinely relevant to them (informative, instructive, inspiring; Padberg 2012) and what they view as hindrances and incentives to participating in research projects. On the other hand, as part of a more service-oriented self-definition it is also the coaching researchers' task to facilitate the practitioners' access to the scientific literature by writing easily readable summaries on the current state of the research in readily available publications.

2.4.2 What Practitioners Should Undertake to Do

- For their part, practitioners must be prepared to leave their own comfort zone and abandon potential defensive tactics and to make their coaching processes accessible to researchers. This also implies answering the critical question as to what extent their claim that protecting the coaching space for the client really is a priority. Is it not in fact merely a useful pretext for refusing to be observed and potentially assessed by external third parties (researchers), a source of some anxiety for the coaches? It is the practitioner's duty to enter into constructive dialog with the researchers and thereby share their own perspectives, ideas and expectations. Perhaps it will be helpful that there is a growing external pressure and that, in the foreseeable future, the demands for the systematic evaluation and quality assurance of coaching will certainly increase—from clients, companies and certifying professional associations.

- Corresponding to the publication service by researchers for practitioners, practitioners for their part must be receptive to suggestions regarding systematization as well as quality criteria such as will be put forward by scientists. This particularly applies to the large number of single-case descriptions that can scarcely be systematically incorporated into the stock of knowledge due to their disparity and their lack of connection to extant research. This is where first guidelines are made available by scientists, for example with regard to how single-case analyses (McDowall and Short 2012) ought to be shaped so that they can be more easily adopted and integrated into the stock of knowledge of coaching.

References

Alvey, S., & Barclay, K. (2007). The characteristics of dyadic trust in executive coaching. *Journal of Leadership Studies, 1*(1), 18–27.

Anderson, M. C. (2011). Evaluating the ROI of coaching: Telling a story, not just producing a number. In G. Hernez-Broome & L. M. Bohon (Eds.), *Advancing Executive Coaching—Setting the Course for Successful Leadership Coaching* (pp. 352–369). San Francisco: Jossey-Bass.

Arthur, W., Jr., Bennett, W., Jr., Edens, P. S., & Bell, S. T. (2003). Effectiveness of Training in Organizations: A Meta-Analysis of Design and Evaluation Features. *Journal of Applied Psychology, 88*(2), 234–245.

Baron, L., & Morin, L. (2009). The coach-coachee relationship in executive coaching: A field study. *Human Resource Development Quarterly, 20*(1), 85–106.

Baron, L., & Morin, L. (2012). The working alliance in executive coaching: Its impact on outcomes and how coaches can influence it. In E. de Haan & C. Sills (Eds.), *Coaching relationships* (pp. 213–226). Farringdon, UK: Libri.

Behrendt, P. (2004). Wirkfaktoren im Psychodrama und Transfercoaching. Diplomarbeit am Institut für Psychologie der Albert-Ludwigs-Universität Freiburg (Gewinner des Deutschen Coachingpreises).

Blattner, J. (2005). Coaching: the successful adventure of a downwardly mobile executive. *Consulting Psychology Journal: Practice and Research, 57*(1), 3–13.

Böning, U., & Fritschle, B. (2005). *Coaching furs Business*. Bonn: ManagerSeminare.

Bono, J., Purvanova, R., Towler, A., & Peterson, D. (2009). A survey of executive coaching practices. *Personnel Psychology, 62*(2), 361–404.

Bourdieu, P. (1988). *Homo Academicus*. Frankfurt/M.: Suhrkamp.

Boyce, L. A., Jackson, R. J., & Neal, L. J. (2010). Building successful leadership coaching relationships: Examining impact of matching criteria in a leadership coaching program. *Journal of Management Development, 29,* 914–931.

Bozer, G., & Sarros, J. C. (2012). examining the effectiveness of executive coaching on coachees' performance in the israeli context. *International Journal of Evidence Based Coaching and Mentoring, 10*(1), 14–32.

Carey, W., Philippon, D., & Cummings, C. (2011). Coaching models for leadership development: An integrative review. *Journal of Leadership Studie, 5*(1), 51–69.

Cavanagh, M. J. (2010). The four factor model of leadership: empirical foundations and practical application. *Paper presented at the international conference of applied psychology* (ICAP 2010), July 13, 2010, Melbourne, Australia.

Cerni, T., Curtis, G., & Colmer, S. (2010). Executive coaching can enhance transformational leadership. *International Coaching Psychology Review, 5*(1), 81–85.

Cox, E., & Patrick, C. (2012). Managing emotions at work: how coaching affects retail support workers' performance and motivation. *International Journal of Evidence Based Coaching and Mentoring, 10*(2), 34–51.

Curtis, D. F., & Kelly, L. L. (2013). Effect of a quality of life coaching intervention on psychological courage and self-determination. *International Journal of Evidence Based Coaching and Mentoring, 11*(1), 20–38.

De Haan, E., & Duckworth, A. (2012). Signalling a new trend in executive coaching outcome research. *International Coaching Psychology Review, 8*(1), 6–19.

De Haan, E., & Nieß, C. (2012). Critical moments in a coaching case study: Illustration of a process research model. *Consulting Psychology Journal: Practice and Research, 64*(3), 198–224.

De Haan, E., Culpin, V., & Curd, J. (2011). Executive coaching in practice: what determines helpfulness for clients of coaching? *Personnel Review, 10*(1), 24–44.

De Haan, E., Duckworth, A., Birch, D., & Jones, C. (2013). Executive coaching outcome research: The contribution of common factors such as relationship, personality match, and self-efficacy. *Consulting Psychology Journal: Practice and Research, 65*(1), 40–57.

De Meuse, K. P., Dai, G., & Lee, R. J. (2009). Evaluating the effectiveness of executive coaching: beyond ROI? coaching: An international journal of theory. *Research and Practice, 2*(2), 117–134.

Dreyfus, H. L., & Dreyfus, S. E. (1987). *Künstliche Intelligenz. Von den Grenzen der Denkmaschine und dem Wert der Intuition*. Reinbek: Rowohlt.

Eagleman, D. (2011). *Incognito. the secret lives of the brain*. Edinburgh: Canongate Books.

Ellam-Dyson, V., & Palmer, S. (2011). Leadership Coaching? No thanks. *I'm not worthy. The Coaching Psychologist, 7*(2), 108–117.

Ely, K., & Zaccaro, S. J. (2011). Evaluating the effectiveness of coaching—a focus on stakeholders, criteria, and data collection methods. In G. Hernez-Broome & L. A. Boyce (Eds.), *Advancing executive coaching—setting the course for successful leadership coaching*. San Francisco: Jossey-Bass.

Ely, K., Boyce, L. A., Nelson, J. K., Zaccaro, S. J., Hernez-Broome, G., & Whyman, W. (2010). Evaluating leadership coaching: a review and intergrated framework. *The Leadership Quarterly, 21,* 585–599.

Feldman, D., & Lankau, M. (2005). Executive coaching: A review and agenda for future research. *Journal of Management, 31*(6), 829–848.

Finn, F., Mason, C., & Griffin, M. (2006). Investigating change over time—The effects of executive coaching on leaders‘ psychological states and behaviour. Vortrag auf dem 26th International Congress of Applied Psychology, 16.–21. Juli, Athens, Greece.

Freitag, T. (2011). Coaching in der Schweiz. Ein Praxisforschungsbeitrag zur Marktsituation. In R. Wegener, A. Fritze & M. Loebbert (Hrsg.), Coaching entwickeln. Forschung und Praxis im Dialog (S. 200–230). Wiesbaden: VS Verlag.

Geißler, H., Hasenbein, M., & Wegener, R. (2013). E-Coaching: Prozessund Ergebnisevaluation des "Virtuellen Zielerreichungscoachings". *Organisationsberatung Supervision Coaching, 20*(2), 125–142.

Gentry, W., Manning, L., Wolf, A., Hermez-Broome, G., & Allen, L. (2013). What coaches believe are best practices for coaching: a qualitative study of interviews from coaches residing in asia and europe. *Journal of Leadership Studies, 7*(2), 18–31.

Grafe, K., & Kronig, R. (2011). Internes coaching bei SAP. *Coaching Magazin, 12*(1), 8–24.

Grant, A. M. (2012). ROI is a poor measure of coaching success: towards a more holistic approach using a well-being and engagement framework. *Coaching: An International Journal of Theory, Research and Practice, 5*(2), 74–85.

Grant, A. M. (2013a). The Efficacy of Coaching. In J. Passmore, D. B. Peterson, & T. Freire (Eds.), *The Wiley-Blackwell Handbook of the Psychology of Coaching and Mentoring* (pp. 15–39). Hoboken: Wiley-Blackwell.

Grant, A. M. (2013b). Autonomy support, relationship satisfaction and goal focus in the coach-coachee relationship: which best predicts coaching success? *Coaching: An International Journal of Theory, Research and Practice*, published online October 2013, 1–21.

Grant, A. M., Green, L. S., & Rynsaardt, J. (2010a). Developmental coaching for high school teachers: Executive coaching goes to school. *Consulting Psychology Journal: Practice & Research September*, 62(3), 151–168.

Grant, A.M., Passmore, J., Cavanagh, M.J., & Parker, H. (2010b). The state of play in coaching today: a comprehensive review of the field. *International Review of Industrial and Organizational Psychology*, 25, 125–167.

Greif, S. (2008). *Coaching und ergebnisorientierte Selbstreflexion*. Göttingen: Hogrefe.

Greif, S. (2013). Conducting organizazional-based evaluations and mentoring programs. In J. Passmore, D. B. Peterson, & T. Freire (Eds.), *The Wiley-Blackwell handbook of the psychology of coaching and mentoring* (pp. 445–470). Hoboken: Wiley-Blackwell.

Hall, J. B. (Ed.). (1991). *Ioannis Saresberiensis metalogicon*. Turnhout: Brepols.

Haubl, R. (2009). Unter welchen Bedingungen nützt die Supervisionsforschung der Professionalisierung supervisorischen Handelns? In R. Haubl & B. Hausinger (Hrsg.), Supervisionsforschung. Einblicke und Ausblicke (S.179–207). Göttingen: Vandenhoeck & Ruprecht.

Ianiro, P., & Kauffeld, S. (2011). Black-Box Coaching-Prozess: Beziehungsaufbau und—gestaltung auf Grundlage interpersonaler Basisdimensionen. Vortrag beim 2. LOCCS-Symposium, 27.–29. Mai 2011, München.

Ianiro, P. M., Schermuly, C. C., & Kauffeld, S. (2012). Why interpersonal dominance and affiliation matter: an interaction analysis of the coach-client relationship. *Coaching: An International Journal of Theory, Research & Practice, 6*(1), 1–22.

Joo, B. (2005). Executive coaching: a conceptual framework from an integrative review of practice and research. *Human Resource Development Review, 4*(4), 462–488.

Jowett, S., Kanakoglou, K., & Passmore, J. (2012). The application of the 3 + 1Cs relationship model in executive coaching. *Consulting Psychology Journal: Practice and Research, 64*(3), 183–197.

Jüttemann, G. (1990). *Komparative Kasuistik.* Heidelberg: Asanger.

Kaufel, S., Scherer, S., Scherm, M., & Sauer, M. (2006). Führungsbegleitung in der Bundeswehr—Coaching für militärische Führungskräfte. In W. Backhausen & J.-P. Thommen (Eds.), *Coaching, durch systemisches Denken zur innovativen Personalentwicklung* (pp. 419–438). Wiesbaden: Gabler.

Kauffeld, S. (2010). Nachhaltige Weiterbildung. Betriebliche Seminare und Trainings entwickeln, Erfolge messen, Transfer sichern. Berlin: Springer.

Kelly-Irving, M. (2014). A Research Frontier. http://researchfrontier.wordpress.com (abgerufen am 27.2. 2014).

Kieser, A. (2005). *Wissenschaft und Beratung*. Heidelberg: Universitätsverlag Winter.

Kines, P., Anderson, L. P., Spangenberg, S., Mikkelsen, K. L., Dyreborg, J., & Zohar, D. (2010). Improving construction site safety through leader-based verbal safety communication. *Journal of Safety Research, 41*(5), 399–406.

Kochanowski, S., Seifert, C. F., & Yukl, G. (2010). Using coaching to enhance the effects of behavioral feedback to managers. *Journal of Leadership and Organizational Studies, 17* (4), 363–369.

Kotte, S., & Möller, H. (2013). Coaching im Kontext von Führungsentwicklungsprogrammen. In R. Wegener, A. Fritze & M. Loebbert (Hrsg.). Coaching-Praxisfelder. Forschung und Praxis im Dialog (Online-Teil, S. 31–49). Wiesbaden: Springer VS.

Kühl, W. (2014). Wirkungen von Führungskräfte-Coaching in der Sozialen Arbeit. *Organisationsberatung Supervision Coaching, 21*(1), 39–53.

Künzli, H. (2009). *Wirksamkeitsforschung im Führungskräfte-Coaching. Organisationsberatung Supervision Coaching, 16*(1), 1–15.

Kurz, S. (2013). Implementierung von Einzel-Coachings im Rahmen eines Führungskräfteentwicklungs-Programms in der öffentlichen Verwaltung. *Organisationsberatung Supervision Coaching, 20*(2), 205–216.

Ladyshewsky, R. K. (2007). A strategic approach for integrating theory to practice in leadership development. *Leadership & Organization Development Journal, 28*(5), 426–443.

Leichsenring, F. (2004). Randomized controlled versus naturalistic studies: A new research agenda. *Bulletin of the Menninger Clinic, 68*(2), 137–151.

Leonard-Cross, E. (2010). Developmental coaching: Business benefit—fact or fad? An evaluative study to explore the impact of coaching in the workplace. *International Coaching Psychology Review, 5*(1), 36–47.

Libri, V., & Kemp, T. (2006). Assessing the efficacy of a cognitive behavioural executive coaching programme. *International Coaching Psychology Review, 1*(2), 9–18.

Linley, P., Nielsen, K. M., Gillett, R., & Biswas-Diener, R. (2010). Using signature strengths in pursuit of goals: Effects on goal progress, need satisfaction, and well-being, and implications for coaching psychologists. *International Coaching Psychology Review, 5* (1), 6–15.

Looss, W. (2006). Unter vier Augen: Coaching für Manager (korr. Neuausgabe). Bergisch Gladbach: EHP.

McDowall, A., & Short, E. (2012). New case study guidelines—a call to arms for practitioners, Coaching: An International Journal of Theory. *Research and Practice, 5*(2), 154–159.
McGovern, J., Lindemann, M., Vergara, M., Murphy, S., Barker, L., & Warrenfeltz, R. (2001). Maximizing the impact of executive coaching: Behavioral change, organizational outcomes, and return on investment. *Manchester Review, 6,* 1–9.
Milner, J., Ostmeier, E., & Franke, R. (2013). Critical incidents in cross-cultural coaching: The view from German coaches. *International Journal of Evidence Based Coaching and Mentoring, 11*(2), 19–32.
Möller, H. (2012). Was ist gute Supervision? Kassel: kassel university press.
Möller, H., & Hausinger, B. (Eds.). (2009). *Quo vadis Beratungswissenschaft?*. Wiesbaden: VS-Verlag.
Möller, H., & Kotte, S. (2011). Die Zukunft der Coachingforschung. *Organisationsberatung Supervision Coaching, 18*(4), 445–456.
Möller, H., Kotte, S., & Oellerich, K. (2013). Coaching-Praxis und Wissenschaft—ein unüberwindlicher Gap? *CoachingMagazin, 1*(2013), 35–39.
Neukom, M., Schnell, K., & Boothe, B. (2011). Die Arbeitsbeziehung im Coaching—ein Stiefkind der Forschung. *Organisationsberatung Supervision Coaching, 18*(3), 317–332.
Padberg, T. (2012). Warum lesen Psychotherapeuten keine Forschungsliteratur? *Psychotherapeutenjournal, 1*(2012), 10–17.
Riedelbauch, K. (2011). *Theorie und Förderung transformationaler Führung. Selbstdarstellungstheoretische Interpretation und Wirksamkeit von Gruppenworkshops und Einzelcoachings*. Dissertation, Otto-Friedrich-Universität Bamberg.
Scherf, M. (2010). Strukturen der Organisationssberatungsinteraktion. Interdisziplinäre Beratungsforschung. Göttingen: Vandenhoeck & Ruprecht.
Scherm, M., & Scherer, S. (2011). Feedbacksysteme im Coachingprozess: Forschungsergebnisse und Praxis. In R. Wegener, A. Fritze, M. Loebbert (Hrsg.), Coaching entwickeln. Forschung und Praxis im Dialog (S. 135–147). Wiesbaden: VS Verlag.
Schermuly, C. C., Schermuly-Haupt, M.-L., Schölmerich, F., & Rauterberg, H. (2014). Zu Risiken und Nebenwirkungen lesen Sie … Negative Effekte von Coaching. *Zeitschrift für Arbeits- und Organisationspsychologie, 58*(1), 17–33.
Seiger, C., & Künzli, H. (2011). Der Schweizerische Coachingmarkt 2010 aus der Sicht von Coachs. Züricher Hochschule für angewandte Wissenschaften [Online]. http://pd.zhaw.ch/hop/544183222.pdf (abgerufen am 21.02.2014).
Sherlock-Storey, M., Moss, M., & Timson, S. (2013). Brief coaching for resilience during organisational change—an exploratory study. *The Coaching Psychologist, 9*(1), 19–26.
Smither, J.W., London, M., Flautt, R., Vargas, Y. & Kucine, I. (2003). Can working with an executive coach improve multisource feedback ratings over time? A quasi-experimental field study. Personnel Psychology, 56, 23–44.
Spencer, L. (2011). Coaching and training transfer: A phenomenological inquiry into combined training-coaching programmes. *International Journal of Evidence Based Coaching and Mentoring, Special Issue, 5,* 1–18.
Stewart, L. J., O'Riordan, S., & Palmer, S. (2008). Before we know how we've done, we need to know what we're doing: Operationalising coaching to provide a foundation for coaching evaluation. *The Coaching Psychologist, 4*(3), 127–133.

Theeboom, T., Beersma, B., & van Vianen, A. E. M. (2014). Does coaching work? A meta-analysis on the effects of coaching on individual level outcomes in an organizational context. *The Journal of Positive Psychology, 9*(1), 1–18.
Van Oorsouw, W., Embregts, P., & Bosman, A. (2013). Quantitative and qualitative processes of change during staff-coaching sessions: An exploratory study. *Research in Developmental Disabilities, 34,* 1456–1467.
Wallis, G. (2010). Does a "blended" programme of development and coaching produce sustainable change? *International Journal of Evidence Based Coaching and Mentoring, Special Issue, 4*(2010), 105–113.

Author Biographies

Dr. phil. Silja Kotte Dipl.-Psych., supervisor (DGSv), further education in group dynamics (DAGG), consultant and trainer in international development cooperation, personnel developer in the industry, freelance work in supervision, coaching, personnel diagnostics and training. Since 2010 a research fellow in the theory and methodology of consultation at the University of Kassel, conducts research and lectures on consultation, groups, and management.

Katrin Oellerich Dipl.-Psych., coach (dpa), freelance work as a coach and trainer specializing in career development, management, and gender equality. Since 2012 a research fellow in the theory and methodology of consultation, University of Kassel, Institute for Psychology. Currently working on doctoral dissertation on the negative effects of coaching and their causes from the perspective of the organization. Research and lectures on consultation involving the living/working environment and conflict management.

Denise Elisabeth Hinn M.Sc., coach-in-training (dpa), freelance work as trainer and moderator. Research fellow in the theory and methodology of consultation at the University of Kassel, Institute for Psychology. Research and lectures on consultation concepts involving the living/working environment, personnel and organizational development.

Prof. Dr. Heidi Möller Dipl.-Psych., doctoral dissertation in the field of psychology on total institutions, post-doctoral dissertation on quality criteria in supervision, TU Berlin, teaching therapist for psychoanalysis and gestalt therapy, teaching supervisor, organizational consultant and coach. 2002 professorship for communication psychology and psychotherapy, 2004 founding dean of the Faculty of Pedagogy at the University of Innsbruck, since 2007 professor for the theory and methodology of consultation at the University of Kassel, Institute for Psychology.

Hard to Evaluate: Coaching Services

3

Siegfried Greif

Abstract

Coaching is a service which is co-produced in interaction with the client as well as being both intangible and confidential. Coaching processes are characterized by a high level of complexity and disparity and are as a result almost impossible to standardize. Taken together, these characteristics lead to coaching being a service that is hard to evaluate for both the customer and the client. As a result, coaching is often only informally evaluated, which brings with it the risk that these assessments turn out to be devaluing and indeed for the client even discriminatory. Professionalism demands that the particularities of coaching are accommodated by the use of sound scientific methods of evaluation. An evaluation model will be presented here that encompasses the three criteria of structural, process and result quality.

3.1 Controversies Surrounding Coaching as a Service, and Evaluation Methods

"Coaching is not a service", but rather an "another useful form of interaction", coaching pioneer Looss (2014) recently and trenchantly declared in his keynote speech at a coaching congress. He justifies his thesis with the point that coaching is difficult to rate in terms of categories of achievement. He did not fundamentally

S. Greif (✉)
Am Pappelgraben 78 B, 49080 Osnabrück, Germany
e-mail: sgreif@uos.de
URL: http://www.home.uni-osnabrueck.de/sgreif

A. Schreyögg and C. Schmidt-Lellek (eds.), *The Professionalization of Coaching*, DOI 10.1007/978-3-658-16805-6_3

speak out against the assessment of coaching in his conclusions with regard to the possibility of evaluating coaching; however, in his view such evaluations are often "desperate and moving attempts to make life predictable". He is presumably not the only one to hold this critical view. Not a few professional coaches evidently have a lot to say against evaluation methods. Schmidt-Tanger (2014), for example took the view at the same congress that coaching, in her professional understanding, should never be conducted in a standardized form. It would have a negative impact on the non-standardizable coaching relationship if the human resources section of a company were to ask the clients to rate their coaching with predetermined standard questions. In this way, standardization of the coaching process would be encouraged.

How legitimate are these or similar frequently heard fundamental objections and reservations regarding the evaluation of coaching? Must a new third category of paid work be created for coaching beyond the classical differentiation between goods and services? One that encompasses forms that provide services that are not generally tangible? Should coaching associations press for coaching not to be evaluated, or at least not using standardized methods, or should they go with the scientists who hold that the scientific assessment of coaching is necessary in order to make the "best practices" usable for clients, as demanded by Stober and Grant (2006), the international protagonists of a scientifically-based coaching profession. The questions concerning the professionalization of coaching that are dealt with in this contribution refer to the clarification of complex contradictions and conflicts within the profession as well as to the issue of whether a professional self-perception of coaching is conceivable without practical and scientific evaluation. The following section offers an overview of the term "evaluation", its meaning and various approaches and methods. After a brief introduction to the term and to the general significance of evaluations, the term service is considered as well as the question as to what constitutes the particularities of coaching in comparison with other services and why coaching is hard to evaluate. Finally, the reader is invited to enter into the discourse between science and practice regarding the further development of a professional self-perception as well as take an active part in the participation in evaluation research as an important basis for professionalization.

3.2 The Term Evaluation and Its Meaning

3.2.1 Various Methods of Evaluation

"Evaluation" is generally understood as "an inquiry process for collecting and synthesizing evidence" for an assessment of the value, worth, or quality of an object, person, or process (Fournier 2005, p. 140). Companies attempt in advance to evaluate the usefulness of coaching before they start the search for coaches and place an order. Often, companies follow the recommendations of credible experts when making their decisions (Stephan and Gross 2011, S. 178). They could however evaluate scientific studies into quality characteristics and the effectiveness of coaching before making their decisions. In order to check whether the expected results have been achieved after the introduction of coaching, they can attempt to evaluate the organization and conducting of the coaching as well as its results. If they are provided with the resources for this, they can carry out a comprehensive evaluation on the basis of an evaluation model and scientific methods or, more pragmatically, implement only a standard questionnaire on customer satisfaction. This decision is not without consequences for the development of the profession, as will be illustrated in the following.

3.2.2 Why Do People Evaluate?

Why do people evaluate products, services and the people and organizations that produce them? In his classical and today still fundamentally important *Social Comparison Theory*, the social psychologist Festinger (1954) assumes, in the manner of evolution theory, that it is an existential need of people to compare their own evaluations with the opinions of other relevant persons (cf. overview of Frey et al. 1993). This comparison of evaluations or "social validation" is necessary in order to avoid misjudgments in a complex and ever-changing world. It enables people to make decisions that are based upon subjectively certain evaluations. This need for comparative evaluation is fundamental. The greater the uncertainty, the stronger the need to evaluate. Festinger differentiates between the two types of criteria that are employed in order to evaluate the correctness of one's own evaluations:

(1) "Objective" criteria (inter-subjectively verifiable data, e.g. physical measurement values, turnover data etc.) and

(2) Social criteria (comparison with the subjective evaluations of other people, for example opinions expressed by other people regarding their experiences with coaches).

According to Festinger, "objective" criteria are generally preferred. If these are not available or appear insufficient for evaluation purposes, a person's own evaluations or judgements are compared with those of other relevant reference persons. Festinger assumed that, for the purposes of social comparison, people are preferred who are similar to the person doing the comparing. According to later studies, other reliable-seeming persons are also consulted according to the object of evaluation (Frey et al. 1993).

With regard to the evaluation of coaching, we can conclude, like Festinger, that evaluations of coaching are unavoidable. They are based on the fundamental need to safeguard one's own opinion. The tendency to prefer "objective data" when evaluating is also, according to Festinger, a basis for decision-making that is recommended not only by scientists. It is in accordance with a natural preference for data the quality of which is uncontested.

3.2.3 Evaluations as Social Constructions

In his theory, Festinger sketches how people construct their evaluations by means of processes of social comparison. In doing so he indicated at a very early point that evaluations do not rest upon "objective" data alone, above all when they relate to complex objects of evaluation. *Complex evaluations are jointly constructed by means of communication with other persons*. This constructivist-style reformulated general conclusion refers not only to the forming of opinions on an individual level but rather also to communication with others.

Greif et al. (2004) describe how judgments of planned change processes in companies are spread by means of *informal evaluation communications* via internal communication networks. They assume that these evaluations of, for example, changes, are much more influential than the official evaluating statements made by the companies. Thus informally communicated evaluations influence readiness to support the planned changes as well as whether employees react with open or concealed individual or collective resistance.

According to the practical observations of the author as an external and internal consultant and coach in various organizations, coaching really lends itself to the spreading of informal stories. Coaching, and the managers who ask for coaching, are even made fun of on the informal office grapevine: "The fact that he needs coaching proves that he is incompetent …". External and internal coaches who are not connected to the internal unofficial channels of communication often have no idea how they and their clients are discriminated against here (especially in the more down-to-earth areas of production).

However, if the need for evaluation is universal, and if evaluations of coaching, as either informal negative or positive social constructions, are unavoidable, it makes little sense to fundamentally go against informal assessments and methodical evaluations. The following case study describes the interplay between informal and formal evaluations.

In 1994, at the firm Felix Schoeller (at that time the global market leader for photographic and special papers), a new position and training programme for shift managers in production was created under the specialist control of the author of this chapter. The training modules were based upon methods of self-organized learning (Greif and Scheidewig 1998). In the first training module the trainee shift managers were to concern themselves with changes that were under way in the firm in order to then inform their staff about the planned changes and discuss with them how they could or would like to be involved. It was a tricky task. The changes had been set in motion by a well-known firm of consultants and were based upon the method still popular then of saving on personnel costs by means of Lean Management. The firm of consultants had managed to set almost the entire staff - right up to the senior master workmen and in part even the production line managers - against them and the planned changes. They did this by means of a concept that was in our view basically insufficiently practicable for this industry, as well as by making big mistakes in their communication of the necessary changes. At the same time it was, even in the opinion of the workers' council, urgently necessary to bring about considerable reductions in costs in order to save jobs.

In the seminar, in agreement with the internal project managers and human resources development, we allowed ourselves the freedom to use a project as an example that was not based upon the Lean Management concept, which was limited to saving personnel costs, but rather a project for internal logistics putting into practice in which no reduction in personnel took place but rather savings in material costs in millions were achieved. It consisted of replacing the plastic packaging of the enormous paper rolls with cardboard rolls, which also happened to be a more environmentally friendly solution. The only idea to be taken up from the Lean Management approach was the idea of an increase in self-organization and the shifting of responsibility to the lower working levels. For the purposes of evaluation of the presentation and discussion of the implementation project by the project leader in the seminar, the trainee shift managers received a short questionnaire with standard scales and open questions on feedback of the type generally used by us at the time for evaluating seminars at the university.

In order to support the trainee shift managers in the preparation of their tricky communication task, we conducted a transfer-coaching process of three to five sessions with them. They knew that their staff would evaluate their information transfer and the discussion anonymously (using the same questionnaire that they themselves

> had used for feedback in the seminar). This type of evaluation of management behavior had never taken place up to this point in the firm.
>
> In the end we had an implementation rate of 100% of the participants, something we had never before experienced in seminars. All of them received an evaluation of good or very good from their staff for their information meetings. These experiences of success have without a doubt increased the motivation and self-confidence of the future shift managers. This was then followed by very positive formal reports on the upper management levels. Even in the informal evaluation communications within the teams, the courageous appearances of the trainee shift managers were a subject of discussion. Previously there had been doubt and many informal complaints on almost all levels (including the management levels) about what shift masters were being trained as "shift managers" for, who were then even "needed coaching". These discriminatory informal evaluation communications ended from that day on.

This case study is an example of how against the background of Festinger's theory a simple evaluation method can make an explainable and very constructive psychological contribution towards increasing the evaluation certainty of the people involved. It additionally demonstrates how in this way discriminating and informal evaluation communications about coaching and the client can be halted or at least reduced. According to Festinger, it is psychologically important to use, where possible, objective numbers (in this case 100% implementation, "80% of employees found the presentation to be good or very good" etc.), but also to include and process as feedback non-standardized expressions of opinion given in response to open questions.

This example also demonstrates why evaluations are social constructs. It was already known to us before the evaluation took place that criticism had been expressed informally and at least in part justifiably concerning the change concept. This led to internally agreed re-evaluations and a partial new construction of the target concept. That which was to be achieved and evaluated in the training program was also developed together with the project management and the head of human resources as well as other stakeholders. The questionnaire, which had been kept deliberately short for use in the team, had to be literally constructed and its implementation had to be carefully negotiated with those responsible in the firm as well as the participants (leaders, human resources, workers' council, and participants). Even in the most extensive scientific investigations pragmatic selection decisions cannot be avoided. Evaluations thus always retain gaps and can never be conducted as comprehensively as one might wish.

One result that is regarded as a success by the company management and the other participants or people affected is based in the end on a kind of collage of incomplete data and information that is regarded as reliable in the estimation and evaluation communications of the opinion leaders and participants. This does not mean that such information collages and those overall assessments that are constructed by means of the evaluation are entirely arbitrary. If in our example the evaluation conducted by us were arbitrary or incorrect in the view of the participants (in the way it was carried out or with regard to the result) then we would have found this out very quickly by means of the informal communication networks. If we think further along the lines of the evolution-theoretical assumptions in Festinger's Social Comparison Theory we can happily postulate that scientists experienced in methodology as well as practitioners capable of reflection are able to find an "applicable and professional" combination of data and opinions by means of which the risk of faulty decisions can be reduced. Anyone who carries out evaluations studies in organizations should have learned to construct them so that they improve the certainty of decision-making and at the same time maintain contact with the informal evaluation networks.

According to scientific standards, evaluation studies must be conducted in a manner that is open for unexpected results. It also follows that (at least within the organization) the results need to be communicated transparently and openly, independently of whether they turn out to be negative or positive. Negative results offer the project leaders and participants the opportunity to initiate and manage an open and transparent discussion about the observed weaknesses of the changes and need for improvement in that they themselves first of all suggest improvements before the measures can be sentenced entirely to failure by the no longer controllable informal rejection. Applied to the evaluation of coaching, coaches who fundamentally reject accepted practical or scientific evaluation methods for coaching leave the evaluation in the hands of informal judgments and decisions.

In the following section, those particularities of coaching will be examined that make it so hard to evaluate the interactions within coaching as well as their effects. First of all, however, the question will be gone into as to whether coaching can be categorized as a service.

3.3 Coaching as a Particular Kind of Service

3.3.1 The Term Service

The classical economic differentiation between sectors of the economy differentiates between a primary sector (agriculture and forestry, animal husbandry and fishing) and a secondary sector (manufacturing and processing industries, mining, trades and crafts, energy and water supply). The "tertiary" sector was added as a "category for the rest" in which fall all other paid occupations that do not belong in either the first or second categories (Nerdinger 2011, S. 12). It was only recently that this extremely heterogeneous but economically strong and expanding "remaining sector" came to be known under the common term of "services", and the attempt to find commonalities between the services performed in this sector.

3.3.1.1 The Meaning of the Term "Service"

It is revealing to examine the origins of the term "service" as well as their evolving meanings (Harper 2016). "Servant" has old French roots of "servant" (foot-soldier) and "servire" in the sense of "to do duty toward, show devotion to" (Latin: "be devoted"). We can derive a role constellation from these word meanings that gives the determining role to the service recipient, whereby recognition for the service provider and for that which he provides is certainly also implicit.

3.3.1.2 Scientific Definitions of the Term Service

One may be skeptical as to whether general common features can be found for the heterogeneous sector of "services" by means of which it can be clearly differentiated from "goods". The business economists Meffert and Bruhn (2012, pp. 214–216) describe and discuss various definitions and the "constitutive" characteristics of services. They prefer a definition that (1) includes the necessary potential of the service provider, (2) the process by means of which the service is provided, and finally (3) the result aimed for. They thus define services in a highly complex manner as "independent marketable performances/services that are connected with the provision of (e.g. insurance services) and/or the employment of abilities (an example of *potential-oriented services* is hairdressing services). Internal (for example business premises, personnel, equipment) and external factors (that do not lie within the realm of influence of the service provider) are combined within the framework of the process of creation (*process orientation*). The factorial combination of the service provider is employed with the goal of achieving useful effects (e.g. a car inspection) for people (customers) and their objects (e.g. their cars and *result orientation*)" (Meffert and Bruhn 2012, pp. 238–239; free translation). The authors explicitly emphasize that their demarcation by means of definition does not intend to "imply a homogeneity that is non-existent in the service sector", but rather emphasize the great variety and heterogeneity, which make a more exact differentiation of different types of services necessary.

The definition appears complicated. To put it simply, three main components are addressed: (1) necessary service skills (or potential) of the service provider, (2) internal and external factors the process of production of the services and (3) as a result, "useful effects" (for people and their goals). Coaching can be subsumed very unambiguously and un-problematically under this definition.

The question remains, however, as to whether all goods or products manufactured within a firm can be excluded using this definition. This also has to do with the fact that the manufacturer nowadays even more frequently combines the sale of their products with the provision of services (for example specialist advice helping the customer to install the product and servicing of the appliances at the customer's location). There are also products that would as such fall under the definition offered by Meffert and Bruhn. One might for example think that the manufacturing of a skin cream might demand "skills" as well as the factors generally listed in the definition in the manufacturing process and in particular in the literal sense of a "useful effect" for people. Skin cream is however clearly not a service.

Maleri and Frietsche (2008) point out three characteristics that are more suitable for demarcation purposes: (1) the immaterial nature of the service, (2) the employment of so-called external factors in the production process (i.e., that the clients participate as external factors in the production of the service) and (3) "no raw materials are used".

In the view of the economists quoted here, the evaluation of the quality of the results of services is difficult because services are immaterial or intangible. It follows that the objective measurement values are hardly suitable, and that instead the subjective perceptions and judgments of the customers need to be called upon. Examples are surveys on customer satisfaction, but in particular on customer loyalty and willingness to recommend. These subjective evaluations are taken very seriously by economists because the turnover of service providers has been shown empirically to be positively influenced by them (see Nerdinger's summary 2011, p. 105 ff.).

3.3.2 Characteristics and Various Types of Services

3.3.2.1 Major Characteristics and Types of Services

The defining major characteristics of services are summarized very clearly and succinctly by Schneider and White (2004). The characteristics can be more or less pronounced depending on the service. In the following, these general features are described using quotations from Schneider and White (2004, pp. 6–9). Afterwards, the individual characteristics are regarded by the author of this chapter in relation to coaching and questions are raised with regard to the evaluation of coaching.

(1) **Relative Intangibility**
"Pure services cannot be seen, touched, held, or stored - they have no physical manifestation." Many services have however tangible components, for example car repair, in which a new exhaust pipe is installed. When we apply the major features of services described by Schneider and White (2004) to coaching, then this occupation clearly belongs to those services that are almost entirely intangible. It may be that in individual cases partial exceptions exist, for example when a client takes with him a questionnaire that he has filled in or notes an appointment in his calendar. The evaluation of the quality of intangible services is difficult. As already mentioned above, subjective perceptions and judgments or observable consequences of assumed intangible changes have to be resorted to. How this is possible is described below.

(2) **Relative Inseparability**
Listening to a symphony orchestra or watching a play at the theatre are examples of "pure" services in which their production and consumption by the customer are not separable in terms of time. They are not produced at one time and then stored at another time or in another place for later use. They are produced by the service provider and "consumed" by the customer at the same time by the customer in a delivery experience. This simultaneity is also called in Latin the uno-actu Principle. When the production and consumption take place simultaneously, this decreases the possibilities for testing and improving quality before delivery.

Coaching belongs without doubt to these services that are, according to Schneider and White (2004), partly inseparable services. The service comes about in an interactive process between coach and client. One example is a client who in a moment during the coaching process develops a strong feeling of being understood and supported by the coach. *The process of coaching is a substantial part of the outcome.* However, the clients can also strictly speaking "take something with them" from the coaching process if they keep in mind the support of the coach or a newly won insight or especially if they note down a plan as to how they can finally implement a change in behavior in their everyday lives for which they had been aiming for a long time.

Since the clients play a major part in the interaction and the result generated, one can speak in the case of coaching of a "co-production" of the service. Constructivists prefer to use the term "co-construction" here. However, "construction" is often used in the context of building, e.g. "Street under construction" etc. If one wants to emphasize that at least for the client something new has come into existence during the commonly created service, then one can describe this process as "co-creation". One consequence for the evaluation of the quality of coaching is that not only do the competence and behavior of the coach within the process need to be analyzed in connection with the interaction but rather also that of the client.

(3) **Relative Heterogeneity**
Coaching is extremely heterogeneous und manifold in form, and in the end as varied as the clients and their themes, goals and contexts. Schneider and White (2004, pp. 8–9) emphasize the point that services are more heterogeneous and less open to standardization than goods in their production and delivery: they also depend on the interaction with the client. They must in each case be adapted to the individual expectations, abilities and previous knowledge of the customer.

In Coaching, the difference of the clients or customers that is described by Schneider and White (2004) is no doubt very clear to all coaches, and they attempt to take this into account by adapting their methods and tools. Some feel that in coaching it doesn't make much sense to use tools or standard methods of evaluation. These methods do not however need to be seen as imperative: they can instead be understood as rules of thumb that are useful for orientation purposes but that always need to be adapted for use or as heuristic principles. (This applies explicitly to this author's guidelines.)

It is possible to determine profiles for the different types of services on the basis of the form taken by the feature described, as shown in Fig. 3.1.

In Fig. 3.1, the profiles of three different typical services are compared: coaching, textile sales in a clothes shop for demanding customers and selling burgers in a restaurant from one of the large chains. The coaching profile stands out clearly with its extremely low level of tangibility and high values for inseparability and heterogeneity. Were we however to draw up a profile for psychotherapeutic work, then it would take on a similar appearance. A professional counseling session conducted according to a proscribed standard procedure would however demonstrate a similar profile in terms of tangibility and inseparability (although with significantly less pronounced values), but have a much lower level of heterogeneity. In a burger restaurant, tangible, standardized edible goods are sold. Only the standard design of the restaurant, the outer appearance and taste of the burger, and the friendliness of the personnel would altogether lead to the value for tangibility being located just below the maximum value. Since however the production and consumption of the burger are clearly separable, and since as a result of the standardization of the sale of the burgers makes almost no allowance for the different customers, this service is very similar to the production and delivery of

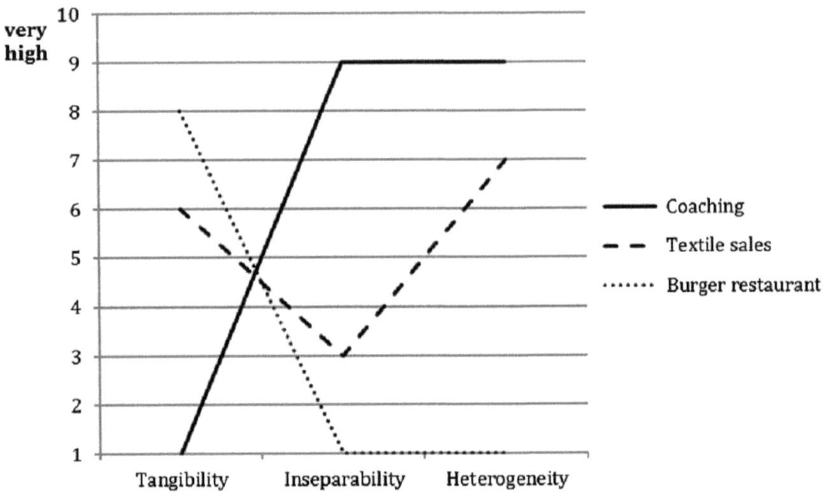

Fig. 3.1 Different types of services

goods in the manufacturing trade. What is interesting is that in high-end clothes shops, the necessity for a psychologically favorable presentation of the current items of clothing reduces the tangibility of this service. The individual and different wishes of the customers must be taken very much into account, which is why the heterogeneity is relatively high.

Research into the particularities of services and the development of methods for evaluating the quality of services is generally still relatively young and not very reliable, as Meffert and Bruhn (2012) found. Schneider and White (2004) rely on research from the field of service psychology (Nerdinger 2011; Schneider and Bowen 1995).

3.3.2.2 Qualifications of the Clients

Schneider and Bowen (1995, p. 93) found that many customers do not understand their role in the co-production of the service. It is therefore necessary to at least enlighten the customers as to the expectations concerning how they behave as co-producer. Schneider and Bowen recommend finding suitable ways of getting across to the customers what exactly is expected of them as co-producer and how they can make a contribution towards more efficient processes and optimal results. This is already common practice for some complex services, for example before a new company software system is introduced: The customers receive a specialist introduction and qualification.

As far as coaching is concerned, it would appear questionable whether the usual short introduction in the first coaching session with information about the general principles of coaching is sufficient, and whether the client is able to implement them straight away in the coaching process. It would appear more appropriate to give staff an introduction to coaching with a special further education module, for example in the case of managers within the framework of their management seminars. In a study project in the field of occupational and organizational psychology at the University of Osnabrück we developed a model of this kind for future managers with three or four "test coaching" sessions. Acceptance and satisfaction on the part of the participants as well as interest in coaching were consistently high.

3.3.2.3 Further Typical Coaching Characteristics

Alongside the general characteristics of services addressed above, the following features are particularly characteristic for coaching:

- *Strict discretion*: Coaches commit themselves to strict discretion with regard to their clients. Unlike doctors and psychotherapists, however, they are not strictly bound by professional secrecy laws. Nevertheless, evaluation studies demand strict anonymity for the participants. This can be ensured by means of strict anonymization procedures and trustworthy evaluators (for example independent scientists).
- *Relative independence of the purchaser and service recipient:* Other than in the case of psychotherapy which is paid for in many countries by the health insurance companies, coaching is, with the exception of private customers, commissioned and financed by firms in a manner similar to company training measures. However, the subjects and goals in coaching are not completely determined by the purchaser, as is the case with training measures, but rather by the clients themselves. The firm's goals are presented to the client in the form of expectations. Because of the discretion aspect, the extent to which they can be taken into account in the process can be controlled only indirectly by the purchaser, for example by means of talks before and after the coaching process. It would be interesting to take a closer look at how often conflicts result from this very particular constellation and whether they affect the level of acceptance of coaching on the part of the purchaser.

3.3.3 Coaching as a Difficult Service to Assess

Meffert and Bruhn (2012) closely examine the complexity of services and its significance for the estimation of the quality of services by the customers. Similar to Benkenstein and Güthoff (1996), they differentiate between five dimensions of complexity: (1) the number of service components (2) multi-personality (number of persons involved), (3) heterogeneity of the service components, (4) length of the period of production and (5) the individuality of the customers (cited after Meffert and Bruhn 2012, pp. 330–341). They use these dimensions to differentiate between types of services. As an example of a service with a high level of complexity in all dimensions they name a heart transplant operation, whereas the dispensing of cash from a cash dispenser scores low on all dimensions. Coaching would be categorized as a service the complexity of which is very high on four of these dimensions. The only exception is the dimension multi-personality, because coaching is normally conducted by only one person.

Complex services can be evaluated only partially and with difficulty by the customers, according to Meffert and Bruhn (2012). This means that their purchase risk is high (Meffert and Bruhn 2012, p. 2611). In order to reduce uncertainty of evaluation as a result of incomplete information, customers rely instead on trust-inducing so called "surrogates" such as for example the quality of the relationship (perceived goodness of the relationship between the service provider and the customer and in particular subjective level of trust on the part of the customer as well as familiarity between customer and service provider, Meffert and Bruhn 2012, p. 991) or simply how well known the provider is or the quality of the brand that he represents (p. 1420).

Coaching can profit as a service from the fact that a high level of trust can be established in the working relationship (Palmer and McDowall 2010), which may then be used by the customer as a surrogate for the evaluation of the goodness of the service. The confidentiality aspect however makes it difficult for the majority of people who have no coaching experience to evaluate complex coaching services in advance on the basis of verifiable information. That which takes place "in secret" can easily be taken as a surface for the projection of accusations and acts of discrimination in informal evaluations. The term "coach", unlike the term "psychotherapist", is not a protected professional term, and the quality of the certificates awarded by coaching associations for coaching qualifications or the status of coach is hardly verifiable for the customer as a measure of quality.

3.4 Coaching as a Profession at the Crossroads

3.4.1 Understanding Coaching as a Particular Form of Service

According to Fietze, from a profession-sociological point of view scientific research into the professionalization of coaching has an important role to play (Fietze 2011, p. 31 and Chap. 1 in this book). Research serves to increase the legitimization of coaching as an independent profession in that it contributes towards clarification of the coaching concept by means of scientific discourse as well as proving its effectiveness by means of scientific evaluation studies (see here Kotte et al., Chap. 2 in this book). More attention should also be paid however in the debate on professionalization to the fact that science not only has a legitimization function for the profession but also a function with regard to orientation, as Fietze notes. This is achieved by means of discourses between practitioners and scientists regarding the professional understanding of coaching as well as with regard to clarifying its constituent features. Comparisons and clarification of boundaries to other professions play a significant role in this.

As has been shown, coaching can be understood as a service and can thus be brought into connection with the interdisciplinary specialist efforts to clarify and research into the characteristics of services as well as into differentiating between different types of services. In summary, five features can be found to be characteristic for the particular nature of coaching:

(1) A very high level of intangibility,
(2) Inseparability (uno-actu principle), and co-creation of the service provided,
(3) A high level of heterogeneity (taking into account the individuality of the client),
(4) Strict discretion, and
(5) Relative independence from the purchaser and service recipient.

When we look at these characteristics, we see that that characteristics profile of coaching differs clearly from that of most other services. A discussion of the similarities and differences between coaching and other services can contribute towards the further development of a differentiated professional self-understanding within the profession and help to clarify "the contours of the professional identity" (Fietze 2011, p. 27, free translation). There are services that are comparable with coaching in not all but many aspects. We can examine here whether these professions struggle with comparable problems relating to evaluation of the service provided. Psychotherapy for example could be discussed as an interesting example for comparison in many respects, even though its solutions can hardly be taken for use as a transferrable model.

In terms of the public image of the profession, it would make little sense for coaching to shut itself out from the current service-sciences' attempts at clarification by regarding itself as a form of interaction or activity that is incomparable to services, when it can obviously be categorized as a service. When in addition service-sciences, and in particular economic analyses, are rejected wholesale, this leads in my view to a dead end in the future of the profession, because it is blind to current scientific discourses. At the current crossroads for the further development of the self-perception of coaching, connecting up with current and economic analyses would be more constructive. It is not true that economists only ever evaluate things in terms of economic figures. The economists quoted here regard services in their standard works through more than just "economic glasses"; instead they analyze in a differentiated manner the difficulties and possibilities with regard to how complex, co-produced, "immaterial services" can be evaluated, communicated and improved in terms of their quality. A closer reference to the language of the economists could even help the coaching profession to overcome communication barriers separating them from their business customers and managers, as well as make comprehensible to them how coaching services can be co-created, evaluated, and improved in terms of quality by means of common efforts.

3.4.2 Taking on the Challenges of Evaluation

The client's difficulty with unambiguously evaluating the quality of coaching or coaches is the downside of the particular features of coaching as a service. Coaches who believe that coaching is impossible to evaluate and that it would be better to do entirely without practical and scientific evaluation do not by doing so get rid of peoples' interest in evaluating coaching. They leave the evaluation of coaching to those informal forms of evaluation that can quickly lead to negative discrimination of the client. These kinds of "evaluation communications" (see above) are very difficult to influence by means of professional evaluations of coaching. The advantage of scientific evaluations is that according to academic standards they are transparent in terms of the methods and criteria used and can thus be criticized very exactly.

Companies mainly rely on personal recommendations, that is, informal evaluative communications, when looking for suitable coaches (Stephan and Gross 2011, p. 168). They attempt to ensure the quality of the coaching by means of "an exact clarification of the task and definition of the goal from the start" (35% of the companies), retrospective ratings of goal attainment (46%), and feedback dialogues (35%) (Stephan and Gross 2011, p. 178; only the highest percentages of the survey of 51 executives in charge of coaching are cited). In the face of such rudimentary criteria for evaluation, which can be easily criticized, we are still a long way away from a professional evaluation of coaches and coaching. It is a challenge for science and the profession to promote the development and use of better-suited systematic methods of investigation and criteria for the evaluation and improvement of the quality of coaching. Evaluation research into psychotherapeutic methods (Hautzinger and Pauli 2009) can serve as an example for how these challenges can be overcome despite perhaps even greater difficulties in terms of evaluation.

With the current state of research, the development of an "evaluation model" is to be recommended as a basis when planning a systematic evaluation (Wottawa and Thierau 1998). When undertaking evaluation of coaching, the systematic and personal preconditions, measures and process characteristics that appear relevant as well as the expected results need to be included and specified in a model of this kind. In the case of services, these differences correspond to the criteria of structural, process and result quality. Suitable methods can then be selected on the basis of this model with which the quality characteristics can then be collected. In a general evaluation model for coaching, Greif (2013, 2017) differentiates the following:

(1) Antecedents of coaching, which influence the outcome before coaching has started (characteristics of coaches, clients and organizations),
(2) Coaching process (coaching relationship, attributes and behavior of coach and client, and their interactions and instantaneous outcome),
(3) Short-term outcome (general evaluation criteria as well as criteria specific to coaching for the clients, coach, and organization),
(4) Long-term outcome (criteria for the clients, coach, and organization),
(5) Favorable organizational context conditions (see also Chap. 2 in this book).

The model can, like any model, be further extended or differentiated as new knowledge is gained.

Attempts have been made by consultants to estimate the economic return on investment through coaching (Anderson and Anderson 2005). The adventurously high estimates (for example an increase of the ROI of 689%) result from estimation artifacts (Greif 2013). Indicators of economic efficiency can probably be achieved by coaching at best indirectly and long-term (when for instance more employees actively participate in organizational changes as a result of a transformational leadership style resulting from coaching).

With regard to the individual criteria of the evaluation model, the current state of research already makes it possible to list examples of recommended instruments and methods that have demonstrated themselves to be scientific and practicable for their assessment (Greif 2013, 2017). In the following, criteria are listed as examples that appear suitable for the evaluation of the short-term results for the client.

The first sub-group of criteria is made up of *general scales*, which can also be used to compare coaching with other services, for example training (for more details see Greif 2013, 2017):

(1) Questionnaires for evaluating customer satisfaction and loyalty. (Here, established national and international scales can be used as recommended by Meffert and Bruhn 2012, for comparative evaluations of services.)
(2) Ratings of the degree of goal attainment or satisfaction with goal achievement. Alongside ratings of customer satisfaction, this is apparently the most commonly used criterion for evaluation coaching.
(3) Scales of positive and negative affect. (With this very short questionnaire people can describe their current feelings. Affect scales of this type are very reliable and "robust" in their practical application, and are used both nationally and internationally in the most varied of fields of application, for example for evaluating psychotherapy and other interventions in the health sector. Coaching appears to reduce negative affect and feelings of helplessness.)
(4) Self-esteem. (This construct is considered to be an important protective mental basis for personality. Coaching can make an increase in strength possible here.)
(5) General well-being. (Scales assessing general well-being are used in many fields of psychosocial research, above all in life or health coaching.)

Instruments and scales also exist with which effects can be measured which are more specific for coaching, such as (for more details see Greif 2013):

(1) Evaluating goal clarity (for example before and after coaching).
(2) Self-efficacy scales. (Here the subjects are asked to what extent they expect to be able to cope with impending tasks effectively and successfully.

Self-efficacy is a beneficial motivational precondition for starting to act. It can be increased by coaching.)

(3) Emotional clarity. (This scale is related to one of the dimensions of emotional intelligence. It is notable that coaching can promote self-perceived clarity with regard to one's own feelings.)

(4) Increase in result-oriented problem- and self-reflection. (These scales ask whether different kinds of problem- or self-reflections have lead to results. Strong effects from coaching could be demonstrated using them. Their application for evaluation is preferable to several standard scales applied in the field, which are problematic because they correlate with rumination and depression, see Greif and Berg 2011.)

The selection put together here only includes scales (Greif 2013) whose statistical reliability and construct validity (that is, that the internal dimensional structure is in accordance with expectations) have been checked. In addition, their correlation with further external criteria has been investigated. Even though they are only based upon the self-report and estimations of the clients, they allow conclusions to be drawn about important changes. Wherever possible, however, the constructs should be secured through a multi-method approach (applying a variety of data types and sources), that is, through additional behavioral data or at least reports from a number of different people: examples would be 360° ratings, or in the case of stress management coaching by measuring blood pressure, heart rate variability or other values that are easy to measure. So far, however, only a few such studies exist for coaching.

Alongside quantitative methods and data, qualitative methods are also always to be recommended in the "method mix" (Greif 2013, 2017). Examples would be interviews in which the subjects freely describe their coaching experiences and results and answer open questions on predetermined subjects. Anonymous case studies can be put together using this method in which it can be shown by means of examples how coaching has been conducted. Clearly described case studies are very important for illustrating intangible and hard to evaluate services and as a basis for the qualification of clients.

One constructivistic method, which activates the client and coach to reflect together about the coaching that has taken place and the perceived subjective causes and results, is the *Coaching-Explorer*.[1] With this method, coach and client can note perceived results and subjective causes of the individual results in key words on small cards (using different colors for positive and not achieved or

[1]Guidelines on the author's website: http://www.home.uni-osnabrueck.de/sgreif/english/downloads.html [retrieved from 24.1.2016].

negative results and related subjective causes). By means of this structure-laying technique, the subjective theories of both the coach and client can be reconstructed and visualized. The structure-images of the coaches and the clients are compared with each other and reflected upon.

When using this method a strong spontaneous interest can be observed on the part of the client when comparing their evaluations and explanations with those of the coach. The clients are happy to invest the additional time necessary in order to do this in the final session. This observation matches the assumption formulated above after Festinger (1954) that people have a strong need to compare their own judgments with those of other relevant persons in order to reduce their evaluation uncertainty. Clients can learn by example how coaching functions and what results can be targeted by means of this joint reflection and the coach's explanations. By means of the visualization using the card technique both coach and client can very quickly decide which of the results noted on the cards can be communicated without problem to the client's boss or colleagues and how the client can effectively explain the coaching process in the case of curious enquiries without giving away anything confidential. The clients thus become coaching experts in their own right as well as disseminators of the method.

3.4.3 Every Coaching Professional Is Called upon

Development of the professional is not a task that can be dealt with by means of well-formulated sentences in the statutes of the coaching federations. Only when it is supported by the attitudes and behavior of the professionals can it be effective. Every coach is confronted with the question as to whether and by means of which practical and scientific methods coaching can in their view be at least partially evaluated, and must answer the question as to how their occupation can be described in all its particularity as well as be distinguished from other services.

Many coaches appear to be content with the status quo of the profession as long as they personally find enough clients who are satisfied with their coaching. They do not involve themselves in the discourse with the scientists or in evaluation research. The question that remains open is not just what consequences such privatization tendencies may have for the profession, but more fundamentally, whether a freezing of the status quo in the development of the profession can be made possible at all through excluding oneself from the scientific discourse. Since society and the sciences continue to develop, this presumably means a backward step and eventually "de-professionalization". At international scientifically oriented coaching conferences, however, a new "spirit of discourse" between scientists and practitioners is becoming tangible. It invites us to continually concern ourselves with the self-conception of coaching and the methods and outcome of evaluation research. Everyone is called upon to join in this discussion and take an active part.

References

Anderson, D. L., & Anderson, M. C. (2005). *Coaching that counts—Harnessing the power of leadership coaching to deliver strategic value*. Amsterdam: Elsevier Butterworth-Heinemann.

Benkenstein, M., & Güthoff, J. (1996). Typologie von Dienstleistungen. Ein Ansatz auf der Grundlage system- und käuferverhaltenstheoretischer Überlegungen. *Zeitschrift für Betriebswirtschaft, 66*(12), 1493–1510.

Festinger, L. (1954). A theory of social comparison processes. *Human Relations, 7*(2), 117–140.

Fietze, B. (2011). Chancen und Risiken der Coachingforschung - eine professionssoziologische Perspektive. In R. Wegener, A. Fritze, & M. Loebbert (Eds.), *Coaching entwickeln. Forschung und Praxis im Dialog* (pp. 24–33). Wiesbaden: VS Verlag.

Fournier, D. M. (2005). Evaluation defined. In S. Mathison (Ed.), *Encyclopedia of evaluation* (pp. 139–140). Thousand Oakes, CA: Sage.

Frey, D., Daeuenheimer, D., Parge, O., & Haisch, J. (1993). Die Theorie sozialer Vergleichsprozesse. In D. Frey & M. Irle (Eds.), *Theorien der Sozialpsychologie - Bd. I Kognitive Theorien* (2nd ed., pp. 81–122). Bern: Huber.

Greif, S. (2013). Conducting organizational based evaluations of coaching and mentoring programs. In J. Passmore, D. B. Peterson, & T. Freire (Eds.), *The Wiley-Blackwell handbook of the psychology of coaching and mentoring* (pp. 445–470). Oxford: Wiley Blackwell.

Greif, S. (2017). Researching outcomes of coaching. In T. Bachkirova, G. Spence, & D. Drake (Eds.), *The SAGE handbook of coaching* (pp. 569–588). London: Sage.

Greif, S., & Berg, C. (2011). *Result-oriented self-reflection—Report on the construct validation of theory-based scales*. Retrieved from Osnabrück http://www.home.uni-osnabrueck.de/sgreif/english/downloads.html (retrieved from January 26, 2016).

Greif, S., Runde, B., & Seeberg, I. (2004). *Erfolge und Misserfolge beim change management*. Göttingen: Hogrefe.

Greif, S., & Scheidewig, V. (1998). Selbstorganisiertes Lernen von Schichtleitern. In S. Greif & H.-J. Kurtz (Eds.), *Handbuch Selbstorganisiertes Lernen* (2nd ed., pp. 347–362). Göttingen: Verlag für Angewandte Psychologie.

Harper, D. (2016). Etymological dictionary Lancaster. Retrieved January 19, 2016 from http://www.etymonline.com/

Hautzinger, M., & Pauli, P. (Eds.). (2009). *Psychotherapeutische Methoden, Enzyklopädie der Psychologie, Psychologische Interventionsmethoden,* (Vol. 2). Göttingen: Hogrefe.

Looss, W. (2014). Die Irrwege der Coaching-Könige: Warum Coaches keine Dienstleister sind, *Kongress Coachig heute: Zwischen Königsweg und Irrweg*. Erding (February 20–21, 2014): Hochschule für angewandtes Management.

Maleri, R., & Frietsche, U. (2008). *Grundlagen de Dienstleistungsproduktion* (5th ed.). Heidelberg: Springer.
Meffert, H., & Bruhn, M. (2012). *Dienstleistungsmarketing: Grundlagen - Konzepte - Methoden: Grundlagen - Konzepte - Methoden. Mit Fallstudien* (7th ed.). Stuttgart: Gabler (Kindle Edition).
Nerdinger, F. W. (2011). *Psychologie der Dienstleistung*. Göttingen: Hogrefe.
Palmer, S., & McDowall, A. (Eds.). (2010). *The coaching relationship*. London: Routledge.
Schmidt-Tanger, M. (2014). Coachen statt Klönen – Emotionale Relevanz und Status im Coaching, *Kongress Coachig heute: Zwischen Königsweg und Irrweg*. Erding (February 20–21, 2014): Hochschule für angewandtes Management.
Schneider, B., & Bowen, D. E. (1995). *Winning the service game*. Boston: Harvard Business School Press.
Schneider, B., & White, S. S. (2004). *Service quality—Research perspectives*. Thousand Oaks, CA: Sage.
Stephan, M., & Gross, P.-P. (Eds.). (2011). *Organisation und Marketing von Coaching: Beiträge des Marburger Coaching Symposiums 2010*. Wiesbaden: VS Verlag.
Stober, D. R., & Grant, A. M. (Eds.). (2006). *Evidence based coaching handbook: Putting best practices to work for your clients*. New York: Wiley.
Wottawa, H., & Thierau, H. (1998). *Lehrbuch evaluation*. Bern: Huber.

Author Biography

Prof. Dr. Siegfried Greif Dipl.-Psych., University of Osnabrück (retired member) and Institute for Economic Psychological Research and Consulting (IwFB GmbH), Osnabrück (managing director for coaching and change management). Fields of focus: coaching research and practice, coaching qualifications, innovative coaching methods. Numerous books, book chapters, and journal articles. Editor of the "Innovative Management" series of books at the publisher Hogrefe Verlag; member of the DGPs, DBVC, ISCP, and IAAP.

The Professional Relationship in Coaching—Polarities and Paradoxes

4

Christoph Schmidt-Lellek

Abstract

In professions, the performance takes place via the interaction between the involved persons—i.e. the client is not a passive recipient; instead, the success of the endeavor relies on his cooperation. Due to this, the relationship between the professional and the client requires special attention; this applies as much to coaching as it does for the other professions. In order to determine the quality of a "dialogical relationship" in a professional context, this chapter will discuss the paradoxes and polarities contained therein. A coach needs to be able to identify paradoxes, such as the "paradox of recognition" and be able to move freely between tension-rich polarities in a manner that is appropriate for each situation. In order to do so, a systematic self-reflexivity is required, which can e.g. be supported by one's own supervision.

4.1 Introduction

If we are to understand coaching as a profession, we will need to view it in the tradition of the classical professions and the characteristics specific to them. Professions are characterized by the fact that they focus on central existential issues people have—in contrast to product-oriented technical occupations (cf. Chap. 1 in

C. Schmidt-Lellek (✉)
Taunusstr. 126, 61440 Oberursel, Germany
e-mail: Kontakt@Schmidt-Lellek.de
URL: http://www.Schmidt-Lellek.de

A. Schreyögg and C. Schmidt-Lellek (eds.), *The Professionalization of Coaching*, DOI 10.1007/978-3-658-16805-6_4

this book). In all professions, the performance takes place via the interaction between the involved persons—i.e. the client is not a passive recipient; instead, the success of the endeavor always relies on his cooperation (cf. DBVC 2012, p. 13). Due to this, the relationship between the professional and the client requires special attention; this applies as much to coaching as it does for the other professions.

The ability to form relationships and appropriate relationship behavior are crucial competencies for coaches. As illustrated by Steinke (Chap. 12 in this book), their relationship competency—alongside numerous other conceptual and expert competencies—are of central importance. A successful professional relationship is also regarded as a significant factor in effectiveness research (cf. Chap. 3 in this book; for psychotherapy cf. Grawe et al. 1994). The actions performed by professions can be seen as a form of "translation work", in that professionals act as an intermediary between the relevant academic knowledge on the one hand, and the individual circumstances and sensitivities, specific situations, contexts, and issues on the other.

Relationships are living phenomena that exist between people, which make them impossible to predict completely. We depend on our spontaneity and intuition in order to be able to react appropriately to the people we encounter in various situations, contexts, and circumstances. However, it is not possible to teach intuition and spontaneity, and they cannot be acquired from attending courses, nor can they be "trained". At the same time, these abilities do not simply fall from the sky or appear out of nowhere, but instead arise from within each person with his history of relationship experiences and evaluational reflections about these experiences; hence, this represents a repository of perceptive, evaluational, and decision-making possibilities. The unique character of the professional relationship can now be seen: it is exactly this unpredictability which is reflexively combined with the relevant specialist competencies—this can be described as aspect of a "*dialogical attitude*" (cf. Schmidt-Lellek 2006; Isaacs 2002). In this manner, a polarity arises between the personal experiences acquired through one's life and the competencies acquired through professional and further education.

In this chapter, I will show that an entire range of polarities and paradoxes need to be considered in order to produce a successful professional relationship. I would first like to explain the meaning of the term "polarity". Together with the "paradox of recognition" as formulated by Jessica Benjamin, this will illustrate a fundamental aspect of dynamics which usually remain hidden in interpersonal relationships. Subsequently, in the section that follows, individual pairs of polar terms will be examined with regard to relationship phenomena in professional settings.

4.2 The Term "Polarity"

In philosophy, "polarity" is used to refer to contrasts that have a complementary relationship with each other. Each of the two poles represents a value. These values are not mutually exclusive, but refer to each other, such that they are able to determine the value/significance of the other in mutual interplay. A polarity describes both a contrast as well as a unit; put differently, each pole also contains its contrary within itself as a possibility and as a corrective. Thinking in terms of polarities is an attempt to neither lapse into the claim of the absolute validity of an individual value system, concept, method, or objective, nor into an arbitrariness in which everything is equally meaningless. Hence, this means departing from an unambiguity which provides safety and instead including the corresponding opposing pole in one's thoughts, feelings, and actions.

The polarities describe *tension relationships* in which the corresponding interpersonal interactions take place. This means that depending on what is made necessary or judicious by the context, the individual situation, the peculiarities of the persons interacting etc., one pole may have a greater weight than the other. According to this, a deformation would not occur by one pole being at the forefront due to the situation, but instead when the other pole is entirely excluded, negated, or invalidated.

If one were to follow Aristotle (Nicomachean Ethics, II, 6; Aristoteles 1983, p. 45–53) and search for the "golden mean" between polar extremes, this would require adapting to the corresponding requirements of the situation, and based on this, deciding where on the scale the "good mean" could be located. Perhaps the idea of *balance* would be a suitable metaphor for illustrating what is meant here: A cyclist will find his balance in a different manner depending on whether he is being driven on by a tailwind, has to battle a crosswind, has to make a sharp turn on a steep downward slope, or has to cycle uphill along a steep road. He will deal with each situation intuitively or reflexively provided that he is skilled enough at riding his bike.

The term "polarity" which we use today has been shaped to a large extent by Schelling (1798/2000) in his "Natural Philosophy" (Naturphilosophie). He saw a universal law in the law of polarity. Thinking in terms of polarities also held a great significance for Friedlaender (1926, p. 355): "A polar manner of thinking and speaking corrects all errors of one-sidedness via the liveliest form of complementarity." Similarly, Martin Buber (1984; see below) also makes a large number of references to this issue. Of particular note is also the ancient Chinese tradition, according to which Yin and Yang (Chin. for "dark" and "light") are understood as being polar cosmological principles. The "*I Ching*—The Book of Changes" succinctly expresses this mindset of thinking in terms of polarities (cf. Wilhelm 1956). Confucianism and Taoism are both also a part of this tradition.

In the field of psychology, the psychoanalyst Mentzos (2009, p. 251) bears mentioning, who formulated a "model of bipolarity" of our endeavors. This model states that our psychological development and our entire existence take place between the two basic needs: of self-referentiality and object referentiality; i.e. on the one hand striving for self-identity and self-cohesion (separate from the object), while on the other the need for ties and belonging (connection with the object). Hence, according to this, living successfully means living one's entire life between these contrasting polarities, i.e. between connectedness and separatedness, and continually finding a balance appropriate for one's age and situation. According to Mentzos (2009), all psychological disorders can be explained by the failure to achieve this particular balance, or the loss of it by veering off to one side or the other.

In the following, with reference to the relationship dynamic between professionals and clients in coaching, I present a list of pairs of polar terms, which may be freely expanded (cf. Schreyögg 2012, p. 208ff.). Being able to move between such polarities and, in a consultation situation, view oneself an advocate of the opposing pole which the client has neglected or is resisting is to be seen as a key characteristic of professionalism (cf. Oevermann 1996, p. 118):

- Autonomy and relatedness
- Asymmetric and symmetric relationships
- Professional function and existential encounter
- Distance and proximity
- Objectivity and subjectivity
- Abstinence and participation
- Confirmation and confrontation
- Directivity and non-directivity
- Transference relationships and real relationships
- Knowing and not knowing
- Predictability and unpredictability
- Activity and passivity, action and inaction
- Emotional experiences as self-reference and as a reaction to others
- Self-protection and accessibility
- Role identification and role distance

Additional specific polarities also bear mentioning for the field of coaching:

- Specialist competency (or field competency) versus process competency
- Cultural familiarity versus cultural alienness

A *dialogical attitude* in professional relationships means perceiving and dealing with the tension between these polarities and finding a balance between them that is appropriate for each situation. It represents a fundamental openness towards others and for that which is alien in others. It refers to the willingness to let oneself be shaken with reference to one's own way of thinking, perceptions and judgments, but without denying or devaluing oneself, or allowing oneself to be debased. Dialogics refers to new challenges from that which is alien and unfamiliar which one encounters, in order to leave the security of that which is known or familiar. Furthermore, it also creates a community of involved parties who have opened themselves up to each other and to the issue to be handled. Seen from this perspective, Dialogics is a basic issue of human existence and/or human coexistence. However, a conscious "dialogical attitude" has a particular relevance for coaching, as in this case the relationship phenomena of the involved persons need to be reflected upon particularly extensively.

Apart from the aforementioned polarities, there are now additional tension-filled aspects to take into consideration for the relationship phenomena in professional contexts. These aspects can be referred to as paradoxes. While *polarities* are relationships of tension between polar opposites, *paradoxes* describe unresolvable contradictions, such as e.g. equality as a person and inequality due to the difference in roles; teachable and learnable knowledge (e.g. of theories and concepts on conflict progression, organization dynamics, intervention techniques etc.), and on the other hand "not-knowing" with regard to the corresponding other party (a person, a team, an organization) and to the problem to be solved in each case; as well as the "paradox of recognition" fundamental to all interpersonal relationships.

4.3 The "Paradox of Recognition"

Benjamin's primary goal was an examination of the relationship of the sexes to each other. In addition to this issue, which is also extraordinarily significant for the professional fields, she also analyzed relationship dynamics, the failure of which resulted in dominance relationships. I wish to retrace some aspects of this, as Benjamin's "theory of intersubjectivity" can be used to illustrate the subtle balance in the relationship phenomena between persons.

In particular, Benjamin (1990) described the *significance of recognition* as a central and lifelong issue of all humans. She builds on Hegel's "fight for recognition" ("Kampf um Anerkennung"), which influences relationships between humans all their lives. The main issues of human life, as is a quintessence of her theory, are on the one hand the *battle for individual self-assertion* as a separate subject, and the *battle for recognition* from others. This corresponds to the aforementioned model of "bipolarity" by Mentzos. There is a "necessary tension" between these two poles (Benjamin 1990, p. 27), as we are dependent on recognition from others in our quest for being ourselves, for independence, and individuality.

The interactive process of recognition is a *reflexive and circular phenomenon.* This process includes the confirmatory response from the other person and the manner in which we accept this reaction and in turn communicate this to the other. This takes place not only through words, but to a significant extent in a non-verbal manner as well, via glances, gestures, tone of voice etc. The "*paradox of recognition*" as Benjamin sees it, "exists in our simultaneous need for recognition and independence: It exists in the fact that the other subject is removed from our control, and yet we still require it" (Benjamin 1990, p. 215). It permeates the entire life of an individual as a central conflict. The paradoxical aspect is that this human need for recognition is only conceivable as a mutual recognition of independent subjects who simultaneously and mutually confirm each other's independence, which in turn ensures one's own self-assertion as an autonomous subject. Hence, throughout a lifetime, one's own self-assertion and independence is dependent on recognition from other independent parties. This therefore means that both subjects perceive each other to be different, and recognize each other. This includes accepting that which is alien, and occasionally also that which is strange and surprising in oneself and others, to not want to get it under control, whether through claims of dominance or symbiotic attempts at harmony.

In our culture, the "paradox of recognition" according to Benjamin will probably never be solved to the extent that the tensions accompanying this conflict can be tolerated in the balance between mutual recognition and simultaneous self-assertion as an independent subject. The historically determined societal order (of the sexes) form various barriers to achieving such a fortunate solution. These barriers lie in the individual and the societal structures themselves. The battle for recognition does not take place among equals and in a domain devoid of power, not even in an academic context.

Benjamin (1990, p. 215) describes two variants of splitting as failed solutions to the paradox of recognition. Splitting is a defense mechanism which we are equipped with biographically already at a very early age, with which conflicts, but also ambivalent feelings can be solved by splitting of a section of the feelings, i.e.

rejecting them and excluding them from one's consciousness. The splitting can take place in two directions:

- Self-assertion is carried too far and, having rejected the recognition, the opposing pole is "deleted". This then results in a perverted form of self-assertion, namely a desire to dominate and control the others. At the same time, one's own dependence on the others is denied, and in doing so, the foundations of empathy are destroyed.
- The other way of solving the "paradox of recognition" is exactly the other extreme: Recognition is perverted through submission and the fundamental need for self-assertion and autonomy is denied.

The following can be derived from this concept for professional relationships in coaching: Here, too, the foundation for successful processes of change is the mutual recognition of the involved parties—in their various roles. It can fail on both sides, on that of the coach and/or the client.

First of all, the client requires the coach to recognize and value him as an independent person. Then, he desires to be perceived and understood where his life problems and his potential for change and development are concerned. But he will only be able to experience this if he is able to perceive and experience the coach as being independent, autonomous, and different: If the other person's statements serve mainly to butter up the client, he will not be able to take his recognition seriously. On the other hand, if the client judges and is only willing to accept the coach's statements and interventions based on whether they correspond to his own expectations, he will not be able to achieve an attitude that can bring about change. However, if all he does is submit to the coach's authority in order to bring about a change, this change will probably not become an integral component of his own autonomous personality.

On the other hand, the coach also requires recognition as an independent person and in his professional role from the client; as without experiencing sufficient recognition, he will not be able to truly activate his potential, or experience himself as having been instrumentalized and/or "misused". On the one hand, the reasons for this may lie in the fact that the coach is, actually, not given any recognition, while on the other, he may not be able to perceive or accept it (i.e. that recognition of the recognition is absent). Here, too, a failure of the paradox of recognition may have an effect in two directions: Through powerful, authoritarian interventions in order to enforce changes on the part of the client (loss of empathy), or through being overly accommodating in order to obtain the recognition of being a "good coach" (loss of autonomy). In both cases, the danger of a burnout increases. As I have shown in other contexts (Schmidt-Lellek 2006, p. 108, 168), the self-interest of the helping person is an integral component of the professional relationship. If this is not acted upon or denied due to biographical, ideological, or contextual reasons, the productive relationship of tensions in the professional interaction, which Benjamin describes as the " paradox of recognition", cannot develop.

4.4 Polarities in a Professional Relationship

In the following section, certain aspects which have a major influence on the relationship dynamic in professional contexts will now be illustrated in more detail. The goal in each case is to find a balance between the relevant polarities in each situation. If a balance is unsuccessful or is lost, the dialogical situation may be damaged. The following aspects serve as an example (cf. Schmidt-Lellek 2006, p. 278 ff. for more details).

4.4.1 Professional Function and Existential Encounter

The most well-known distinction here between the two relationship modalities is attributed to Martin Buber: that of "I–It" and "I–Thou": The former describes the analytical, distant approach with which a therapist encounters a patient in his professional capacity (asymmetric relationship). The latter describes the interpersonal level, the encounter between persons who are equals, which takes place in addition to the various roles and functions (symmetric relationship). This I-Thou relationship can, on the one hand, be understood as an accompanying reality in the professional setting and always be taken into consideration; while on the other, it represents an overarching objective of the process, namely that an interpersonal relationship is no longer defined by the different, asymmetric roles. If the asymmetric role definition is not departed from, this may be construed as the professional's desire for empowerment. "Dialogical relationship" should therefore not mean negating or attempting to conceal a difference in roles defined by the situation, but instead refer to the awareness of a possible switching of the roles that is, *in principle*, possible.

4.4.2 Scientific Objectivity and Experiential Subjectivity

If one has the modern ideals of the scientific approach in mind, it seems particularly difficult to maintain the polarity of "objectivity and subjectivity". This is because—at least in common usage—"objectivity" is associated with "correct, matter-of-fact, rational", while "only subjective" perceptions and statements are seen as deviations from this idea. However, subjective intuitions, perceptions, and assessments generally contain useful clues for the conflict situation to be dealt with; however, they need to be examined with regard to their suitability as well as an interpretation or translation (cf. Chap. 10 on hermeneutics in this book), so that they can be understood intersubjectively and in a manner relevant for behavior.

4.4.3 Transference Relationship and Real Relationship

In coaching, transference phenomena can also influence or impact the interaction between the parties involved to a small or large extent. What we are referring to here are "unconscious reaction patterns", which result from "existing relationship experiences, which sometimes extend far back into the past" (Schreyögg 2012, p. 257). The ability to perceive such phenomena and to deal with them serve to help one understand the other person, whether in a person's current relationship to the coach or in his professional relationships, e.g. with superiors or colleagues. Similarly, it is important that a coach is familiar with and able to reflect on his own reaction patterns and the corresponding interpretative and behavior pattern, with the goal of e.g. being able to competently delimitate himself and not allow himself to be drawn into misleading or destructive encounters. However, if he concentrates his attention exclusively on the transference dynamic with his client, he "implicitly denies him the chance of entering into an authentic relationship with him" (Schreyögg 2004, p. 152). Hence, it needs to be possible to address the actual relationship dynamic in a consultation process where necessary. If the coach does not allow this, transference interpretations may become the coach's immunization strategy, with which he makes himself untouchable.

4.4.4 Abstinence and Participation

This polarity deals with the extent to which coaches "open up to their client or hold back their opinions and feelings" (Schreyögg 2012, p. 215). The abstinence approach, as it was originally formulated in the context of psychoanalysis, refers to the reservation exercised by the analyst with regard to subjective statements in his gestures, expressions, and language; it is meant to ensure that the analyst serves as a neutral projection screen for the transferences of the patient, such that they—as undisturbed as possible by the personality of the analyst—can surface. However, such an approach results in an exaggerated asymmetry between the two parties, which provokes "inappropriate regressions from clients" (ibid., p. 216). Consultation processes require an empathic understanding of the client; however, this can never be separate from the personality of the professional, who also can never be completely "neutral", but who is instead involved in the intersubjective process of understanding (cf. Chap. 10 in this book). Hence, for the coach, intersubjectivity refers to an authentic openness towards the client. This involves the coach expressing the depth of his emotions, his own associations, value systems etc. However, this openness cannot be arbitrary, as this may then interfere with the flow of work and the process of realization. Therefore, what is necessary is a reflected *selective openness* which needs to be adapted to the respective situation and the other person. This is what the opposing pole refers to—withholding one's statements. "Abstinence" continues to mean refraining from an emotional *satisfaction of needs* at the client's expense, e.g. due to a narcissistically motivated instrumentalization of the client.

4.4.5 Confirmation and Confrontation

Confirmation and appreciation are the basic requirements for any professional work, without which dialogical understanding would be wholly impossible. However, confirmation not only refers to the acceptance of the other person as an equal, as well as being who he is, but in the words of Martin Buber, also with his "whole potentiality": Hence, "I not only accept the other as he his, but I confirm him in myself and then in him in relation to his potentiality, that is meant by him, and it can now be developed, it can evolve, et can answer the reality of life" (Friedman 1992, p. 258). Identifying this polarity between currency and potentiality is a key characteristic of professional consultation. "I cannot act in my relationship to him (the client), without this polarity. (…) And there are cases when I must help him against himself" (ibid.). Hence, confirmation is the foundation of a trusting professional relationship, but the professional coach must go beyond this; he needs to find the courage for confrontations, to "interfere" with the other person's habits with regard to how he feels, thinks, and acts, and in doing so initiate an openness towards that which is new.

4.4.6 Knowing and not Knowing

Socrates said: "I know that I know nothing", which is to be seen as the highest level of knowledge. This statement refers to the awareness that all our theories and concepts for action can never be completely understood by another person. Claiming that you have, in your concepts, in your perception and assessment, incontrovertible security, is nothing more than a deception of oneself and other persons, and can interfere with the openness of the dialogical situation. In contrast, a "Socratic" attitude in coaching can mean a joint "exploration" of the issue in question, and that interpretations are to be understood as suggested or possible interpretations which then need to be examined. However, "not knowing" then naturally cannot mean ignorance—the various sources of knowledge which need to be consulted in one's studies, training, and lifelong continued education (cf. Chap. 9 in this book), remain indispensable prerequisites for professional work.

4.4.7 Action and Inaction

The manifold expectations coaching clients and organizations commissioning sessions have of coaching, and often one's own super-ego as well, require from us as coaches to achieve predictable results through our professionally planned actions. Yet the process and results can never be fully predicted, and sometimes it turns out that our targeted actions did not even constitute the decisive factor for change, but instead presence of a dialogical partner to "think along" and "feel along". But it is precisely due to this that some professionals, in their endeavor to achieve something "effectively", feel powerless and subsequently tend to compensate for this feeling with powerful interventions. Chinese Taoism speaks of "action through inaction", and this paradox is illustrated in Laozi's *Dao De Jing*—a masterpiece of paradoxical thought—by the following metaphor: "One forms clay and makes vessels out of it: A vessel's utility lies in the nothingness it contains" (Wilhelm 1921, p. 13). In short, plannable actions are perhaps only the "vessel" for unpredictable processes—but without the artistically shaped "clay", there would be no useful "vessel".

In order to be able to move about within these tension-filled polarities and to find and maintain a balance that is appropriate for each situation, a sufficient degree of systematic self-reflexivity is necessary. In particular, this can be supported via the continuous supervision of one's own professional work. When doing so, the corresponding personal relationship experiences between the involved parties can also be evaluated directly when in the various supervisory settings (teaching supervision, group supervision, intervision with colleagues) in order to make it possible to experience the polarities and paradoxes discussed.

References

Aristoteles (1983). *Nikomachische Ethik.* Stuttgart: Philipp Reclam jun.

Benjamin, J. (1990). *Die Fesseln der Liebe. Psychoanalyse, Feminismus und das Problem der Macht.* Basel, Frankfurt/M.: Stroemfeld/ Roter Stern; Orig.: *The Bonds of Love: Psychoanalysis, Feminism and the Problem of Domination.* New York: Pantheon, 1988.

Buber, M. (1984). *Das dialogische Prinzip.* Heidelberg: Lambert Schneider. (Darin: Ich und Du, 1923; Zwiesprache, 1929; Die Frage an den Einzelnen, 1936; Elemente des Zwischenmenschlichen, 1953).

DBVC – Deutscher Bundesverband Coaching e.V. (Hrsg.) (2012). *Leitlinien und Empfehlungen für die Entwicklung von Coaching als Profession. Kompendium mit den Professionsstandards des DBVC* (4., erw. Aufl.). Osnabrück: DBVC Geschäftsstelle; Engl. version available under: www.dbvc.de/publikationen.

Friedlaender, S. (1926). *Die schöpferische Indifferenz* (2nd ed.). München: Reinhardt.

Friedman, M. (1992). Dialog zwischen Martin Buber und Carl Rogers (1957) (Germ. translation by C. Schmidt-Lellek). *Integrative Therapie* 18 (3), 245–260 (quoted from the unpubl. Engl. original).

Grawe, K., Donati, R., & Bernauer, P. (1994). *Psychotherapie im Wandel. Von der Konfession zur Profession.* Göttingen: Hogrefe.

Isaacs, W. (2002). *Dialog als Kunst gemeinsam zu denken. Die neue Kommunikationskultur in Organisationen.* Bergisch Gladbach: Edition Humanistische Psychologie; Orig.: *Dialogue and the art of thinking together.* New York: Doubleday, 1999.

Mentzos, S. (2009). *Lehrbuch der Psychodynamik. Die Funktion der Dysfunktionalität psychischer Störungen.* Göttingen: Vandenhoeck & Ruprecht.

Oevermann, U. (1996). Theoretische Skizze einer revidierten Theorie professionalisierten Handelns. In: Combe, A., Helsper, W. (Hg.), *Pädagogische Professionalität. Untersuchungen zum Typus pädagogischen Handelns.* Frankfurt/M.: Suhrkamp, S. 70–182.

Schelling, F. W. J. (1798/2000). *Von der Weltseele – eine Hypothese der höheren Physik zur Erklärung des allgemeinen Organismus.* Werke 6, Stuttgart: Frommann-Holzboog.

Schmidt-Lellek, C. J. (2006). *Ressourcen der helfenden Beziehung. Modelle dialogischer Praxis und ihre Deformationen.* Bergisch Gladbach: Edition Humanistische Psychologie.

Schreyögg, A. (2004). *Supervision. Ein integratives Modell (4., überarb. und* (erw ed.). Wiesbaden: VS Verlag.

Schreyögg, A. (2012). *Coaching. Eine Einführung für Praxis und Ausbildung* (7., überarb. und erw. Aufl.). Frankfurt/M., New York: Campus.

Wilhelm, R. (transl.) (1921). *Laotse. Tao te king.* Jena: Eugen Diederichs.

Wilhelm, R. (transl.) (1956). *I Ging. Das Buch der Wandlungen.* Düsseldorf, Köln: Eugen Diederichs.

Author Biography

Dr. phil. Christoph Schmidt-Lellek studied prot. theology, philosophy and pedagogy, doctoral dissertation on the resources of relationship in professional settings, freelance practice in coaching (DBVC), psychotherapy and supervision (DGSv), publications in the fields of psychotherapy and coaching, co-publisher and editor of the journal "Organisationsberatung, Supervision, Coaching" (OSC).

Part II
Coaching in Connection with Other Professional Formats

Coaching in the Context of Social Systems

5

Thomas Dallüge

Abstract

As use of the term coaching has increased, so has the blurring of its substantive meaning. Inflationary use within the professional community has also seen the necessary engagement with professional self awareness fade into the background. This chapter aims to explore coaching from a systems theory background, thereby enabling new professional discussion. To achieve this, different coaching constellations are described and sorted according to dyad, interaction, group/team and organization system types. On this basis, the distinction between multi-person constellation coaching and system coaching is introduced. Various multi-person constellations are discussed with respect to their possibilities and limitations, and a clear distinction is drawn with other consultation professions.

The term "coaching" has gone the same way as many other terms; through frequent use in a wide range of contexts it has lost its communicative meaning. It shares this fate with other wonderful terms such as "organization," "love," "power," etc. Astonishingly, this does not lead to the term no longer being used, in fact, quite the opposite. We can confidently continue to use the term "coaching" without clearly defining it. It will therefore have more of a container function, retaining a broad conceptual framework as well as its own considerable potential. Perhaps this phenomenon is an essential feature of coaching and has contributed to its ongoing popularity. It enables and opens up communication. Only with continuing com-

T. Dallüge (✉)
Trinfactory GmbH, Hufelandstr. 22, 10407 Berlin, Germany
e-mail: thomas.dalluege@trinfactory.com
URL: http://www.trinfactory.com

A. Schreyögg and C. Schmidt-Lellek (eds.), *The Professionalization of Coaching*, DOI 10.1007/978-3-658-16805-6_5

munication a common understanding may crystallize, providing the catalyst for ongoing, meaningful communication. It simultaneously demonstrates that the term "coaching" carries with it a promise of salvation: "It's a good thing, because whatever coaching believes in or does, it aims to improve your current life situation."

This is of course a good thing when discussing professionalism, while remaining deeply unsatisfactory on the other hand. Unsatisfactory, because many stakeholders use the coaching container to provide a framework for their service delivery under the guise of promised outcomes. This is often useful and harmless, but unfortunately can also create or exacerbate problems. For this reason it makes sense to further differentiate the term "coaching" and explore the background of its different meanings. In this task I would like to borrow from a systems theory backdrop, and introduce my own perspective on helpful distinctions. These distinctions enable us to make indicative and action-orientated statements regarding professionalism, lifting the lid on the coaching container and leading to more focused evaluation. In this chapter I would like to highlight five different aspects:

(1) A conceptual sorting of coaching constellations based on the social structures in which they take place, particularly in regard to the social structure in the coaching foreground.
(2) A short reflection on professionalism.
(3) A deeper look at the question of how coaching dyads can be understood from a systematic perspective, and what coaching implications arise from this.
(4) An examination of multi-person coaching with system related selection criteria.
(5) A critical reflection on the overuse of the coaching concept in other consultation disciplines—system coachings are more than the sum of coaching systems.

5.1 A Conceptual Sorting of Coaching Constellations

In my evaluation, the core of coaching lies in 1:1 counseling. In this coaching dyad, the coaching client works through questions of professional performance. That means that two persons enter into direct communication with each other. In the initial evaluation, one person acts as coach and the second person as coachee, customer or client (Fig. 5.1) (I would like to negate all associations with the terms coachee, customer or client and will use them interchangeably.).

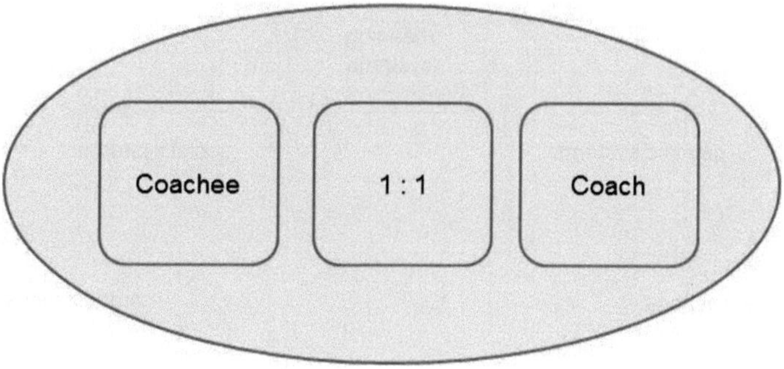

Fig. 5.1 Coaching dyad

If we start with this coaching dyad, we can also recognize a well known phenomenon through this subject, that the unlabeled will always be labeled. So it didn't take long before questions (or practices) arose regarding coaching sessions with several persons. That means that there was not only one coachee, but several who could communicate directly with each other in a room and receive "container coaching". If we follow this distinction, the question arises: Who are these "several persons" and how can we understand them? Here we can resort to systems theory, which offers a typology of social systems (Ameln 2004). Ongoing communication with multiple persons can be described in the context of an interaction system, a group or team system or an organization (we are not considering societal perspectives at this point). The distinction is inspired by Luhmann (1988, 2006), and supplemented by the thematic group and team. In accordance with Wimmer et al. (2014), I express the view that these two models form their own separate emergent structure, whereby the team represents a hybrid structure of the group and the organization (Fig. 5.2).

A small insertion is allowed here because our academic socialization occasionally gets the better of us. The description of the various system types and their related theoretical foundations are an intellectual achievement that equips us with observational perspectives on social phenomena. The theory can enable useful, appropriate and valid descriptions of social phenomena. But it cannot say, "This is how it is". In understanding a social system, it is completely absurd to say: "This is an organization". It is helpful to say, "When I look at this from an organizational perspective, this means…". I make particular mention of this point because in didactic coachings and supervisions I experience coaches searching for an answer what coaching really is, rather for a helpful picture for the client (regardless of how seemingly right or wrong it is—suitability is more the criterion). Here the

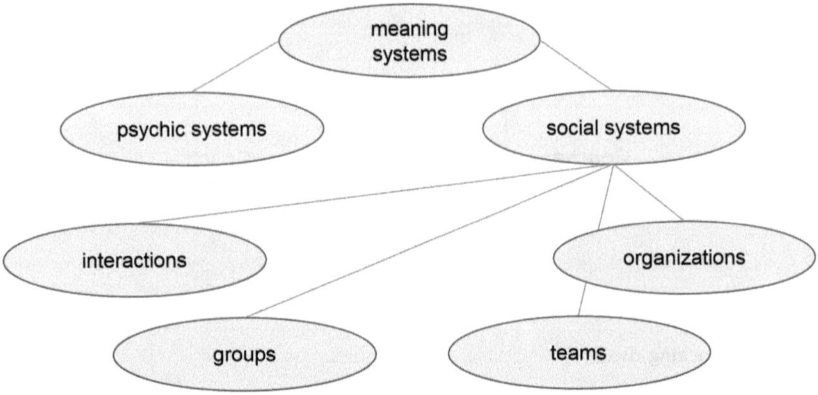

Fig. 5.2 An extract of social systems which are relevant for coaching

distinction between a landscape and a map is sometimes a useful analogy. In coaching, our task is to generate maps rather than describe the real landscape (at this point the constructivist in us would smile quietly).

If we wish to use the aforementioned social systems scheme, we should briefly outline the types of social systems in order to adequately understand them. In the knowledge that extensive books have already been written on each type of system, I will limit myself here to a maximum of 5 SMS lengths per system type.

Social systems are communication systems in which communication continues as events (keyword: autopoiesis), and this continuation forms a system-environment boundary (keyword: operational closure). These social systems process meaning, as they choose a communication method in the context of all possible choices. This selection is echoed in the three dimensions of meaning (subject, social and time).

Interaction systems describe communication between persons present and therefore focus on the development and continuation of communication in the threefold selection of information, communication and understanding. Interaction systems are defined by the physical presence of the parties. It isn't possible for the parties involved to escape the "perception of perception", and it is therefore clear to all parties that any behavior or behavioral failure may be decoded as a communication event.

Groups describe communication systems which are characterized by potentially recurring communication between those present that are "similar". Groups provide themselves with a task or a communication base. Simultaneous with the voluntary nature of participation/group membership, the reduction of complexity in groups follows through individually validated attribution of properties and relationships. This also leads to limitation in group sizes. Internal attempts at differentiation are offset by resymmetrization, which can occasionally lead to significant dynamics.

Teams describe groups in organizations and their associated communications structures. They can be seen as self-organized phenomena of organizations. Hierarchical structures are introduced through the creation of teams, which provide considerable advantages for organizations in complex environments. Simultaneously, linkage possibilities are increased between individuals and the organization through teams. In addition to the many references to the group, there is a distinctive and highly consequential difference: joining a team is not freely chosen, rather it is determined by organization membership. This leaves the team member unable to act "freely", which has a significant impact on group dynamics in negotiation processes. In contrast to the organization it is also significant that leadership is not part of a team. From a leadership perspective we open up an organizational view.

Organizations are communication systems that are made up of continuous decision-making processes. These ongoing decision events can draw on previous decision premises (programs, communication channels, persons). In contrast with groups, persons have become linked with the organizational environment and connected via membership with the organization. Organizations are therefore able to achieve functional internal differentiation. A special feature here is leadership. In this way, leadership is a "limiting function of the organization", responsible for introducing relevant environments and for supplying decisions and decision-making ability.

Against the background of these different system types, "several persons" can be provided with content-based understanding. This means that "several persons" are connected via shared participation in communication or memberships, and now in this context find themselves again in a coaching communication system. There is a common and labeled experiential background (Fig. 5.3).

The resulting coaching systems correspond to the summation of coaching dyads with the physically symbolized presence of background systems. Simultaneously, independent interaction and group systems with their respective dynamics arise

Fig. 5.3 Coaching from a multi-person constellation

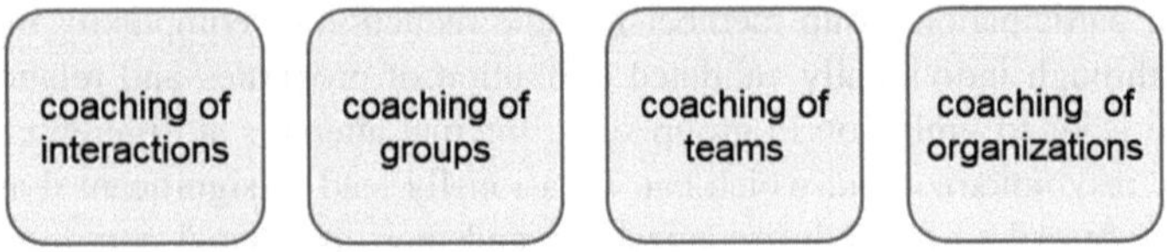

Fig. 5.4 Coaching of different kinds of systems

again around multi-person constellations and the subject of coaching (the deepening of multi-person constellations can be found in Sect. 5.4).

Of course, this distinction draws a further possible line of development or differentiation. Can background systems also be taken into the foreground and coached? This results in approaches to *system coaching* which refer to the respective social systems and not the participating psychological systems. Coaching systems create the "coaching clients" system structure against the backdrop of the social system members who are present (Fig. 5.4). This is a marked difference.

In the following I would like to discuss the coaching of multi-person constellations as well as social systems. Before I expand upon the coaching dyad, however, I will begin with a few thoughts on the subject of professionalization.

5.2 A Short Reflection on Professionalism

For this purpose, I revert back to a suggestion by Kantor (2012). In my view, professional coaching requires inclusion of one's own professional acting in the theoretical map, a model that represents the basis of one's own activities. For an initial approach towards one's own professional self-concept, three questions are helpful:

- What is the subject of my professional acting?
- How does this subject function by itself? This corresponds to the question: what would happen if I do nothing, not in a particular case, but in general?
- How can I act and influence within the context of my professional activities?

Also, at the risk of repeating myself here and sounding prescriptive: From my perspective, being responsive to the questions stated above is a matter of professional duty!

Let us take an illustrative analogy: Craftsmen have things a little easier at this point. For a carpenter, it is quite clear that the object of his activities is the wood with all of its qualities (able to be sawn, flexible, buoyant etc.). When no action is taken on the wood, there are two different possibilities: Either it clings with its roots into the ground, transporting water and nutrients through its own cells, or it rots either in the ground, water or air. I have a diverse range of possible actions. I can carry it from A to B, saw it, split it, join it with screws and nails—all good things. The exciting question now is: How does this look with coaching? What is the object which I can influence? What makes the object of my coaching tick and what possibilities do I have for intervention?

5.3 How Coaching Dyads Can Be Understood from a Systemic Perspective

When I try to answer the questions above (which every coach should be able to do for themselves), the following question arises: How can I understand coaching, and what happens in coaching? In coaching, a communication system forms between the coach and the client. Initial communication continues, and the continuation of this communication generates meaning. This meaning is constituted by the permanent communication choice within the context of all the possible communication continuations. The meaning is highlighted by the fact that we continue our communication in exactly this way as opposed to any other way. We can observe this meaning against the background of its three meaning dimensions. Each continuing communication contains a factual, time and social dimension.

The *factual dimension* describes the content of the communication. This involves the selection of the topic in the context of all other possible topics, which were not selected when the selection was made (this/other). In classic "Business Coaching" it centers around the client's own professional role, which is causing pain and leading to a desire for change, either from the perspective of the organization or the person.

In the *social dimension*, the horizon of choice is spread out between other and ego. This communication always reverberates with questions: What do I think about the person I am currently in communication with, and what do I expect/think that my partner expects from me? These expectation expectations therefore run parallel in the communication. The communication partner (coachee) also makes these associations within the communication. In short, the communication results in an image from my counterpart, and I behave in such a way as to meet their expectations. This is a negotiation and updating process, which continues throughout the course of the communication. As a coaching client my mind runs through what type of coach my counterpart is, what the coach would like from me as a client and how I should position myself in relation to these behavioral expectations. As a result, the client makes the coach an offer how the coach can read himself and his client. In this way, the social dimension describes the continuous updating of the interaction of the coaching roles.

The *time dimension* describes the temporality of the communication system. It covers a temporal dimension between past and future, and thus temporalities can be assigned. During the communication, distinctions run along the timeline such as: From when will things be assigned to the historical past, and until when are you still in the present past? Through references along the time line, the temporalities of the coaching system are processed. The opportunity for coaching to develop its own history and generate a timeline (observation of development) only arises by introducing some degree of continuity.

Important in the observation of a coaching system and in the description of its meaning dimensions is that it deals with the characteristics and references of the communication system, and not the intended characteristics of the persons participating in the communication. At its core, it's about selections, which are updated and manifested through the continued communication. If we take this seriously, we cannot impact directly on the mental and emotional worlds of the coachee during coaching. We can work with clients on creating communicative events that then enable them to (re)construct their worlds in a targeted way.

When we come now to the original question regarding the subject of coaching, we have no choice but to say: "*Coaching is the construction of meaning in the coaching dyad*". This is frightening on one hand, because I really wanted to impact on my coachee's thinking and this now provides striking evidence that I cannot do that. On the other hand, it is an invitation for coaches to live out their passion for coaching through the co-creation of communication, as well as to instigate useful variances in the meaning of coaching.

In summary, we can say that coaching can be understood as a communication system that provides a meaningful framework through a variety of mechanisms, which in turn has a significant impact on coaching efficacy. This leads us to the question of what possible interventions are available to the coach. The goal of coaching is the variance in descriptions (no matter what is described) and the observations of a client. This goes to the core of the factual dimension, i.e., the reason for the coaching.

The client defines the problem and the situation that needs to change. Variance in thinking and observation arises in clients through shared deconstruction and reconstruction of past situations, as well as shared redesign of future scenarios. In the factual dimension there are two basic strategies here:

(1) the contextualization of the coaching issue with other differing perspectives,
(2) the benchmark work relative to the coaching issue, altitude or deep drilling.

The contextualization of the situation describes the facts against different background paradigms. Systemic coaches would question situations against imaginary system theory constructions (e.g. with adoption of perspectives or scaling). Depth psychologists would include their figures of observation (e.g. narcissistic disorders) in the conversation. Business economists or extreme sportspeople would each bring their own professional experience or backgrounds into play in the same way. The aim in each case is to create useful alienation. Unfortunately coaches depend too often on the idea that their explanation patterns really are the right ones (as they often are, of course). At this point we may hopefully rely on the clients' autonomy, so that they do not even have to struggle with the presumed reality of their coaches.

Another approach within the variance of the factual dimension is the deepening, the detailing or the generalization and abstraction, i.e. the benchmark work. This is not about looking at the phenomenon from different perspectives, but working with a zoom. It is necessary to be very careful with this approach. Even detailing needs a map of observation and description, and usually leads the in-depth work to a manifestation of the problem description, and less often to a helpful production of variance (Deepening provides, by contrast, meaning in the description and design of solution worlds.).

At this point I would once again like to highlight that it is vital for professional coaches to have reflected and transparent images, models, analogies, and ways of understanding for people, interactions, behavior, organizations, business worlds, social developments, etc. These maps are the sponsors of their attentions and questions, and the starting point for the common creation of future client worlds—the starting point, because it is not about arranging clients in some kind of "grid", but the helpful creation of a distinction.

These are then the variance opportunities in the factual dimension. Let us now consider the communication system, taking the social dimension into account. In the social dimension it's about the mutual expectations of expectations, and the corresponding fit with the common reason for communication. In coaching, I can follow at least three strategies relating to the expectations of expectations:

- impulses to chang the expectations of expectations of my clients,
- changes of my own expectations of expectations,
- changes in the context of the coaching sessions.

The client has certain expectation to the coach, and thereby forms an image of what the coach expects from a coaching client. To vary this image means to experience the coach in a different way, and to enable new presumed expectations of new perspectives in themselves. Classically, this can be done both by shaping the client relationship (proximity—distance etc.) as well as by the choice of methods/interventions (verbally—analog, etc.).

The change in the expectations of the coach means a change in perspective on the part of the coachee. True to the motto "It can also always be completely different", the coach should consider that one's own picture says more about the coach than it does about the coachee. The fine art of coaching is not in discovering the correct pre-existing image of the coach, but in liquidating pre-existing images in favor of constructing something new.

The context design may have many facets. These range from the design of the place (yoga mat or flip chart), to the integration of special environments (office, hotel, golf course, mountains/nature) to the formation of multi-person settings.

The time dimension describes the temporality of the communication system. This means that there are opportunities here to produce variances with a time perspective towards the past and the future, as well at towards duration and events. Because coaching deals with temporary communication systems, it is possible to choose between different basic formats:

- Coaching as an event. There is no promise of further communication. Each event has to meet coaching expectations.
- Coaching as a common, open ended path. Once enough has been achieved, the path ends.
- Coaching as a defined process with specified dates and a fixed scope.

With specifications on the distance between individual coaching sequences, hypotheses regarding durability and action times are simultaneously brought into observation.

In conclusion, let us say that considering coaching dyads as communication systems and coaching as the co-creation of this communication leads to a wide range of behavioral options for coaches, and in parallel clearly attenuates appreciation of their efficacy.

5.4 An Illumination of Coaching Systems—Multi-person Coaching with System-Related Selection Criteria

With our ideas up to now we have focused on coaching dyads. With the expansion of coaching to "several persons" additional social system logic comes into view:

Coaching of multi-person constellations makes available different system contexts as background paradigms. A certain longevity is necessary for coaching with multi-person constellations because otherwise a coaching constellation makes little sense. For this reason, we can omit coaching of participants in an interaction system.

Coaching of group members describes a setting in which individuals, who are also members of a group, join together in coaching. These may be groups who are constituted around a common theme (friends of XXX), through shared worlds of experience (self-help groups), through common objectives (action groups) or around common professional references (supervision groups). Members of these groups come together and work through questions and topics in a multi-person constellation relevant to their individual, professional or career development. These settings offer the possibility:

- to introduce different worlds of experience against a background of common group experiences in a risk-free way,
- of opening and free space to try out one's own ideas and concepts (individual formulations have relatively limited consequences),
- of being able to expect relatively intention-free feedback,
- to develop supportive relationships directly with the other participants, as the background logic is not so strong.

In parallel, there is a risk that:

- the group and the current group event slide into the foreground,
- group dynamics influence the coaching process,
- potential fluctuations and varying participation make adequate processing of the question difficult,
- the introduction into participant contexts takes a relatively significant amount of time.

This means that the coaching of team members is clearly demarcated by group dynamic interventions. It is not about the processing of relational structures, but the use of a common experience and background relationship for individual development.

Coaching of team members highlights a relevant environment with special system logics and lifts it into the foreground through coaching. The team therefore becomes the relevant context for observing and reconstructing social phenomena through the coachee. From this perspective, particular resources and specific limitations arise in the work content in a team coaching. The following resources, which arise from team member participation, can represent particular added value:

- production of relevant variance in experience, description and evaluation of social situations,
- production of attractive and shared visions of the future,
- production of security and trust for entering uncharted personal territory,
- production of support and anchoring for desired change.

In addition to these resources, the activation of team aspects can also lead to limitations and restrictions. These can be expressed as:

- constrained worlds of thought, focused on team aspects,
- the path dependency of team action,
- the immediate judgmental response towards innovation that may affect the rest of the team (as well as anticipation of these reactions),
- the impossibility of calling onto question team membership, or indeed the team itself.

For the demarcation of Team Development (TD), it is paramount that classic TD topics (e.g. team goals, role negotiation, collaborative agreements) are not brought into common processing between the coachees. They only represent the current respective context for individual actions. TD is commissioned by the responsible manager and places particular demands on the preparation and involvement of team members. Team coaching focuses on the person and use the team as a resource for individual development. Coachees are free to participate in the coaching. They take care of processing their own subjects.

Coaching of organizational members highlights the shared organization as the relevant foreground environment. The specific coaching question then relates to the issue of how one can develop effectiveness within the organization (role and function), and how to adjust oneself in order to deal with its demands and overbearing nature. Through the participation of other members of the organization, the following resources can be incorporated into the coaching:

- getting to know additional organization pictures and different roles designs,
- safeguarding one's own hypotheses on the sustainability and future direction of the organization,
- feedback on one's own design of leadership and organization,
- internal external—perceptions, descriptions of one's own areas and actions.

In addition to this potential, the dark side of the organization can also affect the coaching:

- continuing organizational tensions and conflict lines,
- fear of losing face or of being denigrated because of one's statements (traitor),
- fear of stigmatization (pushover) and therefore reduced future effectiveness in leadership work towards the outside.

In contrast to consulting, this also means that for coaching for organization members, there are no organizational tasks to be processed. Should change impulses arise in the context of coaching, it is the coachee's responsibility to process these issues from their role within the organization. Topics such as leadership, strategy, structure, product development, resource management, etc. can be included as relevant coaching contexts, but not organizational processing. Again, coaching differs significantly from consulting through the type of assignment and the design of processing structure.

The added value of team and organizational coaching lies in the expansion of 1:1 settings, and the intense activation of a potentially useful context for professional role development within the team or organization. Bringing the possible systems perspective limitations into monitoring and processing plays a major role in the success of coaching.

These settings place extensive and specific demands on the coach. It is therefore necessary to resist the temptations of the system overreach and maintain the focus on the coachee. In coachings with multi-person systems, it is not about directly influencing the respective social system, but strengthening and supporting the person in the context of the various system constructions. Coaches need a particular degree of expertise and understanding of team and organization system types when working with team or organization members. They need to understand their own logic and dynamics, as well as the possibility of moving as a person within these constructions. This also presents a particular degree of methodological challenges. Coachings with several team or organization members include a well-balanced mix of group and 1:1 settings. The group value adds with the enlargement of perspectives and in the range of landmarks. The coach ensures that coaches are entitled to their own focusing and interpretation in every case. At the same time coaches also have a group in front of them, with a resulting self-dynamic which is also valid to deal with.

5.5 A Critical Reflection on the Invasiveness of the Coaching Concept in Other Consultation Disciplines—System Coaching

Let us now look at system coaching, the 3rd aspect of the distinction we have introduced. The central difference to coaching systems lies in responsibility being assumed for a social structure. The social structure comes into the foreground. It is about the team, organization or company, and works on team or organizational attributes. It follows that the target goal and assignment are respectively based on the social structure. At the same time, every social structure has its own quality entirely and completely separate action mechanisms. From this fact, one can clearly see a significant point of differentiation with the consultation market (Fig. 5.5).

Phenomena in teams or organizations can usually not be explained by the motivations or skills of individual members. This clearly shows the limits of coaching. I would like to maintain here a clear pleading against its omnipotent presumption of coaches. "Stick to what you are good at" can only mean here: Coach, stick with designing communication situations in which the individual person with their wishes, needs and experience worlds is paramount, stay away from working with social structures. We would also be very reluctant to let a otolaryngologist perform surgery on the spinal cord or the brain. Sure, this may

systems	interaction	group	team	organization
professional role	facilitator	facilitator for group dynamic	team developer	consultant
professional perspective	communication and under-standing	common tasks and relation-ships	organizational goals an cooperation	premises, future decisions

Fig. 5.5 Overview of professional roles

sometimes turn out well, but in most cases it is not really helpful and only leads to more coaching clients. The temptation for coaches in organizational consultation is dealing personally with leadership. Leadership style and personality, biography and past traumatic events are used in an attempt to explain organizational problems. At the same time, stages of organizational development are linked to the emergence of leadership. This leads in most cases to the excessive demands upon persons (that have already been extraordinary) and to the continued ineffectiveness of the organization.

For coaches, it is essential to know about modes of operation and the dynamics of different system types. Firstly, they can offer causes for various social phenomena, and secondly, they are sponsors of images, metaphors and descriptions that can lead clients back to their capacity for acting. It is another matter to want to influence social systems, or to intervene. This is a separate craft, a separate mastery in each case. This can certainly succeed, provided it is based on a solid qualification in the individual professional roles, and describes the requirements of organizational consultation. When advising organizations, I am confronted with the dynamics of all system types, and challenged to act in parallel with them.

Finally, I would like to summarize this text in four central ideas:

(1) Social systems are the central background paradigm when describing client phenomena, therefore offering potential solution images.
(2) The coaching dyad itself can be understood as a communication system. This perspective allows coaching to create useful and meaningful variance. Impulses within the various sensory dimensions are available to the coach.
(3) Coaching of multi-person systems paradoxically increases potentiality and limitation. It requires experience in moderation and group dynamics of the coach.
(4) Coaching of social systems is a risky reduction in complexity. The various social system types and logics require their own professional consultation specialties. Professional roles converge in organizational consultation.

References

von Ameln, F. (2004). *Konstruktivismus: Die Grundlagen systemischer Therapie, Beratung und Bildungsarbeit.* Tübingen, Basel: Francke.

Kantor, D. (2012). *Reading the room: Group dynamics for coaches and leaders.* New York: Wiley.

Luhmann, N. (1988). *Soziale Systeme: Grundriss einer allgemeinen Theorie* (2. Aufl.). Frankfurt/M.: Suhrkamp.
Luhmann, N. (2006). *Organisation und Entscheidung* (2. Aufl., Orig. 1978). Wiesbaden: VS Verlag.
Wimmer, R., Glatzel, K., & Lieckweg, T. (Eds.). (2014). *Beratung im Dritten Modus: Die Kunst, Komplexität zu nützen*. Heidelberg: Carl-Auer.

Author Biography

Thomas Dallüge Dipl.-Phys., Dipl.-Psych., managing director at trinfactory GmbH, consultant specializing in management and leadership, strategy, organizational design, change, coaching (DBVC).

6 Coaching in Relation to Psychotherapy

Christoph Schmidt-Lellek

Abstract

Coaching exists alongside a wide range of other formats of consultation, some of which it competes with, while mutually complementing others. If coaching is to define itself as a profession, clear definitions and hence delineations between it and other professional formats of intervention are necessary. First of all, the difference between it and psychotherapy is clear: Psychotherapy is a curative approach in which personal problems with pathological significance are dealt with, while coaching is a consultation approach which focuses on issues from the working world. However, there are also methodological and thematic overlaps. These include approaches which e.g. attempt to determine how a person's biography has influenced him, but also diagnostic competencies which, where necessary, serve to determine where the limits of coaching lie. This is illustrated by a list of example problems and problem constellations.

Coaching exists today alongside a wide range of other forms of consultation, some of which it competes with, while mutually complementing others. However, the term "coaching" is used to mean a wide range of different things in common usage, which often makes it hard to tell where coaching ends and other forms of consultation and/or treatment begin. But if coaching is to define itself as a profession, clear definitions and hence delineations between it and other professional formats of intervention are necessary. First of all, the difference between it and psychotherapy

C. Schmidt-Lellek (✉)
Taunusstr. 126, 61440 Oberursel, Germany
e-mail: Kontakt@Schmidt-Lellek.de
URL: http://www.Schmidt-Lellek.de

A. Schreyögg and C. Schmidt-Lellek (eds.), *The Professionalization of Coaching*, DOI 10.1007/978-3-658-16805-6_6

is clear: Psychotherapy is a curative approach in which personal problems with pathological significance are dealt with, while coaching is a consultation approach which focuses on issues from the working world. But there are also overlaps between these two formats. They not only include certain methods used by both, but also thematic areas. This is because the various areas of concern for which the respective professions come into question may mutually intersect, and it is quite impossible to clearly define where one ends and the other begins. I will be examining these "intersections" in this chapter. To begin, we will first have a closer look at a number of general aspects regarding the differences between the professions.

6.1 Causes and Motivations for a Consultation

In pedagogical, therapeutic, and consultation occupations (i.e. in all "professions"; cf. DBVC 2012, pp. 11–17; cf. Chap. 1 in this book), the basic premise is always that of people approaching professionals for assistance in coping with their existential issues. Generally, they do this when their own resources are insufficient or do not appear sufficient for resolving the problem. These resources not only include their personal competencies, but also the option of speaking to other persons they are close to, i.e. family members, friends, colleagues etc. about their day-to-day problems and conflicts and to unburden themselves by having these conversations; to consider other opinions, ideas, and options, and to adopt them where necessary. Since time immemorial, this has been one of the most important sources of assistance for dealing with existential issues. In this respect, professionals and their offerings for helping to deal with the relevant problems serve as a replacement for the insufficient or overly taxed personal relationships of a person seeking advice.

The increasing importance of professional consultation in their various forms can be attributed to a range of factors: For one, the increasing isolation of people—i.e. the impoverishment of their communicative resources—is in part responsible for the rise in the number of available consultation and support offerings; and for another, the problems to be solved appear to be growing in complexity, such that a conversation with an understanding friend is no longer sufficient and an expert needs to be consulted.

Generally, however, all our life problems revolve around a few basic issues: health, love, work, the search for meaning, and transience. For all these issues, there are specialists that one can consult when problems are encountered: Psychotherapy is responsible for dealing with conflicts involving love, marriage, sexuality, family relations, friendship, love of oneself and/or issues involving a sense of self-worth (including the "somatized" manifestations of such conflicts); while coaches are the method of choice for dealing with problems involving work, performance, jobs, careers etc.; and ministers and pastors, as representatives of the corresponding religions, are consulted on issues involving the search for meaning and dealing with temporality and transience. However, it is obvious that such a division of labor is inadequate alone from the experience that these various areas of concern encroach upon each other and that it is quite impossible to tell where one begins and the other ends. Psychotherapy has long since started dealing with issues that convention would regard as being the domain of religion, and which cannot be immediately classified according to conventional definitions of illnesses, even though e.g. the experience of futility can certainly lead to illnesses and/or arise as a result of illness.

This would be a differentiation with regard to content-related aspects. A differentiation can also be made according to the goals of the consultation, namely between "*personality development*" and "*personnel development*". Personality development deals with the person and the entirety of their lives, including all intimate, open and concealed, conscious and unconscious experiences and parts thereof, with the goal of achieving the greatest extent of healing and maturity of personality (psychotherapy). Personnel development deals with the work-related aspects of a person, i.e. in his roles and functions within a working organization with the goal of achieving the greatest degree of effectiveness in his work (coaching). But this distinction, too, cannot be made in a precise manner, as the common denominator is the person, who needs to fill in the roles and functions and who is unable to completely separate *internal* conflicts from *external* conflicts (it is precisely because of this that we have presented the concept of "life coaching"; cf. Buer and Schmidt-Lellek 2008; Schmidt-Lellek and Buer 2011).

The mutual overlap of internal and external experiential spheres is particularly significant for persons with management roles (i.e. coaching's target group proper). This is because leadership abilities cannot be measured by specialist competencies alone. Instead, the *personality* with his disposition, talents, interests, and charisma is an important factor for success. What is important here is not only communicative competencies and management techniques, but also the willingness and ability to inspire people for a particular thing or cause, to empathize with others, to connect with them on a deeper level, demarcate clear limits, to confront and criticize others in a manner that allows them to maintain their dignity and without offending them; what is required here is the ability to stand firm in conflict situations, i.e. to neither bury one's head in the sand nor retaliate brutally in order to defend one's one position etc. All this requires a great degree of self-reflexivity, and it is exactly this which coaching aims to help develop and support.

Despite this, the limits between coaching and psychotherapy should not be blurred. For example, coaching is the wrong choice if a client primarily wishes to address personal difficulties. Furthermore, these two formats of consultation each require a different type of relationship with the client: The psychotherapeutic setting implies an asymmetric definition of the relationship if regressive tendencies and a partial dependency of the client on the therapist are to be experienced and processed in longer therapeutic processes (cf. Schmidt-Lellek 2006, p. 297). In contrast, in coaching, we can generally assume a symmetric definition of the relationship, in which both persons involved interact with each other as equals and the client displays a stable ability for self-government. Admittedly, asymmetric elements also play a role here, as the coach needs to structure the coaching process, "particularly where the correction of interpretation and behavior patterns which touch on clients' pre-rational domains are concerned" (Schreyögg 2012a, p. 212); however, symmetry is generally restored at the end of such a session.

6.2 Professional Coaching Requires a Wide Range of Comprehension Paradigms

The specific challenge in professional coaching lies in analyzing the interactions between an organization and a person. Solely looking at the organization with its mode of operation or solely looking at the individual person with his patterns of thinking, feeling, and acting is inadequate for dealing with the complex interactional phenomena between the person and the organization.

For example, in conflict-related coaching, the initial goal is generally determining the possibly manifold causes of a conflict: These causes may be localized in the organization and/or the culture of an organization, while simultaneously arising from the requirements of the organization's environment, as well as from the interaction between the members of the organization, conflicting interests, from open or concealed dynamics of depreciation, from the unfulfilled desires of the persons involved; and sometimes also from members of the organization who are not capable of working in a team or lack communicative ability, and who may be projecting inner conflicts or psychological disorders onto a team. Furthermore, all these possible causes may mutually result in each other. A corresponding expansion of a client's horizon of comprehension may enable him to change his perspective where he was previously accustomed to a familiar point of view, leading to new options of acting.

In order to be able to properly address the complexity of such dynamics, a coach requires a wide spectrum of knowledge resources along with the corresponding comprehension paradigms from the various economics and social science disciplines, as well as from psychology (cf. Schreyögg 2012a, p. 157). He requires comprehension paradigms for the analysis of organization dynamics, of group dynamics (cf. Chap. 13 in this book), as well as psychodiagnostic competencies (cf. Chap. 17 in this book). Particularly when issues of personnel management are involved, simply considering roles and functions is not enough, as they are carried out and/or filled by persons, each with their own unique characteristics, strengths, weaknesses, needs and fears etc.

The extent to which psychodiagnostic competencies are necessary for coaching is initially determined by the coaching concept: The more closely a business coaching is oriented towards an expansion of the client's professional competencies, for which it primarily utilizes the corresponding tools, the less necessary this appears to be—although in this case coaching would continue to be in line with an "*expert culture*". If coaching is, in addition, to serve as a free space for all issues arising in occupational contexts, the person will need to be considered in his entirety, which means that psychological and psychopathological comprehension paradigms will also need to be available to the coach—in this case, the coaching will be oriented more towards a "*professional culture*".

If we wish to understand coaching as a profession, there is an additional aspect: As a consultation format, coaching exists alongside other professions which persons who have encountered problems may seek help from (e.g. lawyers, corporate consultants, doctors, psychotherapists etc. with their specific and relevant expert knowledge). Part of having a sense of professional responsibility is having a *perceptive faculty* for phenomena which exceed one's own field of competence. Such a faculty allows e.g. a doctor to recognize a psychosomatic dynamic in a chronic illness, and hence, in addition to prescribing a course of treatment with medicines, refer the patient to a psychotherapist. However, if he is blind to such dynamics and considers himself alone to be responsible with his medical competence, he may not be able to provide the patient with the care he needs, prolonging the problem instead of solving it. Similarly, a coach may e.g. be able to recognize a narcissistic dynamic behind a manager's drive for success, and need to more precisely differentiate the extent to which this represents a (still) normal, perhaps an even particularly creative form of narcissism, or if it is a pathological form of narcissism which a person may cause damage to himself and others with. If the latter seems likely, he will be able to recognize the limitations of coaching and recommend psychotherapy to the client.

Generally, many typical issues that are handled during coaching require some psychological knowledge (e.g. psychological typologies or concepts of developmental psychology) in order to be able to address clients' unique needs as well as take into consideration their individual life phases. Furthermore, when coaching clients have personal problems, a coach will need to at least be able to sufficiently distinguish a number of things: Not every manifestation of exhaustion is to be classified as a burnout; being dejected is not the same as experiencing depression; the consumption of too much alcohol is not necessarily a sign of addiction, and destructive social behavior is not always indicative of a personality disorder. The distinction between "still healthy" and "already ill" is not an easy one to make, and the resources for coping with stress, uncertainty, and internal or external conflicts vary greatly from person to person. As a general rule of thumb, we can say that coaching reaches its limits when the client no longer shows sufficient ability for stable self-government. In this case, a psychotherapist or doctor should be consulted. As a coach, one does not necessarily need to be a psychologist or a psychotherapist in order to responsibly deal with such phenomena, but being sufficiently and expertly informed in such matters and possessing the ability to perceive and distinguish between psychopathic behavioral patterns is indispensable for professional coaching.

However, the limitations of psychological comprehension paradigms should also be considered, as conflicts in organizations are sometimes unilaterally personalized by coaches with psychotherapeutic training, who then attempt to solve them "only" as individual problems. This may result in the loss of a conflict dynamic's potential to drive change for the organization. It may even serve, as a company's covert goal, to immunize an organizational conflict by pushing it onto a particular person (cf. Kühl 2008, p. 45ff.).

6.3 Common Problem Constellations for Which Psychodiagnostic Perspectives Are Relevant

Generally, for the problem or conflict areas with which persons make use of coaching offerings, there are four different levels which may determine the nature of the conflicts:

(1) The individual, personal level
(2) The interactional level
(3) The institutional level
(4) The societal level.

These may mutually intersect, but although in principle "everything is related with each other", not everything can be lumped together and solved. The required reduction of complexity requires a specific focus—and a decision as to which focus is a priority and holds the greatest promise of initiating change. In any case, psychodiagnostic comprehension paradigms are relevant for conflicts that can be attributed to the first two levels. As long as obvious illnesses or psychological disorders which may impair a client's abilities to act and collaborate are not an issue, it may be wise to include psychotherapeutic perspectives during coaching and to spend a limited number of hours e.g. with a biographical anamnesis for a better understanding of one's own emotional and cognitive patterns. This is because conflicts in the working world are often influenced by psychological conflicts, which are generally attributable to the—rather wide—spectrum of "normal" human functioning.

The following are central issues in coaching which may have a potential interface with psychotherapy, and hence require special consideration:

- *Communication problems*: are the most fundamental problems, and are related with most other issues. Knowledge of how communication functions as a whole and its complexities, such as how dysfunctions in communicative interactions between persons can be identified and overcome, is part of a coach's basic repertoire. The communication model by Schulz von Thun (1981) is of particular utility here. Psychotherapy is to be recommended when a client displays extremely rigid communication patterns, frequently recurring communicative dysfunctions, or a lack of empathy for another person's position.
- *Developmental crises*: may be of a purely occupational nature (e.g. aspirations or fears regarding change at the workplace), but they may also be linked to personal developments: Examples include a mid-life crisis when existing values or purpose in life have lost their meaning, or a transition to retirement, during which a person has to come to terms with the loss of roles and functions. In order for a coach to help clients deal with life tasks that are typical for their age, a sufficient knowledge of developmental psychology is helpful (cf. e.g. Erikson 1977; Faltermaier et al. 1992). Coaching reaches its limits when a client is stuck in such "transitional crises" and/or when neurotic behavior patterns manifest themselves therein. Sometimes, a neurotic pattern which requires psychotherapeutic treatment may also become apparent after the loss of an occupational position in the context of outplacement coaching.
- *Exhaustion, burnout, depression*: Because "burnout" is currently a fashionable term that is being used in a rather inflationary manner, and some clients come or are sent to a coaching session with this (self-)diagnosis, particular care should be exercised in differentiating these three terms from each other in the

diagnostic evaluation. Ordinary exhaustion can be overcome by a period of downtime, managing one's time/schedule differently etc., which often succeeds with the help of coaching. A burnout requires, in addition to this, a deeper reflection and changes in the balance between giving and taking, responsibility for others and responsibility for oneself, the ability to recognize the limits of one's capabilities, and to protect them. If identified in time, a burnout can be handled well with the use of coaching, e.g. by changing the general situation or working patterns. If the symptoms of a burnout are overlooked or not taken seriously, they may lead to depression, which then needs to be handled via psychotherapeutic methods, perhaps even with the use of supporting medication (cf. Behrends-Krahnen 2011 for differentiating between burnout and depression).

- *Addictions*: First of all, this includes substance abuse (alcohol, drugs, medicines) which requires medical or psychotherapeutic treatment if the client is no longer able to control his addiction and this impacts his ability to work. However, the overemphasis on work can also be diagnosed as an addiction ("workaholism"); in this case coaching would have reached its limits if this occurred in combination with a personality disorder. Alcohol problems are frequently accompanying phenomena of other conflicts that have not been solved. If a company recommends coaching to its employee in such a situation, this information may be helpful for making the decision as to whether the alcoholism issue should first be handled with the use of the appropriate therapy before then using coaching to deal with the underlying job-related conflicts.
- *Fear*: can stimulate productive activity, but it can also become paralyzing. If there are insufficient resources for dealing with fear or if fear is compensated for in a destructive manner, a neurotic fear is to be assumed, for which psychotherapy would be competent.
- *Obsession*: is the dark side of a love for order. Reliability, precision, a clear structuring of work and discussion processes are all part of the repertoire of management competencies. However, when they turn into a compulsion, they can have a highly paralyzing effect on the person himself, resulting in the loss of creativity, flexibility, and the ability to identify and deal with complex situations. In this case, psychotherapy is recommended, as compulsive neurotic processing patterns are extremely resistant to change.
- *Mania*: Because people in a manic phase sometimes hold a strong fascination for other persons, an intuition for identifying the subtle differences between mania and a healthy ability to inspire people is important. Manic episodes often have a high pathological significance. However, the affected persons themselves do not notice this at all in this phase—they feel happy, euphoric, charged

with energy, and ready to make quick decisions. Often, such phases are then followed by severe depressive episodes ("bipolar depression").

- *Narcissism*: Narcissistic dynamics can manifest in a wide range of different forms. Because certain occupation roles, but also certain organization types (e.g. in innovative milieus with a high degree of expressiveness) attract narcissistically motivated personalities, coaches are advised to acquire the corresponding knowledge. In particular, it is helpful for coaches to be able to recognize narcissistic backgrounds and their ambivalences in "charismatically" gifted executives and be able to differentiate between their various manifestations. First of all, it is necessary to have a basic understanding of the compensatory function of narcissistic "grandiosity", which often hides a weak or uncertain sense of self (cf. Schmidt-Lellek 2008). A coach should be able to determine if it is at all possible to reach a client with narcissistic tendencies, or if he will only instrumentalize the coaching for his self-validation, without the willingness to actually deal with his own thoughts and actions in a true, critical manner. In addition, it should also be possible to consider narcissism as an interactional phenomenon, because as Steyrer (1995) illustrated in his monograph on "Charisma in organizations", "charismatic" executives often have their delusions of grandeur validated by the corresponding expectations and attributions from their subordinate employees or the public.

6.4 Practical Recommendations

- Coaches without psychotherapeutic knowledge should strive to collaborate with psychotherapists, to which clients can be referred to if necessary. They should inform themselves on and keep a rough overview of the most important psychological disorders and their psychodynamic contexts (e.g. Mentzos 2009). Further education courses providing information on the common diagnosis systems such as the international classification of psychological disorders (ICD 10; cf. World Health Organization 1992) are recommended. Möller and Kotte (2014) also offer a broad overview of the diagnostic approaches relevant for coaching.
- Coaches with a background in psychotherapy are to acquire knowledge of organization dynamics and of economic processes (e.g. Schreyögg 2012b; Mohr 2006).
- If a client requests weekly sessions for a long period of time or mentions health-related symptoms (e.g. cardiac problems, tinnitus, sleep disorders), it is to be assumed that these are issues relevant for psychotherapy.

- In addition to expert psychodiagnostic knowledge, powerful emotional reactions on the part of the coach, e.g. a strong feeling of reduced self-esteem when interacting with the client (which can be understood as a "projective identification") can be taken as an indication that the limits of coaching have been exceeded and that psychotherapeutic measures are to be recommended.
- Regular supervision or intervision (supervision among colleagues) should be seen as a professional standard for coaches. Furthermore, collaboration with colleagues with different basic occupations and professional experiences is recommended.

6.5 Final Remarks

Coaching is an opportunity for productive conflict management with a double orientation towards work-related and personality-related issues. The latter should not form the primary focus in the design of the coaching interactions, but in many cases it can be helpful to expand the perspectives with regard to conflict management in a job-related context or to further occupational development with biographical excursions. Definitely, coaching can never replace psychotherapeutic treatment when serious psychological or psychosomatic disorders impact a person's ability to work. However, coaching is able to provide a free space for all issues that arise in the working world or which are triggered by it, with the overarching objective of integrating one's own personality into one's occupational role by continually reflecting on one's actions, and in doing so simultaneously increasing effectiveness and job satisfaction.

References

Behrends-Krahnen, E. (2011). Burnout – eine Herausforderung im Coaching. *Organisationsberatung, Supervision, Coaching, 18*(3), 333–341.

Buer, F., & Schmidt-Lellek, C. (2008). *Life-Coaching. Über Sinn, Glück und Verantwortung in der Arbeit.* Göttingen: Vandenhoeck & Ruprecht.

DBVC—Deutscher Bundesverband Coaching e.V. (Hrsg.). (2012). *Leitlinien und Empfehlungen für die Entwicklung von Coaching als Profession. Kompendium mit den Professionsstandards des DBVC* (4., erw. Aufl.). Osnabrück: DBVC Geschäftsstelle; Engl. version available under: www.dbvc.de/publikationen/coaching-kompendium.

Erikson, E. H. (1977). *Identität und Lebenszyklus.* Frankfurt/M.: Suhrkamp.

Faltermaier, T., Mayring, P., Saup, W., & Strehmel, P. (1992). *Entwicklungspsychologie des Erwachsenenalters*. Stuttgart: Kohlhammer.
Kühl, S. (2008). *Coaching und Supervision. Zur personenorientierten Beratung in Organisationen*. Wiesbaden: VS Verlag.
Mentzos, S. (2009). *Lehrbuch der Psychodynamik. Die Funktion der Dysfunktionalität psychischer Störungen*. Göttingen: Vandenhoeck & Ruprecht.
Möller, H., & Kotte, S. (Eds.). (2014). *Diagnostik im Coaching: Grundlagen, Analyseebenen, Praxisbeispiele*. Berlin, Heidelberg: Springer.
Mohr, G. (2006). *Systemische Organisationsanalyse. Dynamiken und Grundlagen der Organisationsentwicklung*. Gergisch Gladbach: EHP.
Schmidt-Lellek, C. (2006). *Ressourcen der helfenden Beziehung. Modelle dialogischer Praxis und ihre Deformationen*. Bergisch Gladbach: EHP.
Schmidt-Lellek, C. (2008). Charisma, Macht und Narzissmus. Zur Diagnostik einer ambivalenten Führungseigenschaft. In C. Schmidt-Lellek & A. Schreyögg (Hrsg.), *Praxeologie des Coaching* (S. 61–75). Wiesbaden: VS Verlag (also available in: www.Schmidt-Lellek.de).
Schmidt-Lellek, C., & Buer, F. (Eds.). (2011). *Life-Coaching in der Praxis. Wie Coaches umfassend beraten*. Göttingen: Vandenhoeck & Ruprecht.
Schreyögg, A. (2012a). *Coaching. Eine Einführung für Praxis und Ausbildung* (7., überarb. und erw. Aufl.). Frankfurt/M.: Campus,
Schreyögg, G. (2012b). *Grundlagen der Organisation. Basiswissen für Studium und Praxis*. Wiesbaden: Gabler.
Schulz von Thun, F. (1981). *Miteinander reden*. Störungen und Klärungen. Allgemeine Psychologie der Kommunikation. Reinbek: Rowohlt.
Steyrer, J. (1995). *Charisma in Organisationen*. Campus: Sozial-kognitive und psychodynamisch-interaktive Aspekte von Führung. Frankfurt/M.
World Health Organization. (1992). *The ICD-10. Classification of Mental and Behavioral Disorders. Geneva; Germ. Edition: Internationale Klassifikation psychischer Störungen: ICD-10* (8. Aufl., 2011). Bern: Huber.

Author Biography

Dr. phil. Christoph Schmidt-Lellek studied prot. theology, philosophy and pedagogy, doctoral dissertation on the resources of relationship in professional settings, freelance practice in coaching (DBVC), psychotherapy and supervision (DGSv), publications in the fields of psychotherapy and coaching, co-publisher and editor of the journal “Organisationsberatung, Supervision, Coaching” (OSC).

Coaching in Consultation of Companies

7

Thomas Dallüge

Abstract

This chapter sets itself the task of discussing coaching in the context of consultation processes. For this purpose, the first section briefly outlines the terms company/organization, leadership and consultation. In the second section, we will further differentiate consultation in the context of useful distinctions (core consultation dimensions, change game types) and provide practical examples. The question is raised as to how coaches can be a helpful resource for involved and affected leaders in a consultation context. We also simultaneously consider how consultation and coaching processes can be coupled together as they take place.

7.1 Introduction

The article sets itself the task of putting the characteristics of coaching with consultation processes in perspective. The aim is to widen the perspective of consultation for coaches, and therefore to assist coaches in usefully categorizing their clients' questions.

From my perspective, coaching is increasingly taking place in the context of consultation processes in companies. This is hardly surprising, as change processes with the support of external consultants produce both significant change and

T. Dallüge (✉)
Trinfactory GmbH, Hufelandstr. 22, 10407 Berlin, Germany
e-mail: thomas.dalluege@trinfactory.com
URL: http://www.trinfactory.com

A. Schreyögg and C. Schmidt-Lellek (eds.), *The Professionalization of Coaching*, DOI 10.1007/978-3-658-16805-6_7

considerable uncertainties within companies, which both the responsible and affected individuals need to deal with. Similarly, it can be observed that there are two different coaching orientations in terms of consultation processes: Firstly, coaching takes place simultaneously with, but independent of the consultation process. Also, there is coaching which is integrated into consultation processes, and in my view there is a rising demand for this type of coaching. Integrated coaching consists of the following two aspects:

- It is about coaching a leader who is responsible for implementing a change process involving consultation, and it occurs in coaching on this topic. (As we can already see, it can be a bit tricky when the coach is also the consultant.)
- Coaching as a change process element or as an employee development instrument.

With integrated coaching, the coaching leaves the shelter of the company and is a hidden or open player in organizational processes. Coaching is therefore confronted with major complexity, which it must deal with professionally.

As a coach, in order to act with leaders who are confronted with such situations, it is helpful to have one's own understanding of consultation and the associated requirements and conditions. For this reason, it makes sense to deal with the relevant terms and their related understandings, either through reflecting on one's own consultation experiences, or through relevant qualification formats. Coaching during a change process can be easily compared with support provided during a birth: Someone would probably be of only limited help at a birth if they have never had a child themselves, or studied as a midwife. As we set out as coaches in the professional support of "birth processes", it will surely not harm us to be concerned with consultation of companies.

I do not wish to discuss the coaching term itself at this point, as it has already been defined many times. I refer here to the definition of DBVC (2012, p. 20 f.), as well as to Chap. 5 of this book. An understanding of organizational consultation requires an understanding of the terms "company", "organization", "leadership" and "consultation". The terms and our understanding of organization and leadership are of considerable importance for this purpose. Companies are a special type of organization, and in order to understand them, we need an idea of what organizations are and how they work. Organization and leadership are inextricably linked—they are the two sides of the same coin. We will therefore consider the following questions in the first section: (1) How can I understand companies? (2) How can I understand leadership? (3) How can I understand consultation?

Consultation is further differentiated in the second section, after introducing a basic understanding of these concepts. This deeper understanding is useful in better grasping the implications of coaching. Firstly, we will observe consultation in accordance with its core dimensions. These core dimensions are based on the dimensions of meaning in communication (in the knowledge that consultative processes of organizations can be understood as communication processes). The core consultation dimensions include a factual, a social and a temporal dimension (cf. Wimmer et al. 2014). As in any communication, these dimensions are simultaneously processed and intertwined in consultation communications. In addition to the core dimensions, it is also helpful to distinguish the consultation processes in accordance with the nature of the change. With this we bring the temporal dynamics of change processes and their radical nature into view. We will pay particular attention to the category of radical transformation. The established distinctions are discussed using two examples. In the third section, we will bring the perspectives together and describe the consequences for coaching.

7.2 Definitions

7.2.1 Company

How can we understand companies? Companies are special organizations that act as addresses for economic matters in a functionally differentiated society. They can therefore be understood as social systems. Companies derive their existence from the production of goods that meet a need, and to which a certain value is attributed to their possession. They act in the code of having vs. not having.

In the concept of "social systems" (Luhmann 1988), organizations are operationally closed, autopoietic communication systems. This is a significant shift in observation. We are practiced in assuming that organizations consist of a collection of individuals who provide a certain framing and organization. The individuals have defined characteristics and are in relationships with each other. Another type of observation focuses on the continuous communication of decisions and the resulting structures. Through the introduction of a system-environment border in internal communications, it is possible to align the communication process based on images of one's self and constructed external images.

For company consultation, or in other words, consultation of economic organizations, the following aspects are of particular importance:

- Organizations are answers to social problems. Their current constitutions are a fitting response to all previous requirements (otherwise the organizations wouldn't exist).
- Organizations can be understood as ongoing decision communications. These decisions sit in relation to the decisions that premise the organization. The decision paths of the past are available to the organization as decision premises (conditional programs, purpose programs, communication channels, personnel, culture) (cf. Luhmann 2006).
- Organizations depict an internal complexity (internal differentiation), which corresponds to the organizational environment and its own task.
- Organizations are historical structures. Everything that has happened so far justifies the way things are now, and probably should best remain so into the future.
- Individuals couple themselves to the organizational communication through functions. This coupling is regulated through organizational membership.
- Individuals are structurally coupled environments of organizations. They represent a perception reservoir for organizations, since they are linked to relevant environments.
- It is the responsibility of the organization itself what and in which way becomes part of the organizational communication.
- The organization generates sense of future communication frames through previous communication, recent decisions and associated decision horizons.
- Changing organizational demands emerge in the relevant environments.

7.2.2 Leadership

In accordance with the understanding of an organization as described above, leadership is a function within an organization. Leadership can be understood as a phenomenon of self-organization in organizations that is responsible for "introduction of the relevant external" and "appropriate decision communication". The fundamental objective of leaders is to implement coordinated behavior for their livelihood.

From this perspective, leadership in organizations is less a result of individual passion, but a phenomenon that results from organizational development. And of course we need individuals who can appropriately couple to these leadership roles, fill them, and make arrangements with the organization for further development. This understanding of leadership is most likely based on the understanding of "postheroic management" (Baecker 1994). It allows considerations of personal and characteristic-based management styles fade into the background, and considers rather the design of communication and decisions against the backdrop of a relevant context design. Stated somewhat strikingly, it is no longer about the question, "How can I maintain my heroism?" but the question "How do I take care of the organization with appropriate leadership?"

This service delivery places uncertainty at the core of the decision. Leadership has precisely the task of deciding on the (rational) undecidable. Here, central leadership tasks have sprung up around the paradoxes needing to be managed in organizations—so you will never be finished! (cf. Krusche 2008; Table 7.1).

This task list is a useful tool in many coaching situations. It transforms the question, "How do I lead?" into the question, "How I take care of my leadership challenges?" and offers a wonderful anchor for a looking at both the organization and personal leadership performance. With this organizational and management understanding is also clear that consultancy processes may only be commissioned by responsible leadership. The management of change processes is a non-delegable management task, as it relates to leadership!

7.2.3 Consultation

In discussing the consultation concept, I refer to advice from companies and commercial organizations. In my view, consultation can initially be outlined in two extremely concise but striking ways:

Table 7.1 Leadership responsibilities and paradoxes

Scope of duties	Paradox
Strategy development	Securing the future with the unpredictability of the future
Marketing	Assessment of the market and relevant environments with a lack of market transparency
Resource management	Sustainable profitability with short-term optimization
Organizational development	Powerful structures and processes with flexibility and the ability to change
HR management	Encouraging initiative while at the same time conforming to a position
Controlling	Controlling self reflection with a lack of transparency around the relevant factors

(1) Consultation is coupled variance. That is, the task of consultation is in providing and enabling difference in decision making premises. At the same time, this difference must be communicated in a way that it can be further processed by the organization.
(2) Consultation is observation of observations. That is, that consultation will take into consideration how the organization looks at itself, at environments, at the future and the past. On this basis, alternative creations or creation routines are brought into communication.

Consultancies are brought on board into a company (and its communications) through leadership, and form a new communication system, "the consultation system". The starting point of consultation processes are target-actual differences, which, from the perspective of the organization, are to be worked through with the support of an external organization. The consultation system is constituted in the form of a target-actual difference relating to a tangible issue. In addition, there are guidelines as to which way this consultation system plays out, and with what kind of temporality the consultation system is intended. The consultation system now provides for organizing an innovation and experimentation field—a comparatively sheltered, results-based observation room. Here, new decision logics can be developed, tested, created, observed, rated and optionally connected to company communications. Perhaps they don't have to be—it is up to following communications within the company as to how the consultation outcomes will be referred to. Simultaneously, new self-observation settings (external or internal) arise during the consultation that broaden decision horizons in any case, as long as they do not lead to any real changes.

From the very beginning of its constitution, the consultation system processes its meaning. Through the path of current decisions against the background of all possible choices, the meaning of this consultation develops. The meaning of the consultation can be reconstructed around the three core dimensions (technical, social and time). In the technical dimension, it lies in the expansion of expertise for the organization. In the social dimension it comes down to changes in mutual expectations of personal involvement, and in the time dimension to the temporal reference points and shelf life of decisions.

If one observes consultation from a (meta) perspective, the redundant discussions about claims of "better" consultation between expert and process consultation also end (Königswieser et al. 2006). Technical consulting is aimed more at factual/time dimensions and process consulting, rather on social and temporal dimension. Due to the requirements that arise in companies, it is necessary during the discussions to take a wholistic perspective of organizations, and consequently, in consultation. The focus of expert or process consultation is on already anticipated solutions, which may or may not succeed. Wholistic consultation observes organizations in all three core dimensions, and in balance (see consultation in the third mode; Wimmer et al. 2014).

In summary, we can say:

- Companies are unique communication systems that make sense within economic systems.
- Leadership is a function that ensures an appropriate supply of decisions within companies.
- Consultation allows future issues to be dealt with in a different way.

For coaching, this means that leaders in consultation processes face significant challenges. It is about the existence of the company. It is about highly consequential decisions during uncertainty. It is about adapting to the future without knowing what that future holds. This alone can cause a leader to go weak at the knees. The task of coaching is to create a space for leaders where they can rise to these challenges, and empower them with possibilities for description and options for action. A truly challenging task!

7.3 Further Differentiation of Consultation

7.3.1 Core Dimensions of Consultation and Coaching

Let us take the idea of the three core consultation dimensions, so we can describe company deficiencies in decision communication that are processed as part of a consultation project. In addition to all the core dimensions that are always processed in a consultation system, individual dimensions come to the fore depending on the task and the course of the change process. Accordingly, leaders can be charged with solving the following organizational problem descriptions:

- There is a lack of knowledge and expertise within our organization (technical dimension).
- We don't utilize the potential of involved individuals when making company decisions (social dimension).
- The dynamics that we display on a daily basis don't work (temporal dimension).

As coach, I have to confront my leaders with the following illustrative questions that arise from the organizational change process:

Regarding the technical dimension

- What is the problem?
- Where can I get the relevant knowledge from?
- How can I separate the important from the unimportant? What is a priority?
- How can I highlight relevant knowledge?
- How can I use the expertise of the organization?
- How accurate and detailed does the knowledge have to be?
- When do we know enough?

Regarding the social dimension

- Who do I bond with, who do I tend not to bond with and why?
- How much can I give of myself and still be taken seriously?
- What will others think of me?
- How can I move others to be honest?
- Do others think that is a good thing here?
- What type of invitation is needed for different types of involvement?
- What unspoken loyalties are in the room?

Regarding the temporal dimension

- How long will it take?
- When can it be finished, and will it still be relevant?
- Will we get it done on time?
- How do we construct the process?
- How far should we look back?
- How far forward should we make predictions?
- How should we deal with possible disruptions?

It is important for coaching that these issues have their origins in the consultation and change processes of the organization. They are rarely seen or heard as questions because of low self-worth, or because of the individual incompetence of the coachee. At first glance they have their sources in organizational dynamics. They are the result of organizational phenomena. And as "social problem processors" in a dynamic environment, organizations are filled with them. Especially as the solutions of today are often the problems of tomorrow.

As a coach accompanying leaders through a change process, I am faced with the task of being a suitable sparring partner to the coachee in relation to these questions. This is against the background of questions that are usually associated with complex corporate issues (strategy, market, lean etc.), with complex structures (multiple hierarchical levels, divisional logics—functional, regional, etc.) and a specific culture. As a coach, this means that I need to be equipped with descriptive patterns for organizations in consultation processes, and to be able to reconstruct the accompanying social phenomena in the context of different system types.

I want to emphasize this aspect with an example that I often bring into coaching training: In a medium-sized organization (approximately 5000 employees, €450 million turnover) I got talking with a leader on the subject of "my office". His office consisted of two experienced office workers and two engaged personal assistants. The office was increasingly making errors (travel arrangements, dealing with priorities), and the climate in the office was icy (notice of dismissal in the desk). His question to me was: "What can I do?" When I give a specific description of the situation and the question to the training participants, the intentions of almost all the coaches go in the direction of: "It needs much closer guidance, more attention, there is a lack of leadership capability etc.". In summary, a strong focus on the leader as a person. The organizational aspects are hardly even examined. In the actual case, the striking breakdown of work within the office proved to result from a clash of different business cultures. While the current management had a rather managerial decision making logic, the previous several decades had been dominated by a presidential decision making logic. The office staff brought previous logics and loyalties with them as well as the contrasting new expectations. The change made logical sense for the future as well as the changing conditions of the organization (the new leadership was brought on board for this reason), but the company clearly needs more time to establish the change in premises and decision routines. As a result, the office realigned and renamed itself "core leadership team", and took on the task of being a centralized interface for conveying this cultural change.

Questions were processed in the coaching process with the leader which can be assigned to the core consultation dimensions:

- Where does my office get the necessary expertise from?
- Who should I include within this process?
- How long will it take and how much time do I have to invest as a leader?
- How do I synchronize these questions in order to achieve a performing office?

Here I was asked as a coach and as an expert in organizational change processes. On the one hand I had the job of bringing these issues to a point where they could be appropriately discussed, and secondly to activate the coaching system so as to bring the leadership from the original question towards a meaningful capacity for acting.

7.3.2 Types of Change Processes and Coaching

In addition to the core consultation dimensions, it also makes sense to differentiate the consultation processes by their dynamics and the depth of their change. The dynamics can be distinguished by low and high time pressure. The depth of change can be distinguished between 1st level and 2nd level changes. This results in four varieties of the intended change, which make very different demands on leaders (Fig. 7.1).

A 2nd level change gives leaders the paradoxical challenge of implementing a new style of leadership while acting in their previous style of leadership. This is not only true for a small area, but affects the entire organization. Therefore there is no alternative safe place in the organization. The basis for safety during radical transformation is mainly provided by each responsible manager, and is based more on personal trust than on organizational attribution.

The same applies to the changes under considerable time pressure. This is where leaders undertake the paradoxical challenge of finding the right solution in the shortest possible time, and making the necessary decisions. These solutions or decisions should actually be well weighed and processed appropriately within the organization. Particularly challenging is when both dynamics coincide and the company faces a radical transformation.

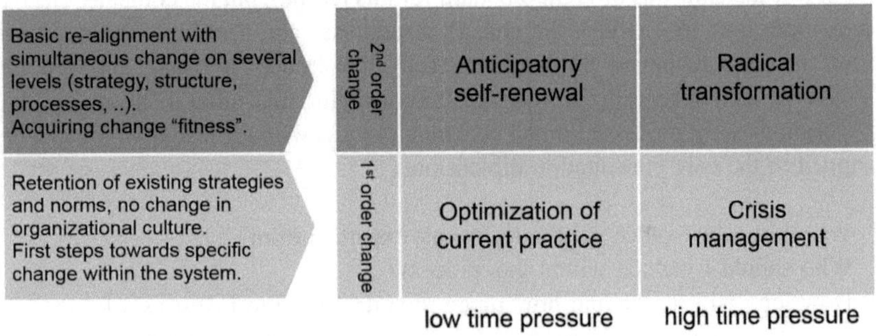

Fig. 7.1 Four varieties of change

Leaders are under considerable pressure and to some extent have personal responsibility towards their employees. The outcome of the transformation is open, and leaders do not know whether they will still have a role, or whether they will even want to have a role in the "new" organization. In addition to the "integration of the former" and the "opening of the new" in the context of the change process, it is not uncommon to find a "search for the other"—the search for another job, possibly in another company.

The relevance for coaching processes is self-evident. In addition to the typical requirements of a coaching process (enabling understanding of the situation and expanding options for action) there comes the added demand of expectation-free communication. Leaders have the opportunity to put every thought into words, without this leading to any consequences in the coaching.

I would like to explain the relevance of this distinction through a second *example*: In a media company, significant changes had taken place over five years. There had been acquisitions, comprehensive restructuring (shared service centers, migration processes, introduction of a new process-oriented organizational design) and downsizing. Several consultancies had been actively involved in the change processes of this company. Overall, this was a case of radical transformation. It was about a pattern change, which affected the entire company. The dynamic component resulted from the financial situation of the company. After a long history of strong profits they were now in the red. Leading the company back to profitability while at the same time equipping them with appropriate options for the future was a matter of urgency.

My client was the member of a management team, and was responsible for several product areas and core functions. Because of a high personal responsibility, he played a key role in implementation of the change process. In coaching, it became clear that this organizational restructure placed extraordinary demands on the client. There was considerable resistance and uncertainty within the company. The previous structure had to be dissolved and a new structure introduced. The difficulty was the fact that the new structure left many questions still unanswered, and the employees had no experience within it. Achieving the change meant setting out on an open and stormy sea with a collection of materials, building the boat during the trip and arriving on time at the destination. It is not an easy task for the captain to find a crew for the crossing or to keep them on board. Against this background, the coaching task was to build strength as well as a rumble strip.

If we look now at the aforementioned distinctions in change dynamics, we recognize features that are important in coaching. In radical transformations is more about individuals dealing with the consequences of their own actions. The timing of necessary decisions is so important (permanent marking of the new) that there is scarcely a chance for reflection. In processes without this time pressure, there are opportunities for testing and integration of reflection and feedback. Radical transformations allow hardly any breathing space. For this reason, the coaching session allows the concrete possibility to draw breath (and to exhale!), form one's own thoughts, and to examine important situations and decisions from various perspectives. Following the established coaching impulse of slowing down a client's world makes little sense at this point. When entering the company, these plans would most likely be swept away by the avalanche of transformation.

The second distinction was the radical nature of the changes. A specific feature of radical transformations is that the leadership system is also dramatically changed. There are changing areas of responsibility, and new mechanisms by which decisions are processed. This can lead to a situation where managers are responsible for the transformation, while at the same time knowing that there won't be a suitable position for them following it. The uncertainty regarding one's own role goes along with radical transformations. For this reason, we often encounter questions in coaching such as: "Can I meet these new requirements? Am I the right person for the job? What will happen if I am not?" That is usually the starting point for looking outwards, for beginning the parallel search for a new position in another organization. These questions are sponsored by changes within the organization. If you keep this in mind, it is important in coaching to support clients in dealing with the encroachments of the organization.

Radical transformations constantly puts leaders on a stage. Every behavior is observed and interpreted. For this reason, there is a need among leaders for unbiased and professional dialogue, that doesn't simply lead to further points on the to-do list. Coaching sessions can be a good place also for this.

7.4 Coaching and Consultation

What these aforementioned concepts and distinctions mean for coaching leaders in consultation processes? Four questions come to the forefront:

(1) What expectations do leaders have from coaching? Is it about a person-oriented view and/or an organizational or consultation oriented view of the leadership role? This effects the understanding of the coach's role.
(2) What frameworks will be put in place by the consultation process?

- What questions and which core dimensions are in focus? This has an effect on the design of the coaching system. Working through issues in the social dimension requires other processes than those used with technical issues.
- With what dynamics and radicalism do these processes impact the organization, and therefore the leaders? This has an effect on the orientation of the coaching. Coaching should make a difference and be sufficiently coupled to the experienced of organizational realities at the same time.

(3) Where do my loyalties lie as a coach? In coaching my loyalty and attention is clearly with the client, even when it comes to him leaving the organization. In contrast, my loyalty and attention in consultation is clearly with the organization and its future viability, knowing that organizations tend to considerably wear out their employees and leaders.

(4) Integrated coaching or more independence from the consultation process? Based on the previous points, it is important to clarify whether or not it makes sense to coach independently or as part of an integrated consultation process. Both options have advantages and disadvantages. A clear indication that integrated coaching is not indicated is reflected in the conflicted loyalties of the coach. At this point, we refer to the added value of supervision. A distance should also be taken from integrated coaching when reevaluations arise within the organization, that are neither helpful for the consultation or suggest the coach or consultant is acting in their own interests.

In summary, one can say that the combination of coaching and consultation involves a significant increase in complex perspectives. For professional implementation, it is helpful to understand consultation and coaching as two different fields of work. They focus on different things (person and organization) and have different intervention methods. At the same time, coaching and consultation require a variety of competencies, and therefore different types of professionalism.

References

Baecker, D. (1994). *Postheroisches management: Ein Vademecum*. Berlin: Merve.

DBVC—Deutscher Bundesverband Coaching e.V. (Hrsg.) (2012). *Leitlinien und Empfehlungen für die Entwicklung von Coaching als Profession. Kompendium mit den Professionsstandards des DBVC* (4., erw. Aufl.). Osnabrück: DBVC Geschäftsstelle; Engl. version available under: www.dbvc.de/publikationen.

Königswieser, R., Sonuç, E., & Gebhardt, J. (2006). *Komplementärberatung: Das Zusammenspiel von Fach- und Prozess-Know-how*. Stuttgart: Klett-Cotta.

Krusche, B. (2008). *Paradoxien der Führung: Aufgaben und Funktionen für ein zukunftsfähiges Management*. Heidelberg: Carl-Auer.

Luhmann, N. (1988). *Soziale Systeme: Grundriss einer allgemeinen Theorie* (2. Aufl.). Frankfurt/M.: Suhrkamp.

Luhmann, N. (2006). *Organisation und Entscheidung* (2. Aufl., Orig. 1978). Wiesbaden: VS Verlag.

Wimmer, R., Glatzel, K., & Lieckweg, T. (Eds.). (2014). *Beratung im Dritten Modus: Die Kunst, Komplexität zu nützen*. Heidelberg: Carl-Auer.

Author Biography

Thomas Dallüge Dipl.-Phys., Dipl.-Psych., managing director at trinfactory GmbH, consultant specializing in management and leadership, strategy, organizational design, change, coaching (DBVC).

8 Coaching in Projects

Ulrich Schueler

Abstract

Working in projects increasingly becomes a common everyday work practice. In the first part of this chapter psychological aspects of project work will be discussed. It will be argued that project coaching is a most suitable means to support learning and feedback processes. Further, structural aspects of project organization and processing will be described, as these form essential conditions for project success and thus also for project coaching processes. These coaching processes can be managed most efficiently by an external coach. The specific requirements a coach has to deal with will be described. The chapter will close with an analysis of motives, aims, framing conditions, and ways to progress in project coaching.

8.1 Introduction—Projects as Standard of Work Life

Working in projects grows more and more to a central way of work organization in today's work life. You can hardly find a professional area that does not claim to currently work on a certain kind of project. Certainly, it would be wrong to state that the practice of working in projects is the most common way to organize work today. Still, there are many areas, where project organization is not applied, think e.g. about industrial serial production or services (for a discussion on project vs.

U. Schueler (✉)
Am Schwarzen Berg 9, 22955 Hoisdorf b. Hamburg, Germany
e-mail: ulrich.schueler@pm-sp.com

A. Schreyögg and C. Schmidt-Lellek (eds.), *The Professionalization of Coaching*, DOI 10.1007/978-3-658-16805-6_8

non-project organization see Schreyögg 2008; Kerzner 2009). But even in these areas you will find out, if you ask the workers, that many of them are busy with personal projects of various kinds.

So, what is it that makes working in project settings so attractive? First of all, it is the fact, that a project is always connected with a vision about reaching a desired target state. People conduct projects as they wish to gain something better than the present reality, that eases work or life conditions, that helps simplifying life, or that simply generates more financial profit. And with a project people explore uncharted waters. That is what makes it a kind of adventure.

Projects are defined by doing something very new that has not been done so far. With a project we create unique things, like a new product, a new service or a new organizational structure. In opposition to that all other activities can be labelled as production or re-production. At the start of a project it is anything else but apparent, how to reach project targets. So the project members need to find new ways, steps that need to be done, have to be thought out and need to be planned. That is, what makes project work so creative and challenging? And, with regards to Maslow (1981) in his motivation approach, it is within the concept of self-actualization one of the basic human needs in an otherwise rather secured life environment.

Last but not least, project work means working in a social environment. Project are embedded in a social context, in a continuous interaction with other humans. This satisfies another basic human need, that of belongingness.

Certainly, it would be oversimplifying to reduce the advantage of working in projects to psychological needs only. The art of project work in its professional way, and that is in a clearly structured approach, is one of the most efficient ways to stay capable of acting in a constantly changing environment. The work modus of project work perfectionalizes basic feedback-oriented activities and perception patterns for highly complex social-, technical-, or trans-cultural challenges. It is clearly in accordance with the basic psychological approaches of various action theories, like the TOTE model (Miller et al. 1960) or the action regulation theory, as well as the Gestalt approaches.

8.2 Psychological Aspects of Handling Projects

Let us stick for a little while to psychological considerations of handling projects. In a second step we will see, that project handling, considered as a more or less mechanical technology with strict procedural instructions and fixed procedural steps may be required, but does not necessarily lead to the expected project success. Success will not be granted, if further substantial criteria will not be systematically accounted for, or will just accidentally be included into the project processes. These additional criteria are clearly of a psychological nature and refer to learning and feedback processes between the acting persons within a project. And I would dare to say, that these processes can be best supported through psychological coaching processes.

Referring to Navis (1987) and Westermayer (2009) describe in an extended Gestalt cycle, how the cycle between experiencing and acting integrates the distinct steps of thoughts, of detecting, evaluating, and integrating into a rule system. And exactly this happens continuously in project work (cf. Fig. 8.1). Becoming aware of an object, or a phenomenon, will result in a specific attitude within the person, who is becoming aware of that specific object or phenomenon. The resulting attitude is then guided by one or more of the previously named steps of thought: Something very new will be detected; something familiar will be rated, or something will be semantically integrated into the person's individual knowledge. Whether actually there might be a characteristic sequence of abduction, induction, and deduction in the following action and evaluation sequences, as Westermayer describes, is not essential for our discussion. What is relevant for us in this psychological approach is, that we find here some essential characteristics of project work: Starting with the (often emotionally) reasoned awareness, followed by generating an intention to act, flowing into a rationally reasoned action, and ending with the evaluation of the outcome of that action. This outcome sometimes implies

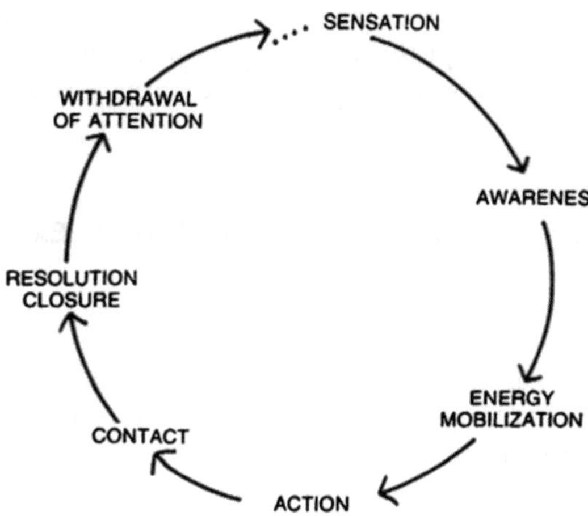

Fig. 8.1 Gestalt cycle (Navis 1987, p. 2)

simply a change in perspective on a given object or situation, or a clear semantical categorization of a realized phenomenon.

Let me introduce an example of my personal project experience: In software development projects it happens that after a recently delivered software component the users of the software application report system errors to the project team. The reported errors are certainly immediately checked by support members of the team. And quite often it happens that a reported error cannot be reproduced by them. Provided, that a certain customer frequently reports errors of that kind, most supporters tend to judge any new report of that user as inadequate—and sometimes accompanied with an emotional component (like: "…OK, again this one… This guy really doesn't understand our system at all!"). As a result of this attitude often the supporter tends to react inadequate, even to a legitimately reported error. Those cases induce inefficient and time consuming project execution processes, including all facets of a change process in individual attitudes (probably passing the stages of "dump user", through "technical misconfiguration of the system by the user", up to "Oh, that's really a bug!").

The principle of abduction, as described by Westermayer, i.e. the fashion of reasoning when surprising experiences or facts arise, seems quite enlightening for our purposes:

> Abduction is a mean to gain awareness over assumptions that are already tied up with perception, or in other words: Curiously self-inquiring about the underlying assumptions to explain a phenomenon that cannot be understood instantly, is the process of abduction. (Westermayer 2009, p. 97; translated by U.S.)

Curious inquiry as a method? For sure, questions and certain styles of questioning are part of the basic techniques within a coaching process (Schreyögg 2012; Grant 2012). But before I address the principles of a project-coaching process, I would like to discuss the structural conditions of a professional project execution.

8.3 Structural Aspects of Project Execution

Working in projects, and especially managing a project have been an investigation topic since many years. There is an ongoing investigation about suitable procedures, applicable for project managers, in order to gain the optimal result from a project. Already in the 1960s in North America as well as in Europe procedural directives were established on how to efficiently conduct projects. The first approaches to standardized procedures in project management were created when the International Project Management Association (IPMA) was founded in 1965 in Europe. In the USA a standardization started with the Project Management Institute (PMI) in the USA in 1969. Today we find a great number of project management institutions all over the world that provide education and certifications in project management. With PRINCE2, PMBoK, ISO 21500, and other documents we can find several documented standards for project management.

8.3.1 Process Organization of Projects

There is a common agreement within all approaches on project management, although with a varying naming of the phases that any project conduction can be structured in initializing processes, followed by planning processes, then execution processes accompanied by monitoring and controlling processes, and finally closure processes. The resulting phases are sometimes sequentially, other times cyclically conceptualized. And there is a common understanding that executional phases can be partitioned into further sub-phases, depending on the complexity of the project topic. Here, each sub-phase can include a recurring structure of all previously named project steps.

Let me focus for now on a procedural approach to projects as provided by the PMI Project Management Body of Knowledge (PMBoK, PMI 2013). This approach is quite useful for practicing project management because it propagates very flexible recursively defined procedures in project execution. It describes 10 different knowledge areas, classified within 5 standard process groups. This structure is shown in Table 8.1.

If, from a psychological point of view, acting target focussed, oriented on strategical issues in order to reach a complex project result, can be described as a typical cycle of

> Perception ➞ awareness (about the tasks to be executed) ➞ execution ➞ evaluation of (interim-) results ➞ perception (deduction of further tasks) ➞…,

the procedural perspective on what a project defines mirrors exactly this cycle. A project manager as well as the project team will be as efficient, as they manage to develop compatible perceptions as well as a compatible awareness about the the project tasks to be executed in the course of the project. The complexity of a project forces all participants to synchronize perceptions and actions. Most projects do not fail because of a poor project plan, but because of a missing awareness about the tasks and the order of tasks to be conducted.

Table 8.1 PMBoK project management process groups and knowledge areas (PMI 2013, p. 423)

Project management knowledge areas	Initiating process group	Planning process group	Executing process group	Monitoring and controlling process group	Closing process group
Project Integration management	Develop project charter	Develop Project management plan	Direct and manage project work	Monitor and control project work; perform integrated change control	Close project or phase
Project scope management		Plan scope management collect requirements define scope create work breakdown structure		Validate scope control scope	
Project time management		Plan schedule management; Define Activities; Sequence activities; Estimate activity resources; Estimate activity durations; Develop schedule		Control schedule	
Project cost management		Plan cost management; Estimate costs; Determine budget		Control costs	
Project quality management		Plan quality management	Perform quality assurance	Control quality	
Project human resource management		Plan human resource management	Acquire project team; Develop project team; manage project team		

(continued)

Table 8.1 (continued)

Project management knowledge areas	Initiating process group	Planning process group	Executing process group	Monitoring and controlling process group	Closing process group
Project communication management		Plan communication management	Manage communications	Control communications	
Project risk management		Plan risk management; identify risks; perform qualitative risk analysis; Perform quantitative risk analysis; Plan risk responses		Control risks	
Project procurement management		Plan procurement management	Conduct procurements	Control procurements	Close procurements
Project stakeholder management	Identify stakeholders	Plan stakeholder management	Manage stakeholder engagement	Control stakeholder engagement	

The real value of applying standard procedures in a project is the following: If professionally applied and accepted by all participants, everybody can rely on important conditions with an essential impact on the project to be registered systematically. Therefore, proper follow-up actions can be derived. But still it is essential, that a sheer mechanical execution of work steps without considering the individual perceptions of the project participants does not lead to project success. Again and again all participants, and this includes all stakeholders of the project, need to be geared towards the shared project target. Only, if compatible views exist about what, when, and how to do between all stakeholders throughout the whole project term a project has a higher probability of success. Again and again it is necessary to re-establish the compatibility of views, and to assure each other of sharing the same perspective. This, for sure, is one of the most important tasks of a project manager, and it is the same for the project participants. This continuing process can be very well supported through coaching.

Two examples: (1) Consider the development of a mechanical part (like a screw) within a technical construction project, which needs to be produced in higher quantities. Here, it is necessary to specify dimension tolerances in the production process. Tolerance definitions are mostly the result of empirical findings, very often through statistical studies. Statistical values always imply variances. Thus, a tolerance value is simply the agreement between experts - which can for a given project prove to be useless.

(2) Whether a software system, designed to support a user in his daily work, shows acceptable response times, is, especially with a rising complexity of the application, a matter of reconciliation between the system engineer and the user. Consider a strictly requested 3 s response time (which is actually a fixed threshold in some formal standards), independent on how complex the computational context is, many operational applications would have to be turned off - even if they sufficiently serve the purposes of these operations. Here, too, the common appraisal between the project members during the development process on the adequacy of the project goals need constantly to be verified. Thus, it is essential to constantly renew the definition of quality criteria to be applied. This is a main task of quality management in a project, called "quality assurance". Exactly here lies a big potential of conflicts. It can be mitigated with coaching.

Since 2001 a common understanding was reached, that project success not so much depends on formal organizational defined parameters, as propagated in the past. It obviously depends on the extend to allow and support co-operation and communication paired with a shared understanding between the project members about the necessary work to be done. The new paradigm of agile project processes arose (i.e. Agile Manifesto, Beck et al. 2001; Cohn 2009). Agile project processes contrast quite clearly to traditional project proceedings. The latter ones propagate a phase oriented proceeding with a characteristic (and quite often inflexible) sequence of goal definition, planning processes, design processes, execution processes, and delivery. In the agile process model the project team proceeds in short development cycles. Project teams are conceptualized as autonomous, self-referential groups with a minimum of hierarchical structures. The role of a project manager is more that of a facilitator and supporter. Relevant project decisions shall be made as much as possible by the project team. Project targets will initially be only broadly defined. They become refined during iterations, whereby each iteration is restricted to a manageable time span of 2–4 weeks. Each iteration results in a (potentially shippable) iteration product. Each following iteration starts with a team decision about the next subgoals to be targeted.

8.3.2 Structural Organization of Projects

Apart from the question of a suitable procedural structure of projects, certainly the problem of a suitable formal structure of a project is relevant. It is non-controversial today that a strictly functional, and hierarchical structure is not the best precondition for project success (Schreyögg and Geiger 2015; Jones 2013; PMI 2013), as usually the project members remain bound to the standard daily business while conducting the project. The project lead virtually does not have the sole authority here to create plannings as well as make decisions. He is more a kind of an assistant to his superior. He must always expect that on shortages in the standard business he as well as the other project members have to postpone project activities. Thus any project proceeding is difficult to calculate. The matrix organization seems to be a better variant for a project conduction, as the project members can be involved more flexible and more reliable from out of their regular organizational unit.

Although the matrix organization today is more common for project conduction, the projectized structure in a given organizational project environment is more beneficial for a project, as this assures the optimal independence of the project team and the project lead from other organizational units. The responsibility of planning, budgeting, decision making, as well as the responsibility for the result lies at the project manager (or even the whole team in agile environments). Thus, the project needs full time resources for the administrative tasks and finally reaches the state of fairly autonomous endeavour. Certainly, this unit needs to be controlled by a superior unit, the steering committee, which acts here as the supervisory board.

From a psychological perspective and a perspective of group dynamics all previously mentioned types of organizations have specific coaching-relevant aspects. With a functional organisation coaching demand arises predominantly on an individual level and especially for the project lead. Very often the line manager of the project lead acts independent from the project. He is usually not part of the project team and provides the team sometimes with directives that are counter-productive with regards to the project. The subordinates cannot but follow those directives restraining their range of actions and decisions within the project. Therefore, coaching will concentrate on developing an individual strategy in order to process existing restrictions and stay capable to act at the same time. Teams will always simply be functional teams. The group dynamics here will usually be strongly determined by the lead person and the formal frame. As the project lead in the functional organization owns a buffer function upwards to his superordinate and downwards to his team, quite regularly conflict management is part of the coaching process.

Looking at the matrix and the projected organization coaching demand can arise on various levels. The increased autonomy of the project leads to increase the demand of self-organization. Coaching is here centered either on specifics of group dynamics: It is to discover potentials of the group and concurrently support a close co-operation of the group members. Another focus will be brought to the issue of individual potentials and how to utilize these potentials within the project. This even may include only peripherally involved stakeholders of the project. Both areas are substantial success factors for a project success. Under the condition of a matrix or a projectized organization coaching may include the topics of leadership, team dynamics, conflicts, as well as individual development. As it is a common fact that with the advance of a project time management becomes a critical issue, the topic of work-life-balance becomes quite regularly a theme for coaching. It is a very interesting fact, that with rising time pressure in a project increasingly career issues will be addressed by the coachees. Last but not least, also methodological and procedural aspects of project conduction are regularly addressed in coaching sessions.

8.4 Coaching as a Profession

Coaching is, as commonly accepted, a way to support individual development processes. Coaching supports—if not even enables—learning and feedback processes, individually as well as group oriented. It is useful then to ask: What can coaching contribute to project success? It obviously can contribute, where standard project work and project management reach their limits: in mutually understanding each other, trying to avoid misunderstandings, and "synchronizing" perceptions of the project members.

In literature the label "coaching" comprises several quite different procedural approaches. The kind of procedures depend on the perspective on what coaching should be (cf. DBVC 2012, p. 20). Learning as well as performance processes, two major factors in projects, can be supported according to the definition of psychological coaching. Working on patterns of perception, of communication, of behaviour, and of solutions are central themes in coaching. Coaching follows the aim to increase the individual efficiency, and sometimes only to preserve this (especially, when personal or occupational crises arise).

The perceptions on what coaching is, seem to converge. In the past it was a pure human resource development tool. Today we find a broader scope of it: Coaching is consultation, offering support in every aspect of individual development, on the personal area as well as on the corporate area. The latter is reflected in terms like "Life Coaching" or "Work-Life-Balance". We are currently in a development phase of the coaching profession, where we identify specializations on various areas.

Project coaching is accordingly the special area in the field of coaching, which supports project workers in their professional and individual development while conducting a given project. Operational, procedural knowledge of the coach is an indispensable part of the coaching process.

PMBok, the project standard of the Project Management Institutes (PMI 2013), established as worldwide standard, being an ANSI standard, and the main foundational source of the ISO 21500, emphasizes for the core processes in human resource management, that it is one of three main tasks of a project manager to promote the individual development of the project members. Unfortunately, there is no hint within this standard, whether the project manager should be promoted here as well, and who should do that.

In the Anglo American region the concept of coaching is quite interwoven with the concepts of counseling and mentoring: Coaching is then the selection and the training of the right personnel; counseling is the consultation of problematical staff; mentoring is the promotion of best performers (Stone 2007). Coaching equals in this view very often to senior coaching, done by the senior to the newcomer. Internal coaching is preferred to external coaching by an organizationally foreign coach (for a discussion about internal vs. external coaching in Germany see Schreyögg 2015; Rauen 2007). Internal as well as senior coaching to my experience is to a certain extent an important and effective instrument for successful human resource and business development. Both, Schreyögg and Rauen, emphasize regarding the external coach, that he receives a leap of faith that is usually not granted to the internal coach. This leap of faith is mostly restricted, though, on personal relational topics and is often not true for the operational aspects within coaching, which play undoubtedly an important role within coaching and especially within project coaching. Here it is essential for the coachee to assume a shared knowledge base with his counterpart. In order to gain a corresponding leap of faith it is of advantage for the coach to have already been engaged in the past in that organization or at least in the domain of the current organization. That is true also for inter-cultural conditions, especially, when workers grant a greater experience to the internal coach in the current work environment.

> A couple of years ago I conducted a bundle of related software development projects in Canada as a program manager with multi-national teams. Part of the teams were added by our customer and they all were Canadians, all of them used to work in multi-national teams. Our Germany based team was multi-national as well, commuting between Germany and Canada. I commuted on a monthly base between our project locations, having my home base in Canada. Both teams worked closely connected on the projects. On my visits in Germany as well as in Canada we regularly talked about the modes of co-operation with the respective remote located teams.
>
> One of our software developers in Germany complained in one of our meetings that a colleague in Canada provided him constantly with unacceptable requirements specifications, as these documents always showed too much ambiguity about the expected results. Soon I arranged a joint meeting with these two guys, where it turned out, that the colleague in Canada did so, as he deliberately wanted to provide tolerances, in order to gain the best technical results from the developers. This meeting even lead to a new common practice between the team: They agreed on having regular meetings where they discussed about specification documents and derived technical solutions. Futhermore, they agreed on having regular meetings, where the (Germany based) developers presented their advances in software development to the Canadian users.

Was my intervention in this case coaching? Can a project manager coach his team? Hackman and Wageman (2005) argue that team coaching is a central task of a lead person. But I think, this does not apply regardless from the given organizational frame, in which supervisor and staff act. In strongly formalized organizations (so called "taylorized" ones; cf. Schreyögg 2008) is coaching, provided by the lead person, hardly conceivable. Here, the organizational layout implies a strict separation between planning and execution, which limits any decision space of the staff. The individual acts within a given working order provided by the manager. Whether to coach or not, is here simply beyond question.

More and more organizations evolve into networked systems of action units, where responsibilities and decision making is increasingly stronger bound to the individual members. In a projected organization this turns even to be the standard. One result of this is, that the supervisor (the project manager) is no more just the authority for the staff. He should also be interested in providing his staff with the optimal environment to identify and accomplish task goals. In many project topics and situations the project manager is no more the lead person, but the one being lead. This necessarily demands, that the staff is enabled to develop themselves within their fields of responsibilities—and not only from a sheer operational point of view.

To the degree the supervisor is aware about his assignment to support the development process of his staff, which includes to support each project member to unfold their individual potentials, he should act as a Coach (Dörr et al. 2014). According to Whitmore the coaching process between supervisor and staff can work quite informally and becomes, if applied properly, the most effective method of management (Whitmore 2009, p. 53f.).

But can a supervisor really take the function of a coach? Certainly, he should support the development of his staff. On the other hand, he should lead strategically and efficiently oriented towards specific results. Thus, the focus of a supervisor is always primarily not focussed on the development of his staff, but more focussed on his own strategic goals and the results to be generated, utilizing the potentials of his staff. So, the interaction between supervisor and staff is to a great extent about exercising influence and less about development work that focusses on a person. Although we find quite sometimes in theory the concept of the manager being a coach for his staff, it is in reality hardly to realize, as it will become sooner or later a conflict of interests for the manager.

In agile approaches of project management the role of the project manager (sometimes called "project owner", sometimes called the "master") as well as the role of the project sponsor of being "the boss" is no more valid. Both are here part of the project team with dedicated duties. The role of the sponsor is more strategically defined, as he should be the one to determine the specific project goals throughout the project. The role of the project manager ("the master") is more coordinative and supportive. He moderates the processes and cares for a smooth project execution, clearing off all kinds of (organizational) problems and difficulties. The team decides jointly about the path to work on and the division of labour in order to meet the project goals as prioritized by the sponsor. Professional project coaching cannot be done here out of the core team. Neither the project manager nor any other team member can constantly take the role of the coach. Consequently, in agile projects it is advisable to coach the project manager regularly in a "coach the coach" setting. Team coachings and individual coachings are further elements of an accompanying coaching process.

8.5 Reasons for Project Coaching

It is obvious that project coaching is central within agile projects. When a new project starts, processes of group dynamics will start as well processes that can be straightened with coaching. For a project manager (in the approach of the agile method "Scrum" also called "scrum master", Schwaber 2007) individual coaching is especially helpful in the initial iterations of a project. Project teams always work under strong time and success pressure. Here, three topics can become relevant in the coaching process:

(1) Professional basics of project execution. Core themes are here regularly: What are suitable project methods and tools for a given project situation;
(2) Individual dispositions, preferences, and potentials in project execution. Here, very often a suitable time and task management is an important topic to the project members, individually as well as within the group.
(3) Conflicts. Here are operational conflicts as well as personal conflicts to work on. Sometimes standard psychological coaching themes like career development or work-life-balance are proactively addressed by project members during project coaching sessions.

Project coaching will become all the more important, the lesser the projects are hierarchically structured. This also counts for projects that do not apply an agile approach.

8.6 Goals, Basic Conditions and Courses of Project Coaching

There are diverse goals of project coaching: With the project endeavour the basic project goals have to be part of any coaching target agreement. These goals are mainly to create a qualitatively high class project result (usually measured by the degree of satisfaction of the project customer), and to be efficient (usually measured by consumed project budget and needed time). Further goals can be determined in social processes within the project team: Role finding, and the improvement of cooperation and team coherence, as well as the degree of self-organization of the team. Finally, individual development goals of project members can be part of the coaching target agreement.

The scope of methods and tools in project coaching are quite the same as in any other psychological coaching process. There are not many restrictions looking at the published methods and tools as referred in Rauen (2008, 2009). The scope of applied methods and tools is only restricted by the knowledge, the experience, and the preferences of the coach. A systematic investigation of the effectiveness of different methods with a project environment would be desirable, but is up to now an open issue. The frame conditions for a coaching setting should be delimited formally as well as locally from the daily project setting of the coachee or the team. During project execution it is an advantage, if the location allows for fast and shortly scheduled sessions. Individual coachings need to be performed in an environment that allows for privacy. Group coachings need to be performed in a room where the group members can disconnect from their daily work environment.

A suggested standard process structure in project coaching accounts for 5 phases:

(1) *Preliminary talk about the Coaching order*: This talk should be done with the constituent and—if already determined at this point of time—with the project manager. Contractual partner is usually the project owner, not the project manager. The following points need to be addressed: What are the project goals? Which actors can already be named? What are the coaching targets within the project? How should the coaching be aligned to the project (in terms of organizational alignment and time structure)? The following formal coaching agreement should include clear statements to these questions.

(2) *Become acquainted with the project members*: It is worthwhile to have an introductory session with the project members. While any information about an accompanying coaching in a project should already be provided at the project kick-off meeting, this session is dedicated to the team expectations on the coaching, to the coaching targets, to the frame conditions, as well as to procedures of coaching within the project.

(3) *Planning work*: This focusses on the analysis of the project schedule and on critical risk factors of the endeavour and the stakeholders (stakeholder analysis: project manager, the team, other parties). The analysis is based on the ongoing planning processes, but with a focus on the soft facts of individual or group oriented issues. This should be done, because in traditional risk management those issues usually play only a subordinated role. Furthermore, the standard stakeholder analysis leads only to a formal stakeholder management, (i.e. mode of inclusion of stakeholders and reporting modes).

(4) *Accompanying coaching of the project team*: This is the core phase of the coaching process. Having periodic individual coachings with the project manager as well as demand driven coachings of team members the project advance is accompanied by the coach. Periodic team coachings should be included here as well.
(5) *Evaluation of the coaching process*: The evaluation of the coaching efficiency should not wait to the end of the project, but should be conducted several times within the project term. A good point of time for an intermediate evaluation is when a project milestone has been reached, or when a project iteration has been finished. The final evaluation of the coaching success must be done with project closure.

8.7 Conclusion

Working in projects will increase in our globalized economy in future. Formal methods and tools to support project execution are well established and standardized. Still, many project fail today. Obviously, a formal structure is not a warrant for project success. Every project success depends on the people, who jointly work on the project. Thus, the psychology of project work is an important factor for project success. Professional project coaching that focusses on these factors will increasingly contribute to the success of projects. Today the ways to accompany a project with coaching is not yet standardized. It is the assignment of a professional project coach to align standard procedures within a project with the capabilities and the potentials of the project members.

References

Beck, K., et al. (2001). *Manifesto for Agile Software Development.* http://www.agilemanifesto.org. Retrieved 09 March 2017.

Cohn, M. (2009). *Succeeding with Agile. Software Development using Scrum.* Boston: Pearson.

DBVC—Deutscher Bundesverband Coaching (Hrsg.) (2012). *Leitlinien und Empfehlungen für die Entwicklung von Coaching als Profession* (4., erw. Aufl.). Osnabrück: DBVC-Geschäftsstelle; Engl. version available under: www.dbvc.de/publikationen.

Dörr, S., Schmidt-Huber, M. & Maier, G.W. (2014). Wirksam führen – Motive, Fähigkeiten und vertrauensvolle Beziehungen. *Wirtschaftspsychologie aktuell, 21*(1), S. 21–26.

Grant, A. M. (2012). Making Positive Change: A Randomized Study Comparing Solution-Focused vs. Problem-Focused Coaching Questions. *Journal of Systemic Therapies, 31*(2), 21–35.

Hackman, J. R., & Wageman, R. (2005). A Theory of Team Coaching. *Academy of Management Review, 30*(2), 269–287.

Jones, G. R. (2013). *Organizational Theory, Design, and Change* (7th Ed.). New York: Pearson.

Kerzner, H. (2009). *Project Management. A systems approach to planning, scheduling, and controlling*. New York: Wiley.

Maslow, A. (1981). *Motivation und Persönlichkeit*. Reinbek: Rowohlt.

Miller, G. A., Galanter, E., & Pribram, K. A. (1960). *Plans and the structure of behavior*. New York: Holt, Rhinehart, & Winston.

Navis, E. C. (1987). *Organizational Consulting. A Gestalt Approach*. Cleveland: Gestalt Institute of Cleveland Press.

Project Management Insititute (2013). *A Guide to the Project Management Body Of Knowledge*. (5. Aufl.). Newtown Square, PA.: PMI.

Rauen, C. (2007). Varianten des Coaching im Personalentwicklungsbereich. In C. Rauen (Hrsg.), *Handbuch Coaching* (S. 111–136). Göttingen: Hogrefe.

Rauen, C. (2008). *Coaching-Tools* (6. Aufl.). Bonn: Managerseminare.

Rauen, C. (2009). *Coaching-Tools II* (2. Aufl.). Bonn: Managerseminare.

Schreyögg, A. (2012). *Coaching. Eine Einführung für Praxis und Ausbildung* (7. Aufl.). Frankfurt/M.: Campus.

Schreyögg, A. (2015). Organisationsinternes Coaching. *Gruppendynamik und Organisationsberatung, 46*(1), 63–77.

Schreyögg, G. (2008). *Organisation. Grundlagen moderner Organisationsgestaltung* (5. Aufl.). Wiesbaden: Gabler.

Schreyögg, G., & Geiger, D. (2015). *Organisation. Grundlagen moderner Organisationsgestaltung* (6. Aufl.). Wiesbaden: Gabler.

Schwaber, K. (2007). *Agiles Projektmanagement mit Scrum*. Unterschleißheim: Microsoft Press.

Stone, F. M. (2007). *Coaching, Counseling & Mentoring*. New York: Amacom.

Westermayer, G. (2009). Freude! Oder wie man die Götterfunken auch im Betrieb durch die betriebliche Gesundheitsförderung (BGF) und in der Politik durch Town Meetings zum fliegen bringen kann. In P. Schulthess & H. Anger (Hrsg.), *Gestalt und Politik* (S. 71–100). Bergisch Gladbach: EHP.

Whitmore, J. (2009). *Coaching for Performance. GROWing human potential and purpose* (4. Aufl.). London, Boston: Nicolas Brealey.

Author Biography

Prof. Dr. rer. nat. Ulrich Schüler Dipl.-Psych, Dipl.-Inform., Professor for Information Management at the Applied University of Economics And Management (FOM), Hamburg. Managing Partner of pmsp—projektmanagement dr. schueler & partner. Core area: Project consulting and coaching in IT projects.

Part III
Knowledge and Competencies in Coaching

Experience—Science—Philosophy Three Types of Knowledge for Conceiving Consultation

9

Ferdinand Buer

Abstract

A good consultation concept needs to combine three types of knowledge with each other such that it contains everything a practitioner actually needs in order to perform his job; i.e. to be able to properly manage a one-time process. For one, this includes refined experience. A practitioner can achieve this by reflecting on his own consultation processes as well as discussing relevant aspects with his colleagues. Secondly, he needs to continually include and take into consideration the tangible and useful findings of scientific research. Thirdly, he will also need well-founded guidance for his actions: He not only needs to have internalized the appropriate quality standards, but also possess ethically motivated standards for correct behavior. With the help of philosophical pragmatism, it will be shown how these three types of knowledge can be combined with each other.

What kind of knowledge do we need in order to draft consultation concepts which, for one, include the requirements and conditions in current practice, but which also set counterfactual standards where necessary and open up new target perspectives which are to be striven for with good reason? For this, we need three very different but equivalent types of knowledge: The experiential knowledge of the practitioners, the knowledge of the scientists, and the reflective knowledge of philosophy. In most publications, these three types of knowledge occur only individually or unrecognizably interwoven. I contend, however, that the benefits are much greater if we first clearly separate them and then relate them to each other. This is

F. Buer (✉)
Alte Schanze 46, 48159 Münster, Germany
e-mail: info@ferdinandbuer.de

A. Schreyögg and C. Schmidt-Lellek (eds.), *The Professionalization of Coaching*, DOI 10.1007/978-3-658-16805-6_9

because they are then relativized, and generate knowledge that holds a greater degree of validity after this mutual relativization process. In this context, my concepts focus on the consultation formats of supervision and coaching.

In the following, I will first illustrate the advantages and disadvantages of these three types of knowledge. After that, in the spirit of pragmatism, I will outline how these three types of knowledge can be meaningfully related to each other.[1]

9.1 The Three Types of Knowledge

9.1.1 Refined Experience—the Practitioner's Contribution

The advantage of the practitioner certainly lies in the fact that they were actually there. They possess experience, in particular with the passing of the years. Their job requires that they continually reflect upon what they have done, and constantly revise what they intend to do for each new process. Certainly, one could also simply neglect this endeavor and attempt to compensate for the related deficits via suggestive enactments—indeed, this could also be well-received by the clients. Furthermore, the published experience reports could also be embellished. And it may also be the case that the self-awareness process could be obscured or even systematically channeled despite a trained self-exploration competency—at least temporarily.

When these limitations are then removed in control supervision processes, realizations will definitely be made that are in fact "near the mark". Hence, a large field of knowledge formation via coaching and/or supervision is a logical choice, which should be used more systematically than has been the case thus far.

Despite these limitations, these refined experiences from practitioners are the most important source of knowledge we possess. And if we have a closer look at the publications—particularly in the major specialist journals—we will find a large number of experience reports: They mostly show how and why a particular way of acting worked. And many practitioners read these reports in order to feel validated in their own practices or to obtain new stimuli for their practical work. When these texts then refer to scientific theories and findings—often only for reasons of legitimization—the reader often simply stops paying attention.

This experiential knowledge is certainly also tangentialized by knowledge that has been obtained scientifically, because the practitioners have taken part in the

[1]This text is based on Buer (2008).

relevant scientific socialization. However, after a number of years, authentic categories are formed, with the help of which one's own practices are independently shaped. But this does not become visible in publications in such a way, as evidenced by discussions among colleagues. Unfortunately, this is related to a certain science devotion of many practitioners. They have allowed themselves to be convinced—mostly by scientists—that professionalism is reflected primarily by the academization of their practices. It is in this spirit that the idea of "supervision as an applied social science" (e.g. in Schreyögg 2004) or "coaching as applied psychology" (e.g. in Lippmann 2006) came into being. However, this gives the sciences a certain predominance, which is not justified at all.

And this is unfortunately why there is an—often unconscious—collusion between science devotional practitioners, and scientists who are interested in maintaining this predominance. Many practitioners are glad to be able to transfer the responsibility for the respectability of the format of consultation they are selling to the sciences. And many scientists are glad to have a rewarding field of research and theory formation assigned to them. However, if this is the only way this works, practitioners should not be surprised that findings of this type of science often prove to be of little use in practice.

9.1.2 Elaborated Research—The Scientist's Contribution

There are no scientific fields responsible for supervision or coaching per se. More comprehensive research and theory-building processes often take place in the form of further qualification measures at universities. Hence, they need to focus on the scientific fields in which the candidate is getting his doctoral or post-doctoral qualifications. In these contexts psychology and pedagogy play the main role. Furthermore, the academic advisors and examiners are often not experts in supervision or coaching themselves. In addition, the (post-)doctoral candidates often have not completed any training in the format of consultation they intend to investigate, and very seldom have any long-term practical experience to speak of. Hence, the issues examined and the approaches taken in these theses all too often leave out the interesting topics.

When there are positions for professors at universities specially for supervision and coaching, these scientists also need to be practitioners—after all, they also need to train students in these formats of consultation. This group is definitely the source of the most publications, particularly those of greater length. However, when we take a closer look, these publications are most often concepts (including e.g. Buer 1999; 2004a) or initial approaches to the formation of a critical theory (e.g. in Buer 2004b), and are only seldom research projects in a narrow sense (e.g. with regard to supervision: Giesecke and Rappe-Giesecke 1997; Berker and Buer 1998; Gaertner 1999; Möller 2001; Petzold et al. 2003; Siller 2004, 2008; DGSv 2006; e.g. with regard to coaching: Feldmann and Lankau 2005; Künzli 2009; Greif et al. 2012). The problem is that research in this field—at least to date—is only very seldom supported by research associations or foundations, and almost everything needs to be done with the means available. And I do not foresee this situation changing.

The advantage of scientifically elaborated research would hence be that it could devote more time and funds to examining more sophisticated issues. This could allow aspects to be discovered which practitioners often overlook. And this also allows comprehensive amounts of knowledge to be processed, evaluated, and made available. However, this research is often oriented towards the paradigm of only one discipline in a one-sided manner, despite the fact that it needs to be multi-disciplinary.

If practitioners entrust the safeguarding of their knowledge to university academics, they must also accept the fact that these academics also provide training (Kersting 2004). The identity of these academics is then established primarily through their discipline, and not through a format, as is the case with practitioners. In order to expand their field of responsibility, they tend to combine multiple formats in their training measures: supervision, coaching, and consulting of organizations. Competent then is a "consultation science" (Möller and Hausinger 2009). This means that the professional formats created in practice and anchored here tend to be negated, and the identities of supervisors and coaches called into question. Hence, academization means the following: Shaping of knowledge by only one discipline, relativization of the specific format-related knowledge, and devaluation of practical knowledge in favor of abstract knowledge.

Hence, those who place their hopes for the generation of tangible and practical knowledge that is generally recognized entirely in the sciences have placed their bets on the wrong horse.

9.1.3 Well-Founded Guidance—Philosophy's Contribution

Even when scientific knowledge on supervision and coaching is currently not particularly well differentiated, and even though the practical knowledge does not appear to be particularly self-critical in specialist publications, one can say the following: We still possess so much knowledge that it is possible to perform our jobs responsibly. But what is still missing are well-founded, justified standards for "good practices". This is because these quality standards do not simply come into being from determining what the current state of affairs is. When something that is to be is derived from what currently is, this results in the famous "naturalistic fallacy". Such a fallacy is seen in Möller when she extrapolates the "characteristics of excellent supervision in a stationary setting" from the examination of the path supervision takes in three instances (Möller 2001, p. 290 ff.). Through research, science provides *descriptions*, while philosophy is able to create and substantiate *prescriptions*. And concepts offer plans for how something should be done. They are based on values and contain standards, the expediency of which first needs to be made plausible.

Practitioners may have experience as to what works well in practice. They certainly strive to draw the right conclusions for their future practice from this experience. But is that which works really the best option? Scientists can also determine what is seen as "best practice" not only by the client, but also by specialists. But are these quality criteria truly substantiated? After all, it is not merely about what is seen as "state of the art" by specialists. Because supervision and coaching are concerned with professional ant management personnel who hold positions with a great deal of responsibility, and who have an (immense) influence on the work and lives of many persons (Buer and Schmidt-Lellek 2008), these measures must not only be substantiated by professional knowledge, but also ethically and socio-politically.

An ethical substantiation not only includes how consultation processes need to be designed in order to prevent inflicting damage, but also how they can provide great benefits. The target group not only needs to receive standards and guidelines for their own practical work, according to which they can evaluate their own actions and behavior in a well-founded manner. These evaluations must not only include the legitimate interests of these target groups, their orderers, employees, and clients. It must also be considered how such practices impact the development of the society in which all these people live. Hence, the issue here is also a social or political ethics which contains concepts of how a good society could look like, or at least what is to be prevented at all costs.

This philosophical reflection is either avoided with the remark that it is unscientific and only leads to noxious moralization or even politicization. Or it is only done indirectly: Certain criticisms that are raised affectively can be used to extrapolate different political blueprints for society (e.g. in Gaertner 2004; or in Gröning 2004). It would be great if these socio-ethical and socio-political debates could be carried out explicitly more often. But this presupposes that arguments are exchanged in a discourse based on reason, and if this proves unproductive, that delineations are carried out fairly. These debates may also bring about approximations which would at least enable alliances in certain issues.

However, excluding certain exceptions, academic philosophers are not concerned with supervision and coaching. Therefore, practitioners and scientists from this field will need to philosophize on their own. Standards for good practices can be obtained solely by doing this (Buer 2011).

9.1.4 Overview of the Three Types of Consultation Knowledge

These three types of knowledge can be represented as follows (Schmidt-Lellek and Buer 2011, p. 20) (cf. Table 9.1):

Guiding knowledge provides answers to the question of "What should I do?" It is nurtured by philosophical reflections, and in the case of some, by the faith in a religion. Both types of knowledge are developed and furthered by various *communities*. This knowledge appears in convictions and leads to characteristic attitudes towards life (e.g. as appreciation of life or pessimism).

Explanatory knowledge provides answers to the question of "How do I explain what I encounter?" It is nurtured by the research findings of the relevant sciences and is generated and safeguarded by the corresponding *scientific communities*. This knowledge appears in interpretive aids (theories, mental models, interpretative patterns, constructions etc.) which help us understand and/or explain worldly concepts.

Knowledge possessed provides answers to the question of "How can I deal with the insights?" It is nurtured by the experiences of practitioners, which are gained from the application of procedures (such as psychodrama) in certain consultation formats (e.g. supervision or coaching) (Buer 2007a). This format knowledge is stored in professional associations (e.g. Deutscher Bundesverband Coaching—German Federal Association of Executive Coaching) and presented at a societal level. The procedure knowledge is safeguarded in specialist associations (e.g. Deutscher Fachverband Psychodrama—German Specialist Association for Psychodrama). This knowledge appears in praxeological action models that more or less regulate ability.

This trichotomy of knowledge is reflected in a long occidental tradition which goes back all the way to antiquity. The Ancient Greeks distinguished between

Table 9.1 The three types of consultation knowledge

	Question	Types of knowledge	Sources of knowledge	Knowledge communities
Guiding knowledge Beliefs lead to attitudes	What should I do?	Philosophies, in particular ethics	Reflection	Scientific communities
		Religions	Faith	Religious communities
Explanatory knowledge Interpretive aids lead to knowledge	How do I explain what I encounter?	The sciences	Research	Scientific communities
Knowledge possessed Praxeological action models lead to ability	How can I deal with the insights?	*Formats* What kind of operational framework will I need to set?	Experience	Professional communities: professional associations
		Procedures How should I maneuver within this framework (know-how)?	Experience	Professional communities: specialist associations

- *philosophía*, the committed striving for wisdom,
- *epistéme*, findings that are confirmed by science,
- *téchne,* the art of practical creation.

Even today, these three types of knowledge are obtained in different ways, safeguarded in different communities, and follow different forms of logic. They are independent and are not to be subject to any hierarchy. At the macrosocial level, cooperative dialogs between the three discourse groups are required to create connections. At the microsocial level, each coach needs to take responsibility for combining these three types of knowledge in good conscience.

However, in order for this to succeed, a metaperspective is required. It can be safely assumed that there are various possibilities to do so. I only wish to recommend those that I have found helpful over the long term (Buer 2007b, 2010, p. 109 ff.; Buer and Schmidt-Lellek 2008, p. 176 ff.).

9.2 Pragmatism—A Model for Combining the Three Types of Knowledge

This school of thought was founded in the USA in the 1870's by Charles Peirce, William James, John Dewey and Georg H. Mead (Nagl 1998; Schubert et al. 2010). It rapidly influenced the fields of psychology, sociology, pedagogy, philosophy, and political science in the USA. In Germany, it was initially met with skepticism, probably because its reception was hindered by numerous misunderstandings. Today, however, it not only plays a prominent role in pedagogy (Bohnsack 2005), but also in philosophy (Fellmann 1991; Craig 1993; Rorty 1994; Joas 2000). Of course, the various authors all have different positions on the matter. However, they all agree on the following aspects:

- *Pragmatic thinking is antifundamentalist.* It denies the assumption that there can be "ultimate substantiations", fixed apriorities and invariantly valid "absoluta". In doing so, pragmatism takes a stand against transcendental philosophical, metaphysical, or scientistic positions.
- *Pragmatic thinking criticizes any universalizations of deterministic explanatory paradigms.* Every social development is the result of historical contexts, all of which could have turned out differently. Experiences cannot be used to extrapolate laws, only maxims for action.

- *Pragmatic thinking is pluralistic.* It opposes the reduction of various types of knowledge and scientific disciplines to a single knowledge ideal, which then often quickly consolidates itself to become orthodoxy. Rather, appropriate realizations may be present in all types of knowledge.
- *Pragmatic thinking wants to guide practice.* The idea is not to accumulate knowledge or create a permanent, comprehensive theoretical structure, but instead concerns itself with what is useful in the here and now, in order to perform the next steps boldly and appropriately: a concept of action.

Hence, pragmatism shows a great affinity with deconstructivism, postmodern philosophy, and social constructivism (cf. Neubert 1998). In our context, the following three aspects are of key importance:

9.2.1 "Experience"—The Foundation of All Knowledge

Since ancient times, the dualities of theory vs. practice and culture vs. nature have dominated European thinking. In each case, theory and culture were seen as being of greater value, and hence became the central topics of traditional philosophy. Pragmatism, on the other hand—in this case primarily as Dewey (1929) sees it—views practice and nature as the primary elements, from which everything else develops in an evolutionary fashion (Engler 1992; Neubert 1998; Jörke 2003), that which humans as natural beings undergo in their daily activities in their lives are experiences. These primary experiences are emergent products of nature, we could also say of the corporeality of humans (Shusterman 2000). Experiences are what we actually have, which is experiences of "being in the world". This primary experience is experienced as a whole, as an interplay between activity and passivity in each concrete situation. It is only when a confusion occurs in the immediate experience, such that an adjustment to adapt it to the environment can no longer take place according to familiar paradigms that humans begin to think. It is only in this reflexive problem-solving process that the initial immediate unity of experience is separated. Subject and object are moved apart for analytical purposes until the reflection is concluded and the direct experience is re-established.

However, the quality of human experience is related to the societal circumstances in which humans have their experiences. Hence, experiences in the modern world are often inherently torn apart, incoherent, and uncompleted. When actions then result in modifications, new opportunities and ideological horizons are opened up. The consequence of this is the growth of human experience. If a balancing of activity and passivity then takes place, or more precisely between routine and creativity, this secondary experience is experienced as a new unity which is completed in itself and balanced. In this way, it attains an aesthetic character (Dewey 1934). Hence, what Dewey is referring to is not more knowledge from, but instead for the growth of qualitative experience.

When practical problems are not solved only through routine or simple trial and error, but instead through innovative creations, Dewey speaks of intelligent action. The vital doubt leads to thinking, which, when it is successful, defeats doubt and establishes a new habit. Thinking or recognizing is hence in itself a form of action; i.e. the interaction through which other natural interactions are subject to regulation. Hence, the knowledge has an "instrumental" function: It is to control the action such that it leads to an enrichment of immediate experience. The secondary experience once again becomes a primary one. We can also state the following: A secondary experience is only true if it enriches the primary experience qualitatively. William James (Diaz-Bone and Schubert 1996) expresses this thought as follows:

> Truth is "something that is fundamentally linked to the manner in which a particular moment of our experience can lead to other moments, the achievement of which is worth the effort. (…) When any moment of our experience motivates us towards a true thought, this means that, sooner or later, and led by this thought, we will once again plunge into the unique characteristics of the experience and form advantageous connections with it" (James 1907/2001, p. 134f.). "Truth *happens* to a notion. It *becomes* true; it is made through by an event. Its truth is in fact an event, a process: namely, the process in which it makes itself true, its veri-*fication*. The validity of a notion is nothing other than precisely this process of self-validation" (l.c., p. 133).

What does this all mean for our problem? The practicing supervisors and coaches are to have positive experiences. But these are bound to practices that also give their clients positive experiences. However, if they have negative experiences, they will need to reflect on their practices. If they find creative solutions for these practical problems, their truth value lies in the fact that they actually give the clients better experiences in the context of their practice. Hence, this is a circular process between theory and practice, the value of which can be measured by an improved practice of the clients.

When an individual coach is able to keep this process going smoothly (perhaps with supervisory support), then everything is in order: a growth in the qualitative experience of his clients is guaranteed. It is only when these processes are seen as unsatisfactory on a wide front by the clients, but also the coaches themselves, that a collective event becomes necessary. In this context, the collective external aid from individualistic self-help may be of assistance. In this context, secondary research could be helpful to the primary research.

What holds true is: Experience is not only the starting point of all endeavors for obtaining insight. It is also the goal. The objective is not to continually amass knowledge about supervision or coaching. The goal is to allow the addressees of these formats to have better experiences through improved practices. That is the criterion.

9.2.2 Research as Inquiry on All Levels

Good supervisors and coaches are hence to be viewed as the primary researchers: In joint processes, they have experiences together with their clients; experiences which are to modify the former experiences of the clients. This is because the clients have doubts about their own experiences. They have carefully considered their negative experiences, but have not found any solution that has proven itself or "held true" for them in practice; i.e. that could cross over to primary experience. Hence, they have turned to someone who is able to provide them with professional guidance in this process of inquiry. The supervisors and coaches may utilize various procedures in this professional inquiry, but this process can still be described as a research process (cf. Niemeyer 1987; Fuhr 1992; Krall et al. 2008), which according to Dewey's (1938) model consists of five phases (Krüger 2000):

(1) *The unidentified situation:* The mutual relationship between organism and environment in a certain situation has entered a state of imbalance.
(2) *The identification of the problem:* A distinction needs to be made: What can be seen as being certain, what is problematic? The questions of the inquiry have to focus on these aspects.
(3) *Identifying the solution to the problem:* First of all, a background of solid convictions is to be identified which can be used for obtaining solutions of the open questions. The search for solutions is then focused on anticipations of possible consequences from initial conjectures. These will then become clear ideas via a comparison between conceptual thinking and empirical observations.
(4) *Logical thought and rational discourse:* The idea for the solution is then compared with existing knowledge and operationalized such that it can be verified experimentally, and its possible consequences made visible.
(5) *Restoring the unproblematic situation.*

Dewey does not call this process *research*, but instead *inquiry*; i.e. an examination, an investigation. Hence, the process of obtaining insight is always conceived as a learning process: The findings are to be transferred to thinking and behavioral habits, which are automatically considered in similar situations.

All processes of obtaining insight can be related to this model; from the daily process of thinking which can be performed alone or in a dialog with related persons, via a process of inquiry which is led by professionals in their work, up to elaborate research projects conducted by scientists. The differences between these three levels are not defined matter of principle in this model, but arise gradually. Hence, the processes of inquiry in supervision range between everyday thinking processes and scientific research. The central mode of inquiry is *abduction*, as opposed to induction and deduction as described by Peirce (Nagl 1992, p. 107 ff.). In Dewey's model, abduction is located on the 3rd level of the research process:

The client cannot advance with his solution models thus far. A new one needs to be found. And it is this process that is a creative one; it cannot be described logically, and exactly because of this, it also cannot be planned. After all, Peirce calls this process "guessing". Because the search for a new solution cannot be carried out in the form of inference according to fixed logic, one can only adopt an open attitude towards the emergence of a new idea. The social researcher Reichertz (2003, p. 66) describes this attitude as follows:

> The abductive inferer is curious; he observes intensively and a great deal, and is always ready to be surprised. If he encounters something unusual and disappointing when it comes to his expectations, he does *not* quickly attempt to make sense of it. Instead, he does exactly the opposite: he continues to observe, speaks with himself and others, searches his memories for similar experiences, lets his entire knowledge "float" and waits for a possibly consistent interpretation of all or at least a large number of surprising details to appear.

Is this not a wonderful description of the professional work done in supervision and coaching? In this case, the process of obtaining insight is not solipsistic, but instead conceived as being dialogical and communicative: Both the professional and the client move together in this process of inquiry. First of all, both examine if traditional patterns of thinking (interpretation patterns, mental models, interpretation aids) can be applied to this case and if solutions can be generated via induction or deduction. It is only when this does not succeed that abduction comes into play. In this case, the professional is to ensure a correspondingly creative learning space in which both he and his client can allow solution concepts to rise to the surface. And because guaranteeing such a space is exactly the most difficult part of a professional's work, he will require a process that suits him: It should make him creative as well, such that his creative frame of mind is transferred to the client, loosens his rigid patterns of thinking, sensing, and acting, and allows new ideas to emerge.

This process of inquiry can be understood as action research (cf. Moser 1995): The working contexts of the client are more or less comprehensively relived "naturally" in the process in order to cooperatively examine concrete processes in concrete situations and to develop concepts and competencies into a better formation in the future.

Hence, supervision and coaching serve first and foremost to examine and improve external experiences. At the same time, this process itself must always be observed and also reflected upon. From the client's feedback and/or his own observations, the supervisor or coach can then ascertain the efficacy of his endeavors. From these experiences, he can then determine what will help and what will not. If this takes place in a methodologically guided manner, one can justifiably speak of research. In this respect, professional relationship workers are the primary researchers in this field. Compared to them, research from scientists is always secondary. They can document this primary research process more accurately and comprehensively than practitioners are generally able to, and subsequently analyze them in a more sophisticated manner (e.g. Möller 2001). In addition, they can also subject many reports from practitioners to a secondary analysis (e.g. Petzold et al. 2003). Hence, the closer they remain to the experiences of the practitioners, the more useful the results will be for real-life applications.

However, scientific examinations often do not really serve to improve real-life practices; instead, their role is that of legitimation: They serve to show that the correct application of a particular form of consultation is in fact expedient; i.e. that an investment is worth the effort and costs (cf. Künzli 2006). Yet it cannot be concluded from efficacy research of this type that the type of coaching that Ms. X offers Mr. Y will proceed exactly as planned, and hence achieve causally predictable results. Hence, the employer's skepticism cannot be dispelled by referencing research findings of this type.

I therefore contend that the complaint that supervision and coaching have yet to be adequately researched, and that both forms of consultation are still in a pre-professional stage, is entirely inadequate. What is needed here is not only secondary research by the *scientific community*, but also to encourage the *professional community* to take their primary research more seriously and to document them in a more sophisticated fashion. For this purpose, cooperation on both sides is necessary.

9.2.3 Goal-Setting as a Democratic Process

But what *should* supervision and coaching achieve? Pragmatism gives a simple answer: These formats of consultation, together with their tools and in their framework, are to contribute to their clients having better experiences in the future. And this is to take place in that they trigger processes of insight in which practical opportunities come to light, the implementation of which will probably also result in the involved persons having positive experiences. And they are to be made competent and encouraged for this verification. They should therefore have learned something.

Hence, what better practices are and what positive experiences are need to be anticipated in the supervision or coaching sessions. This can best take place via a role reversal with the involved person. This process results in practical intentions, and the client will need to take responsibility for their implementation. But because not all reactions can be predicted, and there is always a possibility that a number of things may crop up, the experiences had will in turn need to be evaluated, such that corrective consequences for future practice can be determined.

In this process, the professional is bound to the interests of his clients. However, he also has an obligation towards his professionalism and professional ethics. He therefore needs to find a way to be responsible to himself and his profession. This results in limitations. Yet the process of obtaining insight is entirely open within these limitations. Beyond status and position, each participant in a supervision or coaching process can take part as equals. Ultimately, the person from whom the case originated will need to decide what is to be viewed as good practices. However, he will need to submit to an evaluation by others.

Even in the working world, everyone involved in this new practice and those affected by it generally need to be included in an evaluation. Solutions that are decided democratically with a contractually safeguarded acceptance of the predetermined primary objective of the respective organization of work are a good choice.

It is because of this that democratic negotiation processes are initiated in both supervision and coaching, because only they are able to provide humane and enduring solutions. Supervision and coaching are therefore forms of consultation through which a democratization process is advanced, in the working world as well. This wide and fundamental definition of democracy was propagated primarily by Dewey (cf. Jörke 2003; Hartmann 2003).

9.2.4 The Practitioners' Responsibility for Providing Good Concepts

The result of all these considerations is: What ultimately counts are positive experiences. And positive experiences are primarily what the clients of the supervision and coaching processes should have, but also those who are affected by their practices. Practitioners are to pay attention to this. By doing so, they too will have positive experiences. They are therefore the primary researchers. The scientists are to provide them with secondary support. However, because this knowledge is obtained via a variety of means and subject to various filter processes, a systematic and continuous interaction between these two types of knowledge is important. Hence, in future, there should not only be congresses for scientists or conferences for practitioners. An increasing number of events should be held at which both groups can compare and contrast their independent bodies of knowledge. After all, the professionalization of an occupation is not identical to its academization (Buer 2012).

The goal here would be an improvement in how supervision and coaching are carried out in practice. And in order to do so, what is primarily needed are concepts that are based on experience-rich knowledge, but also value-bound guiding principles. And these guiding principles simply cannot be extrapolated from that which is. A philosophical reflection is required in this case. This is where I currently see the greatest deficit, not only for practitioners, but also for scientists. Hence, a greater number of philosophers who are ready to direct their reflections towards practical consultation issues should be consulted. Coaches and supervisors with a philosophical or theological background already exist. They should not conceal this knowledge, but instead make it available explicitly. It is only in a dialog among these three groups that a mutual critical examination of the various types of knowledge as equals would be possible.

Because good concepts are crucial for good practices, it is primarily the practitioners who bear the greatest responsibility for collating the required knowledge. They should not be allowed to shirk this responsibility and shift it onto the sciences. Naturally, they can ask that the scientists fulfill their responsibility and make their due contribution. But it is more important that they shape their own research process appropriately. And they should not allow the standards and target perspectives to be prescribed by their clients alone. They need to independently determine—on their responsibility alone—the manner in which a constant stream of improvements to their practices can be identified; improvements that ensure a growth in qualitative experiences for as many people as possible. But such a concept is a promise that has yet to be fulfilled.

References

Berker, P., & Buer, F. (Eds.). (1998). *Praxisnahe Supervisionsforschung*. Münster: Votum.

Bohnsack, F. (2005). *John Dewey. Ein pädagogisches Porträt*. Weinheim: Beltz.

Buer, F. (1999). *Lehrbuch der Supervision*. Votum: Der pragmatisch-psychodramatische Weg zur Qualitätsverbesserung professionellen Handelns. Münster.

Buer, F. (Ed.). (2004a). *Praxis der Psychodramatischen Supervision. Ein Handbuch* (2nd ed.). Wiesbaden: VS Verlag.

Buer, F. (2004b). Über die professionelle Kompetenz, Professionalität kompetent darzustellen. Und welche Rolle die Supervision heute dabei spielt. In F. Buer & G. Siller (Hrsg.), *Die flexible Supervision* (S. 161–201). Wiesbaden: VS Verlag.

Buer, F. (2007a). Zehn Jahre Format und Verfahren in der Beziehungsarbeit. *Zur Rezeption einer bedeutsamen Unterscheidung. OSC, 14*(3), 283–300.

Buer, F. (2007b). Unsicherheiten im Beratungsdiskurs. Wozu Berater und Beraterinnen Philosophie brauchen – Pragmatismus zum Beispiel. In A. Schreyögg & C. Schmidt-Lellek (Hrsg.), *Konzepte des Coaching* (S. 163–188). Wiesbaden: VS Verlag.

Buer, F. (2008). Erfahrung – Wissenschaft – Philosophie. Drei Wissenssorten zur Konzipierung von Supervision und Coaching. In H. Krall, E. Mikula & W. Jansche (Hrsg.), *Supervision und Coaching* (S. 223–238). Wiesbaden: VS Verlag.

Buer, F. (2010). *Psychodrama und Gesellschaft. Wege zur sozialen Erneuerung von unten*. Wiesbaden: VS Verlag.

Buer, F. (2011). Life-Coaching als Ort der Besinnung: Was Fach- und Führungskräfte dazu bewegen kann, gute Arbeit zu leisten. In C. Schmidt-Lellek & F. Buer (Eds.), *Life-Coaching in der Praxis* (pp. 51–83). Göttingen: Vandenhoeck & Ruprecht.

Buer, F. (2012). *Rezension. OSC, 19*(3), 359–366.

Buer, F., & Schmidt-Lellek, C. (2008). *Life-Coaching. Über Sinn, Glück und Verantwortung in der Arbeit*. Göttingen: Vandenhoek & Ruprecht.

Craig, E. (1993). *Was wir wissen können. Pragmatische Untersuchungen zum Wissensbegriff*. Frankfurt/M.: Suhrkamp.

Deutsche Gesellschaft für Supervision (Hrsg.) (2006). *Der Nutzen von Supervision – Verzeichnis wissenschaftlicher Arbeiten*. Köln: Eigenverlag.

Dewey, J. (1929). The Quest for Certainty. *Gifford Lectures*. New York: Minton, Balch & Comp.; Germ. transl: *Die Suche nach Gewißheit*. Frankfurt/M: Suhrkamp, 1998.

Dewey, J. (1934). *Art as Exeperience*. New York: Capricorn Books, G.P. Putnam's Sons; Germ. transl.: *Kunst als Erfahrung*. Frankfurt/M.: Suhrkamp, 1988.

Dewey, J. (1938). *Logic: The theory of inquiry*. Carbonale: Southern Illinois University Press, 1986; Germ. transl.: *Logik. Die Theorie der Forschung*. Frankfurt/M.: Suhrkamp, 2002.

Diaz-Bone, R., & Schubert, K. (1996). *William James zur Einführung*. Hamburg: Junius.

Engler, U. (1992). *Kritik der Erfahrung: Die Bedeutung der ästhetischen Erfahrung in der Philosophie John Deweys*. Würzburg: Königshausen u. Neumann.

Feldman, D. C., & Lankau, M. J. (2005). Executive coaching: A review and agenda for future research. *Journal of Management, 31*, 829–848.

Fellmann, F. (1991). *Symbolischer Pragmatismus. Hermeneutik nach Dilthey*. Reinbek: Rowohlt.

Fuhr, R. (1992). *Plädoyer für alltägliches Forschen* (pp. 84–95). Sonderheft Forschung: Gestalttherapie.

Gaertner, A. (1999). *Gruppensupervision. Theoriegeschichtliche und fallanalytische Untersuchungen*. Tübingen: edition diskord.

Gaertner, A. (2004). Supervision in der Krise – Expansionismus, Unschärfeprofil und die Ausblendung der Selbstreflexion. In F. Buer & G. Siller (Eds.), *Die flexible Supervision* (pp. 79–100). Wiesbaden: VS Verlag.

Giesecke, M., & Rappe-Giesecke, K. (1997). *Supervision als Medium kommunikativer Sozialforschung. Die Integration von Selbsterfahrung und distanzierter Betrachtung in Beratung und Wissenschaft*. Frankfurt/M.: Suhrkamp.

Greif, S., Schmidt, F., & Thamm, A. (2012). Warum und wodurch Coaching wirkt. Ein Überblick zum Stand der Theorieentwicklung und Forschung über Wirkfaktoren. *OSC 19*(4), 375–390.

Gröning, K. (2004). Institutionelle Modernisierung und die flexible Supervision. In F. Buer & G. Siller (Eds.), *die flexible Supervision* (pp. 63–76). Wiesbaden: VS Verlag.

Hartmann, M. (2003). *Die Kreativität der Gewohnheit. Grundzüge einer pragmatistischen Demokratietheorie*. Frankfurt/M.: Campus.

James, W. (1907). *Pragmatism: A New Name for Some Old Ways of Thinking*. Cambridge, MA: Hackett Publishing 1981; Germ. Transl. *Pragmatismus. Ein neuer Name für einige alte Denkweisen*. Darmstadt: Wiss. Buchgesellschaft, 2001.

Joas, H. (Ed.). (2000). *Philosophie der Demokratie*. Suhrkamp: Beiträge zum Werk von John Dewey. Frankfurt/M.

Jörke, D. (2003). *Demokratie als Erfahrung. John Dewey und die politische Philosophie der Gegenwart*. Opladen: Leske & Budrich.

Kersting, H. J. (2004). Masterstudiengänge Supervision an Hochschulen. Chancen und Probleme. In F. Buer & G. Siller (Hrsg.), *Die flexible Supervision* (S. 203–216). Wiesbaden: VS Verlag.

Krall, H., Mikula, E., & Jansche, W. (Eds.). (2008). *Supervision und Coaching. Praxisforschung und Beratung im Sozial- und Bildungsbereich*. Wiesbaden: VS Verlag.

Krüger, H. -P. (2000). Prozesse der öffentlichen Untersuchung. Zum Potential einer zweiten Modernisierung in John Deweys „Logic. The Theory of Inquiry" (1938). In H. Joas (Hrsg.), *Philosophie der Demokratie* (S. 194–234). Frankfurt/M.: Suhrkamp.

Künzli, H. (2006). Wirksamkeitsforschung im Führungskräftecoaching. In E. Lippmann (Hrsg.), *Coaching. Angewandte Psychologie für die Beratungspraxis* (S. 280–294). Heidelberg: Springer.

Künzli, H. (2009). *Wirksamkeitsforschung im Führungskräfte-Coaching. OSC, 16*(1), 1–15.

Lippmann, E. (Ed.). (2006). *Coaching. Angewandte Psychologie für die Beratungspraxis*. Heidelberg: Springer.

Möller, H. (2001). *Was ist gute Supervision? Grundlagen – Merkmale – Methoden*. Stuttgart: Klett-Cotta.

Möller, H., & Hausinger, B. (Eds.). (2009). *Quo vadis Beratungswissenschaft?*. Wiesbaden: VS Verlag.

Moser, H. (1995). *Grundlagen der Aktionsforschung*. Freiburg: Lambertus.

Nagl, L. (1992). *Charles Sanders Peirce*. Frankfurt/M.: Campus.

Nagl, L. (1998). *Pragmatismus*. Frankfurt/M.

Neubert. S. (1998). *Erkenntnis, Verhalten und Kommunikation. John Deweys Philosophie des „experience" in interaktionistisch-konstruktivistischer Interpretation.* Münster: Waxmann.

Niemeyer, C. (1987). Der Praktiker als Forscher. Psychoanalyse als Erkenntnistheorie und als Metatheorie psychologischen und pädagogischen Erkennens und Handelns? *Psyche, 41,* 193–237.

Reichertz, J. (2003). *Die Abduktion in der qualitativen Sozialforschung.* Opladen: Leske & Budrich.

Petzold, H., Schigl, B., Fischer, M., & Höfner, C. (2003). *Supervision auf dem Prüfstand.* Opladen: Leske & Budrich.

Rorty, R. (1994). *Hoffnung statt Erkenntnis. Eine Einführung in die pragmatische Philosophie.* Wien: Passagen.

Schmidt-Lellek, C. & Buer, F. (2011). Einführung (S. 13–24). In C. Schmidt-Lellek & F. Buer (Hrsg.), *Life-Coaching in der Praxis. Wie Coaches umfassend beraten.* Göttingen: Vandenhoeck & Ruprecht.

Schreyögg. A. (2004). *Supervision. Ein integratives Modell. Lehrbuch zu Theorie und Praxis* (4., überarb. u. erw. Aufl.). Wiesbaden: VS Verlag.

Schubert, H. -J. et al. (Hrsg.). (2010). *Pragmatismus zur Einführung.* Hamburg: Junius.

Shusterman, R. (2000). Dewey über Erfahrung: Fundamentalphilosophie oder Rekonstruktion? In H. Joas (Hrsg.), *Philosophie der Demokratie* (S. 35–62). Frankfurt/M.: Westdt. Verlag.

Siller, G. (2004). Ökonomisierungsprozesse im Sozial- und Gesundheitswesen und ihre Folgen für die Supervision aus individueller Perspektive – Empirische Forschungsergebnisse. In F. Buer & G. Siller (Eds.), *Die flexible Supervision* (pp. 35–62). Wiesbaden: VS Verlag.

Siller, G. (2008). *Professionalisierung durch Supervision. Perspektiven im Wandlungsprozess sozialer Organisationen.* Wiesbaden: VS Verlag.

Author Biography

Prof. Dr. Ferdinand Buer worked as a social scientist and an education specialist at the University of Göttingen and the University of Münster, as a training lecturer in the fields of supervision, coaching, psychodrama, and constellations at various private and public institutes in Germany and Austria, as well as a supervisor, coach, and trainer in private practice.

Hermeneutics for Coaching 10

Christoph Schmidt-Lellek

Abstract

One significant aspect of professional interaction in coaching is the initiation of processes of understanding in order to enable the desired changes in perceiving, thinking, feeling, and acting. For this purpose, the philosophical discipline of hermeneutics (the science of understanding, the art of interpretation) may provide valuable insights. This chapter will first retrace a number of basic topics in hermeneutics which are of particular relevance to professional practitioners as well. Subsequently, using the trinity "Experience—Expression—Understanding", which is fundamental for interpersonal interactions, it will be shown that in professional practice, there is also the option of taking into consideration other, in part unconscious forms of expression (e.g. body language, dream language, symptoms of illnesses, organizational culture) in addition to a person's verbal expression for the hermeneutic process.

10.1 Preliminary Remarks

One significant aspect of professional interaction in coaching is the initiation of processes of understanding in order to enable the desired changes in perceiving, thinking, feeling, and acting. When doing so, the objective is to understand the

C. Schmidt-Lellek (✉)
Taunusstr. 126, 61440 Oberursel, Germany
e-mail: Kontakt@Schmidt-Lellek.de
URL: http://www.Schmidt-Lellek.de

A. Schreyögg and C. Schmidt-Lellek (eds.), *The Professionalization of Coaching*, DOI 10.1007/978-3-658-16805-6_10

relevant situation to be discussed together with its contexts, to understand oneself with one's biographically acquired patterns of thinking and acting, to understand the desired goals and the methodological paths to reaching it, and also to acquire an intersubjective understanding between the persons involved who have to be attuned to each other during the coaching process. As in all professions, the coach "performs a ‚translational task', in that general knowledge has to be applied to a particular case with its own specific characteristics" (DBVC 2012, p. 13). This means that the specialized knowledge acquired from the various disciplines cannot be used directly, but instead needs to be adapted for each specific situation—and most of all, the client needs to understand this information in order to be able to transpose it to his daily life.

For this, the philosophical discipline of hermeneutics may provide valuable insight. The question "What does it mean to understand?" has been a central issue in philosophy since ancient times, which since the 17th century and particularly since Schleiermacher (approx. 200 years ago) has been dealt with under the term "hermeneutics". Hence, it is a worthwhile effort for coaches to consult these rich philosophical sources in order to obtain a clear idea of the structures, methods, and also the risks of processes of understanding by reflecting on one's own professional actions.

In this short presentation of hermeneutics, my first source and point of orientation will be a book by the Canadian philosopher Grondin (2009), who provides a concise overview of the developments in philosophical hermeneutics. With the help of this book, I will first retrace a number of basic topics in hermeneutics which are of particular relevance to professional practitioners. Grondin does not refer specifically to the areas of application of hermeneutics in professional interactions. However, in this book, the reader will find a great deal of advices on how certain problems and paradoxes in professional practice can be better analyzed and handled. The second part of this chapter is dedicated to this issue.

10.2 The Concept and History of Hermeneutics

Hermeneutics is the philosophical term for "the science of understanding"—the discipline which deals with the possibilities, forms, and processes of understanding. The term "hermeneutics" comes from the Greek word *hermeneúein*, which means "to explain, translate, interpret" (lat. *interpretes* = translator). Etymologically, the word (presumably) comes from "Hermes", the divine messenger who imparts the secret knowledge of the gods. The first mention of the term can be found in Plato's writings: the art of translation/interpretation (*hermeneutikè téchne*;

Epinomis, sec. 975c; cf. Symposion, sec. 202e). Plato emphasizes that hermeneutics does not provide any information on the truth value of that which is interpreted, as this is the domain of metaphysics, which refers to the "ideas" as opposed to the "phenomena", i.e. the concrete "manifestations".

Since the 17th century, the term was first picked up by protestant theologians in Germany (much later by the catholics): Compared to "exegesis", which focuses more strongly on word meaning and grammatical structure, hermeneutics endeavors to interpret a bible text for one's contemporaries; i.e. provide a translation into current cultural and social contexts. At the same time, hermeneutics was also of importance for other ancient texts.

Friedrich Schleiermacher (1768–1834) defined hermeneutics as being the "art of understanding" (he differentiated between hermeneutics and critique). He was the first to develop a systematic and generalized form of hermeneutics as a scientific method that could also be applied to non-ancient texts—"an artistic theory of understanding" which "utilizes the simple fact of understanding arising from the nature of language and the basic conditions of the relationship between the speaker and the listener to develop its rules in a closed context" (Schleiermacher 1838/1977). The interpreter of a text must be familiar with the conditions under which the author wrote it and the reasons that resulted in it being written; he must be able to put himself in the author's shoes. Corresponding to the combination of general factors (language) and individual factors (thinking) in each utterance, one needs to differentiate between the two moments of grammatical and psychological interpretation during understanding. Understanding is the inversion of the action of mental production. Because this often takes place subconsciously, one needs to "first understand the utterance just as well, and then better than its speaker" (ibid., p. 94).

In the 19th century, Wilhelm Dilthey (1833–1911) had to deal with an entirely new situation, as the humanities were now confronted with the issue of providing a methodological justification in the face of the rapidly growing natural sciences. For this purpose, Dilthey distinguished between "to explain" and "to understand": The natural sciences attempted to *explain* the causality of phenomena and to infer them from general rules, while the humanities' goal was to *understand* the historical individuality in the phenomena (cf. Grondin 2009, p. 26). Correspondingly, Dilthey opposed the opinion of contemporary psychologists that psychological relationships could be explained in the same way as causal relationships in nature. Because psychological phenomena should be examined as a whole, understanding should be the method employed in psychology.

Following Schleiermacher, Dilthey defined hermeneutics as being "an artistic theory of the understanding of written life utterances" (Dilthey 1883/1990).

The interpretation of a text aims to understand the "singularity" which the author expresses therein. Accordingly, understanding means "recreating the author's experience within oneself" (Grondin 2009, p. 27). Hence, while an author attempts to express his experience in a fixed, written form, the interpreting reader attempts to return to the experience via the words expressed. Dilthey considered hermeneutics with this "trinity of experience, expression, and understanding" (ibid.) as being the methodological basis of the humanities, as they always arise from language.

Consequently, hermeneutics was expanded on in particular by Martin Heidegger (1889–1976) in his existential philosophy, which concerned itself not only with the understanding of texts, but also human existence itself. In this case, hermeneutics primarily means the understanding of one's self; i.e. of existence in its temporal and finite limits. Hermeneutics aims to "bring human existence out of its self-forgetfulness, in which it is so fond of hiding" (Grondin, p. 127). Heidegger's turning away from the metaphysics tradition is due to the fact that metaphysical concepts of human existence close their eyes to existential "facticity", in particular to the finiteness of existence, which Heidegger describes as "self-forgetfulness".

This "existential turning point" had a deep impact on all future discussions on hermeneutics, which was most comprehensively carried out by Hans-Georg Gadamer (1900–2002), the most well-known representative of philosophical hermeneutics in the 20th century. Grondin devotes the most time to describing "Wahrheit und Methode" (1960, "Truth and Method"), his magnum opus.

Gadamer describes understanding not as one of man's many modes of behavior, but instead as a central, significant activity of human existence. When hermeneutics e.g. attempts to understand history, this can only succeed if it also takes into consideration its own historicity (Gadamer 1990, p. 305): Understanding is not only the comprehension of the respective subjective meaning of a historical or literary text; instead, it means entering a transmission process in which the past and the present interact (ibid., p. 300).

In particular, Gadamer emphasized the "hermeneutic circle", which refers to the fact that in processes of understanding, one's own prior understanding or "prejudice" with its own historicity also influences the process. However, this does not mean that one should—in accordance with the ideal put forth by the Enlightenment—eliminate this prior understanding in order to obtain a correct, unprejudiced understanding of that which one encounters. Instead, the challenge is now to become conscious of one's historically resp. biographically formed prejudice structures; i.e. to understand oneself, through which "glasses" one views and attempts to understand the world. However, the question is now if there is perhaps nothing other than these "glasses", as radical constructivism would assume ("all perception is a construct"), or if there exists a contact with the facts, beyond the "glasses", constructs, perspectives,—to phrase it in a classical fashion: if there is a adequacy (lat. *adaequatio*) between the subject and the object of perception. Here, Gadamer speaks of a "merger of horizons", which results that a true understanding of the other person necessarily has a retroactive effect on oneself, because one learns to recognize and question one's respective prior understanding.

Hence, understanding possesses a *dialogical structure*, where an external text causes the interpreter to confront his own prior understanding, which he also brings into the text. This "hermeneutic circle" cannot be circumvented:

> A person who wants to understand a text is (…) prepared to learn something from it. Hence, one must be receptive to a hermeneutically trained consciousness for the "otherness" of the text from the outset. However, such receptiveness presupposes neither factual "neutrality" nor self-effacement, but instead includes the distinguishing acquisition of one's own prior opinions and prejudices (Gadamer 1990, p. 273 f.).

When you replace the word "text" with "person" in this quote, it can be applied directly to the encountering of the otherness of another person, and hence also to professional interaction in coaching and other consultation formats.

Furthermore, I find the debate between Gadamer and Jacques Derrida in April 1981 in Paris to be of particular importance to practitioners. This debate clearly illustrates a fundamental issue, which Grondin gives a comprehensive treatment of. One of Gadamer's central statements is: "Existence which can be understood is language." This means that "everything which can be understood is an existence that expresses itself in language. (…) First of all, it is language which allows the existence of the world to come to light, as it makes it possible to develop the language of things itself" (Grondin, p. 66 ff.). Hence, hermeneutics is more than a method in humanities; rather, it has become "a universal philosophical reflection on the linguistic character of our experience of the world and the world itself" (ibid.). In doing so, Gadamer rejects a nominalist view in which language and the world ultimately remain separate and language merely serves as a tool in the hands of the subject which is used to tackle and control things or other people.

It is exactly this which Derrida is insinuating that hermeneutics does when he diagnoses a will to dominate in the desire for understanding with the help of language, including its systems and structures. This has to do with his "deconstruction" of occidental metaphysics and its "totalizing assertion of existence" (ibid, p. 97), a central issue of "postmodern" philosophy. For Derrida, understanding is a "form of violence that is imposed on the other". And his question for Gadamer is as follows: "Does the desire to understand not force the other to bow down, to adapt his thoughts to the constructs I impose upon him and which—in doing so—completely miss his specificity?" In short: "Is it the *other person* I am understanding when *I* understand him?" (p. 107).

As Grondin then describes, Gadamer partially revised his position, and also stated it more precisely in reaction to Derrida's criticism. He later appears "more aware of the danger of understanding, which the other person, in acquiring that which is *other*, may possibly exert violence on his otherness (Grondin, p. 110; cf. Gadamer 1990, p. 305, note 230 in the new revised edition). According to Gadamer, however, the aim of hermeneutics is to "open up to the otherness of the other", and hence, as Gadamer now highlights, due to the fundamentally linguistic nature of understanding, one must recognize the limits of language—that "we can never entirely say what we want to say" (Gadamer 1995, quoted in Grondin 2009, p. 111). Hence, as Grondin concludes: "Meaning is always a meaning of things themselves, of what they say and indicate, a meaning which certainly extends beyond our pitiful interpretation attempts and the limited horizon of our respective linguistic abilities" (p. 131).

10.3 Relevance for the Practice of Consultation

But what relevance do these analyses have for a professional coach in his daily work? First of all, the trinity of *experience—expression—understanding* is fundamental: The experience of a person or client yearns to be expressed; a form of expression through which he himself can process the experience and tell an interested listener or counselor about it. Hence, this can be characterized as a process of translation from an experience into an expression of this experience, whatever the medium may be (see below). A listener can, by interpretatively assimilating such an expression, participate in the client's experience and by doing so recreate it within himself—the perceived expression is therefore "back-translated" into experience and at the same time linked to his own experiential patterns. Hence, understanding is more than just passive assimilation. Instead, it is also a creative act, because in addition to the opening up of oneself to the client's experience, it also simultaneously always represents an interpretative inner resonance. If this resonance is in turn expressed, it can open up the client to a change in his own understanding of his experience. After all, this is the overarching goal in any consultation, as it is in psychotherapy: that a client acquires a changed, more intensive, clearer understanding of himself. The above is a brief description of the "dialogical structure" of processes of understanding between persons.

However, for professional interactions, the hermeneutics for the philosophical perspectives described above will need to be expanded such that it takes into consideration that consultation and therapeutic work is not *only* concerned with language. Instead, understanding should take into account all forms of human experience and self-expression: It is only with corporeal and sensory experience and non-verbal expression that the verbal components of the communication are given the comprehensive meaning that correspondingly needs to be understood by the relevant other person (cf. Schulz von Thun 1981). This is because, in the interaction between two persons, and particularly between a person seeking advice and aid and a professional counselor, the aim is not only to understand a *spoken text*, but to understand the *speaker* and his life situation with all its dimensions of experience.

This expansion of the horizon of hermeneutics was also addressed in philosophical debates. In the following are a few examples of this:

- Susanne Langer (1942) differentiates between a "discursive", language-related symbolization (or form of expression) and a "presentative", image-related symbolization. Both require their own specific approaches for achieving understanding, as linguistic utterances are always subject to the passing of time, while an image allows for a stationary perception as a whole.
- Maurice Merleau-Ponty (1945/1976) bases his theory of language and dialog on corporeal expression, as "our body is our overall medium for participating in the world", i.e. living in the world and experiencing the world (Merleau-Ponty 1976, p. 176).
- Georg Picht tears down the walls between thought, sensory perception, and affect with his reflections on modern art by insisting: "the senses think" (Picht 1986, p. 336). He speaks of the "hermeneutics of affect", which is "neglected by all modern philosophers" (ibid., p. 257), and he examines all artistic forms of expression as a "presentation" of something which would otherwise remain hidden from perception and understanding (ibid., p. 393).
- Hermann Schmitz (1989, p. 28ff.) speaks, with regard to the success of psychotherapy, of "corporeal communication" as a term which should encompass linguistic, sensory, and emotional forms of expression.

For therapeutic practice, Petzold (1992) is in favor of "multiperspectivist" hermeneutics in order to not only be able to access reality through language, but also through images, signs, movements, attitudes, feelings, odors, noises etc. However, here too we should consider that our understanding always takes place in conversational and interpretative communities, and that, as a context- and situation-related phenomenon, it can always only be temporary. Hence, this *context* is also to be included in the hermeneutic concept, as Hermann Argelander attempted to do so with his concept of "scenic understanding": In addition to the "objective information", i.e. the biographical facts, and the "subjective information", i.e. the personal interpretative factors, the "scenic information" is necessary in order for a person's understanding. This concerns "the experiencing of the situation with all the feelings it evokes and conceptual processes" (Argelander 1970, p. 14).

Hence, recognizing and understanding psychological, communicative, institutional or organizational phenomena not only involves the perception and interpretation of spoken words and of texts, but also of a wide range of other modes of expression in which life processes are articulated. However, for consultation practice, this requires the corresponding *methodological approaches*. The following are a number of examples of this:

Body language: A direct communication between persons contains non-verbal components in addition to verbal components, the "body language", i.e. facial expressions, gestures, vocalizations, rate of speech, body position, body contact, autonomous body reactions (e.g. turning red, turning white, sweating etc.); these may comment, intensify, or even contradict the verbal utterances. These generally have an involuntary and direct effect on the other person, who usually also reacts to them involuntarily. Communication in professional contexts requires a counselor or psychotherapist to be able to consciously perceive these non-verbal "messages" and also react to them consciously in order to comprehend the complexity of the self-expression and do justice to the other person's expectations with the greatest amount of understanding (cf. Argyle 1975; Schulz von Thun 1981). This competency not only has diagnostic relevance, but can also strengthen the intensity and authenticity of the communicative processes in all curative and counseling professions.

Dream language: The language of dreams is a main source of information about the unconscious components of a personality. Dream language often uses coded, sometimes drastic and appalling symbols, but remains a significant form of expression of personality. For many people, it initially appears to be closed to them—a "foreign language" which requires "translation" ("hermeneutics"), i.e. the interpretation of dreams. That this has been a special art and a form of wisdom since ancient times is illustrated by stories such as e.g. the story of Joseph in the Old Testament (Gen. 40–41). In addition to modern (e.g. brain psychology) research, a number of diverse approaches have been developed for the interpretation of dreams in the field of psychotherapy: For Freud (1900), dreams generally represented a fictional fulfillment of suppressed or censored drives; the method of "free association" attempts to make an interpretation possible. According to C.G. Jung, dreams provide access not only to the individual, but also the collective unconscious, such as e.g. the "archetypes"; i.e. general human structural patterns which are articulated in symbols. A methodological approach in this context requires a great deal of familiarity with the symbols in mythology, cultural history, religion and art (cf. Jung 1968). In F. Perl's Gestalt therapy, dreams are seen as existential messages and as a presentation of the inner reality of the person, in which emerging possibilities which have not yet been realized by the consciousness can also manifest themselves; an experience-related method of achieving understanding takes place e.g. via a scenic presentation of the dream as well as via dialogs with the individual dream components in order to be able to recognize them as dispossessed parts of themselves and integrate them into the consciousness. Specially for coaching, Bernd Schmid presented a more playful and associative approach together with a work on dreams which has a double objective: an "understanding and processing aspect" and a "reality-shaping aspect" (Schmid 2005, p. 384).

Signal value of illnesses: Illnesses, too, can represent what are expressions of personality in their corporeal and mental unity which are hidden from the consciousness, provided that one is able to interpret them. For example, Viktor von Weizsäcker (1886–1957), one of the founders of psychosomatic medicine, was of the opinion that basically every illness is to be understood the expression of an existential conflict of the person, as illnesses are a wholly "psychosomatic" phenomenon (v. Weizsäcker 1973). By conducting a wide range of research studies, it was possible to deduce connections with certain typical conflict dynamics for a number of psychosomatic diseases (v. Uexküll 1979). Hence, for a doctor or therapist, as well as for the affected person, understanding the signal value of an illness is a hermeneutic task. The purpose of doing so is not only to overcome the symptom of the illness, but also to identify the existential conflict that lies behind it and to find a solution for it. Methodically, this requires, in addition to the usual specialist diagnostics, an intensive interview with the patient in order to achieve an understanding of his existential situation that is as broad as possible via his subjective sensory contexts (Jaspers 1965, p. 687). Of course, coaching sessions are not the place for analyzing psychosomatic medical histories and treatments that should be carried out by doctors or psychotherapists. However, coaches can sensitize themselves to such situations and point this out to clients, such as when the issue is the limits of stress resistance or a burnout. The goal here would be the willingness and the ability to understand health-related disturbing factors as a reaction to external disturbing factors or conflicts in one's own life and to initiate the corresponding changes.

Organizational culture: Institutions and companies function not only thanks to the rationally planned formal aspects of the organization, but are also strongly influenced by their corresponding organizational culture, which contains non-formal systemic phenomena that mostly have not been reflected upon. Hence, the members of the organization are not entirely conscious of them, even though their behavior is of course subject to them. They therefore serve as a collective template for orientation; for e.g. how issues are to be understood and described, how the members of the organization interact with each other etc. However, when familiar cultural patterns have become charged with conflict or become dysfunctional in processes of change or in the case of a merger of companies, they need to be brought to light and made accessible through a confrontation. What is being done here is a "system diagnosis" in order to achieve "cultural understanding" (Schreyögg 1995, p. 29). Schein (1995, p. 142ff.) describes a process for this with which a consultant or researcher, particularly through interviews with members of the organization, can achieve an "unveiling of common basic premises" (p. 142), in order to also be able to change them.

The efforts made to achieve understanding can hence also refer to such—often unconsciously intended—modes of expression. With their help, a great variety of phenomena may manifest themselves which would otherwise not be accessible to conscious perception and processing. Generally, these non-verbal modes of expression are first verbalized in order to be able to deal with them and, if necessary, change them. However, in counseling and therapeutic settings, there are also non-verbal and pre-verbal methodical approaches towards obtaining understanding: For example, an empathic understanding of another person and his problems can be activated through role-playing. In actionist procedures such as psychodrama (according to Moreno), complex problem constellations and developments can be acted out with multiple roles, such that the scenes experienced by the protagonist are recreated by the role-players, allowing for the situation to be understood by being re-experienced, and enabling "corrective" scenes to be devised (cf. Buer 1989). Similarly, as part of family therapy, the method of the "family sculpture" was developed, where role-players illustrate the constellation of the family systems, allowing its effects on the members of this system to be experienced.

When we once again return to the aforementioned trinity of "experience—expression—understanding", the method of understanding in these approaches lies in having the feedback-giver (a group member or the counselor) depart from the role of the distant observer of an expression and instead entering the mode of expression himself in order to be able to identify with a role or a family member and better understand the experience of the client, and subsequently be able to illustrate and interpret his own experience in this role. The client (or the protagonist) then has the option of observing his mode of experience from a distance and hence achieving other interpretations. Alternatively, he utilizes the role-changing method to take on another role in a family system or a conflict event in order to identify with a different expression and distance himself from his original experience and learn to understand it in a different fashion. However, such a form of witnessing in turn subsequently requires verbalization in order to identify overarching structural contexts, and finally also to relinquish what is sometimes a powerfully effective identification with a role and return to the position of the observer. The objective of such methodological approaches is the clarification of and a change in patterns of understanding, and hence also in the behavior patterns of a client.

An even more subtle form of "understanding witnessing" is the "container model" of the English group analyst Wilfried R. Bion (1962). According to this model, the thoughts or emotions of the client—via projection resp. "projective identification"—searches for a "nesting site" in the mental life of a "host" (i.e. of a counselor, therapist, supervisor etc.), in which they can be processed or "digested", such that they can subsequently be "fed back" ("feedback") to the client. The "host" must hence have the ability to assimilate the projected thoughts or feelings without judging or explaining them, as well as "tolerate that which is unknown, mysterious, and dubious" without "an irritated grasping for facts and explanations" (Lazar 1994, p. 381). "Hence, if the assimilating object (the psyche of the container) takes in that which is to be assimilated (that which is projected into him, not understood, painful, needy, non-tenable, unimaginable) from the subject into himself, he must be able to first understand this metabolizing, unscrambling process in himself and for himself, in order to be able to feed it back to the subject in a measured manner, such that it can be digested and does not have to be immediately spit back out" (ibid.).

While Bion developed this model primarily with intimate processes between the patient and the psychotherapist in mind, Ross A. Lazar also uses it for the situation encountered in supervision. Supervision also requires a secure, protected, and intimate context, "such that the uniqueness can be experienced and perceived and is not destroyed by fear, envy, competition, or hate" (ibid. p. 382). The supervisor can handle the accounts of the person being supervised in the same manner as the therapist those of his patient. "I attempt to handle the material from the supervisee's accounts as if I myself had to react in the given situation. This means that I attempt to identify with the descriptions so intensively and introjectively as if I myself was standing on the stage of the situation described, in part in the role of the supervisee, in part in that of the patient" (ibid., p. 383). This can also be applied to the situation in coaching.

10.4 Conclusion

In all endeavors to understand other people and their utterances with all aforementioned approaches and methods, Derrida's objection to philosophical hermeneutics should be taken to heart: The respective understanding of a professional should not be imposed on the client or the customer, as this would not allow the professional understanding to lead to a new, authentic, and autonomous self-understanding on the part of the client. However, this danger is often present: A client is given a template for understanding or a diagnosis, but does not feel taken seriously. Even when the client believes in the professional competency and the authority of a psychotherapist, supervisor, or coach, their templates for understanding for him cannot truly be effective until he is able to connect them with his own templates for understanding and competencies. A template of understanding is only helpful for him when it is able to open up a horizon for questions and new possibilities for understanding, which can then lead to new patterns of thought and behavior. This not only applies for individual persons, but also to organizational systems and their representatives, with whom coaches, supervisors or organizational consultants deal with.

In conclusion, it can be said that understanding has a dialogical structure, as Gadamer clearly described: In that the interpreter is caused, by an external "text" (whatever form it may take) to confront his own prior understanding, this confrontation can also be included in the dialogical process of understanding and contribute to an intersubjective understanding. In particular when we are dealing with the understanding of another person, it is necessary to know one's own patterns of understanding well, to not doggedly stick to them, and also to question them in our interactions with others. One can attempt to rise to this challenge by e.g. reflecting on transference and counter-transference dynamics. All this takes place in the context of a professional relationship with tension-filled paradoxes or polarities (Schmidt-Lellek 2006, p. 278 ff.; cf. Chap. 4 in this book). In this manner, the hermeneutic process can be an enrichment for all involved parties.

References

Argelander, H. (1970). *Das Erstinterview in der Psychotherapie*. Darmstadt: Wissenschaftliche Buchgesellschaft.

Argyle, M. (1975). *Bodily Communication*. London: Methuan; Germ.: *Körpersprache und Kommunikation* (Trans. C. Schmidt-Lellek). Paderborn: Junfermann, 1979.

Bion, W. R. (1962). *Learning from Experience*. London: William Heinemann; Germ.: *Lernen durch Erfahrung*. Frankfurt/M.: Suhrkamp, 1990.

Buer, F. (1989). Die Philosophie des J.L. Moreno – Die Grundlage des Psychodrama. *Integrative Therapie, 15*(2), 121–140.

DBVC—Deutscher Bundesverband Coaching e.V. (Hrsg.) (2012). *Leitlinien und Empfehlungen für die Entwicklung von Coaching als Profession. Kompendium mit den Professionsstandards des DBVC* (4., erw. Aufl.). Osnabrück: DBVC Geschäftsstelle; Engl. version available under: www.dbvc.de/publikationen/coaching-kompendium.

Dilthey, W. (1883). *Einleitung in die Geisteswissenschaften. Versuch einer Grundlegung für das Studium der Gesellschaft und der Geschichte*. Ges. Schriften, Bd. 1 (9. Aufl. 1990). Göttingen: Vandenhoeck & Ruprecht.

Freud, S. (1900). *Die Traumdeutung*. Studienausgabe Bd. II. Frankfurt/M.: Fischer, 1982.

Gadamer, H.-G. (1990). *Wahrheit und Methode. Grundzüge einer philosophischen Hermeneutik (6., durchges. u* (erw ed.). Tübingen: Mohr.

Grondin, J. (2009). *Hermeneutik*. Göttingen: Vandenhoeck & Ruprecht, UTB.

Jaspers, K. (1965). *Allgemeine Psychopathologie* (8th ed.). Berlin, Heidelberg: Springer.

Jung, C. G. (1968). Zugang zum Unbewussten. In C. G. Jung et al. (Eds.), *Der Mensch und seine Symbole* (pp. 18–103). Olten: Walter-Verlag.

Langer, S. K. (1942). *Philosophy in a New Key: A Study in the Symbolism of Reason, Rite, and Art*. Cambridge, Mass.; Germ.: *Philosophie auf neuem Wege. Das Symbol im Denken, im Ritus und in der Kunst*. Frankfurt/M.: Fischer, 1984.

Lazar, R. A. (1994). W.R. Bions Modell „Container-Contained" als eine psychoanalytische Leitidee in der Supervision. In H. Pühl (Hrsg.), *Handbuch der Supervision 2* (S. 380–402). Berlin: Edition Marhold.

Merleau-Ponty, M. (1976). *Phänomenologie der Wahrnehmung*. Berlin: de Gruyter (Orig. 1945).

Petzold, H. (1992). Konzepte zu einer mehrperspektivischen Hermeneutik leiblicher Erfahrung und nicht-sprachlichen Ausdrucks in der Integrativen Therapie. In R. Kühn & H. Petzold (Eds.), *Psychotherapie & Philosophie – Philosophie als Psychotherapie?* (pp. 475–549). Paderborn: Junfermann.

Plato (1967). *Sämtliche Werke*, 3. Bde. (5. Aufl.). Köln, Olten: Jakob Hegner.

Picht, G. (1986). *Kunst und Mythos*. Stuttgart: Klett-Cotta.

Schein, E. H. (1995). *Unternehmenskultur. Ein Handbuch für Führungskräfte*. Frankfurt/M., New York: Campus; orig.: *Organizational Culture and Leadership*. San Francisco: Jossey-Bass, 1992.

Schleiermacher, F. (1838/1977). *Hermeneutik und Kritik*. Mit einem Anhang sprachphilosophischer Texte Schleiermachers. Frankfurt/M.: Suhrkamp, 1977.

Schmid, B. (2005). Träume im Coaching. Ein Beispiel und ein Leitfaden für kollegiale Traumdialoge. *Organisationsberatung, Supervision, Coaching, 12*(4), 383–396.

Schmidt-Lellek, C. (2006). *Ressourcen der helfenden Beziehung. Modelle dialogischer Praxis und ihre Deformationen*. Bergisch Gladbach: EHP.
Schmitz, H. (1989). *Leib und Gefühl. Materialien zu einer philosophischen Therapeutik*. Paderborn: Junfermann.
Schreyögg, A. (1995). Organisationskulturen von Human Service Organizations. Begriff, Charakteristika, Einflussvariablen, Implikationen für die Organisationsberatung. *Organisationsberatung, Supervision, Coaching, 2*(1), 15–34.
Schulz von Thun, F. (1981). *Miteinander reden. Störungen und Klärungen. Allgemeine Psychologie der Kommunikation*. Reinbek: Rowohlt.
Uexküll, Th. v. (Hrsg.) (1979). *Lehrbuch der Psychosomatischen Medizin*. München u.a.: Urban & Schwarzenberg.
Weizsäcker, V. v. (1973). *Der Gestaltkreis. Theorie der Einheit von Wahrnehmung und Bewegung*. Frankfurt/M.: Suhrkamp.

Author Biography

Dr. phil. Christoph Schmidt-Lellek studied prot. theology, philosophy and pedagogy, doctoral dissertation on the resources of relationship in professional settings, freelance practice in coaching (DBVC), psychotherapy and supervision (DGSv), publications in the fields of psychotherapy and coaching, co-publisher and editor of the journal "Organisationsberatung, Supervision, Coaching" (OSC).

The Potential Diversity of a Coach's Roles

11

Astrid Schreyögg

Abstract

In contrast to Schein's *expert abstinence* and to the "midwife role" of a coach, this article advocates a diversity of roles on the part of the coach that is tailored to the client's issues and problems. Already due to pragmatic aspects, this would be a limitation placed on this form of consultation, as many clients expect the coach to provide specialist expertise. But even under normative aspects, this would also be a restriction, as even clearly asymmetric methods can be justified if the subject status of the client is maintained. Symmetry/asymmetry on the one hand and intersubjectivity on the other are, namely, not congruent. It is due to this—as will be shown in a case study—that directive coach roles can also be justified, as long as they do the client justice as a subject.

11.1 Introduction

In the debate concerning the coaching of specialist and management personnel, there is to a large extent a consensus that the coach should serve as a dialog partner for his clients (e.g. Birgmeier 2009; Lippmann 2005; Rauen 2005). But what does this mean exactly? In which role should the coach present himself to his clients? Which consultation model should serve as the standard? Some coaches, such as

A. Schreyögg (✉)
Breisgauer Str. 29, 14129 Berlin, Germany
e-mail: info@schreyoegg.de
URL: http://www.Schreyoegg.de

A. Schreyögg and C. Schmidt-Lellek (eds.), *The Professionalization of Coaching*, DOI 10.1007/978-3-658-16805-6_11

Radatz (2000), give a detailed warning against assuming the role of a "know-it-all", against providing counsel, and where applicable, against any form of expert advice. However, Enoch (2011, p. 376) is of the following opinion: "The systemic and solution-oriented consulting approaches" which Radatz refers to "virtually postulate intentional decontextualization and ignorance at the beginning of the consulting process". In contrast to this, the author can prove that it is exactly this—namely the coach making available appropriate knowledge which he possesses—which makes the success of the consultation at all possible.

In the milieu of psychotherapists, particularly since Rogers (1972), the maxim prevailed that counselors should refrain from expressing any of their own opinions, and perhaps also from providing any stimuli at all. The idea was that the client himself knew best what was right for him. The counselor was only relevant in the role of a "midwife" or a structural companion. But how did this credo also come to influence professional forms of consultation such as consulting for organizations, supervision, and coaching, and how can it even be implemented in these contexts? For the topics and issues in these forms of consultation obviously are more closely related to professional expertise as compared to psychotherapy. For example, an engineer who feels extremely vexed at the situation after his company has merged with another will find it rather unhelpful if his coach were to simply nod his head in a friendly manner and say nothing other than an encouraging "mmh" in response. Such and many other specialist and management personnel who consult a coach are generally looking for a dialog partner who listens closely to them, but who also occasionally provides an assessment or opinion, gives recommendations on how the events in question could be viewed from a different perspective, who can provide and assist with alternative behavior patterns, and where necessary, is also able to suggest role-play sessions and perhaps also offer advice.

In this article, I aim to show that ideally, a coach utilizes a consultation model that has a high degree of role diversity and variability, which he should adapt to the consultation process according to the client's issues and options as well as his own potential. However, it is important that he maintains the subject status of the client. (1) In the first step, I will describe the historic genesis of "expert abstinence" according to Schein (2000) with its specific "midwife role". (2) Subsequently, I will show that, for qualified coaching, the coach should include his own expertise at various levels of the process due to *pragmatic aspects*. (3) Also, I wish to show that a *normative perspective* can in fact include asymmetries of the intersubjectivity between the coach and the client, and can often also involve aspects of expert consultation. (4) Furthermore, I attempt to clearly show that the normative positions of various processes that are useful in coaching generally need to correspond to the needs of intersubjectivity, even if they can involve asymmetry. (5) Finally, the postulated role variability of the coach will be demonstrated in a case example.

11.2 The Original Conceptual Basis for the Expert Abstinence of Counselors

Many authors of the coaching debate refer directly or indirectly to Edgar Schein (2000), who already references Rogers and his "non-directive" therapy in his early writings on organizational development (1969). In his first few publications, which were written in the context of the American human resource movement, he and a number of his colleagues, e.g. Argyris (1975) and Likert (1975), searched for alternatives to traditional forms of consulting for organizations. In particular, they drew attention to the fact that the form of consulting practiced in corporate settings often met with *resistance to change* from members of the organization. The situation in such cases was as follows: Representatives from notable consulting firms such as McKinsey or Boston Consulting, acting as experts, "prescribed" the members of the organization a new organizational structure that was pretended to be more effective. In contrast, Schein advocated a novel form of corporate consultation in which the counselors did not see themselves as experts, but instead one in which the members of the organization were involved dialogically in a complex social process, and at the very most as "experts in themselves". This new form, which was practiced as "process consultation", then formed the conceptual foundation for a new type of consultation for organizations, now called "organizational development".

Schein, who was also part of the early group movement (Reddy 1997), names Lewin and Rogers as the most important advocates of "process consultation" and the concepts related to it. Lewin and his colleagues had conducted a comprehensive examination of social processes of change under the shadow of fascism (Lewin 1947). From the Lewin school of thought, Schein adapted the postulate of a high degree of participation on the part of the members of the organization. And from Rogers, one of the most prominent representatives of the movement of humanistic psychology, Schein adopted his normative orientation. These movements were decidedly against positivist trends and emphasized, as part of a phenomenological understanding, that every consultation necessarily existed in a subject-subject relationship between the counselor and the client. Furthermore, the counselor would need to withhold his dominance to the benefit of the client, such that the client can shape the consultation process to the maximum possible extent. Temporarily, Rogers even advocated an extreme deprofessionalization of psychotherapy, in which each human-human conversation with the maximum degree of intersubjectivity is beneficial (Rogers 1972). From Rogers, Schein also adopted his specific form of dialogical guidance, which however can only be seen to a limited extent as the "guidance" of dialogs. Its most important methodological approaches were:

- Passive listening
- Active listening with verbalization (=the coach summarizes the client's utterances) and paraphrasing (=the coach summarizes the client's utterances and provides a minimal amount of interpretation)
- Posing targeted questions.

It is significant that Schein emphasizes till today that "process consultation" is not so much a method as a "philosophy of assistance" (Schein 2000, p. 13), which is valid in a variety of counseling situations. In doing so, he advocates a practical philosophical/ethical position for the counseling relationship, which exists in a subject-subject relation (cf. Chap. 4 in this book).

Although Schein and his successors have received great acceptance till today, traditional expert consulting still remains dominant where consulting for companies is concerned. In contrast, organizational development as conceived of by Schein rarely takes place. Instead, it primarily influenced systemic consultation—a form of organizational development which is enriched by systemic concepts (Kühl and Moldaschl 2010). Today, one other large faction of organizational developers prefers to practice coaching as person-oriented counseling. In this manner, the consultation model of process attendance in coaching was able to become well-established. In the so-called solution-oriented consultation, it was even able to develop into a more extreme form, namely that of abstaining from any form of guidance or providing any expert advice.

11.3 The Significance of Expert Advice in Coaching

However, even Schein tempered his position by saying that the provision of expert advice remains appropriate if the client requires any information or expert service which he himself is unable to provide. And this fact plays a much greater role in coaching than most protagonists of solution-oriented approaches assume. This already applies at the beginning during the identification of objectives, as well during further progress for the handling of the client's new patterns of interpretation and behavior.

(1) In fact, in many cases the identification of the objective—i.e. the question of what the client wishes to deal with specifically—is already a point in the consultation process where specialized expertise of the coach is required. We have to realize that clients develop special systems of meaning via their daily interactions through which they see and judge certain issues or problem constellations. They then enter the consultation process with exactly these patterns. And as Bourdieu (1973) already described, these patterns are characterized by an extreme amount of inertia. However, they often become useless for the person in question when they are confronted with new situations or when they experience new problem constellations. For example, psychotherapists, who are used to dealing with the problems of individual persons in their work, also tend to individualize problems which they encounter in their own work. Hence, it is a fundamental duty of the coach to first comprehensively *reconstruct* the issue described by the client. In many cases, it is only through such reconstructions that the problem can be formulated correctly (Schreyögg 2007). Naturally, the coach requires a diverse range of structural patterns for such reconstructions which allow him and the client to examine an issue from multiple perspectives and using multiple paradigms. Hence, for example in the case of conflicts, it has proven to be extremely prudent for the coach to take the initiative to reconstruct an issue which has been described not only as an individual, but also as an interactive and systemic phenomenon.
(2) However, the coach must also include his own specialist expertise later on in the coaching process. As with the formulation of the problem, it will also become apparent when dealing with an issue further along the line that humans continue to hold on to primarily formed patterns of interpretation and behavior. In this case, it is also the coach's duty to encourage a widening or restructuring of these patterns. Suitable for this purpose are e.g. experience- and action-oriented approaches from corresponding processes such as psychodrama and gestalt therapy in conjunction with specialist expertise on the part of the coach.

11.4 On the Relationship Between Intersubjectivity and Symmetry Versus Asymmetry in Coaching

Among counselors, there is a strong tendency to assess dialogical sequences in which counselors, supervisors or coaches provide their specialist expertise to clients as an ethically indisputable objectification of clients. In this case, there is the (mostly) implicit assumption that dominance, such as in the sense of a psycho-educative attitude, includes the objectification of clients. After all, in such sequences, the coach does indeed take on the role of guiding the client, and no longer acts on equal footing with the client.

Two lines of argumentation from practical philosophy/ethics can be used to refute to the idea that dominance is to be equated with objectification.

As Habermas demonstrated in 1981 using psychoanalysis as an example, professional interactions such as psychotherapy and related forms of consultation (which coaching is unquestionably a part of) are special forms of communication. In psychotherapy, the client takes on the role of a psychologically ill person; i.e. a clearly subordinate role in his interaction with the therapist, and the idea is for him to grow stronger through their interaction. Ideally, there then exists symmetry between both parties at the end of the therapy. This is also how it works in coaching: Clients turn to coaching due to a situation where a deficit exists in the hope of being able to eliminate this deficit through the interaction with the coach. Here too, it is the coach's task to help the client reduce or eliminate the deficit altogether. Hence, he will initially need to submit to an asymmetry in order to enable the client to achieve more symmetry through the interaction.

This was already pointed out by the phenomenologist Strasser (1962): that the asymmetry between persons does not necessarily result in objectification. For example, children can absolutely be taken seriously as subjects in their respective developmental stages by their "superior" parents or teachers. This is proven by reports by famous child therapists, such as Bettelheim (1977). Even "confused" schizophrenic patients should ideally be seen as subjects with their own intentions by psychotherapists where their speech and actions are concerned (Laing 1974). This also applies today for qualified work with persons suffering from dementia in old age or nursing homes. For all persons whose self-structuring does not yet function or no longer functions adequately due to their young age or due to illness, the professional helper, as an adult person, is to compensate for the missing self-regulation and/or to promote its continued development. In doing so, the helper takes on responsibility for a person whose subject status, despite the situation, is to be maintained (cf. Schreyögg 2010).

11.5 Which Understanding of Roles Should Be the Standard for a Coach?

From the very beginning, the coach has to fulfill a wide range of roles. He needs to enter into a *dialog* with the client which is primarily characterized by *intersubjectivity*. However, depending on the process step, he practices various forms of *symmetry* versus *asymmetry*, which are in turn characterized by *action* and *reaction* on his part.

- In a first step, the coach is mostly passive and allows his inner self to be touched by the client, who takes the lead with regard to content in this case.
- The coach is now simply receptive to the client and his reactions.
- He then also anticipates his own effects on the client, including verbal and non-verbal aspects.
- In the first sequences of the encounter, the coach will also need to ask a range of questions, i.e. be active in order to connect with the client's issues. However, in this case, there is always a dominance on the part of the client with regard to content.
- Over the course of this question-and-answer sequence, the coach attempts to identify with the client as smoothly and quickly as possible, and while he interacts with him, he attempts to get involved with the client at various levels of his consciousness.
- As the sessions progress, and when the client has more precisely stated his issue, the coach will suggest a suitable methodological measure according to his diagnosis. The client can decide to accept this proposal or not; i.e. each intervention is only an offer for the client.
- During the execution of the intervention, e.g. role-play sessions, the coach will be in charge of the structural management of the interaction, but the client will retain control of the content-related aspects.
- After the completion of the intervention, the coach asks the client to reflect back on what he has just experienced, and what effect and meaning it had on/for him. Here, too, the client remains the master of his own perspectives and realizations etc. The coach only takes a structural lead.

The process in which the professional is comprehensively receptive to the client was called "containment" by Bion (1990) (cf. Sect. 10.3 in this book). In his role theory, Mead (1973) also describes both the conscious and unconscious mutual guidance phenomena between two persons interacting spontaneously. Still, the coach will also need to carefully take into consideration a formal role as a professional consultant in accordance with Parsons' structural role theory (1951, cited in Dreitzel 1979). This includes all expectations placed on him resulting from his education, preparatory training, his professional convictions and professional standards. In this case, he will combine various meaningful methodological approaches from various processes to the client's benefit depending on the issue and his diagnosis. However, the normative basis must always serve to retain the subject status of the client; i.e. he is never to be objectivized by the coach.

Hence, the coach needs to maintain a sensitive balance between various role requirements:

- First of all, there are formal role requirements which guide his regular acting as a professional coach with the corresponding professional patterns of interpretation and behavior.
- However, he also needs to open up as a human being in the sense of containment in order to comprehend the client with all of his senses at all levels of his consciousness.
- Furthermore, he also needs to involve himself as an entire person in his interactions with the client in order to create an authentic relationship as described by Mead.
- In addition to all that, as a professional actor, he needs to repeatedly put himself in an excentric position (Plessner 1966) with regard to the overall situation in order to comprehend the interaction between himself and the client in the respective context, and to guide it professionally.

11.6 A Case Example

I would like to use the following case example to demonstrate the potential variety in the roles of the coach and then use the numbers in brackets to assist in naming the roles:

A 35-year-old medical professional came to me when she wanted to prepare to "sing for her supper", i.e. at an interview at a university. For this purpose, she came to me for a period of two days.

(1) Her concern was as follows: Although she was active in a discipline in which her expertise was practically unrivaled, she was unable to assert herself. Specifically, she had already submitted her documents to two universities and given presentations there, but had not been appointed despite her great number of highly-qualified publications. "Apparently, there is something about me that makes me unsuitable for the position."

(2) We considered a number of possible reasons, including the question of whether she was perhaps unable to gain a foothold because it was a male-dominated field. She then reported that after every appointment procedure, she had contacted an equal opportunity representative, but despite that, she was still not awarded the position.

(3) I then suggested to the client that she should present the presentation that she had prepared for the next round of auditions to me. It was not the content I was interested in, since I would not be able to comprehend most of it anyway, but instead the impression she made during the presentation. Hence, I asked her to imagine that she was in a corresponding presentation setting in my office and to begin.

(4) Suddenly, I had a violently gesticulating young woman who spoke her sentences in a staccato fashion. Almost immediately, I felt a knot in my stomach and the need to gain as much distance between her and myself as possible.

(5) "Stop, stop," I said, now breathing heavily myself, "I feel like I am being clobbered by your rapid-fire speech, why are you going at such a breakneck pace?" "Oh, I always have much too little time to develop my arguments. They are so unusual for my field that I am afraid that they are not listening to me." "But it seems to me that it won't work in this way not at all", I said.

(6) I now explained to her as exactly as possible what sensations I had over the course of her presentation. "I myself felt breathless, as if your hectic pace had infected me somehow. I felt like I was being forced to listen to you and was not allowed to present counter-arguments. Somehow, I had the feeling that you are not ready for any confrontation." The client listened to me with a hurt expression and said "yes, that is true somehow, but what should I do?"

(7) "Let us calmly examine what gets you all hectic and riled up, and then perhaps you can try to give the presentation in an entirely different fashion." She then told me of her origins in a petite bourgeois family of late Romanian repatriates. Her parents and siblings had always found her a little strange with her ambition in school and at university. When she came home, she always had the feeling that they "weren't even listening, and I have to speak quickly, or they'll no longer be paying attention." Even later with

friends, she was always worried "if they are actually listening to me." These experiences led to her being so pushy and penetrating in her presentation.

(8) I now asked her to first take a deep breath so she felt it all the way to her abdomen. In the hour that followed, I first showed her how she could achieve calmer and composure through breathing exercises. Subsequently, I practiced with her how to make her style of speaking appear more inviting to her audience with regard to tone, facial expression, and gestures.

(9) We then once again set up the presentation situation. Furthermore, I asked her to imagine a friendly colleague she knew well, and to once again give her presentation just to this one person. She now came across significantly more adequate. Her voice was lower, she no longer gesticulated around as wildly etc. Furthermore, I asked her to switch roles with this colleague and allow him to speak about her presentation. In the role of this colleague, she made comments of acknowledgment. "Oh, I really need to get feedback on my work more often," she then said. The client then told me that she would soon be giving a presentation at a convention in English in front of an international audience. "That is wonderful", I said, "it will give you the chance to practice for the interview."

(10) We agreed that she would do her breathing exercises half an hour before her presentation in a quiet place and then, when she was in the auditorium, that she would then first imagine that she was giving her speech to that friendly colleague she knew, and that she would consciously interact with that person before later addressing the rest of the audience.

(11) Finally, I asked her how she would be dressed for the presentation as well as the interview. "Well, as I would normally", she said, surprised. "What do you mean by 'normal'?", I ventured. "Oh, the way I am dressed right now." She was wearing a long, dark gray skirt, a blue and yellow blouse, and a blue V-necked sweater. "Really, you intend to go as you are?", I asked incredulously. "Have you seen how women dress for a presentation in your faculty?" "Hmm, yes, once. She was dressed up a little." She then clumsily explained to me that her colleague had worn a dark blue suit with a white blouse matched with white pumps. "She looked good," she said pensively, "but do you think I should get something like that too?" "Maybe," I said. "Think of the impression you want to make on the auditorium. You should definitely dress yourself in order to make that impression." She now seemed to be at a loss, as she had never seriously considered this question before.

(12) Over the course of a longer dialogical sequence, we looked for business wear at various online clothing stores. She then showed a large amount of enthusiasm and expressed great interest in a close-cut dark blue pantsuit

with a white blouse and a band collar. "Oh, that would look good on me, I'll order that online." After this sequence, she expressed her satisfaction and confidence.

A few weeks later, she sent me an e-mail informing me that her presentation was extremely well-received. And half a year later, she wrote me a card that she had received a high-ranking position as a university professor.

In (1): the coach as a process companion, as a passive and active listener
In (2): the coach as an empathic dialog partner, who poses various questions
In (3): the coach as a person who perceives attentively and with great concentration
In (4): the coach as a container
In (5): the coach as someone who confronts
In (6): the coach as a feedback giver
In (7): the coach as an explorer and a passive listener
In (8): the coach as a breathing therapist and trainer
In (9): the coach as a psychodrama leader
In (10): the coach as a trainer
In (11): the coach as a fashion advisor
In (12): the coach as someone who encourages.

11.7 Diversity of Roles as the Basis of Intersubjectivity Despite Plurality of Methods

This case example clearly illustrates that the client, with her issue, generally remains the subject of the coaching interaction. However, the coach varies his behavior between directivity and non-directivity depending on the selected methodological measure. While at the beginning he assumes the role of the process companion and finally the role of a container until the client has explored all avenues of her issue including all its implications, he then switches to a very active role involving support and confrontation, as is common in gestalt therapy. In order to explore the depth of the issue, he then once again assumes the role of the process companion in order to then act in an active role, this time even in that of a trainer. Furthermore, he repeatedly assumes the role of a psychodrama leader by stimulating imagination and eliciting action while in various roles. Finally, the coach even initiates a confrontation with the client about her outfit.

For process companionship, I initially postulated that it is to be managed based on a subject-subject relationship. However, this postulate also applies to the other two processes mentioned, namely gestalt therapy and psychodrama. These two therapeutic procedures both originate from the humanistic psychology, for which the subject-subject relationship forms a foundational basis (Schreyögg 2010). In contrast to Rogers' original intention with regard to non-directivity, these two procedures were already conceived as being directive at the outset. In the later development of what we call client-centered therapy, a relatively directive variant was also developed among the "Rogeranians", which now takes the form of "Focusing" (Gendlin and Wiltschko 2007). This is because here too, practitioners were convinced that intersubjectivity was not to be equated with non-directivity. Furthermore, in the case example, the coach also takes on an expert role. This applies not only to the dialog concerning university issues, but also the guidance provided for appropriate breathing, the conversation about the client's outfit, and of course, for the selection of the semi-therapeutic form of consultation in the coaching sessions.

References

Argyris, C. (1975). Das Individuum und die Organisation: Einige Probleme gegenseitiger Anpassung. In K. Türk (Ed.), *Organisationstheorie*. Wiesbaden: Westdeutscher Verlag.
Bettelheim, B. (1977). *Gespräche mit Müttern*. München: Pieper.
Bion, W. R. (1990). *Lernen durch Erfahrung*. Frankfurt/M.: Suhrkamp (Orig.: *Learning from Experience*. London, 1961).
Birgmeier, B. (Ed.). (2009). *Coachingwissen. Denn sie wissen nicht, was sie tun?*. Wiesbaden: VS Verlag.
Bourdieu, P. (1973). *Die feinen Unterschiede*. Frankfurt/M.: Suhrkamp.
Dreitzel, H. P. (1979). Rollentheorie. In A. Heigl-Evers (Hrsg.), *Lewin und die Folgen*. Die Psychologie des 20. Jahrhunderts, Bd. 7. Zürich: Kindler.
Enoch, C. (2011). Wissensvermittlung in Beratungsprozessen. *OSC, 18*(4), 369–383.
Gendlin, E. T., & Wiltschko, T. (2007). *Focusing in der Praxis. Eine schulenübergreifende Methode für Psychotherapie und Alltag* (3rd ed.). Stuttgart: Klett-Cotta.
Habermas, J. (1981). *Theorie kommunikativen Handelns*, 2. Bd. Frankfurt/M.: Suhrkamp.
Kühl, S., & Moldaschl, M. (Eds.). (2010). *Organisation und Intervention. Ansätze für eine sozialwissenschaftliche Fundierung von Organisationsberatung*. München, Mehring: Hampp.
Laing, R. D. (1974). *Das geteilte Selbst*. Erice: Editione Continua (orig.: *The Divided Self. An existential study on sanity and madness*, 1960).
Lewin, K. (1947). Subjective and objective elements in the social field. Three steps procedure. *Human Relations, 1*, 5–41.

Likert, R. (1975). *Die integrierte Führungs- und Organisationsstruktur*. Frankfurt/M.: Campus.
Lippmann, E. (Ed.). (2005). *Coaching. Angewandte Psychologie für die Beratungspraxis*. Heidelberg: Springer.
Mead, G. H. (1973). *Geist, Identität und Gesellschaft*. Frankfurt/M.: Suhrkamp (orig.: *Mind, Self, and Society*. Chicago 1934).
Plessner, H. (1966). Soziale Rolle und menschliche Natur. In Ders. (Hrsg.), *Diesseits der Utopie. Ausgewählte Beiträge zur Kultursoziologie*. Düsseldorf: Diederichs.
Radatz, S. (2000). *Beratung ohne Ratschlag: Systemisches Coaching für Führungskräfte und BeraterInnen*. Wien: Verlag systemisches Management.
Rauen, C. (Ed.). (2005). *Handbuch coaching*. Göttingen: Hogrefe.
Reddy, W. B. (1997). *Prozessberatung von Kleingruppen. Wie der Berater erfolgreich interveniert*. Leonberg: Rosenberger.
Rogers, C. R. (1972). *Die klientenzentrierte Gesprächspsychotherapie*. München: Kindler (orig.: *Client-centered Therapy*. Boston: Houghton Mifflin).
Schein, E. H. (2000). *Prozessberatung für die Organisation der Zukunft*. Köln: EHP (orig.: *Process consultation revisited*. Reading, Mass.: Addison-Wesley, 1999).
Schreyögg, A. (2007). Wie viele „Brillen" verwenden Berater? Zur Bedeutung von Mehrperspektivität in Supervision, Organisationsberatung und Coaching. In A. Schreyögg & C. Schmidt-Lellek (Eds.), *Konzepte des Coaching (OSC Sonderheft 1* (pp. 91–116). Wiesbaden: VS Verlag.
Schreyögg, A. (2010). Ist Coaching reine Prozessberatung oder sind hier auch andere Beratungsmodelle relevant? *OSC, 17*(2), 119–133.
Strasser, S. (1962). *Phänomenologie und die Erfahrungswissenschaft vom Menschen*. Berlin: de Gruyter.

Author Biography

Dr. phil. Astrid Schreyögg Dipl.-Psych., psychotherapist, supervisor, coach; head of research at the German Academy of Psychologists of the BDP for Supervision and Coaching; domestic and international fellow; trainer for supervision and coaching; textbook author; publisher of the journal "Organisationsberatung, Supervision, Coaching" (OSC).

Competency Requirements for Coaches

12

Ingo Steinke

Abstract

This article is concerned with the competencies a coach is required to have. Competency has become a core concept in further education and corporate management, particularly in the selection, evaluation, and development of human resources. In everyday language, people are said to be competent when they make the impression of being truly capable. In addition, we need to be able to answer the question of what are important coaching competencies. This question is also important for further education in coaching: With which competencies should a coach be equipped in order to be regarded as competent? Is "competency" even the right term here for the result of further education, or should we instead be speaking of requirements, qualifications, and teaching and course content? This article offers answers to these questions.

What is the purpose of addressing the issue of competency with regard to coaching? (1) Competency has become a core concept in further education and corporate management, particularly in the selection, evaluation, and development of human resources, such as when competency models are being referred to. This is certainly related to the fact that competency always implies a judgment of quality: In everyday language, people are said to be competent when they make the impression of being truly capable. (2) As a coach, the question is: Am I competent (for this task)? In addition, a coach needs to be able to answer the question of what are important coaching competencies. (3) Furthermore, when coaching quality and

I. Steinke (✉)
COATRAIN, Graustr. 1, 21029 Hamburg, Germany
e-mail: i.steinke@coatrain.de
URL: http://www.coatrain.de

A. Schreyögg and C. Schmidt-Lellek (eds.), *The Professionalization of Coaching*, DOI 10.1007/978-3-658-16805-6_12

quality management in coaching are being discussed, people often speak of particular (often controversial) competencies a coach should have which are regarded as crucial for the quality of coaching. (4) This leads to yet another important point: Coaching in further education and in teaching. Those who provide training should consider what kind of training is being provided. Which competencies should an aspiring coach be equipped with in order to be regarded as competent? Is "competency" even the right term here for the result of further education, or should the reference be to requirements, qualifications, and teaching and course content (cf. Krautz 2009)? Thus, it would be helpful to take a closer look at the concept of competency.

12.1 The Concept of Competency—Historical Background

The words "competency", "competent" and "competence" are derived from the Latin word *competere*, which has several meanings: (1) to be capable of something, to suffice for something, (2) to be entitled to something, to be due to someone. This explains the double meaning: On the one hand, competence/competency means the same thing as skill or ability ("The project manager is competent enough to manage this task"), while on the other hand it also means jurisdiction, authority (e.g. "This decision does not lie within the project manager's competence").

The evolution of the concept of competency encompasses various disciplines in the social sciences. According to Heckhausen (1989) and Oerter and Montada (1995), it was White (1959) who introduced the concept of competency in the field of psychology: White sees "a primary motivation of humans as experiencing themselves as effectors; as causers of changes in their environment. (…) Competency is the result of a fundamental *effectance motive* to grapple with the environment ceaselessly in order to assert one's own effectiveness" (Heckhausen 1989, p. 362, 457). Ultimately, this leads to a *sense of competence* and *self-determination*. Thus, striving towards competency is explained as resulting from basic motives, and can already be observed in small children. The feeling of competency exists when "people attempt to affect the environment in a targeted, selective and persistent manner in order to achieve certain desired consequences" (Oerter and Montada 1995, p. 1127f).

One milestone in the field of pedagogy was marked by Heinrich Roth, who significantly shaped the concept of competency in this field. He introduced three competencies as identifying characteristics for a person's maturity or ability to assume responsibility: (a) *self-competence*, which is the ability to act for yourself in a responsible manner, (b) subject-matter competency, which is the ability to be able to judge and make decisions in various matters, thereby being able to assume responsibility for them, and (c) social competency, which refers to the ability to judge and make decisions in material or social areas that are socially, societally and politically relevant, as well as be able to assume responsibility for them" (Roth 1971, p. 180).

However, it is McClelland who is seen as the founder of the modern competencies movement in psychology: Inspired by the competency-based education movement which began in the US in 1970, he developed a method for identifying the *actual success-relevant characteristics for a job* which go beyond exam grades and (talent and) test results. He called these characteristics competency variables (McClelland 1973; Sarges 2001). From this arose, via a number of different stages (in particular Boyatzis 1982; Spencer and Spencer 1993), a widespread movement in academia and in organizational practice which focused on developing the appropriate competency structures for various purposes—so-called competency models—which up until the present day "are often generated intuitively and without reference to well-established expertise and knowledge from organizational psychology" (Krumm et al. 2012, p. 1).

Today, competency is commonly defined as a "*professionally or job-relevant, behaviour-related and measurable characteristic of a person*" (Sarges 2001). Hence, a competency is simultaneously an aspect of personality, linked to behaviour, job-related—and hence also specific to a particular role. This means that competency is not clearly distinguished from the terms value, motive, attitude, characteristic, behaviour, and performance. But what we should always bear in mind is: Competency is a construct, a *disposition*. It cannot be observed directly. The only thing that can be observed is its effect, namely actions. But they must first be turned into indicators of competencies so that it is possible to speak of competencies. Therefore, from a social psychology standpoint, competency is also always something that someone attributes to a person. In other words, it is a projection. When in doubt, competency tells us more about the person who recognizes it than the person who has it. This is something that designers of competency models within companies should take into account more strongly.

Hence, for persons who are attempting to identify competencies, it is recommended that they first collect *characteristic indicators* (Sarges 2001), which are generally concretely identifiable behaviours, today called *behavioural* anchors. This collection should always be carried out by experienced persons who have a good understanding of the job for which competencies are being developed. The indicators are clustered and a term is searched for which truly expresses the *common denominator* of the collection. If it is possible to add the words "ability" or "capacity" to this term (e.g. problem-solving ability, evaluation capacity)—at least conceptually, a position close to a competency has been reached. (Other syllables in English include "-ivity" or "-ability", such as sensitivity or sociability.) In this manner, it is even possible to develop competencies company-wide (generic competence models; cf. Sarges 2001); this is not detrimental to the quality of a competency model. Naturally, this presupposes that it is possible to develop both domain-specific and role-specific behavioural anchors. This means that for example customer orientation means something different for a salesman than for a project manager. In the meantime, the competency clusters created can be very well validated with the aid of theoretical constructs in the social sciences, or with the aid of psychological tests or other instruments for competency measurement (for an overview see for example Sarges 1995; Erpenbeck and von Rosenstiel 2007).

12.2 Requirements and Aptitude Instead of Competencies

It should be mentioned that the concept of competency that is prevalent in the English-speaking world has not met with much acceptance in the German-speaking world. Instead, people here speak of qualifications and requirements. While people in Germany are used to proving their qualifications in the form of certificates according to the motto "Show me what certifications you have and I'll believe that you can do it," the principle in the English-speaking world is generally "Show me that you can do it and I'll believe that you're the one for the job." However, by the 1990s, it was already apparent in the field of professional education in Germany that a shift had taken place from professional qualifications to professional competency; i.e. the ability to actually work successfully in a particular area of responsibility (cf. Arnold 1997). Similarly, the current definition of the term "professional qualification" also points in this direction: "An overarching term for all performance-related characteristics of a person for successfully mastery of work-related requirements. Primary characteristics generally include specific expertise, action competency, and skills" (Greif 2014). Even before the PISA studies, there has been a continual emphasis placed on the necessity to shift away from the current "input-orientation" in curricula, teaching materials and methods to an "output- orientation" of educational standards, which are to be defined in the form of verifiable competencies (Schott and Ghanbari 2008, p. 9). According to this, teachers should teach in such a manner that during lessons participants have the opportunity to learn the things they will need to be competent in after the lesson. Furthermore, tests and examinations should be competency-oriented; i.e. test learning in ways that show the extent to which participants have actually achieved the competencies which were the objective of the lesson. Are these also standards that should be used in further education courses for coaching? (for a critique of this approach cf. Krautz 2009).

Notable representatives from the field of work and organizational psychology in the German-speaking world rarely speak of competencies; instead, they speak of requirements: requirements which apply to personal characteristics, to behaviour, job-specific and overarching requirements, and requirements for certain roles such as management personnel. In the DIN standard 33430:2002, which defines the standards for judging professional aptitude, the word "competency" does not appear. "In general, 'aptitude' always means an aptitude for something," postulates Schuler (1996, pp. 59–69), among others. And this something should be "described in such a way that it can be contrasted with the relevant characteristics of persons" (ibid.). For this, a work and requirements analysis is required at the task level, the behavioural level (also the importance, frequency or duration of behaviour) and the characteristics level (which can be identified through, for example, psychological test procedures). The analysis then takes place either in an experience-led and intuitive manner (dealing with the "material" of the tasks), in an analytical, job-related and empirical manner (e.g. formalized in the form of a survey booklet), or person-specific and empirically (e.g. in the form of tests).

The concept of requirements contrasts the person and the situation more strongly with each other: This is the manager, those are the requirements. "I'll try to fulfil the requirements then," is the reflex that frequently results. The person can, rather impartially, start attempting to fulfil requirements– or question them. The concept of competency shifts the requirements more strongly towards personality and then more or less "tacks" them onto a person. "He is X and can do Y", is often the resulting knee-jerk reaction. Or the other way round: "He is an introvert, how will he ever be able to sell himself?" The concept of competency generally ignores the category of possible behaviour (Holzkamp 1985, pp. 234–237); i.e. the extent to which, in (the sense of) a particular profession, organization and situation mechanisms for getting things done and possible ways of behaving in order to act in a competent manner are available. Furthermore, competencies have a positive connotation per se and are harder to question than requirements. People are exposed to the suspicion of being incompetent, and who wants to do that? By contrast, requirements can be either correct or false. The meaning of requirements offers more possibilities for consciously viewing oneself in relation to them and accepting or rejecting them.

12.3 Competency and Behavioural Context

Hence, Reischmann (2004, p. 1) recommends defining competency as a "reflected ability to act in a describable, action-facilitating context, which also includes responsibilities and resources as external factors." This is important to avoid inadmissible personalization or psychological analysis precisely where coaching is being carried out. After all, coaching often takes place in a context that can range from action-facilitating to action-impeding. Distinguishing between possibilities and impossibilities, which themselves in turn could lead to other possibilities—this is what coaching is all about. This definition is also interesting because a person's role also comes into play; i.e. the responsibilities and resources connected with a certain role. And suddenly competency once again has this double meaning of "capable" and "authorized to do something". But this would mean that competency does not exist without a specific context! How would it then be possible in principle to judge if a coach were competent in general? Or develop a competency model for the further education of coaches, when they work in such greatly varied fields as senior management, commercial production, psychiatry and the church? Do these environments all have something in common?

Sarges (2001) is of the opinion that the concepts of competency and requirements do not differ in any significant fashion. However, he sees requirements analyses as being past-oriented, while competencies also allow strategically relevant requirements to be integrated into them which can be related to the desired future situation and, in this manner, equip companies for the future. He prefers competencies, as "competencies are often formulated much more strongly in the language of the working world than in concepts of disposition or ability in psychology" (ibid.). He also points out that competencies are easier to measure, as they are more personality-specific, and thus more enduring complexes of characteristics. Krumm et al. (2012, p. 12) are also in favour of integrating both approaches for reasons of practicality: Competency clusters form something like a surface structure, while the underlying structure is made up of specific requirements and observable behaviour. This makes particular sense when designing specific, operational competency models.

Furthermore, this is also related to a further debate, namely the debate on "organizational capabilities" and recently also on "dynamic capabilities" in the field of business management. However, this refers to the specific, unique—often strategically significant—competencies of a company which are responsible for its success. "Today, when we speak of competencies in strategic management, we are talking about templates for combining resources or problem-solving architectures that have proven to be successful. These paradigms of action are of historical origin, intrinsically complex and difficult to comprehend, but have repeatedly made success possible" (Schreyögg and Kliesch-Eberl 2012). In this case, once again the way competencies are embedded in an "action-facilitating context" is being through to the end. For present purposes, this shows that "a good coach" is by no means good and suitable for every corporate context, but must first demonstrate competency in a particular (strategic) field of action in a specific company.

12.4 Structural Models for Coaching Competencies

When searching for a structural model, the question that should be asked is: What do we see as being of crucial importance and how do we categorize and structure coaching competencies independent of specific contexts, i.e. before making selections and placing emphases in a context-specific manner?

12.4.1 Key Qualifications and Core Competencies

The extent to which the discussion of competencies diverges is shown by a movement within organizational psychology led by John Erpenbeck, Volker Heyse, and Lutz von Rosenstiel, who reserve the concept of competency, entirely in contrast to "organizational capabilities", for something which previously used to be called a "key qualification" (Mertens 1974; Lang 2000; Eilles-Matthiessen et al. 2007). Erpenbeck and von Rosenstiel (2007) define competency as a meta-ability which makes it possible to deal with fundamental abilities and skills. They base this, among other things, on the European Qualifications Framework (European Commission 2006). According to this qualifications framework, competency is the "proven ability to utilize knowledge, skills, as well as personal, social, and/or methodological skills in work or learning situations and for professional and/or personal development" (ibid., p. 17ff.). In this context, they define the following (2007, p. XI): "Competencies are self-organization dispositions of mental and object-related action." Despite support for the self-organization debate in constructivism and systems theory (cf. Probst 1987)—self-organization is insufficient to serve as a central determining characteristic for competency. Viability (Glasersfeld 1996, p. 43), the "usefulness of reality constructs" as a point of reference for behavioural competency, would have been better in this case. The concept put forward by Erpenbeck et al. is also at an entirely different level from the definitions which have been discussed so far. They distinguish between what they call competency classes:

(1) Personal competencies (loyalty, normative and ethical attitude, credibility, individual responsibility)
(2) Activity- and implementation-oriented action competencies (drive, mobility, readiness to act, initiative)
(3) Socio-communicative competencies (communicative ability, cooperation skills, relationship management, adaptability)
(4) Expert and methodological competencies (expert knowledge, knowledge of the market, planning behaviour, cross-disciplinary knowledge).

In addition, they also name 48 additional competencies which can simultaneously be categorized into two of the competency classes just mentioned (ibid., p. 512). While doing this they emphasize that the concept of competency they use is "to be explicitly distinguished from the concepts, which originate in professional education and are often used among the general public, of material, methodological, social, and personal competency "(ibid., p. XIII). But this is not entirely correct. Furthermore, it strongly resembles the concept of key qualifications: "Key qualifications are cross-disciplinary competencies for shaping current and future work and life situations" (Eilles-Matthiessen et al. 2007, p. 15). Key qualifications are seen as a combination of personality traits, abilities and skills which centre around work-relevant and economically relevant requirements and, due to societal changes, are subject to dynamic shifts (ibid., p. 18). The general self-organizational competencies and/or key competencies previously mentioned contain interesting elements, but are insufficient for a succinct description of coaching competencies. In this case, we notice that competencies obviously not only need to be formulated for a specific organizational, company-specific action context, but also require a certain proximity to the relevant occupational field.

12.4.2 Requirements for Further Education in Coaching

In their study on further education courses in coaching, *Stiftung Warentest* (a prominent German consumer organization which investigates and compares goods) chose to formulate requirements without a competency model. These were requirements further education courses in coaching, and indirectly also qualified coaches, were to fulfil. The organization listed a total of 13 dimensions: (1) basic professional ethical and coaching principles, (2) the coaching process, (3) coaching settings, (4) role competency, (5) psychology, (6) change and career development (7) coaching techniques, (8) personal competency, (9) positioning in professional field, (10) organizational competency, (11) leadership and management, (12) crisis management, (13) conflict management (cf. text inset, p. 8).

These criteria appear to be a collection of widely varying topics and competencies. To the credit of those who designed this study, they did intensively inform themselves about the curricula and learning materials of various further education institutes, after which they put together a panel of experts to discuss and validate the essentials of these concepts. The study appears to be free of ideology, to include all institutes, and be independent of any professional association, which all speak in its favour. It focuses on three things that have not received sufficient attention in either academic or practice-oriented discussions on coaching to date:

- Coaching and further education in coaching need to involve a plurality of methods. However, the sociological concept of a profession already requires this (cf. Chap. 1 in this book). Philosophies or tools from only one single school or school of thought in the social sciences are insufficient.
- Coaching requires not only psychological and/or psychotherapeutic methodological competency, but also coaching-specific know-how from organization theory and management theory (coaching expertise).
- Coaching exists in the form of various coaching variants. It is no longer appropriate to speak of "coaching" or show how "coaching" functions in demonstrations. For example, conflict coaching involves different approaches, techniques (tools) and attitudes from career coaching. In coaching, friction does not arise between different schools of thought in the social sciences, but instead between different coaching variants, which need to be distinguished from each other and taught differently.

Criteria for good further education courses in coaching according to *Stiftung Warentest*

(1) *Fundamentals*: This includes an introduction to professional ethical principles, values and attitudes, an overview of disciplines related to coaching such as psychotherapy and mediation, as well as issues concerning occupational law and drafting contracts.

(2) *Sequence of events in coaching and phases of coaching*: The focus here is on the course of events in a coaching process, from initial contact to identification of the objective and tasks at hand, all the way to planning

individual sessions and methods for identifying the objective and tasks at hand.

(3) *Settings*: The various constellations in which coaching can take place such as individual, team, or group coaching are to be examined.

(4) *Role concepts*: All coaches need to be conscious of their role as a coach. They also need to clearly recognize the various role aspects which are relevant in the client's professional life and be able to include them in the reflection. For this purpose, coaches need to deal with the subject of role concepts.

(5) *Psychological aspects*: Coaching has a lot to do with psychology. That is why topics such as basic principles of personality development and behaviour modification as well as the development and analysis of potential should also be taken into consideration. It is also important to clearly distinguish between coaching and psychotherapy.

(6) *Processes of change*: People who attend coaching sessions are generally seeking to change themselves on a professional or personal level. This means prospective coaches should have comprehensive knowledge of professional transitions, life paths, and career paths.

(7) *Intervention techniques and tools*: Participants should become acquainted with a sufficient number of the many existing intervention techniques and tools. These include methods of building a good relationship with their client, techniques for identifying the objective and tasks at hand, and of course questioning and feedback techniques.

(8) *Personal competency*: The qualification course should help every participant develop a professional attitude as a coach. This includes approaching clients in an unbiased and respectful manner. Self-reflection, self-criticism and willingness to work on oneself are also aspects for which awareness must be raised in a course.

(9) *Positioning in the occupational field*: Those who wish to make a living as a coach will need a coaching concept, a network, and a marketing strategy in order to obtain clients. A qualification course should also help them with these aspects of the profession.

(10) *Organizations*: Participants should become familiar with various types of companies and organizations (e.g. profit/non-profit) as well as being made aware of a range of corporate cultures and typical stress triggers in organizations.

(11) *Leadership and management*: Coaches need to be acquainted with various management styles and also be able to help their clients work out their own understanding of management, as well as provide them with support in

increasing their management skills. The differences between men and women in management should also be discussed.

(12) *Crises*: Conflicts can turn into crises. It is therefore important that prospective coaches also gain proficiency in dealing with emotions. Coaches should be able to be able to distinguish a non-pathological crisis from a serious psychological disorder. In the case of the latter, the matter is no longer within the coach's purview. Furthermore, a coach should have a good knowledge of stress and stress management.

(13) *Conflicts*: A client's conflicts may also be an issue in coaching. Therefore, prospective coaches may sometimes need to study the diagnosis and handling of conflicts as well as conflict management in an organizational context.

However, the summary of *Stiftung Warentest*'s requirements also reveals that a theoretical foundation is lacking—i.e. a metatheory of coaching (cf. Schreyögg 2012, p. 160ff.) with which it would be possible to justify why which competencies and content are important. It exists implicitly for most coaches and further education providers for coaching, but is rarely made explicit. It can be expected that various metatheories will appear over the coming years—initial attempts have already been made (cf. Backhausen and Thommen 2006)—which will then give rise to the corresponding understanding and/or models of competency.

12.4.3 Competency Certification for Coaches?

Roth (1971) was the first to introduce a type of structural model through his categorization into material, self- and social competency. Hülshoff (1996) builds on this and defines action competency as (a) expert competency (possessing expert knowledge, being able to utilize this knowledge in a manner appropriate to the situation, and being prepared for expert discussions), (b) methodological competency (knowing which path to take, being able and willing to take this path), (c) *social competency* (being able to perceive thoughts, feelings, and attitudes, being able to make oneself understood in a situation- and person-specific manner, and being willing to work towards understanding) and (d) *personal competency* (having a realistic world view, being able to act according to one's own convictions, and being willing to take social responsibility) (Hülshoff 1996).

It is exactly this structural model of competencies which serves as the foundation for a DIN standard—the DIN SPEC (PAS 1029:2008)—Field of competency, individual coaching, of the German Institute for Standardization (DIN 2008, pp. 18–23): This is a technical rule (PAS = publicly available specification), which basically contains a list of (a) expert competencies, (b) methodological competencies, (c) social competencies, (d) personal competencies, and (e) professional action competencies (perception competency, communication competency, reflection competency) on four pages. Coaches who possess the competencies listed in PAS 1029 can indicate this by using the DIN institute's logo, although this guideline is not a quality standard in a conventional sense, but instead simply a list of competencies. Accredited authorities can use these guidelines as a basis for carrying out personal certification as long as they themselves are recognized according to the international ISO 17024 standard, which defines standards for authorities which certify persons (cf. German Institute for Standardization 2002). In this case, coaches who have had their competencies approved are allowed to call themselves "DIN-Certified Business Coaches", which I find rather misleading. This is misleading because the PAS standard is not a DIN quality standard in the conventional understanding of the word. Further education institutes for coaching use it in advertising to, promise a competitive edge for course participants—in a manner which is often no less misleading: "ISO makes the difference—for clients, partners, and employers. Get in the (career) fast lane with ISO (…) The ISO certification 17024—Competency certification for coaches—is a professional certification program for coaches" (from a flyer from a member of the quality conference of further education providers for coaching of the DBVC).

The PAS 1029:2008 defines the various fields of competency as follows:

(1) *Expert competency* is understood as the ability required for dealing with things (methods, instruments, knowledge) and carrying out specialized tasks, which in addition to theoretical knowledge also includes practical know-how (general knowledge and relevant preliminary knowledge), and requires intellectual and manual skills and abilities.
(2) *Methodological competency* is understood as the knowledge and mastery of various methods (planned procedures) which can be used to successfully complete tasks set in changing situations when dealing with things, persons, and groups, as well as to solving problems. Methodological competency includes acquisition strategies and/or learning strategies, metacognition for reflection and monitoring, as well as organizational strategies (design of the learning environment, time management, utilization of information sources).

It is necessary for the planning, management, examination and safeguarding of processes, procedures, and sequences in a company.

(3) *Social competency* is understood as the ability which makes it possible for a person to act successfully and react appropriately when approaching another person or interacting with others. Hence, it includes the ability to perceive thoughts, feelings and attitudes and to make oneself understood in a situation- and person-specific manner, as well as being willing to work towards understanding. Social competency refers to the ability to deal with conflict, make and maintain contact, and to work in a team.

(4) *Personal competency* can be understood as the ability to act for oneself in a responsible manner. This includes aspects such as value systems, the development of motives and self-image, but also self-assessment, aptitude, motivation, and creativity. It also includes autonomous experience (freedom of action is experienced positively), competency experience (experiencing self-efficacy), effort (endurance, comprehensiveness of knowledge, desire to quit), motivation (curiosity, setting your own objectives, interest), and attention (concentrating on the goal).

(5) *Professional action competency* specifies expert, methodological, social, and personal competencies involved in competency-based quality aspects which are important to a coach:

    (a) *Perception competency* is concerned with the sensibility for current psychological situations and the mental state of a person, or the ability to perceive verbal and non-verbal signals. In this case, the authors also understand this as the ability to recognize emotions as the totality of physical reaction patterns, feelings, evaluative thoughts and behavioural patterns.
    (b) *Communication competency* is concerned with communicative paradigms of action for the creation of relationships between persons, things, and topics in a specific situation. It includes the ability to maintain communications particularly in difficult situations.
    (c) *Reflection competency* includes analytical ability as well as the ability to examine situations or scientific findings with regard to a goal or a certain question or issue. It also refers to the ability to self-reflect (evaluation) (DIN 2008, pp. 18–19).

When the minimum requirements with which each field of competency is operationalized (see text box) are examined it is striking that hardly any more competencies are formulated here. Instead, it involves topics and training content which every coach should know and also be capable of implementing. Hence, the PAS appears to be more of a curriculum for further education in coaching than a competency model. It appears instead to be a standardization of further education content which institutes that produce "DIN-certified coaches" can use as an orientation. There is no clear-cut distinction between expert and methodological competencies: A part of expert competency is the ability to utilize methods and instruments (theoretical knowledge and practically applicable know-how), while methodological competency is introduced as involving familiarity with and mastery of various methods which can be used to successfully complete tasks and solve problems. In this context, expert competency would be better defined as "specialist knowledge from social science disciplines" and methodological competency as "coaching process knowledge", i.e. as knowledge of what needs to be done in which phase of a coaching process, and how. But this is insufficient as defining the methodological competency of a coach. Perceptual competency and communication competency are very well-described, but should clearly be categorized as part of personal and social competency. Reflection competency is inadequately defined, yet it represents a significant area of expertise which touches upon or pervades all other fields of competency, as can be seen at the end of the following summary.

Minimal requirements for each field of competency as defined in the PAS 1029:2008
Expert competency

- understands and is able to implement the roles and tasks in the field of coaching
- is familiar with various coaching approaches
- understands and is able to implement the legal and formal aspects in the field of coaching
- understands and is able to evaluate and select important methods, procedures and diagnostic instruments used in science and in practice
- is familiar with and able to utilize questioning techniques
- is familiar with and able to utilize the applicable intervention techniques in coaching, as well as their limits
- is familiar with and able to utilize methods and knowledge related to identifying and formulating an objective, as well as subsequently coming up with a concrete plan of action

- is familiar with the fundamentals of leadership, psychology, stress and conflict management, and organizational and personal development, and is able to use them to develop client-oriented approaches
- is familiar with and able to utilize various communication techniques.

Methodological competency

- Is able to determine if coaching is the right instrument, if the coach is suitable for the task at hand, and if all required general conditions are fulfilled before beginning a coaching measure
- able to analyse the initial situation and evaluate the chances that a coaching measure will succeed
- able to set realistic goals and specify concrete success and measurement criteria for evaluation, as well as communicate realistic expectations with regard to the objective identified, as well as provide an outlook on the possible scenarios
- able to make it possible for the person being coached to work out his or her own approaches and a concrete plan of action
- able to create documentation that includes the objectives and plan of action
- able to help the person being coached to put a plan into action
- able to carry out a regular evaluation (current vs. target comparison) as well as determine the result in a closing evaluation
- able to achieve a transfer of the results to the professional and/or private environment
- able to recognize changes in the context of the task at hand and integrate them into the coaching sessions
- able to manage him- or herself.

Social competency

- ability to recognize the rights of other persons without restrictions and to orient him- or herself accordingly
- able to build up a respectful and trustful relationship
- able to act in a responsible and confident manner
- ability to collaborate with a social attitude that is cooperative, goal-directed, and helpful
- is perceptive with regard to other people and able to perceive their needs, accept their opinions in a tolerant manner and reflect on them
- ability to behave towards others in a manner that is understanding, cooperative, and considerate

- able to work in a solution-oriented manner and show fairness when doing so
- possesses the ability to deal with conflict, make and maintain contact, and to work in a team.
- able to utilize linguistic, professional and intercultural competencies in a manner beneficial for the person being coached.

Personal competency

- ability to perceive and reflect upon him- or herself (person, role, organization)
- able to act in a responsible manner
- able to carry out a realistic self-assessment and orient his or her own actions accordingly
- able to responsibly regulate his or her own experience of autonomy, competency, and effort
- able to include motivation and attentiveness in the coaching process.

Perception competency

- possesses psychological sensitivity and is able to show it
- ability to perceive verbal and non-verbal signals
- able to recognize, reflect on, and communicate emotions (physical reaction patterns, evaluative thoughts, and corresponding behavioural patterns).

Communication competency

- able to build relationships between persons, things, and topics through communication
- ability to maintain communication even in difficult situations.

Reflection competency

- ability to analyse and examine situations and scientific findings with regard to a goal or certain question or issue
- able to carry out a self-evaluation as part of self-reflection, and implement the findings
- able to reflect on and evaluate his or her own role in the coaching process
- able to reflect on the environment, the person being coached as a person, his or her roles and how he or she is embedded in the organization

- able to assess the relationship with the person being coached, the client, the course of events in the coaching process and the influence of the environment.

12.4.4 Competency Model for Coaching Leadership Personnel

One of the few empirical investigations on the topic by Merz and Frey (2011) is more consistent than the PAS in identifying and defining coaching competencies. For this purpose, the authors surveyed experts and closely examined a comprehensive selection of published literature to ascertain which competencies are mentioned as being necessary for coaches. Their "Empirically based competency model for the field of coaching for leadership personnel" (title) also referred to a subcategorization of professional action competency into (a) expert competencies, (b) methodological competencies, (c) social competencies and (d) self- or personal competency, and they justified this using a statement from Kauffeld (2006): "This subcategorization from real-life professional practice is clearly consistent with theoretically sound systematizations of learner outcomes in professional training measures in Anglo-American literature and has more or less established itself in practice." With reference to multiple authors (Bergmann 1999; Sonntag 2004; Sonntag and Schaper 2006), they describe what they call the competence dimensions they identified in their study as follows (Merz and Frey 2011, p. 26ff.):

(1) *Professional action competency* is "the ability of an employee to, on the one hand, comprehend the increasing complexity of the professional environment, and on the other, to shape it via targeted, self-confident, reflected and responsible actions."
(2) *Expert competencies* refer to the "knowledge, skills and abilities which apply across professions and organizations, but which are also task- and job-specific; (…) the ability to solve problems using expert knowledge and technical skills, (or more generally), all specific knowledge, skills and abilities which are required to carry out tasks belonging to a particular job."
(3) *Methodological competency* is defined as "cognitive abilities which apply across all situations and which can be used flexibly, which enable a person to deal with tasks independently, (…) the ability to make methods and tools available in order to handle tasks and to utilize these methods and tools."

(4) *Social competency* refers to “communicative and cooperative modes of behaviour or skills which allow goals to be achieved in social interaction situations; (i.e.) the ability to successfully interact with others in social situations.”
(5) *Self- or personal competence* comprises “personality dispositions which manifest themselves in the form of attitudes, values, needs and motives. They apply primarily to the motivational and emotional management of professional decision-making and behaviour.”

Merz and Frey’s concept is factually well-researched, and (in my opinion) it meticulously summarizes all available opinions and publications on coaching competencies to date—even from international research contexts. At the same time, it is apparent that the competencies are not always located on the same level of abstraction. When speaking of, for instance, “cognitive abilities” or “emotional intelligence”, it is clear that these are located on a different level from for example “counselling methods” (questioning techniques, active listening) or “dealing with resistance effectively”. However, Merz and Frey’s work serves as a good starting point for example developing a specific competence model in the committees of associations or other groups of coaches, as well as in companies that are establishing organization-internal coaching. This refers both to an overarching structural model as well as core competencies for coaching, as well as behavioural anchors which define and operationalize the competencies.

But it is surprising that, despite surveying experts, including practitioners, Merz and Frey assign field competency only a very low level of importance by subcategorizing it under expert competency as one of many points. In the debate on supervision, the relevance of field competency was already established in the mid-1980s: “In addition to subject competency and counselling competency, field competency is discussed as a fundamental competency of a supervisor. Beginning with the guiding principle that field orientation and method orientation, in a state of polar tension, have contributed to the professionalization of social work, (…) maintaining the distinction between field and method is today seen as being below the required professional standard. Correspondingly, field competency is defined as the perception, understanding, and active contribution to a particular specific field dynamic. Field dynamics are defined as the interaction between client dynamics, professional dynamics, and institutional dynamics” (Berker 1992). Field competency includes implicit experiential knowledge and abilities for dealing with the specific culture of a professional field, an industry, an organization, or a company. This experiential knowledge has not always been fully reflected on and is not always accessible. However, it allows the coach to plug into a social system and the standards which apply there, achieve acceptance for himself as a person and his intervention, to interpret the processes and cultural phenomena relevant for his client in an adequate fashion, and to include them in the coaching process.

12.5 Competency Requirements

The danger of lapsing into a normative discourse is considerable when discussing coaching competencies. What does being competent entail? Which coach can still be seen as being competent? In my opinion, we are still far from being able to answer these questions in a matter that is theoretically or scientifically well-founded. Hence, I advocate speaking of competency requirements: Requirements can be accepted or rejected from a critical and reflective distance. The competency requirements for coaches will be different, regardless of whether we like this practice or not: Depending on the competency model which a coach, a further education provider for coaching or a company uses, differing competencies will be emphasized. The following outline can serve as a general framework for a discussion on coaching competencies.

In this case, we define *coaching competency* as the *ability to reflect and act* in the context of person-oriented dialogical counselling of persons in the working world. By doing so, we emphasize on the one hand an activity- and/or action-orientation, i.e. the ability to practice or implement something. This also refers to "the ability to integrate one's own emotions, motivations, abilities and experiences and all other competencies (…) into one's own impulses of will and to successfully realize actions" (Erpenbeck and von Rosenstiel 2007, p. XXIV). On the other hand, we also emphasize (self-) reflectivity in social relationships and "conscious behaviour towards" conditions, meanings, and possible courses of action. They are not activity determinants for a coach; he is "by no means rigid in his actions, … (but instead) always has the 'alternative' to not act or to act differently" (Holzkamp 1985, p. 235ff). This also includes being able to reflect on when, how, and why a course of action or "reacting this way" is appropriate (cf. Reischmann 2004, p. 6). All too often, coaching goes no further than providing the client with the results of this (self-) reflection without the use of special methods.

This coaching competency comprises multiple components (Fig. 12.1): (1) subject-matter competency, (2) methodological competency, (3) social and communicative competency, (4) personal competency, (5) field and role competency (cf. *Stiftung Warentest* text inset, p. 8).

(1) *Subject-matter competency* is the ability to be able to reflect on and make judgment calls within the confines of certain expert fields or areas. Coaching requires knowledge structures, primarily from the social sciences. We need to select and define what these structures are. In this case, Buer (Chap. 9 in this book) speaks of explanatory knowledge; i.e. being able to categorize and evaluate interpretative aids from the sciences and research in a meaning-oriented manner (cf. Erpenbeck and von Rosenstiel 2007, p. XXIV). Subject-matter competency also provides a coach with the background for reflection and interpretation: A coach needs to be able to understand and categorize the experiences from (professional) roles, social systems and organizations that the client recounts. Subject-matter competency can usually be documented in the form of qualifications or certificates. Why subject-matter competency and not expert competency? No definition available on the market is able to make a satisfactory distinction between expert and methodological competencies. In the social sciences, expert competencies are, to a considerable extent, methodological competencies. Instead, what we are much better able to do is to distinguish between knowledge, reflection, assessment on the one hand, and practicing, applying, and implementing on the other. After all, both refer to actions and have the same significance for decision-making ability.

A coach's subject-matter competency covers a wide body of knowledge from the social sciences, in particular from psychology, pedagogy, economics, sociology and philosophy. In particular, these are: knowledge of psychological and/or management diagnosis and evaluation, psychotherapy and development psychology (e.g. symptoms of clinical disorders and intervention methods, see below), work and organizational psychology (e.g. methods of work analysis, aptitude judgments), knowledge of social psychology (e.g. group dynamics, conflict research), pedagogy (didactics) and the neurosciences. Of significance are also economic traditions of thought (e.g. Smith, Keynes, Friedman), knowledge of organization theory and management theory (e.g. planning the structure, culture, and processes of an organization, leadership and management activities), knowledge of business concepts (e.g. income statements, activity accounting systems and performance statements, calculation and liquidity planning), as well as knowledge of philosophical and sociological traditions of thought (e.g. phenomenology, hermeneutics, systems theory, theory of communicative action) in order to be able to locate and reflect upon one's own actions and behaviour as a coach. Subject-matter competency also includes general legal knowledge (e.g. social and contract law, tax law, liability law, and labour law). Subject-matter competency

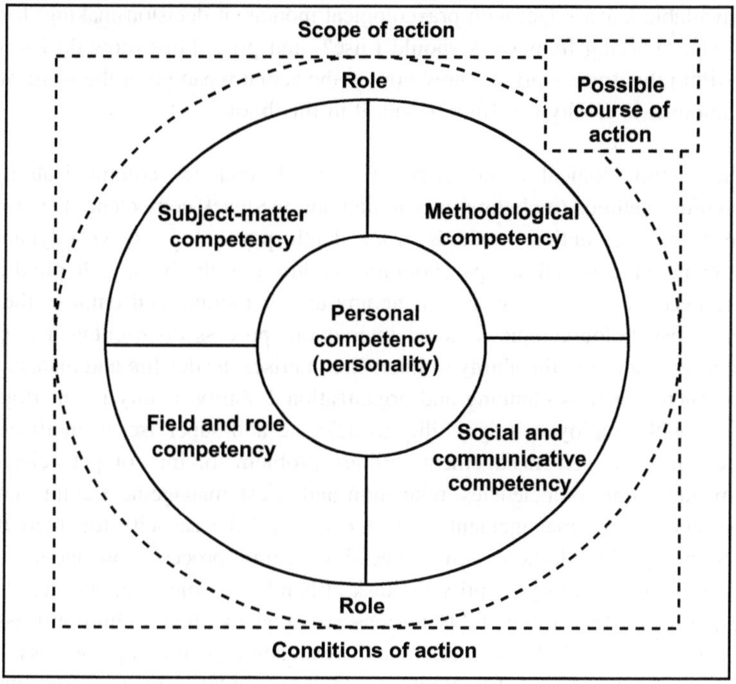

Fig. 12.1 Components of coaching competency

now also includes comprehensive knowledge from practice of and research on coaching, such as definitions, approaches and the history of coaching, theories, (process) models, contract and framework design, tools and intervention methods, ethics and business integrity, market analysis and marketing in coaching, quality management and the current status of coaching research. Subject-matter competency is expressed via the educational background and verifiable expert qualifications of a coach, which also include further education in coaching.

(2) *Methodological competency* is the ability to utilize strategies and approaches in an independent manner in order to deal flexibly with tasks, solve problems and put plans into action in changing situations, as well as to (further) develop strategies and approaches independently. This is nothing more than ordering activities systematically with regard to an objective. The system is based on subject-matter competency and reflection. In this case, we are dealing with

available knowledge; with praxeological models of decision-making: formats (what working framework should I use?) and procedures (how do I proceed within this framework?), know-how in the actual meaning of the word, which amounts to ability (cf. Buer, Chap. 9 in this book).

The methodological competency of a coach includes communication and counselling methods (including questioning and feedback competency), as well as mastery of intervention methods from depth psychology (psychodynamics), client-cantered counselling, psychodrama and/or gestalt therapy, hypnotherapy (where necessary, NLP), behaviour therapy and/or rational and emotive therapy, systemic psychology, topic-cantered interaction, process counselling and group dynamics; in addition the ability to intervene in crises, leadership and management competencies such as planning and organizational ability, ability in entering into dialogue with employees (e.g. ability to delegate and supervise, to motivate and inspire), time and self-management abilities, problem-solving competencies, conflict management competencies, relaxation and stress management competencies, project and change management competencies, and the capacity for intercultural understanding. In addition, come special coaching process competencies: the ability to unambiguously identify the task at hand, the objective, and the client's issues, contract design, the ability to consciously shape the coaching process, the ability to intensify (self-)perception and awareness, positioning, process counselling, the ability to identify topics in an issue-cantered manner (didactics of coaching), carrying out behavioural experiments (e.g. in the form of role-play), supervision of learning processes, as well as the ability to ensure transfer, evaluation, and quality assurance.

(3) *Social and communicative competency* is the ability to perceive oneself and others in intersubjective relationships, to consciously shape relationships and interactions with other people, and to make oneself understood discursively and instrumentally in relationship with other people (i.e. in a purpose-oriented fashion) (cf. Habermas 1981). Social and communicative competency is the ability to make and maintain contact and to collaborate, even in controversial interpersonal situations. This also includes being able to assess other people and social situations, as well as ability to make contact or establish rapport with others; i.e. adjusting the type of interaction to various roles and contexts (e.g. familial or organizational contexts).

The social and communicative competency of a coach includes communicative competency, including the ability to distinguish nuances of non-verbal body language. An elementary aspect is the ability to make and maintain contact and relationships, i.e. to enter into interpersonal relationships, to be respectful in a trustful relationship, and to change and end relationships. Role competency is—particularly for work with persons with high-ranking positions in organizations—of importance; i.e. being able to actually deliberately assume various roles, to fulfil them, to change between them and to relinquish them (cf. Chap. 11 in this book). Emotional process competency is what characterizes a coach, in this case in particular sensitivity and empathy in conjunction with a pronounced ability for self-perception with regard to feelings, motives, values and attitudes, as well as emotional reflexivity, even during the course of interactions. The ability to deal with criticism and confrontation (paired with honesty and a certain swiftness) and to deal with conflict, the ability to dissociate and/or change perspectives and (micro-) political tact, i.e. the ability to handle power, resistance and (micropolitical) tactics, are important. A coach's social and communicative competency also includes sociability and ability to cooperate.

(4) *Personal competency*, in this case, is understood as the characteristics of the personality of a person which make the person capable of coaching. It also includes the ability to realistically assess oneself and one's capacity for action, to reflectively compare one's self-image and others' images of oneself, and to correct the self-image. In the context of social and communicative, but also personal competencies, we can utilize a wide range of constructs which were developed in for example psychodiagnostics, particularly in the design of personality tests, through which make a certain degree of quantifiability possible. A number of descriptions of social and communicative competency and a great many on personal competency were written by Merz and Frey (2011, pp. 121–155), based on research in the form of studies and surveys of experts.

The personal competency of a coach entails a developed self-reflective ability; a conscious self-inclusion on the part of the coach. In addition, it also includes curiosity and attentiveness, quick thinking and a pronounced capability for intellectual thinking, flexibility and adaptability, authenticity, and the ability to be selectively open, independence and integrity, authority and credibility, and the ability to deal with (emotional) stress. Clear principles, values, and ethical guidelines are also part of this competency. Stamina, a goal- and solution-oriented orientation, ideological openness, tolerance, liberality, striving towards professionalism, discretion and confidentiality, willingness to take risks, the ability to deal with criticism, creativity, self-confidence and assertiveness, a sense of responsibility and autonomy, optimism and a well-balanced frame of mind, humour, tolerance for ambiguity and frustration, intuition, helpfulness, and reactions that are swift and appear natural.

(5) *Field and role competency* comprises deep and far-reaching experience and abilities which originate from encounters with and intensive discussions on and examinations of specific fields of work and/or decision-making levels, their requirements and scope. They arise from the reflexive processing of successes and failures in the use of (potentially) all other competencies as well as of restrictive and emancipatory coping strategies which are developed by modifying existing competencies. They refer concretely to specific areas of expertise, methods, social and communicative forms of interaction and personal requirements in specific contexts,—in roles and positions, (sub-)cultures and social milieus, organizations or other social systems and societal fields of action (such as for example industrial sectors) with their own specific dynamics: psychological, group, and system dynamics. In this case, field and role competencies (related to the organization) may contradict existing material and methodological competencies (of the profession) or social and communicative and personal competencies (of a person) and endanger or deform them (*déformation professionelle*).

Initially, a coach's field and role competencies build on personal professional and life experience, and then later on contacts with the fields of work, decision-making levels, organizations, roles, processes, tasks etc. of clients. The more reflected and specific the field experience of the coach with regard to the client's issues and problems, the more comprehensively the coach will be able to provide the client, in the role of an advisor or sparring partner, with orientation-providing "insider knowledge" from the very beginning. The field competency of a coach is crucial for credibility and acceptance in the client's field of work, and hence often also for the quality of the interface and the shaping of the relationship in coaching. And field competency is the central reason for hiring internal coaches to work within an organization. However, the disadvantage here is an "organizational blindness"; i.e. unreflected or insufficiently reflected and/or inaccessible, implicit field experience.

The field and role competency of a coach consists of the components cultural experience, industry experience, business experience, organizational experience, divisional experience (e.g. sales and production experience), role experience in leadership and/or management positions categorized according to hierarchy levels (e.g. as a team leader or a board member), as well as in other social roles (e.g.

father of a family, board member in an association), career (development) experience as well as experiences in various social milieus (e.g. as the son of a board chairman or daughter of a works council member). In addition, a coach also requires general processed and reflected experience (e.g. reflected childhood experiences, experiences with sibling roles, adolescent experiences, experiences with threshold situations in the course of life, starting a family, having a life companion, growing old and old age) and crisis experiences (e.g. experience in dealing with serious illnesses and/or psychological crises, unemployment, drug use, violence, debt, separation, loss, caring and providing for family members, and death). That is why the age of a coach often plays a key role when the client system assesses the field or role competency as well as the suitability of a coach.

12.6 Conclusion

Regardless of the varying, in part inadequate, concepts for the definition and description of competencies, not to speak of coaching competencies, and due to pragmatic considerations, we are faced with the task of considering which competencies we mean when we speak of a "competent coach" or when we provide courses for "coaching competencies" that are independent of a coach's specific job environment. For the latter, we could simply formulate teaching materials and hence, at a concrete level, requirements for a qualification course, or define our coach's competencies in a solution-oriented manner based on a company's competency model. However, we would then be missing the theoretical underpinning, as was the case with *Stiftung Warentest*'s attempt. Why and for what purpose should we choose certain sections of content and not others? Or should we create some form of competency certification as attempted via DIN-PAS, as an increasing number of associations which are developing their own competency models and translating them into expert assessor guidelines are doing? This appears arbitrary and has very little scientific basis. Furthermore: "Competencies are pure functional abilities which are value-independent: I can acquire reading competency using "Romeo & Juliet" or an instruction manual for an MP3 player. So far, we have assumed that instruction manuals do not have the same educational value as Shakespeare's plays, which is why the latter are included in school curricula, but not the former. When the sole purpose is to acquire functioning abilities, questions of value are meaningless. What is learned is valueless" (Krautz 2009).

The definition of coaching competencies based on a quasi-scientific study such as the one by Merz and Frey or on one which satisfies scientific quality criteria provides us with a conceptual framework. However, this always involves making certain meta-theoretical assumptions. The field and role competency of a coach then, in certain circumstances, does not appear in the investigations, for example because the research participants or persons surveyed are not as advanced in their own establishment of categories. Furthermore, when using a scientifically founded framework as a basis, we must not fall into the trap of thinking that we will always be right and successful in every specific corporate context. After all, each company needs its own "organizational coaching capabilities": The secret of how this company can, through the targeted coaching of the development of its capabilities, be more successful than its competitors.

Ultimately, the meta-theory of a coach or further education provider for coaching will also determine how and which coaching competencies are to be emphasized, how they are to be defined, and their significance contextualized. Currently, three trends exist: (1) interactionist theoretical constructions which are influenced by attitudes and methods from psychotherapy, (2) business-oriented theoretical constructs which are influenced by organizational and management theory, (3) tool-oriented approaches which see coaching techniques as an extension of the behavioural repertoire in traditional roles (e.g. as manager, mentor, or management consultant) without having to switch into a (professional) coach role. The problem: The meta-theories which are developed cannot be aligned unilaterally with a particular school within the social sciences, as none of these schools covers the entire spectrum of theoretical fundamentals required for coaching. Not even a construct such as humanist psychology is sufficient, as it contrasts personal development and realization with societal, organizational, systemic expectations, structures, and dynamics. By contrast, coaching deals with how people in roles, in expectations, structures and dynamics can be capable of action, through which they can transform these.

We face the challenge of abandoning one-sidedness and the polarization and ideologies it produces. No matter how much they have functioned as mental guidelines until now, and have given us support and an orientation. No matter to what extent recognition value and thus marketing effects or journalists serve as simply structured reference points for readable articles in the public debate. Coaching is nothing other than a term for developing something that is simultaneously methodologically integrative and transformative on a philosophical, socio-scientific and methodological level, and which adds something simple to the diversity and complexity of our work and (experiential and) living environments which maintains this complexity. As someone once so aptly said: Simplicity before complexity is worthless, but I'd give everything for simplicity after complexity.

References

Arnold, R. (1997). Von der Weiterbildung zur Kompetenzentwicklung. In Arbeitsgemeinschaft Qualifikations-Entwicklungs-Management-Berlin (Hrsg.), *Kompetenzentwicklung 97* (S. 253–307). Münster: Waxmann.

Backhausen, W., & Thommen, J.-P. (2006). *Coaching. Durch systemisches Denken zu innovativer Personalentwicklung*. Wiesbaden: Gabler.

Bergmann, B. (1999). *Training für den Arbeitsprozess. Entwicklung und Evaluation aufgaben- und zielgruppenspezifischer Trainingsprogramme*. Zürich: vdf.

Berker, P. (1992). Felddynamik. *Supervision, 21*, 3–9.

Boyatzis, R. E. (1982). *The competent manager. A model for effective performance*. New York: Wiley.

DIN Deutsches Institut für Normung (2002). *Anforderungen an Verfahren und deren Einsatz bei berufsbezogenen Eignungsbeurteilungen. DIN 33430:2002.* Berlin: Beuth.

DIN Deutsches Institut für Normung (2008). *Kompetenzfeld Einzel-Coaching. PAS 1029:2008.* Berlin: Beuth.

Eilles-Matthiessen, C., Janssen, S., Osterholz-Sauerlaender, A., & El Hage, N. (2007). *Schlüsselqualifikationen kompakt. Ein Arbeitsbuch für Personalauswahl und Personalentwicklung*. Bern: Huber.

Erpenbeck, J., & von Rosenstiel, L. (Hrsg.) (2007). *Handbuch Kompetenzmessung. Erkennen, verstehen und bewerten von Kompetenzen in der betrieblichen, pädagogischen und psychologischen Praxis.* Stuttgart: Schäffer-Poeschel.

Glasersfeld, E. v. (1996). *Der Radikale Konstruktivismus. Ideen, Ergebnisse, Probleme.* Frankfurt/M.: Suhrkamp.

Greif, S. (2014). Qualifikation, berufliche. In M. A. Wirtz (Hrsg.), *Dorsch – Lexikon der Psychologie.* Göttingen: Hogrefe. http://www.portal/hogrefe.com/dorsch/qualifikation-berufliche, Download am February 25, 2014.

Habermas, J. (1981). *Theorie des kommunikativen Handelns*. Frankfurt/M.: Suhrkamp.

Heckhausen, H. (1989). *Motivation und Handeln* (2., überarb. u. erw. Aufl.). Berlin: Springer.

Holzkamp, K. (1985). *Grundlegung der Psychologie*. Campus: Frankfurt a.M.

Hülshoff, T. (1996). Das Handlungskompetenzmodell. *WSB intern. Zeitschrift des Weiterbildenden Studiengangs Betriebspädagogik und der Gesellschaft für Betriebspädagogik.* 2/96, S. 37–45.

Kauffeld, S. (2006). *Kompetenzen messen, bewerten, entwickeln. Ein prozessanalytischer Ansatz für Gruppen*. Stuttgart: Schaeffer-Poeschel.

Krautz, J. (2009). Bildung als Anpassung? Das Kompetenz-Konzept im Kontext einer ökonomisierten Bildung. *Fromm Forum, 13*(2009), 87–100.

Krumm, S., Mertin, I., & Dries, C. (2012). *Kompetenzmodelle*. Göttingen: Hogrefe.

McClelland, D. C. (1973). Testing for competence rather than for intelligence. *American Psychologist, 28*, 66–69.

Kommission der Europäischen Gemeinschaften (2006). *European Qualification Framework (EQF). Europäischer Qualifikationsrahmen.* Brüssel.

Lang, R. W. (2000). *Schlüsselqualifikationen. Handlungs- und Methodenkompetenz, Personale und Soziale Kompetenz.* München: Deutscher Taschenbuch Verlag.

Mertens, D. (1974). Schlüsselqualifikationen. Thesen zur Schulung für eine moderne Gesellschaft. *Mitteilungen aus der Arbeitsmarkt- und Bildungsforschung, 7,* S. 36–41. Stuttgart: Kohlhammer.

Merz, C., & Frey, A. (2011). *Empirisch fundiertes Kompetenzmodell für den Bereich des Führungskräftecoachings.* Aachen: Shaker.

Oerter, R., & Montada, L. (1995). *Entwicklungspsychologie. Ein Lehrbuch.* Weinheim: Beltz.

Reischmann, J. (2004). *Kompetenz lehren? Kompetenz- und Performanz-Orientierung in der Andragogik zwischen Didaktik und Organisationsentwicklung.* Bamberg: Universität Bamberg. http://www.uni-bamberg.de/andragogik/interne_links/publikationen.htm. Download am 30.12.2013.

Probst, J. B. (1987). *Selbst-Organisation. Ordnungsprozesse in sozialen Systemen aus ganzheitlicher Sicht.* Berlin, Hamburg: Paul Parey.

Roth, H. (1971). *Pädagogische Anthropologie. Bd. II: Entwicklung und Erziehung.* Hannover: Hermann Schrödel.

Sarges, W. (Ed.). (1995). *Management-Diagnostik.* Göttingen: Hogrefe.

Sarges, W. (2001). Competencies statt Anforderungen—nur alter Wein in neuen Schläuchen? In H.-C. Riekhof (Ed.), *Strategien der Personalentwicklung* (pp. 285–300). Wiesbaden: Gabler.

Schott, F., & Ghanbari, S. A. (2008). *Kompetenzdiagnostik, Kompetenzmodelle, kompetenzorientierter Unterricht.* Münster: Waxmann.

Schuler, H. (1996). *Psychologische Personalauswahl. Einführung in die Berufseignungsdiagnostik.* Göttingen: Verlag für angewandte Psychologie.

Schreyögg, A. (2012). *Coaching. Eine Einführung für Praxis und Lehre* (7., überarb. u. erw. Aufl.). Frankfurt: Campus.

Schreyögg, G., & Kliesch-Eberl, M. (2012). Das Kompetenzparadoxon. Wie dynamisch können organisationale Kompetenzen sein? *Revue für postheroisches Management, 3,* S. 6.

Sonntag, K.-H. (2004). Personalentwicklung. In H. Schuler (Hrsg.), *Enzyklopädie der Psychologie* (S.827–893). Göttingen: Hogrefe.

Sonntag, K.-H., & Schaper, N. (2006). Förderung beruflicher Handlungskompetenz. In K.-H. Sonntag (Ed.), *Personalentwicklung in Organisationen* (pp. 270–311). Göttingen: Hogrefe.

Spencer, L. M., & Spencer, S. (1993). *Competence at work. Models for superior performance.* New York: Wiley.

Stiftung Warentest (2013). *Coachen im beruflichen Kontext. Was eine gute Einstiegsqualifizierung bieten sollte.* test.de, Download (zur Verfügung seit 26.09.2013).

White, R. W. (1959). Motivation reconsidered: The concept of competence. *Psychological Review, 66,* 297–333.

Author Biography

Ingo Steinke Dipl.-Psych. Management Coach (DPA), Quality Manager (DIN-ISO), TQM Assessor for Business Excellence (EFQM), Change Manager (CTU), Systems-Based Supervision and Organizational Consulting (NIK). Work as Corporate Consultant, Head of Qualification Department, and since 2000 Managing Shareholder of COATRAIN coaching & personal training GmbH, Senior Coach (DBVC).

Coaching and Group Dynamics 13

Thomas Bachmann

Abstract

The following article examines concepts and models of group dynamics from three different perspectives for the coaching context. In the first part, group dynamics training sessions are described as a learning setting in which persons who work, e.g. as consultants or coaches, interact and have intensive and reflection-rich experiences of their own. The second part examines group dynamics models and theories which are regularly of particular relevance when coaching persons with leadership responsibilities who lead groups or teams, or are themselves a part of groups and teams. Finally, in the last section, methods and intervention options will be presented which allow the dynamics of groups to be shaped and/or influenced.

13.1 Introduction

Group dynamics now looks back on a tradition that has lasted more than 70 years. The ideas, experiments and theories of Kurt Lewin (1890–1947), which he developed at MIT in his Research Center of Group Dynamics, are the most well-known in this field. Those seen as the fathers of group dynamics include Jacob Levi Moreno (1889–1974), the inventor of psychodrama and sociometry, as well as the Austrian Raoul Schindler (*1923) with his rank structure model for groups. Group dynamics findings, models and theories, principles, settings, exer-

T. Bachmann (✉)
artop, Humboldt-Universität, Christburger Str. 4, 10405 Berlin, Germany
e-mail: bachmann@artop.de

A. Schreyögg and C. Schmidt-Lellek (eds.), *The Professionalization of Coaching*, DOI 10.1007/978-3-658-16805-6_13

cises and games have become extremely popular since psychology's entry into learning, work, organizational, leadership, therapy, and consultation contexts in the middle of the last century. Listing all the developments and representatives here would go beyond the scope of this article, which is why I have focused on the aspects of group dynamics which are relevant for coaching as a form of consultation.

The concept of group dynamics can be viewed from three different perspectives: (1) as the interactions and the course they take in a group of persons, (2) as a method and learning setting for creating and facilitating the experience of group dynamics and (3) as a scientific sub-discipline, e.g. in social psychology or therapy research, which describes and investigates these interactions and the course they take. These three perspectives are also reflected in the examination of group dynamics and coaching, hence emphasizing the significance which group dynamics experience, group dynamics action competency and theoretical knowledge of group dynamics hold for coaching. Hence, this chapter will examine the group dynamics learning setting for self-experience, group dynamics theories and models for counseling for persons with leadership roles for teams, and group dynamics action competency in the context of multi-person settings, such as in group or team coaching.

13.2 Self-experience in the Group Dynamics Learning Setting

Contrary to other attempts that serve to standardize coaching, to define it as a service that can be called upon at will, or to demonstrate that it is equivalent to a pill with effects and side effects (e.g. Schermuly et al. 2014), coaching remains a dialogical consultation process that cannot be controlled directly, and which is more appropriately characterized as "the art of relationship" (cf. Schmidt-Lellek and Buer 2011; Buer 2012). Building a counseling relationship based on trust, acceptance and respect, but which simultaneously can also give rise to irritation, confrontation and consternation is a process that requires a coach to have a great deal of experience and faith in himself as a person. In addition to methodological, process-related and specialist competencies allowing a coach to decide when he should do or refrain from doing something, and to determine what is a part of coaching and what is not, what is needed here is above all a form of professional contact management which allows a thematic and emotional depth to be achieved in a relatively short time frame of a few sessions, in which the client's major issues are dealt with, and reflections, confrontations, or even solutions can be offered or come up with (cf. Schein 2012).

Building a helping relationship in which contact occurs and where someone is prepared to enter uncharted terrain and explore solutions with another person requires a great deal of experience and reflection from the coach regarding his own behavior during contact, as well as his own inner unresolved issues, favorite hypotheses, desires to improve the world, driving forces and projections of all shapes and forms. This is because, all tips and tools aside, coaching is primarily a dialogical form of reflection with a consultant who is competent and professional where the client's issue is concerned, and with whom there exists no other relationship contexts, thereby allowing him to act in an unprejudiced and impartial manner with regard to clients, issues, change, and solutions. This turns the coach as a person into *the* "tool" in the coaching process. His contact behavior, emotions and responses, questions, feedback, confrontations, interpretations and advice (cf. Dehner 2009) are the material that result in a fruitful coaching process.

There is a further important aspect that refers to the coach as a person: In coaching, we encounter people in borderline situations. A coach is generally not sought out during "normal operation". However, when conflicts escalate, important decisions are looming, the management of employees is not working out, poor results were received during 360°-feedback, one's own role is unclear, or any other problematic situations or situations of change are about to take place, coaching is offered—particularly in large organizations—or a coach is sought out on one's own initiative. A coach must be familiar with such situations—with regard not only to their content-related, but also to their emotional aspects. Specifically, this means knowing and being able vividly to empathize with how it feels to be involved in a conflict that has escalated, when one receives negative feedback, or when one simply does not know what to do next and imminent decisions have simply become too much to handle. The empathy skills required for this cannot be learned in any seminar, nor in any qualification course for coaching; instead, they are acquired when a person has experienced similar situations and evaluated them together with others in a professional context. Professional coaches and consultants ensure that such personal space for reflection is created in supervision and intervision groups. In addition, the group dynamics learning setting provides a very special and productive opportunity for intensive reflection on one's own self as a person (König and Schattenhofer 2012; Königswieser et al. 2013).

Training group design, which was developed by Lewin, is a classic aspect of this: A group dynamics learning setting stretches out over several days, where people work together in groups of approximately ten persons who meet up now and then in a plenary session to reflect on the group process or to give and/or receive feedback. The process in the groups is kicked off by one or more trainers and accompanied passively, that mean not with active instruction what to do or what the goal is. With the "initial uncertainty" that the participants are now on their own and do not receive any instructions from the trainers, learning begins in a group process that develops in a self-organized manner. In order for this to work, the setting is defined with the participants via a contract and a spatial and temporal structure. However, within this structure, there are no requirements or strict guidelines. Naturally, there are numerous variants for organizing such processes which differ primarily in the amount of management, input and confrontation on the part of the trainer, and the extent to which the group dynamics are steered or intensified with the use of certain exercises (Brosius 2009; Antons 2011).

But what does learning in a group dynamics setting entail? When a group of strangers comes together and is made to give this state of being together meaning over a long period of time, an interesting process can be observed: Cautiously, the first comments are made, and the persons who utter these comments to the group hope for follow-up communication. Control attempts are made to give the communication process a certain direction. On the other hand, others send counter-stimuli into the group in an attempt to anchor the development of other meanings (cf. Luhmann 1984). There are active and passive, dominant and submissive, sympathetic and not so sympathetic forms of behavior (cf. Scholl 2013a); some attempt to coalesce with others, while others attempt to draw a line in the sand, some withdraw, and others project objectives out into the world and hope that the group follows them (cf. Bachmann, in prep.). Gradually, communication patterns develop in the group, resulting in certain persons being linked with certain roles. The process takes its course, and passive and crippling phases are followed by phases of enthusiasm and energy. Conflicts arise, feedback is given, people speak of patterns, roles, fears, desires, as well as surprising and familiar things. Ultimately, a very close and trusted atmosphere results in which each individual can open up and receive support and feedback from the other members of the group. It is not unusual for the tension in this unusually familiar situation to result in unburdening emotional reactions. All participants receive feedback from each other, intensive relationships are formed; finally the group is closed after a few days and stops existing. The members, now rich with experiences, feelings and findings, take their leave from each other. During all this, learning takes place at multiple levels, and its specific characteristics and intensity come from the fact that each of the participants shapes the dynamics of the group, while also simultaneously being "at its mercy". However, this method also has risks, which were pointed out by Königswieser et al. (2013).

First of all, each individual receives extremely direct *behavioral feedback* on how he involves himself in the group process, in a context that did not exist before, in that none of the participants have a history with each other, and the social status and education background of each individual are a guess at best. Unlike in other contexts, one acts here initially "without a role", as there do not exist any specific conventions in the group yet. One does not play the accustomed part of consultant, management executive, parent, or friend. Each individual is there "simply" as a person and needs to develop a role. Furthermore, one can only utilize practiced roles from one's own professional background to get through the situation for a limited amount of time. At the very latest, after a few hours, each participant will be faced with the task of personally involving himself in the process and shaping it. This shaping and coming up with one's own role while simultaneously receiving direct feedback from the group is a valuable learning result so compact and intensive that it is practically unheard of in any other context.

Yet another learning level deals with the experiencing of one's own effectiveness with regard to the *influenceability of the group process.* Attempting to influence a social system with stimuli that lead to a desired effect can be an extremely intensive, interesting, and satisfying, but also frustrating learning experience. What happens with my ideas, requests, suggestions and attempts to influence a group? What is well-received, what goes unheard, and what is turned down? Who will ally with me, and who is against me? Where do I feel safe? It was precisely for initial situations in group processes that Richter (1993) developed his famous list of questions. Reflecting on these questions at a suitable point in time in the group is a significant and meaningful experience. Königswieser et al. (2013) describe one major learning effect as being the experience for the group members resulting from such processes—that there is often a large difference between the intention and effect of certain behavior, and that contrary to one's own intentions, one's actions often have exactly the opposite effect. Self-images and external images can therefore be individually examined and compared with each other. Hence, the experiencing of the elementary process of group genesis, its phases, the progress and crises, as well as one's own role in this process and reflecting on it with the other group members enables in-depth social learning.

The third learning level is the level of *observation.* In a group dynamics learning setting, one is simultaneously a designer and observer for the entire length of time. One experiences one's own thoughts and feelings in this process and simultaneously also the "togetherness" with other group members. It becomes possible to experience and observe group processes directly, which, combined with the corresponding theoretical reflection, leads to a deeper understanding of groups with regard to the roles that evolve, interaction patterns, phases encountered, formation of structures, as well as the development of standards and "group culture" (cf. also Amann 2009).

The participation in group dynamics training sessions, as previously described, should therefore be an integral part of qualification courses for coaches, trainers and consultants, as well as the (further) development of persons in positions of leadership (cf. Königswieser et al. 2013). As before, this also includes regular participation in supervision and intervision groups with peers, whose setting may not create the same density and intensity with regard to the group experience, but which also enables emotional and professional learning in a group process (Schreyögg 2004).

13.3 Group Dynamics Aspects When Coaching Persons in Positions of Leadership

Almost all persons with leadership and management responsibilities lead groups. It could be a group of employees, a project team, a group of management executives, or another constellation in which multiple persons come together for a common purpose, are organizationally linked, or need to work together as a team. Such groups exist not only within organizations, but could also be stakeholders such as clients, oversight committees, or the clients or cooperation partners of organizations. For example, property managers need to regularly manage the group in a homeowners association meeting, caregivers for the elderly a group of relatives, management boards and CEOs need to work together with advisory boards or oversight committees etc. At the same time, all persons have leadership and management roles and are simultaneously also members of groups, making them both the designers of and parties affected by the dynamics that arise in each group. Group dynamics processes influence the behavior of organizational members and the course and results of decision-making processes in a variety of ways. These include ingroup-outgroup dynamics, groupthink phenomena, status rivalries, clique formation, and various types of informal structure formation and communication (cf. Schreyögg and Koch 2007).

Generally, the following holds true: There are no groups without group dynamics. However, whether these dynamics are observable, how they are expressed or the intensity with which they manifest themselves depends on a variety of factors. Wimmer (1998; cf. Königswieser et al. 2013) emphasizes the time factor in this case, and distinguishes a short-term or sporadic meeting of persons from an obligatory and continuous association over a longer period of time. This distinction was also made by Luhmann (1984) when speaking of fleeting interaction systems and other social systems. According to Wimmer, the phenomenon of groups is an emergence phenomenon which arises over the course of the social process over time and develops characteristics which we then identify as being typical for a group: interaction patterns, internal distinctions and the formation of boundaries with the environment are examples of this (cf. Campbell 1958).

Not only do those with leadership and management responsibilities need to be able to "steer" groups while at the same time also being members of them, but the importance of groups and teams in the world of work and organizations in general is also experiencing an overall increase. This is not a new discovery, but remains a significant one nonetheless. Relevant here are not only the classic advantages of group decision making as compared to individual decisions made by a solitary person in a position of leadership—namely the inclusion of more information, more perspectives and hence more premises in a decision. In addition, social systems benefit, being more susceptible to influence and management, when as many of their representatives as possible are included in the decision-making processes as possible (cf. also Scholl 2004, Chap. 6; Scholl et al. 2013). Another important aspect of the potential of groups has been broached by Senge (2008) with his concept of a "learning organization". According to Senge (2008), "team learning" is one of the most significant factors allowing learning and change to take place in an organization. Organizations require the group dynamics, relationship-orientedness and hence the personal aspect of the teams they consist of in order to initiate change, as the organization itself is not capable of learning and reflection. On the contrary—via a contract—it forces (to put it simply) its members to reproduce practiced patterns (routines, programs, procedures and structures) under the threat of losing their membership in the organization. Changes to these patterns (i.e. learning) can only take place by making it possible for the relevant environments in the organization, i.e. the teams and leadership personnel, to be involved in decisions, to have leeway to act, freedom and responsibility, and to feel safe when exercising these freedoms and responsibilities, so that creativity and innovation can develop (Scholl 2004, 2013b). In this context, team leadership plays a particularly central role. Its objective is to find the right middle ground between rules, control, and authority on the one hand and lawlessness, the absence of obligation, and symmetry on the other in order to use the flexibility, creativity and learning ability of groups to the organization's advantage (Wimmer 1998).

The coaching of persons with leadership and management tasks is at the same time therefore always the coaching of groups and teams, only in this case it is conveyed via the client being coached. Hence, many of the issues which arise when coaching clients also have direct and indirect relevance for the phenomena and processes of group dynamics. These phenomena may include conflicts, resistance, rivalries, incompatibilities, and divisions within a group. It is therefore often the coach's job to analyze such phenomena together with the client; i.e. to produce useful descriptions, explanations and evaluations in order to generate possible courses of action for the client. In addition to methods and techniques for asking questions, structuring, or reconstructing as part of the coaching process, it is particularly important here for a coach to have profound theoretical knowledge of groups, teams and their dynamics in order to be able to act in a helpful and competent manner when dealing with such issues.

At this juncture, it becomes apparent that the difference between groups, teams and organizations needs to be defined more clearly. Consequently, I wish to examine more closely the most important models and theories of the dynamics of groups which may be relevant in coaching, thereby compiling a list of the fundamental tools for a "Theory of the Thing" for coaches.

13.3.1 Groups and Teams as Social Systems

A *group* is a social system which consists of more than three but a maximum of 12–14 members. Similar phenomena may be observed in dyads or triads as in a group, but despite this, it is still expedient to distinguish them from groups because these interaction systems develop extremely specific patterns and other dynamics are generally able to evolve in them. With regard to interaction patterns in triads, the reader may wish to consult von Schlippe and Schweitzer (2012) or the transaction analysis and the "drama triangle" developed by Karpman in this context (cf. Schlegel 1993). Furthermore, when there are only three persons, not all positions can be filled so that (at least in the short-term) stable internal distinctions may be made within a group. Hence, it only makes sense to speak of a group when there are at least four persons. Once the number of members increases beyond a certain point, the group begins to split up into sub-groups and the significance of the group dynamics processes become blurred among the great number of individuals and interactions (cf. Fengler 1986). When there are too many individuals it becomes increasingly difficult for the individual member to shape intensive interactional relationships with others and to update them. The same applies for leadership personnel, whose scope of direct leadership should also not exceed 12–14 persons. In training, coaching, and consultations, too, a lot changes when one works with larger groups, as it then becomes necessary to utilize other methods and new social arrangements in order to effectively shape a common learning process or an organizational development project. In order to fulfill these requirements when working with large groups, trainers and consultants have developed a rich repertoire of methods (cf. Seliger 2011).

If the members of a group come together permanently or at least repeatedly due to a particular occasion, the initial (potentially infinite variations of) interactions of the members result in the formation of communication patterns via processes of selection and retention which are unique for each group (cf. Simon 2004). A social system arises from patterns of communication and follow-up communication, and functions and structures now begin to take shape (Luhmann 1984). In order to ensure its continued existence as a system, the group now needs to develop various system functions. These include the ability to adapt, to formulate goals, integration, and structure retention (Parsons 1978). Through its adaptability, the group system regulates its external relationships and sees to it that the group is continually fed with new communication via the group members.

For a system, this means creating synchronicity at the expert, social, and temporal levels in order to remain significant for its members. In short, the common anchoring of meaning needs to reflect the individual assignments of meaning as applied to the group (Luhmann 1984). The goal function allows the group to project goals and to mobilize actions for their achievement, which in turn creates satisfactory states internally; i.e. for example to complete a common task, to have fun, or to learn together.

In order for the goal function to develop, the group requires an internal differentiation so that the symmetric relationship of its members yields at least temporarily to asymmetry for the purposes of goal formulation and decision-making. Individual members provide stimuli, indicate directions, make suggestions, and take the initiative, while others join in, help out, and/or follow. The formation of goals and the switch from symmetry to asymmetry and back under the participation of various members constitute a significant part of the group dynamics.

As an additional system function, the integration function ensures that all group members find a place in the overall system in accordance with their needs; it provides the group with cohesion towards the outside and allows new elements to be included. For this purpose, the system needs to take care of the needs and concerns of the individual in order to retain all persons as far as possible as relevant environments per se, and also to include new ones. Communicatively, this system function is expressed through mutual "confirmatory communication" and other positive responses from the members at the social level. Finally, the function of structure retention together with the development of common group values and standards creates an orientation framework which gives the group system and its members a sense of commitment, orientation and rules, thereby structuring and consolidating the inner workings of the group. All system functions act by means of the system-environment boundary, the maintenance and design of which allows the group system to be distinguished from the environment (cf. Willke 2006; Bachmann, in prep.). This distinction is simultaneously the prerequisite for and result of the existence of a group.

In contrast to a *team*, all these processes of internal differentiation and formation of functions are of an informal nature, as a group is initially not integrated into the context of an organization and does not have a specific goal and/or task. Groups can also exist without a task or decide on a task temporarily, and then later for another. A group initially only represents a continuous, purpose-based communication context. Examples include learning and training groups, supervision groups, self-help groups, spontaneous self-organizing work groups etc. In a team, on the other hand, the fulfillment of a task is at the forefront. It is the purpose of the team, i.e. its reason for existence. The main purpose of any team activity is to solve problems together, i.e. to man a sailboat, to win a football match, or to develop a new product.

Due to this task-orientedness, the focus is shifted from the persons and their requirements to the functions which are required in the team. In the team, the functional coupling of person and task for cooperatively achieving the goal is at the forefront. Roles are no longer negotiated informally, but instead assigned formally. On a sailboat, one is not the ship's cook today and the captain tomorrow. In particular, positions of leadership are formally determined in a team as compared to a group: There is a team leader, a captain, or a management executive. Hence, a team is to be seen as a pre-form of an organization—a sort of hybrid—as it has characteristics of both system qualities: the informal, relationship-oriented and dynamic ones of a group and the formal, functional and goal-oriented ones of an organization.

Finally, *organizations* are formed of multiple teams, have a (leadership) structure, and their processes are formalized and serialized. Almost everything is written down, formal communication predominates, roles and functions are in the foreground, and hence the task as well. Well-formed hierarchies and structures allow many individuals to be coordinated. Concepts such as politics, power, decisions, rationality, leadership, management, strategy, vision, goals, structures, processes, key figures, culture, control, human resources and marketing dominate daily life in an organization and provide us with an impression of the inner workings of such systems.

With these descriptions, it becomes clear how important the dynamics and person-orientedness of groups are for organizations and with what stark contradictions organizations need to reconcile themselves if they wish to promote teamwork, team learning and creativity. Consequently, group dynamics issues and the transmission and/or formulation of action competencies and options hold a high degree of significance in the coaching of leadership personnel who need to solve or tolerate these contradictions anew each day.

13.3.2 A Number of Models for Describing Groups

But which maps can be used to describe group dynamics processes, so that useful descriptions and approaches for solutions are developed from them during coaching? There now exist a wide range of models and theories (cf. Amann 2009). Some may appear outdated and bizarre, for example when psychoanalytically oriented representatives speak of the "wild ancient horde" or "patricide". Other models have become permanent components of trainer and consultant folklore, such as the "team clock".

Fengler (1986) distinguishes the following approaches for the description of groups:

(1) Role theories and function theories (for describing group structures)
(2) Typologies (according to size, tasks, role distribution etc.)
(3) Models for describing groups as systems (interaction systems, organism, social system, production model, control circuits)
(4) Phase models (waveform, cascaded, or spiral-shaped development of groups)
(5) Process models (groups as processes for change, problem-solving, consultation, defense, authority and intimacy, community).

The theoretical superstructure of the following chapter is the theory of social systems (Luhmann 1984). For describing group dynamics phenomena, I will continue to restrict myself to selected models of group phases and/or group developments as well as roles and/or structures. This is a gross simplification, as something as static as a structure or a role of course does not exist in a group. Groups are open, autopoietic systems which are constantly interacting with their environment, and hence constantly becoming, as they exist only in time (cf. Willke 2006). If one could stop time, the persons would still be there, but the group would no longer exist, as the communication patterns can only arise and be maintained over the course of interactions. Hence, structural models are to be seen as momentary snapshots of the group.

The most well-known model of group development is Tuckman's (1965) phase model. In his model, which is also a meta-analysis of numerous investigations of hundreds of therapy and training groups, Tuckman postulates four typical phases which a group undergoes, from the initial contact of the group members up till the disbanding of the group at the end of the group process. The well-known phases are "forming", "storming", "norming", "performing", and finally "adjourning", which was added at a later point in time. The phases describe very succinctly the closeness-distance regulation of the group members, the significance of the role of the group leadership in the individual phases, and the processes of internal differentiation and anchoring of meaning that take place subliminally. Furthermore, possible courses of action can be extrapolated for the group for each individual phase; i.e. for leadership personnel, trainers, and consultants.

The *forming* phase is characterized by uncertainty and tentative communicative convergence attempts made by the group members. Relationships within the group are still unclear. The group members search for orientation in the form of rule or goals. In the *storming* phase, the group begins to differentiate itself internally. The members attempt to find common ground from a distance, and conflicts regarding goals, leadership, and the status of the individual in the group determine cooperation. The group is hardly able to perform any tasks. In the *norming* phase, rules are negotiated implicitly or explicitly (with help from the leadership personnel) and positions are clarified. The group members once again approach each other, and common standards and values arise. In the subsequent *performing* phase, the group is relatively independent of external leadership stimuli. Cooperation and assistance dominate, and the group is able to perform work. Finally, some groups are then disbanded; the *adjourning* phase describes the processes of leave-taking, of how each individual processes and concludes the relinquishing of group membership.

For coaching and consultation, the following implications from Tuckman's (1965) model are of relevance:

(1) With each new member and/or each new task, the group goes through the phases of group development all over again.
(2) In each phase, the leadership personnel can make a specific contribution in order to make it easier for the group to successfully tackle each individual phase.
(3) All phases need to be run through and cannot be skipped.
(4) In order for a group to become or remain effective, the phases need to be completed again from time to time.
(5) Particularly in the storming phase, attacks, challenges, and resistance are often directed at the persons in leadership roles. This is where professionalism and action competency are required in order for the persons in leadership positions to avoid becoming the object of the group dynamics themselves.

(6) Constantly repeating conflicts in a group signify that the norming phase, i.e. the clarification and coming up with a contract, cannot take place. The group members are then permanently stuck in the storming phase and cannot find their position. When this happens, the performance of the group is permanently and negatively impacted.

Furthermore, the model clearly demonstrates the closeness-distance dynamic within groups over the course of their development, as the relationships of the group members alternate between closeness, cohesion, solidarity or harmony on the one hand and distance, differentiation, independence and conflict on the other across the various phases. Both poles are of crucial importance for the development of the group: Closeness means that the group has solidarity, and allows the members to experience a feeling of security and being accepted. However, the group is hardly effective in this state, as the harmony needs to be dissolved through differences in order to make decisions and formulate goals. Differentiation and hence distance and conflicts make developments and the tackling of tasks possible. Efficacy then increases. At the same time, there must also not be too much differentiation, or the group will fall apart. Effective groups regulate this oscillation between closeness and distance simultaneously on the dimension of expertise and the social dimension of communication; i.e. differences in the dimension of expertise are compensated for on the social dimension and vice versa (cf. West's 1996 concept of "full functionality team").

In the last section, the term *team* was consciously avoided, as Tuckman developed his model from group research and for groups. In a team, the person-task coupling and hence the roles are assigned in a fixed or a more rigid manner, and hence are not the result of a group dynamics negotiation process. Despite this, beneath this formal team structure, there always exist the informal processes for the internal structuring of a group, particularly with regard to informal roles, status, or certain—especially relevant—anchors of meaning. Hence, no matter how sophisticated the division of labor is, each team is still a group and also experiences the aforementioned group phases in its development.

Tuckman's (1965) model is primarily of a phenomenological nature. A deeper immersion into the inner processes of a group allows for the modeling of a group dynamics space (Amann 2009). This model is closely related to Parsons (1978) system functions and the patterns of order from the contexts of families and/or the design of organizational structures (Weber 2001). The group dynamics space describes three fundamental dimensions along which groups typically develop conflicts over the course of their development. The conflict dimensions are hierarchy, affiliation, and intimacy. The model postulates that all group dynamics conflicts can be assigned to at least one of these three dimensions.

The dimension *hierarchy* describes the phenomenon whereby members of a group move from what was up till that point in a time a symmetric position into an asymmetric position through initiative, ideas, or suggestions—i.e. through leadership stimuli. The crucial questions here are: Who will prevail? What is being done? Who is being followed? Who leads and represents the group? Who will shape the common standards and values? Who has a higher status than other group members? Groups are, with regard to this dimension, extremely sensitive to a permanent asymmetrization and attempt to re-symmetrize it in good time (Königswieser et al. 2013). The group members permit asymmetrization for as long as they think it is useful for the group. The dimension of hierarchy corresponds to Parsons system function of goal formation, and in the context of system design with the ordering principle "leadership, innovation, and performance take precedence" (cf. Weber 2001). Conflicts in groups regarding which direction to take, goals, truth, approaches, evaluation of a particular matter etc. are therefore often an expression of an inner process of hierarchy formation in which it needs to be decided who—at least for a time—gets to say how the group will proceed and who is to follow.

The second dimension refers to *affiliation*. In this case, conflicts occur when the system boundaries are not clearly defined. Who belongs and who does not? Who is committed, and with which goals? Is everyone going to be involved, or are some just along for the ride? Who is also a member of other rival groups? This dimension corresponds with Parsons (1978) integration function and in the context of (group) design with the "right of affiliation" (Weber 2001). Many teams in organizations have to deal with conflicts in this dimension, because particularly in the context of modern organizations and highly varied structures, it is not always clear who belongs where. However, if a group is to act properly, a clear system boundary is important so that internal qualities such as closeness, a sense of commitment, contact, cohesion and ultimately common values can develop.

The third dimension is called *intimacy*. Conflicts on this dimension primarily address the closeness and distance regulation of the group members among each other. Examples of questions asked for this dimension are: Is everyone's involvement in the group process equally intensive? Is everyone opening up appropriately to the group's purpose—particularly with regard to the sharing of feelings? Have all group members built up an equally intensive feeling of closeness with each other? Differences, as when two group members are very close to each other but keep their distance from the other members, lead unavoidably to tension within the group, as an additional relationship context is immediately presumed.

The dimension of intimacy corresponds with Parsons (1978) structure maintenance function and with the principle of "equalization of giving and taking" in the design context (cf. Weber 2001).

The group dynamics space is a fruitful and effective model for categorizing the conflicts into groups and deriving interventions. During the coaching of leadership personnel, it allows group dynamics problems to be described accurately and for explanations to be developed, as this model refers to the fundamental issues of a social system. It quickly becomes clear to anyone that a team cannot render its maximum performance when it is expending all its energy on maintaining its elementary system functions.

The models presented describe processes that take place in the context of group dynamics. The following models provide an idea of how groups structure themselves over the course of their development and which roles the group members assume in the process. Kantor's (1977) model was the one that broke new ground in this respect. He was a family therapist who investigated the domestic communication procedures of hundreds of families. He then generalized his results for groups and teams, which were then summarized in the famous Kantor model: When the interaction in a group begins, i.e. when, for example, a task needs to be solved, the person who provides the first stimulus, i.e. makes the first suggestion, is called the *mover*. This suggestion is then followed by the next counter-suggestion without much delay. The person who makes the counter-suggestion is called the *opposer*. Subsequently, most of the dynamics then take place between these two positions and are followed by the other involved persons, in that they support the first or the second point of view. Kantor (1977) calls these persons *followers*. They wait to see how the mover-opposer interaction develops, and then support the position that has prevailed. The fourth position refers to what Kantor (1977) calls *bystanders*. They do not get involved in the process and provide comments from a distance without actually involving themselves. They only allow themselves to be involved when the decision of which direction to take has been made. However, the bystanders' comments can be seen as an important reflection of the quality of the process.

With the Kantor model, typical interaction patterns in groups can quickly be identified. In this context, there are a number of interesting questions when working with groups and coaching leadership personnel:

(1) Are the positions in my team always assumed by the same persons or do they change?
(2) Which persons prefer which positions?

(3) Can followers and bystanders be encouraged to also take up other positions?
(4) Which position do I myself often have in groups?

The assumptions of this model lead, when one continues along this line of thought, to an internal hierarchy which emerges in the group through the interaction processes described by Kantor. This allows us to now turn, practically without a transition, to Schindler's (1957) rank dynamics position mode, another classic in group dynamics. Schindler assumes that a group, in order to fulfill a task or to fend off a threat, needs to develop a functional structure internally which makes it possible for goals to be followed, actions to arise, and for as many group members as possible to have the same view of the task which he calls the "other party" (Ger.: "Gegenüber"). For this, the group members occupy certain positions. The term *position* is important, as it signifies that a person can leave it, much like a position on a playing field. Hence, what is being spoken of here is not roles or personality characteristics which are described by this model, but instead functions which characterize a group internally.

The first and highest-ranking position is *alpha*. The person who assumes this position or is assigned the position takes over the task of leading the group towards a goal and of managing the handling of the *other party*. In doing so, alpha acts in an externally oriented manner and depends on the group members following him. In addition, alpha defines the image of the *other party*. The group sees the *other party* equally through alpha, i.e. the reality construct of the group system is heavily influenced by the alpha position.

The *beta* position is occupied by the expert who assists alpha and has a more internal focus. In this case, there is often an ambivalent relationship: Alpha needs beta in order to lead, and beta needs alpha in order to partake of the power (to lead). Hence, there is the potential here of beta's overthrowing alpha in order to seize power for himself.

The actual work is done by the group members in the *gamma* positions, who identify with alpha and share the alpha position's view of the *other party*.

The fourth and particularly interesting position is that of the *omega*. It is important here to not confuse it with the concept of the same name in biology, which uses omega to describe the individual with the lowest rank. Rather, omega is the position opposite alpha, and which hence has a significantly different view of the *other party*, the task or the goal. The gamma positions experience this as a threat, as it disrupts their identification with alpha. Simultaneously, omega is also seen as a threat by alpha and beta, as he calls their leadership position into question. Due to this, omega is often stigmatized as a disruptive factor, and an attempt is often made to exclude him. This is because, in the words of Luhmann (1984), he disrupts the established communication patterns through *re-entry*. The behavior of the omega position and how the group deals with him is indicative of the reflective capabilities of a group with regard to reaching its goal, of how it handles varying points of view, of its cohesiveness, and of how power is concentrated within in the group. Hence, omega is to be seen as corrective of alpha, and simultaneously an indicator for the state of the overall system. In systemic family therapy, such positions are called the "index patient" or the "symptom carrier" (cf. von Schlippe and Schweitzer 2012). The efficacy and development of a group depends significantly on how constructively the conflict between alpha and omega is administered. Should omega become too strong, alpha runs the risk of losing his position; should alpha become too strong, there is no longer a corrective position in the group, and there is a threat of stagnation.

In coaching, it is interesting for leadership personnel to analyze the positions in the employee team in order to better understand conflicts and other patterns: (1) Who holds the informal alpha position? (2) What is the *other party*? Me, the team leader, or the threat which has triggered the current process of change in the team? (3) Who shares which views with whom in the team? Who supports alpha? (4) How can I improve collaboration with alpha, and in doing so obtain better access to the team? (5) Which topics does the omega position address? Are perhaps unclear structures, unresolved task sections or goal conflicts being addressed here which I, as a person in a leadership position, would need to deal with? These and many other questions can be addressed and answered in coaching with Schindler's rank dynamics model.

Wimmer (1998) describes groups from yet another important perspective (cf. also Amann 2009): namely, what can be discussed in the group and what cannot. The communication patterns of a group decide which communications in the group receive a follow-up communication—and which do not. Through the development of patterns over the course of group development, numerous topics slowly disappear into "undiscussableness". Implicit conventions occur on about what one can speak to each and about what not. Topics which are difficult to discuss typically include issues such as criticism of the group's performance, inequality, differences, hierarchy, a need for closeness, fears, or weaknesses of group members, to name a few. When working with groups or during interventions in groups, the distinction between things that can and cannot be discussed are an important and key difference. Particularly in situations involving change, during conflicts in the group or other difficult phases, the number of discussable topics rapidly declines. The group searches primarily in externally directed perceptions for explanations of its situation, which is why the goal of meticulous, professional work with groups involved in processes of change should be to create a context in which more (internal) topics can once again be made discussable.

In the last section, a number of theories and models for understanding group dynamics processes have been presented which can be used during the coaching of leadership personnel. Naturally, there is also a large number of other approaches for describing groups and teams. In the context of teamwork, the reader may wish to refer to West's (1996) approach or Belbin's (1996) model. Introducing additional models would exceed the scope of this text. In conclusion, we can say the following: taking group dynamics theories and models into account is a worthwhile endeavor, even if a coach only works with an individual person. Many issues in coaching also involve groups and their dynamics and can be brought to a fruitful conclusion by also taking into consideration the appropriate knowledge.

13.4 Managing Group Processes in Multi-person Settings

Many coaching assignments take place in multi-person settings. Strictly speaking, the boundary is crossed here into neighboring formats, namely that of organizational consulting and/or training, as working with multiple persons differs fundamentally from the work with individual persons with regard to the topics, the process design, and the methods used. Unfortunately, this situation is compounded by the use of terms such as organizational coaching or team coaching, which imply that everything is somehow also a form of coaching (cf. Bachmann 2012; Chap. 5 in this book). The sustained coaching boom is assimilating neighboring concepts, which unfortunately is not an advantage for the consulting industry overall.

Working with groups requires profound knowledge and competencies in the management of a social system. If the groups are a part of an organization, i.e. a team or a leadership crew, elaborate organizational knowledge and organizational experience are also necessary in order to be able to provide professional counseling. Presenting the entire toolbox of experienced trainers would exceed the scope of this article, which is why I have restricted myself to a number of key aspects. The design, i.e. the planning and execution of group sessions can take place at multiple levels through interventions: (1) the context, (2) the structure, (3) the process, (4) the content, (5) the interactions and (6) the persons. Naturally, an intervention at one level will also always have an effect on the other levels.

(1) Context

Interventions dealing with the *context* of the group session are primarily concerned with how they are embedded in organizational processes (of change), the task at hand, and the goal of the session, expectations of the client and possible "hidden expectations", voluntariness of participation etc. All these context factors are to be clarified in advance and to be influenced as part of professional relationship design, role clarity, and the fulfillment of the task at hand (see chap. 4 or chap. 11 in this book).

(2) Structure

The *structure level* comprises all spatial and temporal characteristics of the session as well as the composition of the participants' system and the consultant's system, the media to be used, fees, contracts, documents etc. Experienced trainers, consultants, and coaches design the setting of their sessions such that the conditions for influencing systems are optimal for themselves as well as the participants.

(3) Process

The *process level* in a group session refers to what is commonly called "dramaturgy" or "leitmotif". From the beginning of the meeting, i.e. such as the round of introductions up till the final feedback given by the participants, the goal is to utilize interventions in the form of techniques or methods with regard to the topic, the group, and each individual in order to create an optimal group process. For this, the field of topic-centered interaction (cf. Cohn 1997) has worked out a good orientation framework and possible courses of action. Interventions at the process level can initially be of a communicative nature, in that the coach asks questions, confronts, mirrors, describes what his own experience is, describes patterns, gives feedback, carries out meta-communication, verbalizes feelings, provokes, instructs, recognizes, supports, sympathizes with the client etc.

The entire repertoire of consultation-related communication skills can be used here, depending on the point in the group process that has just been reached. Unlike when working with individual persons, the reaction here always comes from an entire system with its patterns, often expressing itself in the form of differing reactions to interventions by individuals, which are often not always understandable for outside parties. Hence, interventions with negative connotations are often rejected by many and only shared tacitly, while interventions with positive connotations are generally answered positively by the entire group when there is a positive relationship basis. However, positive interventions can also be viewed with skepticism. This is the case when the participants suspect hidden tasks or are not participating in the sessions voluntarily. Hence, when working with groups it is important to recognize the pattern(s) of the group, true to the statement which is ascribed to Kurt Lewin: "One can only understand a system when one attempts to change it."

Intervening at the process level therefore means recognizing patterns and influencing the communication system of the group to fulfill the sessions' objectives. This primarily takes place by covertly introducing new communication into the system which is easy to follow up on, thereby enabling new perspectives, new points of views and positioning via the contract between the coach and the group. In this, the central challenge is getting the group to make itself the object of reflection, as system learning only takes place when the communication of the system assimilates and processes that which is new and puts itself in perspective. A group or a team does not learn when individually involved persons absorb knowledge or acquire experiences, but instead when the social system makes itself the subject being addressed and communicatively processes the learning content or experiences of the various persons. Of course, the knowledge or experiences of individual persons flow into the communication process and also influence it; however, this does not allow a targeted modification of communication patterns which affects all members to be made. This is clearly shown by the fairytale "The Emperor's New Clothes" by Andersen. Even when all courtiers hold their hands in front of their mouths and whisper to each other what they see, this does not change anything about the actual pattern. The emperor continues to be praised for his new clothes. It is only when the child appears and introduces the communication "But the emperor is naked!" into the system that the blinders are removed from everyone's eyes, and nothing is as it was before. Speaking systemically, what happens is the *re-entry* which was previously mentioned; the verbal re-introduction of the system-environment difference into the system. The influencing of group dynamics in the professional context (i.e. beyond manipulation) of coaching and consultation therefore always means enabling the group to reflect on themselves and in doing so more closely examine its own internal structures and processes. If this takes place in a protected, respected and benevolent context, changes are able to propagate in the communication patterns.

All methods and exercises from the toolbox of trainers and consultants who either make structures visible, reveal process patterns or describe the groups or team culture therefore have the goal of providing the social system with new descriptions and to integrate them into the communication patterns of the group through a common process of explanation of evaluation. Typical methods and exercises include: The sociogram (cf. Höhn and Schick 1976) in all its variants and variations, cooperation and decision-making exercises (cf. Antons 2011) as well as a wide range of creative and projective procedures (impromptu games, creative group images, sculptures etc.). Furthermore, this includes methods in which reflecting positions are able to voice their opinions and provide the group with certain descriptions in a targeted manner. This also includes metadialogs or reflections from the trainer, coach or consultant, the fish bowl, in which a small inner circle reflects on the group as a whole or assumes certain positions, e.g. the fools, the wise men etc. The risk of using exercises always exists in the systemically determined "non-instructionability". This means that not every method always results in the desired effect, i.e. it is not possible to work according to a "recipe book". Experience, intuition and good contact with the group, as well as management competency at the micro-level, i.e. with regard to verbal and non-verbal interventions, are required in order to intervene at the "right" point in the group process and to provide effective stimuli.

(4) **Content**

The influencing at the *content* level takes the form of a meticulous clarification of expectations before beginning with the task at hand as well as a methodologically and didactically appropriate preparation, transfer, and reflection of content in the group process. Luhmann (1984) describes the content level as a communication system's dimension of expertise. This is where a system synchronizes itself with regard to what is currently the topic and what is not. Because a social system needs to be fed constantly with communication in order to maintain its autopoiesis, the dimension of expertise decides if the interest of the involved persons in continuing to contribute to the group is maintained, or if they digress, or introduce a new topic into the communication. Good content preparation, clarification of expectations and the inclusion of all group members and interim feedback are fundamental to forestalling unfulfilled expectations or content that cannot be followed-up upon, thereby disrupting or impeding the process.

(5) **Interactions**

Finally, the dynamics of a group can be influenced at the level of *interactions*, i.e. the individual relationships between its members. Through their relationships, group members experience the social dimension of communication, i.e. the correspondence between "ego" and "other" (Luhmann 1984).

The spectrum of intervention options at the level of interactions is also extremely wide. From a systemic and constructive perspective, the main objective is to address expectation expectations within the interaction relationships of the group members and to calibrate them accordingly. Expectation expectations can be defined as the reality constructs which I assume another person has of me (what do I think you think of me? Or: what do I think you expect of me?). Expectation expectations are therefore social constructs which the members of a social system have concerning each other. They regulate the togetherness, make social relationships predictable and hold social systems together (von Schlippe and Schweitzer 2012). When there exist socially established or traditional contexts for expectation patterns, the expectation expectations often correspond with them in an unspoken manner, such as when eating at a restaurant, at the hairdresser's or when taking a taxi. The taxi driver thinks that the passenger expects to be told of the fare upon reaching the destination. Hence, the passenger is therefore not surprised at all when the driver does announce the fare. In contexts that are less clear, such as in a group or a team, the expectation expectations need to be spoken out every now and again in order to avoid disruptions at the "relationship level" or to clarify them.

The methods of choice for this clarification are the various forms of giving and receiving feedback in the group. This can take place between two or more persons, between partial groups, or among the entire group. One extremely effective intervention for providing assistance when the group dynamics are stuck in a rut in the norming phase is a method in which all group members, simultaneously and in pairs, give short, respectful feedback and/or tell each other of their expectation expectations, then switch partners until each group member has received feedback from every other. The result is a significant and positive change in the group situation, as all relationships have been reactivated and provided with positive communication in the social dimension. The individual group members feel secure again in the group, and the expectations each has of the other are clearer.

(6) **Persons**

Interventions in the context of the dynamics of groups can also be directed at one or more *persons* and their behavior in the group. This also entails asking that individual persons involve themselves more in the group while requesting that others exercise more restraint, getting disruptive persons under control, showing appreciation for positive contributions, and ensuring that all (are able to) involve themselves etc. Therefore, in addition to the management of a social system at the context, structural, and process levels, working with multiple persons also involves, above all, the shaping of one's relationship with each individual group member. Here too, there exist numerous intervention options, beginning with showing appreciation for, providing support to and encouraging individual persons in the group process all the way to conversations for the purposes of clarification or conflict resolution following a workshop that did not go well.

The interventions at the person level serve, among other things, to promote, maintain and secure the acceptance and authority of the coach and hence his effectiveness. Relationship dysfunctions between individual group members and the coach may also be an expression of the group dynamics in this case, as well as an indication that the coach is no longer the one in charge of the group dynamics, but has instead become a part of it.

13.5 Summary

It is inconceivable that coaches who do not possess sophisticated group dynamics experience and competencies should coach persons with leadership and management roles. Specifically, this refers to the reflection and maturing of one's own consultation personality in the social space of a group, the theory-led consultation for persons with group dynamics issues in coaching, and the development of action competencies for managing group processes in multi-person settings. These three application perspectives should be the content and subject of learning, practice, and reflection in the qualification of coaches as part of further education courses for coaching as well as their personal development and continued education. In doing so, it is not necessary to assimilate as many elaborate approaches and theories as possible, but instead, based on useful descriptions, to observe the client's issue or one's own actions and hence build up or strengthen one's own competencies for the client and oneself as a coach. Above all, management of groups and intervention in group dynamics processes require a great deal of experience as well as authority and presence in the role of group leader. These effective qualities arise based on knowledge, method and process reliability and clarity, reflection, focusing, i.e. clarity of roles; and these are exactly the three ingredients which Seliger (2010) describes as being the components out of which professionalism develops.

References

Amann, A. (2009). Der Prozess des Diagnostizierens - Wie untersuche ich eine Gruppe? In C. Edding & K. Schattenhofer (Hrsg.), *Handbuch Alles über Gruppen. Theorie, Anwendung, Praxis*. Weinheim: Beltz.

Antons, K. (2011). *Praxis der Gruppendynamik: Übungen und Techniken*. Göttingen: Hogrefe.

Bachmann, T. (2012). Coaching? Training? Organisationsentwicklung? *Wirtschaft und Weiterbildung, 3*(2012), 38–40.

Bachmann, T. (in Vorb.). *System und Kontakt – Ideen für eine Theorie des Kontakts*.

Belbin, R. M. (1996). *Managementteams. Erfolg und Misserfolg*. Wörrstadt: Bergander.

Brosius, K. (2009). Soziales Lernen in Gruppen. In C. Edding & K. Schattenhofer (Hrsg.), *Handbuch Alles über Gruppen. Theorie, Anwendung, Praxis*. Weinheim: Beltz.

Buer, F. (2012). Die Supervision und das Glück. In. W. Weigand (Hrsg.), *Philosophie und Handwerk der Supervision* (S. 237–245). Gießen: Psychosozial-Verlag.

Campbell, D. T. (1958). Common fate, similarity, and other indices of the status of aggregates of persons as social entities. *Behavioral Science, 3,* 14–25.

Cohn, R. C. (1997). *Von der Psychoanalyse zur themenzentrierten Interaktion*. Stuttgart: Klett-Cotta.

Dehner, U. (2009). *Beratung mit Ratschlag*. Heft: ManagerSeminare. 131.

Fengler, J. (1986). Soziologische und sozialpsychologische Gruppenmodelle. In H. Petzold & R. Frühmann (Eds.), *Modelle der Gruppe in Psychotherapie und psychosozialer Arbeit* (Vol. 1, pp. 33–108). Paderborn: Junfermann.

Höhn, E., & Schick, C. P. (1976). *Das Soziogramm*. Göttingen: Hogrefe.

Kantor, D., & Lehr, W. (1977). *Inside the Family*. San Francisco: Jossey-Bass.

König, O., & Schattenhofer, K. (2012). *Einführung in die Gruppendynamik*. Heidelberg: Carl-Auer.

Königswieser, R., Wimmer, R., & Simon, F. B. (2013). Back to the Roots - Die neue Aktualität der ("systemischen") Gruppendynamik. *Organisationsentwicklung, 1,* 65–73.

Luhmann, N. (1984). *Soziale Systeme*. Frankfurt am Main: Suhrkamp Verlag.

Parsons, T. (1978). *Action theory and the human condition*. New York: Free Press.

Richter, H. E. (1993). *Lernziel Solidarität*. Reinbek: Rowohlt.

Schein, E. H. (2012). *Prozess und Philosophie des Helfens*. Bergisch Gladbach: EHP.

Schermuly, C. C., Schermuly-Haupt, M.-L., Schölmerich, F., & Rauterberg, H. (2014). Zu Risiken und Nebenwirkungen lesen Sie… Negative Effekte von Coaching. *Zeitschrift für Arbeits- und Organisationspsychologie, 58,* 17–33.

Schindler, R. (1957). Grundprinzipien der Psychodynamik in der Gruppe. *Psyche, 11,* 308–314.

Schlegel, L. (1993). *Handwörterbuch der Transaktionsanalyse*. Freiburg: Herder.

Schmidt-Lellek, C., & Buer, F. (Eds.). (2011). *Life-Coaching in der Praxis. Wie Coaches umfassend beraten*. Göttingen: Vandenhoeck & Ruprecht.

Scholl, W. (2004). *Innovation und Information. Wie in Unternehmen neues Wissen produziert wird* (unter Mitarbeit von L. Hoffmann und H.-C. Gierschner). Göttingen: Hogrefe.

Scholl, W. (2013a). The socio-emotional basis of human interaction and communication. How we construct our social world. *Social Science Information, 52,* 3–33.

Scholl, W. (2013b). Vertrauenskultur und Innovationsfähigkeit. In G. Becke, W. Scholl, S. Klinke, C. Funken, & M. K. W. Schweer (Eds.), *Innovationsfähigkeit durch Vertrauensgestaltung?: Befunde und Instrumente zur nachhaltigen Organisations- und Netzwerkentwicklung* (pp. 23–42). Frankfurt/M.: Peter Lang.

Scholl, W., Breitling, K., Janetzke, H., & Shajek, A. (2013). *Innovationserfolg durch aktive Mitbestimmung. Die Auswirkungen von Betriebsratsbeteiligung, Vertrauen und Arbeitnehmerpartizipation auf Prozessinnovationen.* Berlin: Sigma.

Schreyögg, A. (2004). *Supervision. Ein integratives Modell* (4., überarb. u. erw. Aufl.). Wiesbaden: VS Verlag.

Schreyögg, G., & Koch, K. (2007). *Grundlagen des Managements. Basiswissen für Studium und Praxis.* Wiesbaden: Gabler.

Seliger, R. (2010). *Dschungelbuch der Führung.* Heidelberg: Carl-Auer.

Seliger, R. (2011). *Einführung in die Großgruppenmethoden.* Heidelberg: Carl-Auer.

Senge, P. M. (2008). *Die fünfte Disziplin.* Stuttgart: Schäffer-Poeschel.

Simon, F. B. (2004). *Gemeinsam sind wir blöd?! Die Intelligenz von Unternehmen, Managern und Märkten.* Heidelberg: Carl-Auer.

Tuckman, B. W. (1965). Developmental sequence in small groups. *Psychological Bulletin, 63,* 384–399.

von Schlippe, A., & Schweitzer, J. (2012). *Lehrbuch der systemischen Therapie und Beratung.* Göttingen: Vandenhoeck & Ruprecht.

Weber, G. (2001). Organisationsaufstellungen: Basics und Besonderes. In G. Weber (Ed.), *Praxis der Organisationsaufstellungen.* Heidelberg: Carl-Auer.

West, M. A. (1996). Reflexivity and workgroup effectiveness: a conceptual integration. In M. A. West (Ed.), *Handbook of work group psychology* (pp. 555–579). Chichester, UK: Wiley.

Willke, H. (2006). *Systemtheorie I: Grundlagen.* Stuttgart: Lucius & Lucius.

Wimmer, R. (1998). Das Team als besonderer Leistungsträger in komplexen Situationen. In H. W. Ahlemeyer & R. Königswieser (Eds.), *Komplexität managen.* Wiesbaden: Gabler.

Author Biography

Dr. Thomas Bachmann Dipl.-Psych., founding member and senior partner at artop GmbH, the institute for consultation, professional qualifications, and research at the Humboldt University of Berlin, consultant and coach for organizations, management staff, and teams. Senior coach at DBVC and a member of other institutions and associations, and visiting lecturer at the Humboldt University of Berlin.

Emotions in the Context of Coaching

14

Beate West-Leuer

Abstract

Best intentions notwithstanding, managers often fail to change their communicative behavior in a constructive manner. This would require a better understanding of their own and others emotional patterns. An understanding of this type can be obtained through interactional psychoanalytic interventions: The coach selectively makes his authentic emotional reactions available; he helps to identify and clarify the client's emotions; he assumes ego functions, if these are temporarily unavailable to the client. Case studies clearly show how these interventions can improve self-management and self-control. An overview of the findings of basic neurobiological affective research serves as the scientific foundation of the approach.

14.1 Introduction

The manner in which we deal with feelings such as anger, fear or joy has a significant and formative impact on our social competencies—not only in our private, but also professional lives. If coaching is to be used to improve a client's ability to deal with his own emotions and the emotions of other people, the coach will require knowledge about the development of affect, feelings, and empathy. He

B. West-Leuer (✉)
Wehler Dorfstr. 37, 41472 Neuss, Germany
e-mail: West-Leuer@t-online.de
URL: http://www.west-leuer.de

A. Schreyögg and C. Schmidt-Lellek (eds.), *The Professionalization of Coaching*, DOI 10.1007/978-3-658-16805-6_14

will also require methods of intervention that can help the client to decipher affective signals, to resolve his emotions with regard to himself and others, and to modulate these signals in a manner appropriate for the situation. The reasons that prompt such a coaching session are often highly diverse. If a coaching session is recommended by the company, the human resources department which is searching for a coach for the client often indicates various issues such as "personality development", "improvement of ability for self-reflection", "insufficient communicative ability", "discipline problems", or "emotional regulation" (cf. Grimmer and Neukom 2009).

Findings from neurobiological attachment research tell us that the formation of our affect systems takes place when we are infants. Our social experience is activated in real-life mirror-image interactions with the face of our attachment figures in early life and the emotional reactions recognizable in these faces, allowing the neural circuitry for social competencies to develop in the brain. This early emotional attachment has a profound impact on our self-management abilities. These abilities manifest themselves in a situation-dependent manner when interacting with others; with employees, colleagues, and superiors, and range from well-integrated to poorly integrated. This is where the interventions of the interactional-psychoanalytical method come in. In coaching, they aim to stabilize the client's affective systems and to assist him with difficulties encountered in his own self-management. In a selective and authentic affective interaction, the coach demonstrates to the client how he behaves in various relationships, how he handles his affect, and how others may perceive the manner in which he deals with his emotions. In this manner, the coaching relationship repeats and consolidates what neurobiology and attachment research deem necessary in order for affective regulation to be successful.

In the following, this psychodynamic process will be illustrated using cases from the author's coaching experiences. These case studies are embedded in an illustration of the basic theoretical assumptions of the interactional-psychoanalytical method and its possible applications during real-life consultations. An overview of the most salient findings of neurobiological and attachment-oriented affective research will serve as a scientific foundation.

14.2 Improvement of Self-management and Self-government

During coaching sessions, an executive has the opportunity to reenact relationship experiences from his professional life in a safe space. In a dialog with the coach, friendly and inimical emotions that have arisen not only in his private life, but also in daily working life, can slowly be made accessible. This allows the client to improve his self-management and self-government in his professional role and as a person, and to objectify the manner in which he interacts with his superiors, employees, colleagues, and clients.

Coaching presupposes self-management competencies; psychotherapy builds on them (cf. Chap. 6 in this book). Coaching is a suitable consultation format when the client has had sufficiently positive relationship experiences in his early life development. Ideally, the consultation setting creates conditions in which the client activates his internalized, benevolent relationship experiences, enters into an internal dialog with them, and obtains appropriate images of himself as a self-determined and self-determining person. These images then enable him to develop creative action plans and strategies for his professional goals and in his professional relationships (Grimmer and Neukom 2009, p. 128 ff.).

In real-life consultation, however, coaches are increasingly consulted with requests in which their potential clients self-management and self-government are negatively impacted due to the great deal of stress they are under.[1] "High Performers" react with shame and the feeling of having failed when their career stagnates. They suffer from psychological crises or fall into depression (West-Leuer 2009, 2011; Haubl 2007). They then attempt to keep this hidden from themselves and others for as long as possible. This is because psychological crises can have disastrous consequences for their career. Human resources and coaching representatives are aware of this. Hence, they formally insist on separating coaching and psychotherapy, but paradoxically, they value therapeutic interventions as being particularly effective and therefore assume that it is understood that such interventions will be utilized in coaching sessions (Grimmer and Neukom 2009, cf. Chap. 6 in this book). In practice, coaching and psychotherapy can be seen as opposite poles of a consultation service which is "by people, for people" that are linked by the effect factor "relationship" (cf. Chap. 4 in this book).

14.3 From Affect to Feelings and Empathy

Our feelings can be ascribed to the basic affects of fear, anger, joy, grief, and disgust. *Fear* is a hereditary instinct that results in the distancing or fleeing away from a dangerous external object. *Anger* aims to quickly and aggressively destroy a dangerous external object, while *disgust* is meant to expel a dangerous object that has partially invaded a person. *Joy* results in closeness (safety, propagation), and *grief*

[1]For coaching with psychotherapeutic elements, cf. West-Leuer (2011).

takes care of the loss of and the spiritual recovery of the lost object. Transferred to a professional situation, fear of employees or superiors may result in problems, errors in performance, and conflicts not being addressed. In certain cases, options ranging from a retreat to "mentally checking out" are preferred over an objective or professional confrontation. Anger can lead to uncontrolled outbursts that have a permanent impact on employees (or superiors)—occasionally even "traumatizing" them. Disgust can lead to mobbing, such as when a team attempts to expel a team member due to collective rejection. Joy increases motivation and leads to a positive attitude towards work processes and products. Grief is crucial in restructuring, when that which is old and familiar has to give way to new structures and processes. An insufficient or overly zealous management of individual basic affects plays a background role in a great number of coaching requests, as this often results in a significant negative impact on social behavior in daily working life.

We generally learn to deal with these basic affects in our own way from the face of our attachment figures in early life, usually the face of our mothers. If the attention given is empathy-driven and stress-regulated, it results in the optimization and maturation of the stress-modulated neural systems in a child's brain. A process —as technically formulated by Franz (2008)—which can be described as a structure-creating download of emotional information into the dynamic "hardware" of the synaptically linked neural networks of a child's brain In this manner, an infant's state of distress is basically understood "online" and intuitively by a healthy and sensitive attachment figure. This great achievement—i.e. being able to immediately empathize with a child's feelings by paying attention to microsignals (*affect attunement*) —, is a prerequisite for appropriate stress regulation. Furthermore, a sufficiently sensitive person is also able to recreate the corresponding affect state his child is currently experiencing within himself and to empathize with the child's activated affect system in response (*affect sharing*). Subsequently, within fractions of a second, he is able to provide the child with an affect-expressing response signal and therefore also a symbol for what the child himself is experiencing. This takes place very intensively, via his adequately affective facial expression, which is observed by the infant with great concentration.

It is now crucial that the emotional facial expression of the attachment figure does not simply perfectly mirror the e.g. impassive experience of the child like an automaton. The mechanically mirrored affect "fear in child = real, actual fear in the attachment figure's face" unsettles the child just as deeply as closing one's eyes or turning away one's face for a long period of time (Franz 2008). Through the facial expressions he contributes, the attachment figure comments on the negative affect present in the child to some extent, modifies or "digests" it, and represents it on his face in a "cleaned-up" version (Fonagy et al. 2004).

If this process of *affect marking* is successful, the child will subsequently be able to sense the dissimilarity of the other party as not automatically being hostile, and react to it not with narcissistic control or separation anxiety, but instead to empathize with the emotional experiences of the other party, and thoughtfully allow it to be incorporated into his own behavioral management, without questioning or damaging his own identity. The child finds out that the attachment figure is predictable and can be comprehensively manipulated for satisfying its needs. In truth, this is simply an illusion of control which is created when the attachment figure sufficiently satisfies the needs of his child (Franz 2008).

The supervision and mental modeling of the experiences of the other person in one's own ego, in addition to a secure attachment, are crucial fundamentals in the acquisition of socio-emotional, cognitive, and personality structure competencies.

- Socio-emotional competencies include, for example, the ability to develop realistic views of the behavioral motifs of others; i.e. to represent the experiences of the other party within oneself. Emphatic, constructive social behavior, reciprocity in relationships, the ability to work with others, humor, as well as a conscious handling of affects and/or verbal methods of communicating feelings are indicators of such socio-emotional competencies.
- Among other things, cognitive competencies are expressed by separating "wishful thinking" from the ability to simulate the behavior and wishes of others within oneself in a trial "as-if" mode. A reliable perception of facts, curious exploratory behavior, a capacity for abstract reasoning, and the ability to extrapolate general from specialized concepts also indicate that a person has acquired age-appropriate cognitive competencies.
- Personality structure competencies which indicate that children and adults are securely attached and have the ability to "mentalize", are a growing supervisory measure against affective (e.g. aggressive) impulses and lead to a socially well-adjusted regulation of affect, the appropriate handling of fears, a mature tolerance towards frustration and stress resistance, as well as well-developed concentration and learning abilities (cf. Franz 2008).

14.4 Emotional and Interactional Intervention Modes

The precise perception of one's own affective processes and those of other people is a core competency for leadership personnel. It promotes self-reflection and enables a person to shape his own professional role actively and intersubjectively —in his interactions with superiors, employees, and clients (cf. DBVC 2012).

A professional coach requires—among other things—intervention modes that help and encourage his client in perceiving and dealing with affect.

Psychodynamic intervention modes that are not only suitable for therapeutic purposes, but also for forms of consultation, are provided by the interactional-psychoanalytical method (Heigl-Evers and Ott 1998; Streeck 2007). The most significant interventions are *authentic responses, affect identification* and/or *affect clarification* and the *adoption of auxiliary ego functions.* They can enable emotions such as amazement, bafflement, surprise, or dismay, but also irritation, shame, or grief to be experienced in a sophisticated manner within the context of the relationship with the coach, and allow them to be integrated in a person's self-perception. In this manner, negative effects that leadership personnel subject themselves to through the insufficient or overzealous management of individual emotions and affects can be modified gradually.

In the following, the application of the interactional-psychoanalytical intervention modes will be introduced with the help of case studies. Unstable affect systems and affect regulation can interfere with the work process to a particularly significant extent, such as when crises and conflicts between employees and superiors need to be handled, during restructuring and streamlining processes, during breakdowns in communication, as well as in the case of social competency deficits. Particularly in "critical" situations (as opposed to those requiring improvement or relaxed situations) (cf. DBVC 2012), it is not ideal working conditions which these people require at their workplace, but instead authentic (working) relationships (cf. West-Leuer 2007a).

14.4.1 The Mode of an Authentic Response Which Is Selective in the Method of Its Expression

In his authentic reaction, the coach expresses verbally in a modified fashion what the client triggers in him: "When you behave in "manner of behavior", I experience you as being "how coach experiences client" and then I feel "feeling" towards you." The coach shows himself as a different person and the client is acutely aware that he is someone to be taken seriously. The client is confronted with a perspective that is different from his own. An authentic answer that targets the core of the counseling relationship and the issue being dealt with during the consultation procedure is a chance for the client to not only get to know the other party, but also himself from a different perspective.

Mr. A has repeatedly lost his job as a facility manager in mechanical engineering firms. He cannot explain why he is always dismissed from his job after two or three years even though everyone is completely satisfied with his performance. When he is rejected after an interview at an SME, he turns to coaching. He wants to understand why he did not get the job despite his excellent professional qualifications. He speaks of the interview, and tells me that he was interviewed by the owner's daughter in lieu of her father. And then he says: "After the first few sentences, I realized that the daughter was entirely overwhelmed by the situation."

I identified with the boss's daughter and experienced both feelings of being talked down to, as well as anger. My emotional reaction shows me that I am transferring the client's narration to the coaching situation. I wonder if Mr. A is trying to tell me that he feels that anything other than a male colleague with the same specialization as him for a coach is inadequate for a person with a master's degree in process technology. If this were the case, the reason he chose me would have been to unburden himself of his feelings of being devalued, and not to work on himself.

In the case of destructive domination tendencies, I would either terminate the coaching session or subtly ensure that Mr. A decides to cancel all future sessions. In order to avoid this, I reply in the mode of the selective and authentic response: "It appears to me that you are not able to precisely separate your professional competencies from the competencies of others. And that causes you to appear to be slightly condescending. I bristled slightly at your remark about the senior boss's daughter, and transferred your comment to our relationship as an experiment. The result is that I have doubts about whether you really want to use coaching to change something, or if you are instead trying to find out which of us is "on top" and who is "below". If the boss's daughter felt something similar, she would have recommended against hiring you. I am willing to work together with you in coaching sessions. The first goal would then be to deal with each other—despite our extremely different professional competencies—humanely, with respect and as equals".

A client who was at a loss and inexperienced in dealing with relationships quickly surfaced behind the mask of the tough applicant. I was able to ascertain for myself that the devaluation attempts stemmed from his fear of failure. My reply that gestures of superiority, even if they are well-founded from a professional point of view, are generally not accepted by superiors, was neither distancing, nor condescending, but instead successful in establishing contact. In this manner, any previous negative beliefs that he would be "kept in his place" and hence needed to inflate his superiority in order to survive, were neither confirmed nor consolidated, but instead partially alleviated. Consequently, he was able to understand that a demonstration of superior professional knowledge can be perceived by others as arrogance—which is of course unfavorable in a job interview. The result of these short coaching sessions (6 × 60-min sessions) was that the client was able to find a new job. Feedback from him after four years showed that he was able to gradually improve his social competencies, in particular his "understanding" for superiors and employees.

14.4.2 Affect Identification and Affect Clarification

The entire spectrum of our emotions is reproduced in coaching processes. In the intervention mode *affect identification and affect clarification,* the coach allows himself to be reached emotionally by the client, and also conveys this: "You are someone that can speak to me regarding feelings, and elicit emotions within me. Similarly, I am also someone who elicits feelings within you. In this manner, during the consultation process, we will interact, coordinate, and encourage each other, leading to actionable processes which may be of a friendly, critical, or even an aggressive nature." The client can then be addressed with regard to obvious inhibitions and suppression or uncontrolled actions and the exaggeration of affects with the intention of subjecting them to an adequate amount of control and guidance. In short, the goal is as follows:

- To clarify affects and their relationship to the situation, to oneself, and to others
- To modify affective tolerances
- To limit and modulate affects
- To decipher affective signals.

"When employees speak of their boss as being a 'businesslike' or 'cool-headed' person and say that he does not have an emotional relationship with people, this is not true—he does have one, but it is a poor relationship!" (Bayer 1995). In actual fact, the superior described simply has a reduced perception of his own affects and consequently is unable to decipher his employees affects or answer in a motivational manner. Coaching offers the opportunity to carefully "sound out" affects and to transfer these experiences to the relationships at the workplace. Here is a corresponding case study from coaching in SMEs (cf. Chap. 16 in this book).

The scheduling agents in a shipping company "flip out" on a regular basis after telephone calls. They rant about the company's clients in a loud voice. Because they work in a large open-plan office, the other clients currently on the phone also hear these outbursts. Because of this, the young boss hired a communications trainer. When this only results in a short-term change in the behavior of his scheduling agents, he turns to coaching. He reports on the social practices in the company, and says that he makes every effort to be professional and polite. He is also attempting to introduce a democratic management style. His mother's style of management was more authoritarian. She would come to work each day and openly criticize her employees "incompetence" and her son's "soft" management style. These complaints continue to be audible. He then suddenly changes the topic and tells the coach that he read in a yearly horoscope that being a cook was actually the right profession for him. He is now considering changing jobs, even though the company has expanded a great deal recently.

In this case study, the client describes what is clearly aggressive and debasing behavior on the part of his mother, but is initially unable to himself feel or activate anger concerning the situation. His desire to switch jobs indicates that he would rather flee than subject himself to a necessary confrontation. Presumably, he would also not dare to switch companies, because this does not agree with his mother's plans (cf. Chap. 17 in this book). At times, he then flees inwards: the aggression is directed at himself, and the client takes recourse in what is mostly a depressive symptomatic. In this case, the obvious course of action would be to examine the client's "addiction to harmony". This is because the over-zealous management of his grievances and the denial of his emotional wounds have led to his scheduling agents vicariously "flipping out" by (consciously and) insufficiently managing their aggression. When this is addressed during coaching, it is to be expected that the client will attempt to mollify the coach and show "emotion". When confronted with his modified behavior, grief becomes perceptible. It is only after a grieving process that the client is able to stabilize the "good" mother in his emotional landscape, but then also distance himself from her obvious errors in the affective management as his senior boss, and override her mistakes. After the agreed-upon ten sessions, the client stops the consultations. He no longer saw any additional need for coaching at that point in time. However, he considers whether he could benefit over the long term from deep psychology psychotherapy, and contacts the coach after half a year requesting a recommendation for psychotherapy.

14.4.3 Adoption of an Auxiliary Ego Function

In the third intervention mode, the coach primarily adopts ego functions that are not available to the client. These functions include the following:

- Perception and verbalization of needs and desires
- Perception and changes of inner standards and ideals
- Activation of ego functions:

  - Self-perception and-judgment
  - Perception and judgment of others
  - Reality check
  - Regulation of closeness and distance
  - Ability to reach compromises
- Registering and changing dysfunctional resistances.

The adoption of these auxiliary ego functions is an offer of providing assistance and identification: "How about if you try doing it this way?" "I, your coach would react or act differently from you, and instead do this." As in Mr. A's case (see above), the coach notices that the client constantly falls into the same trap. He repeats a particular pattern of behavior, is astonished by the results, comes to the next session and says: "You'll never guess what happened to me!" When the coach then confronts him with reality and says: "Then you have most probably trivialized the situation", the client turns the tables on him. He denies and plays down the issue. In such cases, it is then the coach's duty to carry out the reality check (Ott and West-Leuer 2003).

In this situation, the coach's duty is to utilize the auxiliary ego function to make the client aware of the fact that an alternative strategy is necessary. Particular attention should be paid to resentful affects such as bitterness, resent, grudges, ill will, spite, or feelings of vengeance. If the client is able to identify such affects within himself, he can learn to understand the context of how they arise and process them in an appropriate fashion.

The national human resources chef of an internationally active economics company contacts me abruptly and informs me that he is doing extremely badly. A year ago, he was able to avert an impending burnout with the help of intensive coaching sessions recommended to him by his superior. The need for coaching arose after the group's management decided on drastic personnel cutbacks in the HR department. The client had organized and carried out these cutbacks, causing him to suffer from a great deal of stress. The personnel cutbacks in this department were heavily castigated in the media, but celebrated as a flagship project within the organization. Employees were also dismissed in other areas of the company in accordance with the model developed by the client. The group was on the path towards consolidation, or so it appeared.

Now the client had once again turned to coaching. He is visibly distressed and has tears in his eyes. He asks me whether I knew that the offices where he and the remaining employees were working were going to be shut down. The employees had been offered jobs in another federal state. However, ≈20% of the HR personnel would not be able to resume employment. If the group wanted to retain him, he would have to be offered a job managing the setting up and heading of a profit center with new employees at a different location. His boss had rejected this, and said that he was needed for the restructuring. He is extremely disappointed by his boss. His doctor subsequently placed him on sick leave. His boss had to announce the re-restructuring of his department in his absence.

In addition to empathy, I feel the urge to distance myself. The company is on the brink of economic ruin, and he "flees" by going on sick leave. I can relate to a good counseling relationship, and risk a confrontation. Could it be that your employees feel that you have left them in the lurch? The client is extremely astonished by this assumption. After all, he had been stabbed in the back by his boss. And now he expected him to contact him. I surmise that there is an extortionary power struggle going on, which the client confirms with a thin smile. But he does not realize that he is waging this war on the backs of his employees. "If I were you, I would speak to my boss. After all, the company and your job are extremely important to you." The client is unhappy with the course the conversation has taken, and leaves the coaching session in deep contemplation.

The client's taking refuge in sickness is ego-syntonic, in full agreement with himself, and is nourished by a profound feeling of entitlement which the coach is supposed to share (Hartkamp and Heigl-Evers 1995). In the auxiliary ego intervention mode, the aim is to adopt ego functions which are temporarily unavailable to the client due to development-related reasons. In this case, affects of grief regarding the fact that the consolidation of the company has not been successful so far are unavailable to the client. He feels no fear that he may lose his job, and is instead furious at the company's "impudence" for daring to disband his department. What is significant here is the absence of a reality check and a third-party perspective. He cannot anticipate that his boss cannot show himself as being susceptible to blackmail without losing self-regard, but also the client's respect.

Often, people who turn to coaching have a familiar yet dysfunctional strategy which they are unable to give up (cf. West-Leuer 2007b). When the coach then confronts them with this reality, they put up a dogged amount of resistance. These clients will continually push on with a smoldering conflict in a wide variety of variations and allow it to escalate, even if they risk losing their job in the process. The coach will then relinquish the auxiliary ego position and decide to provide an authentic answer: "I cannot accompany you on your crusade. If I go along with your futile quest, it may cause you more harm than good. And that is neither my duty nor my desire."

14.5 Conclusion: No Coaching Without Emotion[2]

The case studies show that the coach and the client are emotionally involved in a variety of different ways, whether they are aware of it or not. In order to understand this involvement and to utilize it in a manner that is beneficial for the client, psychotherapists take part in numerous training sessions which focus on self-awareness. This is because it is not possible to cognitively acquire the ability to handle emotions in an interactional manner—one can only experience it personally. And even then, it is not easy to engage with the client on an emotional level, while at the same time observing this process from a cognitive meta-level. In "doublethink" (West-Leuer 2007a), the aim is to find out which emotions are currently virulent for the client, which ones for me, the coach, and what these emotions have in common with the client's consultation issues. What makes this all the more difficult is that having emotions or even showing them openly is strongly frowned upon in a company and taboo (Vasella 2014). This illusion of emotionlessness is frequently transferred one-to-one to coaching. In this case, coaches are sometimes discouraged and give up, and say that they do not see how it is possible for them to apply emotional and interactional intervention methods in coaching.

Yet in doing so, they are passing up a good opportunity. Only after precisely perceiving his own and others affective processes does a leader become able to shape his professional role actively and in a self-determined manner. A sufficiently sensitive coach—something every professional consultant will be—is intuitively capable of "affect attunement", "affect sharing", and "affect marking". He can identify with the client as well as the client's employees, customers or superiors; he will trust that his own emotional reactions towards the client will not be very different from the reactions to the client in his professional environment.

If "doublethink" does not seem to work in the beginning, the coach can ask himself the following after the session: Which emotions did I sense from the client and which emotions from myself? The case studies show that the coach's and client's affects cannot always be distinguished accurately. The feelings of inadequacy of the consultant in the first case study—the shame she feels because she thinks she may not meet the requirements—have enabled her to access the client's feelings of inadequacy and fear of failure. Her disappointment and indignation at the client having taken sick leave in the third case scenario acted like a mirror for the indignation and disappointment the client felt at having been "betrayed" by his

[2]Chapter title alludes to Roth (1997): No cognition without emotion.

boss. In the second case scenario, the absence of feelings was striking—in this case the absence of aggression. Due to this, the employees overcompensated by displaying their aggression to an even greater extent. When working with emotions, perceiving and identifying them is the *first step*. The *second step* is reviewing what one has perceived in order to better understand the problem: The scheduling agents "flip out" because they are annoyed at their senior boss and their boss who is unable to show aggression. However, aggression is only acceptable downwards or to the outside, but not upwards (Vasella 2014). Hence, the scheduling agents bad-mouth the customers. In the third step, the coach can formulate an intervention, e.g. in the auxiliary ego mode. In this case, he or she will consider which missing feeling should be addressed: the annoyance at the senior boss, feeling embarrassed (on account of someone else's behavior) due to the insubordinate interference of the mother, or the sadness at the pending intrapsychological separation from the idealized maternal object.

A coach can also practice the "emotional" follow-up of a coaching session by systematically examining the following: Were there affects such as astonishment, curiosity, or interest? Such information-processing affects generally provide constructive help, allowing the coaching process to progress. Were there affects that prompted (impulsive) action, such as anger, annoyance, sadness, and joy, or were they suppressed or even denied? The suppression or denial of feelings may contribute to slowing down the process. Self-reflexive affects of guilt or shame occur in the coach and the client if the path from affect to feeling and empathy was taken in early socialization and an emphatic cooperation is possible. If they become obvious, the coach must resist the impulse to trivialize them out of wrongly understood sympathy. On the other hand, affects involving resentment such as grudges, indignation and outrage are difficult to deal with. This is because they are ego-syntonic and do not allow the client any courses of action. Instead, the expectation that the other person needs to change is at the forefront (cf. Hartkamp 2013).[3]

The interactional identification of striking emotions which do not appear to fit the context at first glance or the apparent absence of contextually expected motions will be drawn on by the coach for hypothesis formation according to their significance in the context of the coaching issue(s). These hypotheses can be provided to the client in a selectively confrontational manner; i.e. without offending or hurting his feelings. If these interpretations appear consistent for the client, they will effect an advanced understanding for his professional situation, and where

[3]For a comprehensive list of emotions in organizations, please refer to Martin Y Troyano (2006), p. 16ff.

applicable, also a behavioral change. Should the interpretations not be accepted, or if they are corrected by the client, the counseling relationship can still be strengthened by this intervention. This is because the client will realize that the coach does not act like a know-it-all. The client always remains "master of his own house".

References

Bayer, H.-P. (1995). *Coaching-Kompetenz. Persönlichkeit und Führungspsychologie.* München: Ernst Reinhardt.

DBVC – Deutscher Bundesverband Coaching e. V. (Hrsg.) (2012). *Leitlinien und Empfehlungen für die Entwicklung von Coaching als Profession. Kompendium mit den Professionsstandards des DBVC* (4., erw. Aufl.). Osnabrück: DBVC Geschäftsstelle

Fonagy, P., Gergely, G., Jurist, E. L., & Target, M. (2004). *Affektregulierung, Mentalisierung und die Entwicklung des Selbst.* Stuttgart: Klett-Cotta.

Franz, M. (2008). Vom Affekt zum Gefühl und Mitgefühl. In M. Franz & B. West-Leuer (Hrsg.), *Bindung – Trauma – Prävention. Entwicklungschancen von Kindern und Jugendlichen als Folge ihrer Beziehungserfahrungen* (S. 15–38). Gießen: Psychosozial-Verlag.

Grimmer, B., & Neukom, M. (2009). *Coaching und Psychotherapie. Gemeinsamkeiten und Unterschiede – Abgrenzung oder Integration?* Wiesbaden: VS Verlag.

Hartkamp, N. (2013). *Affektdifferenzierung, Affektklärung und das Interventionsprinzip Antwort.* Power Point Präsentation im Rahmen der Coaching-Weiterbildung am Institut Psychodynamische Organisationsentwicklung und Personalmanagement Düsseldorf e.V., 24.11.2013

Hartkamp, N., & Heigl-Evers, A. (1995). Feinstrukturen einer analytischen Supervision. *Zeitschrift für Psychosomatische Medizin und Psychoanalyse, 41*(3), 253–267.

Haubl, R. (2007). Wenn Leistungsträger krank werden. Chronische Müdigkeit – Symptom oder Krankheit? In R. Haubl & E. Brähler (Hrsg.), Neue moderne Leiden. Krankheit und Gesellschaft. *Psychosozial* 30 (110), 25–34.

Heigl-Evers, A., & Ott, J. (Eds.). (1998). *Die psychoanalytisch-interaktionelle Methode. Theorie und Praxis.* Göttingen: Vandenhoeck & Ruprecht.

Martin y Troyano, N. (2006). *Emotionen im Kontext der Personalführung. Eine empirische Studie zur Frage, wie Führungspersonen mit den Emotionen einzelner Mitarbeiter und Mitarbeiterinnen umgehen.* http://deposit.fernuni-hagen.de/59/1/Diss_Emotionen_im_Kontext.pdf.

Ott, J., & West-Leuer, B. (2003). "Präsenz, Respekt, emotionale Akzeptanz und Authentizität": Interaktionelle Prinzipien nicht nur für das Coaching im Krisenfall. In B. West-Leuer & C. Sies (Eds.), *Coaching – Ein Kursbuch für die Psychodynamische Beratung* (pp. 125–147). Stuttgart: Pfeiffer bei Klett-Cotta.

Roth, G. (1997). *Das Gehirn und seine Wirklichkeit. Kognitive Neurobiologie und ihre philosophischen Konsequenzen.* Frankfurt/M.: Suhrkamp.

Streeck, U. (2007). *Psychotherapie komplexer Persönlichkeitsstörungen.* Klett-Cotta: Grundlagen der psychoanalytisch-interaktionellen Methode. Stuttgart.

Vasella, D. (2014). *Unter mir die Stadt. Reflexionen über Emotionen in Management und Topmanagement anhand eines Fallbeispiels im Film.* Email vom 06.06.2014

West-Leuer, B. (2007a). *Coaching an Schulen. Psychodynamische Beratung zur Stärkung professioneller Beziehungskompetenz.* Gießen: Psychosozial-Verlag.

West-Leuer, B. (2007b). "Wir sehen immer nur die Spitze des Eisbergs ..." Führungskräfte-coaching und Psychodynamische Beratung. In F. Lang & A. Sidler (Hrsg.), *Psychodynamische Organisationsanalyse und Beratung. Einblicke in eine neue Disziplin* (S. 51–80). Gießen: Psychosozial-Verlag.

West-Leuer, B. (2009). Psychodynamisches Coaching – mehr Chancengerechtigkeit für Fach- und Führungskräfte? In R. Heinz, W. Tress & B. West-Leuer (Hrsg.), Gerechtigkeit – Psychoanalytische Perspektiven eines strittigen Begriffs. *Psychosozial* 32 (116), 65–78.

West-Leuer, B. (2011). Affekt-Coaching. Business-Coaching zur Verbesserung von Selbstmanagement und Selbststeuerung. In H. Schnoor (Hrsg.), *Psychodynamische Beratung* (S. 165–178). Göttingen: Vandenhoeck & Ruprecht.

Author Biography

Dr. phil. Beate West-Leuer senior coach (DBVC), supervisor (DGSv); head of the institute "Psychodynamic organizational development and personnel management" (POP), vice chair of the Academy for psychoanalysis and psychosomatic medicine, member of the university board at the Gelsenkirchen Bocholt Recklinghausen University of Applied Sciences. Freelance consultation practice. Publication specializations: psychodynamic business coaching; psychoanalysis and film. Publisher of the journal "Agora. Düsseldorfer Beiträge zu Psychoanalyse und Gesellschaft".

Part IV
Conceptional Variations of Coaching

Internal Coaching Within Organizations

15

Astrid Schreyögg

Abstract

This article will examine aspects specific to internal coaching within organizations. Today, it is used as a human resources development measure in companies, the public sector, and social service systems. The postulate here is that this form of consultation does not only receive its legitimation from the respective organization, but also its defining characteristics, such as its conception, the goals, functions, settings, and implementation. They are to be adapted to the relevant organization.

15.1 Coaching—A Modern Form of Human Resources Development

Böning (2005, p. 21) speaks of a real "triumph" of coaching as a human resources development instrument. This is because, as Fillery-Travis and Lane (2006) remarked, the "coaching industry" has grown to become a two-billion-dollar market in western industrial nations. While private clients dominated up till the turn of the millennium, coaches today are more often hired by company representatives. These representatives come from companies, the public sector, and social service systems such as those in clinics or retirement homes. And as Segers

A. Schreyögg (✉)
Breisgauer Str. 29, 14129 Berlin, Germany
e-mail: info@schreyoegg.de
URL: http://www.Schreyoegg.de

A. Schreyögg and C. Schmidt-Lellek (eds.), *The Professionalization of Coaching*, DOI 10.1007/978-3-658-16805-6_15

et al. (2011) determined after a comprehensive international baseline study, in all these organizations coaching is not only used to deal with crises and conflicts; in many respects, it is used more often to develop specific skills or competencies. The number of publications on coaching has increased exponentially over the past few years.

As part of this development, forms of internal coaching for use within organizations have established themselves in many organizations in the industry, in the public sector, and in the social sector. Bollhöfer (2012, p. 87) is of the opinion that coaching has finally "established itself as a relevant factor in human resources development" in all types of organizations. However, the author suspects that the reason a particularly large number of persons today are making use of internal coaching offers within organizations is probably because the hurdles associated with utilizing them are much lower than if they were to seek out an external coach on their own.

Hence, the success of the internal variant can certainly also be referred to as a "triumph". However, this success in no way corresponds to the number of publications. On the contrary, one would need to have a genuine interest in this form of coaching in order to find relevant articles in professional journals or the brochures published by professional associations. Why then has so little been published about internal coaching within organizations despite the fact that it is currently so widespread? Two reasons are probably responsible for this:

(1) The majority of publications on coaching to date have been written by freelance or external coaches, primarily for marketing reasons. By having their work published, the authors are generally hoping to increase the number of clients they receive. Internal coaches within organizations, on the other hand, seldom see themselves as market participants. After all, their market is "limited" to their company. Therefore, they assume that clients will come to them whether or not they publish anything. In fact, many of them do not want to advertise coaching offensively, as they fear that they may then receive more clients than they can handle.

(2) One other extremely important reason lies in the fact that many management personnel are disinclined to provide approval for their employees' publications when it can be ascertained from these publications that coaching takes place within their system. In other organizations, relevant publications are only accepted after drawn-out approval procedures.

Hence, such publications come primarily from two groups of persons:

(1) From internal coaches whose company follows a special marketing strategy with this form of coaching, and which therefore are gladly willing to publish such works. This applies e.g. to Hogan Lovells, an international law firm which aims to hire only the very best university graduates, and hence attempts to attract them with sophisticated human resources development measures such as coaching.
(2) The second group of persons includes coaches who deal with the specific aspects of internal coaching as part of their duties when teaching coaching, as it is part of their job scope. This group includes me, the author of this article, as I have been working on the implementation of internal coaching in the public sector, in social service systems and companies for a number of years now. Because of this, I think it is worthwhile to have a closer look at internal coaching within organizations.

15.2 The Influence of the Organization with Its Constituents on Coaching as a Professional Form of Consultation

As is also the case in external coaching, in internal coaching the organization forms the backdrop for all phenomena to be dealt with during coaching. In addition, however, in internal coaching the organization is constitutive for the form of consultation itself. This means that the organization is ultimately a significant factor for all the major defining characteristics of internal coaching:

- for the concept of the coaching sessions, for questions regarding who has influence over the concept, and who gets to decide who is allowed to/who should teach the coaches and with which concept,
- which goals and functions are to be realized through coaching and who determines this,
- who functions as a coach within the organization, the areas in which coaching is established and with which rules,
- who is allowed to utilize coaching,
- the settings in which coaching is to take place,
- how coaching is implemented.

15.2.1 Who Shapes the Concepts of Internal Coaching?

In many social service organizations, such as clinics or large institutions providing psychiatric care, it is common for psychologists or social workers to independently obtain coaching qualifications on their own and then to offer this role within their system. Often, the employer pays for the training, or provides subsidies (e.g. Lellek 1999). When depth psychology concepts dominate, the management staff attach great importance to ensuring that the coaches are trained in a manner that conforms to the relevant concepts.

In the public sector, such as the police force in North Rhine-Westphalia, great emphasis is placed on ensuring that the qualification course satisfies university-level standards. Due to this, the Fern-Universität in Hagen (the only state-maintained distance teaching university in Germany) was charged with the task of providing qualification courses for supervision/coaching in the 1980s by the ministry of the interior of North Rhine-Westphalia. This was where chief commissioners were educated; primarily with regard to conflict management in police squads (Röhring 1999).

Who is commissioned to conduct the qualification courses or which type of coaching qualification courses appear acceptable in the corresponding organization is determined according to the group of persons which is later to assume this role. For example, in each case, the city of Nuremberg hired three to four social workers as internal counselors who previously also received their qualifications from a further education institute with an emphasis on social work, such as the German Association for Public and Private Welfare (Deutscher Verein für öffentliche und private Fürsorge) (Holzberger and Winkelmann 1999). Church associations, on the other hand, attach importance to ensuring that their counselors, too, receive their qualifications from a system that is close to the church (such as e.g. the "Evangelisches Zentralinstitut"). This also applies to the established municipal consultation offices in all protestant and catholic state churches (Knizia 2003).

In many cases, when an organization maintains psychological departments, the leading psychologist turns to the German Academy of Psychologists (Deutsche Psychologen Akademie) for further education courses. For example, the Federal Employment Agency (Bundesagentur für Arbeit) and the German Federal Armed forces (Bundeswehr) have had many psychologists qualified as coaches in this academy since the 1990s. Even the Bavarian Ministry of Culture has sent its school psychologists to this academy to prepare them for supervision and coaching tasks since 1986 (cf. Schreyögg 2000, 2008; Schreyögg and Lehmeier 2003). However, organizations in the public sector are required to publish a call for tenders nationwide first.

In companies, such as Siemens, Volkswagen, in banks and insurance companies, it is common practice today that one or more employees from human resources development plan to obtain coaching qualifications at a relevant coaching course provider which appears attractive to them due to their prior qualifications. In this manner, they expand the scope of their roles, which up to that point in time consisted perhaps primarily of training sessions, in a direction that includes coaching as well. If the courses are subsidized, the company representatives from the human resources department generally present the course concept for approval first. Zaggl (2012) chose yet another form of concept generation in a Tyrolean trading firm: After having obtained their coaching qualifications at the University of Innsbruck, they surveyed all nine management personnel in their company on their wishes and requests regarding coaching. They then independently developed this into a tailor-made concept for their company.

15.2.2 Types of Internal Coaching

However, internal coaches seldom work exclusively in the capacity of a coach in their organizations. For example, a psychologist at the Federal Employment Agency has various duties to fulfill, such as providing expert assessments or personnel selection. In each case, coaching is only a part of his portfolio (Westerwelle 2004). As part of the work the DBVC does, Bollhöfer (2012, p. 93 ff.) surveyed 25 company representatives regarding the implications of internal coaching and identified a number of different types of internal coaching:

(1) **Job enrichment of HR professionals**

Human resources development specialists who deal with the traditional aspects of human resources development (HRD) are asked by management staff to help out with conflict management or dismissals at certain points in time. Such events take place *ad hoc*, and are not seen as coaching in the sense of a professional consultation. However, such encounters encourage the HRD employee to qualify themselves professional for coaching and to later offer it as such in a targeted manner. In small companies, it often does not progress beyond this tentative variant. In large companies, however, it is often the first step to the professionalization of coaching. For example, the insurance provider KKH decided to have an entire group of human resource development specialists professionally qualified to conduct coaching.

(2) **The sector-specific coach**

These coaches are specialists from a certain area of the company, such as sales executives. They then obtain training e.g. in banks as to how clients can be given optimal advice over the phone during the purchase of real estate. Alternatively, they may also be responsible for complaint management in large department store chains. There also exist speech coaches who train opera singers in the pronunciation of a language that is foreign to them. This is a very limited form of coaching; i.e. it deals with a very specific task scope. Due to this, the goal of the work is also very narrowly defined. Before the term "coaching" became popular, such activities were also called "training".

(3) **The coach pool consisting of professionals and "semi-professionals"**

In this case, what is meant is the occupation- and hierarchy-independent groupings within a company. "Employees who meet certain personal and qualificational requirements can, (…) after being approved by HR and HRD employees", be entered into a coaching pool (Bollhöfer 2012, p. 95). In this manner, an attempt is made in large organizations to utilize the specialist competencies of various groups of persons for the benefit of the organization, such as in the university clinic in Frankfurt (Eichhorn 2011). Employees are then relieved by other colleagues with the same job scope for the purposes of coaching. Work that is not done in their core working area due to this is then compensated for by offsetting it with a profit center. This type is only found in very large systems, as it is only in such cases where confidentiality can be guaranteed within the various job scopes.

(4) **Internal coaching as a standard instrument for human resources development**

In rare cases, psychologists, educators or business economists are tasked exclusively with coaching employees within an organization. This only takes place in organizations which have a specific strategy linked to their utilization of coaches. For example, the law firm Hogan Lovells has two coaches in its German department which attend to the needs of all lawyers in Germany. After law firms all over Europe came under intense competitive pressure to obtain the best minds, this company has been attempting to attract aspiring candidates with exquisite human resources development perks (Bollhöfer 2011). Even in organizations in the area of social services, such as in private clinics, attempts are being made to attract first-rate employees by offering full-time internal coaches (Hedlund 2003). At the same time, this also aims to improve the quality of leadership, the way mistakes are handled, or the overall quality of the work. However, coaches can also be hired for general "employee care". For example, in the city of Nuremberg, all employees—from the mayor to the cemetery caretaker—can consult three full-time coaches on any topic (Holzberger and Winkelmann 1999).

(5) The inter-organizational coach pool of internal coaches

Occasionally, we also find organizations which have combined their resources in order to be able to "afford" one or more coaches. The advantage of this constellation is, first of all, that such coaches are fully utilized. This is because only large organizations are able to finance their own coaches. One other significant advantage is that the coach does not become blind to the faults of his own company, as he is confronted with various organizational cultures and subcultures. Although this means that he requires a high degree of adaptability, it also results in him perceiving all phenomena he encounters from an outside position. In turn, this results in his ability to quickly comprehend a wide variety of constellations, to process them smoothly, and to influence them in a beneficial manner.

(6) The psychological coach pool

Psychological expertise is a basic requirement in order to work as a coach. Hence, it is a natural step for organizations which employ a large number of psychologists to use this expertise for coaching as well. For example, the Federal Employment Agency currently has over 100 qualified psychological coaches which are available to its management staff. In the German Federal Armed Forces, approximately 50 troop psychologists have been trained as coaches as well. And the state of Bavaria has had over 200 school psychologists qualified for supervision/coaching. These school psychologists not only coach teachers, but also school principals and school oversight officials. Furthermore, a large number of police psychologists in various federal states have also undergone training to qualify themselves for coaching tasks.

15.2.3 What Goals Should Coaching Have and What Roles Should It Assume?

Similarly, the goals and roles of coaching are determined according to each individual organization. One rarely finds goals that are formulated in detail such as those of the Federal Employment Agency, where coaching is to serve to create "excellent leadership practices" in order to increase the quality of the entire organization. But because coaching takes up a significant amount of resources, some form of profit or benefit is expected in every organization, at least implicitly. Bollhöfer (2012) lists four aspects in this case:

(1) Today, processes of change are taking place almost everywhere in order to "future-proof" organizations. And coaching is indeed an excellent option for supporting change; in fact, the accompanying of planned organizational processes of change appears to be becoming one of coaching's major roles (Klafke 2011).
(2) Furthermore, coaching strengthens the "employer's brand" (Bollhöfer 2012, p. 89). What this means is that coaching still continues to tack on a presupposition of exclusivity, such that employees are to be given a certain exclusive image of their organization through coaching.
(3) In many cases, coaching serves to drive innovation in human resources development strategies. It is valuable as an integrating element in various human resources development measures such as internal career counseling or stress and burnout prevention.
(4) Furthermore, coaching also allows know-how to be created and protected. When there exists competition within a sector of the industry, such as e.g. in insurance companies, coaching generally serves to retain employees with their valuable knowledge within the organization. Coaching can also be used to disperse conflicts within a company, which is why they reduce "personnel-related centrifugal forces" (Kühl 2008), and the employees remain in the system.

Although such goals are also often significant in external coaching; in internal coaching they can be realized in a more compact manner.

15.2.4 In Which Organizational Areas Is Coaching Located and What Are the Regulations?

Internal coaches are generally located in staff departments and are generally commissioned "from the line". Regulations for coaching depend on the type of organization, their size, and their degree of formalization. In a large federal agency such as the Federal Employment Agency, there exist regulations for coaching, but these do not need to be adhered to too strictly. Usually, a superior (e.g. a division head) recommends that an employee (e.g. a team leader) attend coaching sessions. He informs him of this, and after a talk with the employee, he speaks to human resources about booking a coach. The human resources department reports the need for coaching to the head psychologist of a region, who then recommends one to two suitable coaches. The client then receives the dockets of two coach profiles and is asked to decide if he would like to get to know one or both coaches. However, in general it is also possible for a division head or team leader to independently approach human resources regarding a coach. In certain cases, a potential client also approaches a coach on his own. However, the amount of time that a psychologist can make available for coaching is limited by the amount of time he can budget according to his schedule. This means that he cannot commit fully to coaching.

In banks and insurance companies, things are done in a similar fashion: An employee, such as one from the middle hierarchy level, requests e.g. a promotion or a salary increase. Personnel interviews and/or assessment center sessions are then held to decide if the management executive in question should improve his managing abilities or the transparency with which he carries out his management tasks before receiving a promotion. Human resources is then notified of this, who then select a suitable coach.

15.2.5 Who Reports Coaching Needs and Who Is Allowed to Use Coaching for Which Issues?

At Hogan Lovells, which even advertises the fact that it provides internal coaching, every employee is eligible for coaching. All he has to do is notify one of the two internal coaches of this requirement, and will then receive the next available appointment. After an initial interview, the time, location, frequency and number of coaching sessions is agreed upon. Any issue which a client presents is a suitable issue to be dealt with during coaching. Things function similarly in the German Federal Armed Forces. There too, every officer and non-commissioned officer from every hierarchical level can register his need for coaching with a psychologist in his organizational environment, and will then be attended to in due course.

The topics dealt with in internal coaching are as diverse as in external coaching. For example, even in large government agencies, the question of how couples in which both parties are career men/women can reconcile their private and professional lives is playing an increasingly significant role (Jahn 2012). We also find this form of consultation, which has recently come to be called "life coaching" (Schmidt-Lellek and Buer 2011) and which also includes private topics, in the German Federal Armed Forces, particularly after overseas missions. Contrary to popular opinion, the issues in internal coaching center relatively seldom focus on internal conflicts within an organization, and instead more often on a need for support, often before promotions.

15.2.6 Which Regulations Exist for the Selection of External or Internal Coaches?

In many organizations, there is a rule that management staff from lower and middle levels are attended to by internal coaches, while a pool of external coaches is reserved for the highest levels. However, with regard to the fields of expertise and organizational aspects, there are milieus that are so specific that an external coach would find it hard to follow the topics at hand. For example, Pannicke (2008), who himself worked at SAP, states that internal coaches for employees are a much more expedient choice in the IT industry due to their specialist expertise alone. The same applies to the educational sector. It is often the case that teachers and school principals insinuate that persons who do not come from the educational sector have too many prejudices against education-related issues or only have a limited understanding of them. Furthermore, they do not want to spend their own money for their consultations, and wish to use only internal offerings.

As for the question of whether management staff desires an external or an internal coach, the general relationship they have with their organization seems to play a crucial role. Trzaska (2011), who herself is an internal coach in a federal agency, describes that employees who feel that they have been treated well by their company also trust the coach that their company provides for them. Due to this, they do not desire an external coach.

15.2.7 In Which Settings Does Internal Coaching Take Place?

Coaches in organizations where training sessions are commonplace as human resources development measures are often of the opinion that coaching only makes sense in one-on-one sessions. They fear a "dilution" of the coaching formats in group settings. After all, a private one-on-one situation does indeed constitute what is actually exclusive and innovative about coaching. It is precisely this setting that originally made a splash (Loos 1991). And as Kühl (2008) remarks, this one-on-one setting also enjoys an exceptional status with regard to socio-political aspects. This is because in our society, and particularly in the working world, we constantly find ourselves in "forced groups". Being able to speak about one's concerns in a one-on-one situation and to find an attentive ear at the same time is itself an exclusive affair.

Despite this, representatives of a number of large companies have reported a great deal of success with small-group coaching. For example, supervisors at Daimler who are promoted to master craftsmen are offered coaching sessions with six to seven colleagues. At Siemens (Wallner 2004), too, group coaching sessions are conducted for management staff who share the same job scope and/or position in the hierarchy. Koschuth (2011) even recommends the installation of group coaching as a regular human resources development instrument for leadership personnel who have achieved a "career leap" in their company. In particular, being promoted to becoming the boss of one's previous colleagues can then be dealt with more easily. We also find group settings in a number of clinics when nurses are promoted to head nurses.

Using the results of an empirical study on internal group supervision at a regional service provider, Mohr (2012) was able to show that the collaboration, but also self-management and even the personal development of the management personnel could be fostered. The advantage of this setting lies primarily in the fact that all participants bring along similar issues, and not only does a high degree of solidarity develop in the group, but also an intensive learning situation. However, the coach then assumes what is more or less a moderator's role.

In certain large companies or government agencies, internal coaches also offer team supervision and/or team coaching (Elbers 1999; Bäcker 1999; Hamann-Wehe 1999; Höppner 1999). However, in such cases, and more so than in an external context, the coach will need to ensure that no unnecessary opening up or sharing takes place, and that conflicts do not escalate excessively. In cases in which a conflict has reached a particular escalation level where the employees are simply shouting at each other, multi-person coaching is of course no longer a viable option. In such cases, superiors will need to contain the conflict via "interventions of power" (Glasl 1998).

15.2.8 How Is Internal Coaching Implemented?

There have been almost no suggestions in the literature so far addressing this issue, which is why the implementation of internal coaching will be examined in more detail here:

The fundamental dictum is that coaching is never to be offered as a method for deficit compensation. In such a case, coaching would immediately be "burned". In the worst case, every member of the organization would then be wary of approaching the coach's office. Coaching should make an appearance primarily as a constructive measure in human resources development, such as the "fostering of social competencies", the "fostering of communication" etc. Ideally, employees should associate coaching with positive aspects in the organization from the very beginning. The extent to which it fits into the portfolio of all HRD measures should also be clarified (Stenzel 2012). Should it e.g. follow certain training courses or seminars? It has proven effective for coaching to be offered offensively in the introductory phase on topics that are a concern in every organization, such as "support after a "career leap", "support with training new employees" (Schreyögg 2012) or "help with training successors" (Jakobuß 2011).

Depending on the level of professionalization at which coaching is present in an organization, the coaches should utilize all informal networks to announce their offerings. It has proven optimal for high-ranking leadership personnel to proclaim to the organization that they have already used the services of coaches. By doing so, coaching has the best chances of "metamorphosing" into a component of human resources development that is seen as being natural and self-evident.

Internal coaches can make use of a number of possibilities to advertise their profession in the organization:

- Giving short lectures on coaching
- Publishing articles in the employee magazine
- Announcing their offerings at employee meetings
- Distributing flyers in the canteen
- Putting up notices at the bulletin board
- Inserting items asking about coaching requirements in employee surveys
- Utilizing small introductory meetings; e.g. providing support when an employee assumes a new position
- Presenting short vignettes of coaching during training sessions or in seminars
- Presenting coaching to persons in key positions
- Introducing coaching during meetings with company representatives, staff council representatives, and equality officers
- Taking advantage of meeting rituals to spread the word
- Offering coaching during all processes of change.

It should be emphasized once again that coaching can only become a natural and self-evident component of an organization if the highest management level has also successfully been convinced of the utility of this instrument for human resources development. However, the general reputation of the human resources department or the department for human resources development is also a crucial factor for the success of coaching and its image.

15.2.9 The Pitfalls of Internal Coaching

As should be clear by now, internal coaching within an organization brings with it a number of advantages. Field competency, in particular, plays a crucial role. However, as Seiler (1999) and Stenzel (2012) have made clear, it also has a number of disadvantages. First of all, there is the problem of "organizational blindness" which internal coaches are hardly able to escape, as it is generally difficult for them to assume an outside position when dealing with their own company. After all, once a certain amount of time has passed, they themselves become part of the system. Hence, they are hardly the right choice when the members of the organization are to be encouraged to innovate.

One other problem is that of hierarchical interferences. Internal coaches, like all other members of an organization, have a particular status in the system. Hence, when they coach persons of a higher status, a certain amount of friction may arise between them and their interaction partners. This is because, in coaching, the counselor generally has to frame the relationship, as the client would otherwise not be able to benefit from the consultation. Therefore, the coach is not allowed to transform into a merely reacting dialog partner (cf. Haley 1978). However, this is difficult for coaches who are of a lower rank. Due to this, it is often helpful when the coach at least hast a high level of education.

Internal coaches also quickly run into conflicts of loyalty when a client heavily criticizes their shared employer. If he simply agrees with everything, he may trigger a loyalty conflict with his employer; if he defends the company, he may lose the client's trust.

Internal coaches are also often subject to "temptation from authority". After all, many coaching sessions, even internal ones, start with a meeting involving three persons, where the superior begins by informing the coach, in the presence of the client, of particular consultation needs he feels the client has. It is then often the case that superiors, as part of a "parental conspiracy", later approach the coach and ask how the client is doing. This quickly results in problems involving confidentiality, particularly when the coach feels flattered by his own importance for his superior. Other traps for the coach include being enticed by the compliment that he is the one who has best been able to deal with particularly difficult topics, or topics that have been unsolvable thus far.

Problems of confidentiality also often occur when the counselor coaches individual persons within a single department who are at different hierarchical levels (Franzke and Schauf 2009). In such cases, he is the keeper of a large number of secrets, and needs to keep a close watch on what he tells to whom. Often, this is also linked to the danger that the internal coach's professional standards are eroded through informal phenomena. A problem may also arise when the coach's clients are aware that he is advising multiple persons within a single department. If this happens, it is a good idea to avoid "interfacing" topics that are interrelated (Esse 2011).

Naturally, there exists a particularly high risk that internal coaches are misused or allow themselves to be misused as agents for adapting the clients to untenable organizational conditions. It is not seldom that they are even expected to compensate for a leadership vacuum or structural grievances.

One fundamental problem of internal coaching, however, lies in the consequences of failure. While an external coach can more easily "shake off" the failure of a consultation, in the case of an internal coach this may lead to his image being tarnished overall under certain circumstances. Due to this reason, Seiler (1999) recommends that internal coaches should pay particular attention to the stipulations in their contract and the clarification of roles. When a consultation interaction fails, it is important that the coach is backed by the HRD department. In certain cases, it may even be expedient for him to "borrow power" from the head of human resources and/or to obtain moral reassurance or legal insurance from a higher authority. Esse (2011) notes that the organization's regulations for internal coaching should already serve as a form of conflict prevention.

15.2.10 Quality Assurance and the Evaluation of Internal Coaching

Ideally, quality assurance takes place in the form of regular further education measures for coaches. Furthermore, coaches should have their work supervised at particular intervals.

However, the evaluation of coaching overall has proven to be a problem (Greif 2008). Simple surveys on how satisfied clients are relatively useless, as consultation is an "ensemble formation" from a sociological point of view (Kühl 2008), i.e. due to the intimacy of consultations, clients tend to always give positive statements. In addition, more stringent forms of evaluation are not an option alone due to the fact that the number of persons involved is usually small, and it is quite impossible to carry out verification with a control group. Ultimately, demand itself is also a standard of measure here, as even the internal coach experiences himself in a market subject to supply and demand, even if it is an internal market.

Finally, I also wish to remark that, contrary to the opinion of a number of freelance coaches, internal coaching is neither of poorer quality, nor is it cheaper. In fact, particularly in large companies or large government agencies, coaches need to subject themselves to a comprehensive critical verification process right at the very beginning. Furthermore, their work is also constantly monitored and assessed by their clients and supervisors, whether directly or indirectly. They too, need to prove their worth constantly. Also, full-time coaches, as employees, not only cost their companies a monthly wage, but also social contributions which do not apply for external coaches.

References

Bäcker, R. (1999). Internes Konfliktmanagement bei einem Arbeitsteam. *OSC, 6*(1), 27–39.

Böning, U. (2005). Coaching: Der Siegeszug eines Personalentwicklungs-Instruments – Eine 15-Jahre-Bilanz. In C. Rauen (Ed.), *Handbuch Coaching* (3rd ed., pp. 21–36). Göttingen: Hogrefe.

Bollhöfer, G. (2011). Praxis des organisationsinternen Coachings. *OSC, 18*(1), 97-109.

Bollhöfer, G. (2012). Organisationsinternes Coaching. In Deutscher Bundesverband Coaching (Hrsg.), *Leitlinien und Empfehlungen für die Entwicklung von Coaching als Profession* (4., erw. Aufl., S. 87–96). Osnabrück: DBVC Geschäftsstelle.

DBVC – Deutscher Bundesverband Coaching (Hrsg.) (2012). *Leitlinien und Empfehlungen für die Entwicklung von Coaching als Profession* (4., erw. Aufl.). Osnabrück: DBVC Geschäftsstelle; Engl. version available under: www.dbvc.de/publikationen.

Eichhorn, A. (2011). Implementierung des internen Coaching-Pools am Klinikum der J.W. Goethe-Universität Frankfurt. *OSC, 18*(1), 67–81.

Elbers, K. (1999). Leichen im Keller. Wie Teamsupervision zur Förderung eines positiven Arbeitsklimas beitragen kann. *OSC, 6*(4), 345–355.

Esse, T. (2011). Wie den strukturell bedingten Herausforderungen des internen Coachings begegnet werden kann. *OSC, 18*(2), 173–180.

Fillery-Travis, A. F., & Lane, D. (2006). Does coaching work or are we asking the wrong question? *International Coaching Psychology Review, 1*(1), 23–36.

Franzke, A., & Schauf, M.-A. (2009). Personenorientierte Beratung über mehrere hierarchische Ebenen. Inwieweit kann ein Supervisor mögliche latente Probleme eines einzelnen Klienten objektiv erkennen und beheben. In K. Galdynski & S. Kühl (Hrsg.), *Black-Box Beratung? Empirische Studien zu Coaching und Supervision* (S. 221–256). Wiesbaden: VS Verlag.

Glasl, F. (1998). *Konfliktmanagement* (4th ed.). Bern: Haupt.

Greif, S. (2008). *Coaching und ergebnisorientierte Selbstreflexion.* Göttingen: Hogrefe.

Haley, J. (1978). *Gemeinsamer Nenner Interaktion.* München: Pfeiffer.

Hamann-Wehe, K. (1999). Teamsupervision mit unvollständigen Teams. *Chancen und Risken, OSC, 6*(4), 355–373.
Hedlund, S. (2003). Zur Bedeutung von Supervision bei stationärer Psychotherapie. *OSC, 10* (2), 145–155.
Holzberger, R., & Winkelmann, C. (1999). Institutionalisierte Supervision bei der Stadtverwaltung. *OSC, 6*(1), 53–63.
Höppner, K. (1999). Die Grundsätze des Handelns in der BfA. Kulturschock. Sinnfindung und/oder Handlungsanweisung? *OSC, 6*(4), 373–385.
Jahn, N. (2012). Coaching von Dual Career Couples als organisationsinternes Angebot. *OSC, 19*(3), 295–309.
Jakobuß, L. (2011). Kombinierter Einsatz von Wissenstransfer und internem Coaching in einem Großunternehmen. *OSC, 18*(2), 161–173.
Klafke, M. (2011). Coaching von Führungskräften in Changeprozessen. *OSC, 18*(1), 5–17.
Knizia, F. (2003). Zugänge eröffnen, Verstehen ermöglichen. Überlegungen zur Geeindeberatung und Organisationsentwicklung evangelischer Kirchengemeinden. *OSC, 10*(4), 315–329.
Koschuth, A. (2011). Ein Plädoyer für Coaching vor dem Karrieresprung als fest installiertes Angebot in Organisationen. *OSC, 18*(2), 145–161.
Kühl, S. (2008). *Coaching und Supervision. Zur personenorientierten Beratung in Organisationen*. Wiesbaden: VS Verlag.
Lellek, S. (1999). Überlegungen zur internen Supervision am Beispiel eines Kinder- und Jugendheims. *OSC, 6*(1), 21–27.
Loos, W. (1991). *Coaching für Manager. Problembewältigung unter vier Augen.* Landsberg/Lech: Moderne Industrie.
Mohr, G. (2012). Internes Coaching in der Gruppe. Eine Studie zu Wirkungsbedingungen, Auswirkungen und Effekten auf die Unternehmenskultur. *OSC, 19*(3), 261–283.
Pannicke, D. (2008). *Coaching in der Software-Branche. OSC, 15*(1), 40–56.
Röhring, L. (1999). *Institutsinterne Supervision bei der Polizei. OSC, 6*(1), 39–53.
Seiler, D. (1999). Wachsam sein. Zur besonderen Situation der internen Supervision in einer Behörde. *OSC, 6*(4), 329–345.
Schmidt-Lellek, C., & Buer, F. (Eds.). (2011). *Life-Coaching in der Praxis. Wie Coaches umfassend beraten*. Göttingen: Vandenhoeck & Ruprecht.
Schreyögg, A. (Ed.). (2000). *Supervision und Coaching für die Schulentwicklung*. Bonn: Deutscher Psychologen Verlag.
Schreyögg, A. (Ed.). (2008). *Konfliktcoaching und Konfliktmanagement in der Schule.* Bonn: Deutscher Psychologen Verlag.
Schreyögg, A. (2012). *Coaching. Eine Einführung für Praxis und Ausbildung (7)* (überarb ed.). Frankfurt/M: Campus.
Schreyögg, A., & Lehmeier, H. (Eds.). (2003). *Personalentwicklung in der Schule*. Bonn: Deutscher Psychologen Verlag.
Segers, J., Vloeberghs, D., Henderickx, E., & Inceoglu, I. (2011). Structuring and understanding the coaching industry: The coaching cube. *Academy of Management. Learning/Education, 10*(2), 204–222.

Stenzel, S. (2012). Leitfragen zur Implementierung von organisationsinternem Coaching. In Deutscher Bundesverband Coaching (Hrsg.), *Leitlinien und Empfehlungen für die Entwicklung von Coaching als Profession* (4., erw. Aufl., S. 99–101). Osnabrück: DBVC.

Trzaska, E. (2011). Die Bedeutung von Vertrauen im internen Coaching. *OSC, 18*(2), 129–145.

Wallner, I. (2004). *Gruppencoaching für Führungskräfte. OSC, 11*(3), 275–283.

Westerwelle, G. (2004). Interne Supervision und Coaching in der öffentlichen Verwaltung. *OSC, 11*(3), 267–275.

Zaggl, V. (2012). Einführung von internem Coaching in die Organisation eines Handelsbetriebes. *OSC, 19*(3), 283–295.

Author Biography

Dr. phil. Astrid Schreyögg Dipl.-Psych., psychotherapist, supervisor, coach; head of research at the German Academy of Psychologists of the BDP for Supervision and Coaching; domestic and international fellow; trainer for supervision and coaching; textbook author; publisher of the journal "Organisationsberatung, Supervision, Coaching" (OSC).

Coaching in SMEs—The German *Mittelstand* Professional Counseling "from Next Door"

16

Cornelia Seewald

Abstract

Aspects specific to German SMEs (the *Mittelstand*) are described from a historic, cultural, and quantitative perspective, as well as the particular demands such special requirements situations place on the coaching intervention and the profile of an appropriate coach. Brief descriptions of three very different real-life case scenarios serve to illustrate these points. These case scenarios each represent diverse aspects that are typical for German SMEs. Correspondingly, the coaching intervention also shows considerable variation. The analysis of the case scenarios result in generalized suggestions for methodological approaches that work towards a corresponding long-term solution. Particular emphasis is placed on six factors that are indispensable for success in the intervention that is coaching in SMEs, with the primary target categories of survival, disencumbrance, professionalization, and growth.

In order to illustrate the topic of coaching in the *Mittelstand*, this chapter will concentrate on a few central perspectives which give an exemplary insight into the specific situation of coaching in German SMEs. Three real-life scenarios outlined in brief will help the reader picture various aspects that are typical for German SMEs, which are then described accordingly. But first of all, what is the *Mittelstand* and what are SMEs?

C. Seewald (✉)
Sternstr. 32, 40479 Düsseldorf, Germany
e-mail: seewald@costconcept.de
URL: http://www.costconcept.de

A. Schreyögg and C. Schmidt-Lellek (eds.), *The Professionalization of Coaching*, DOI 10.1007/978-3-658-16805-6_16

16.1 Background

When people speak of the German *Mittelstand* (≈ SMEs) in the globalized economy, they refer to more than just small- and medium enterprises as defined by facts and figures. The German *Mittelstand* has become a term that has taken on a meaning of its own, and describes a historical, qualitative, and cultural phenomenon unlike any other.

It is practically impossible to keep an overview of the wide range of operational structures, degrees of professionalization, industries and niches, the sheer variety of financing concepts, property and ownership structures, degrees of organizational maturity and fidelity to tradition: start-ups, consulting agencies, skilled trades, service companies, engineering firms, research institutes, industrial companies, associations, chains, and many more. Equally varied are the challenges and conflict situations faced in these SMEs, something which Classen and Happich (2013, p. 253 ff.) have clearly pointed out.

Historically, the *Mittelstand* is characterized by early and individual entrepreneurship, which is based on trade, skilled crafts, and agriculture. Industrialization and mechanization have enabled the expansion of businesses run by master craftsmen and of forms of trade, and also resulted in the development of new products and services. New technologies such as the internet have revolutionized traditional trade structures and enabled numerous innovative products and services. Even among the liberal professions (doctors, lawyers, tax consultants etc.), as they are called, company forms of significant economic importance have also emerged. At the same time, over the past 20 years, we have observed an increasing number of one-man companies—the "I Inc."—which are also generally considered part of the *Mittelstand*. Officially, the *Mittelstand* is defined as companies which have up to 250 employees and up to €50 million in turnover each year (Institute for *Mittelstand* Research (IfM)). However, in general usage and in companies' self-assessment, there are also globally successful companies consisting of ≈5000 or more employees who consider themselves part of the *Mittelstand* (Simon 1991). 92% of German companies are owner-run, family-run, or partially family-run and family-controlled companies, and the vast majority of them are part of the *Mittelstand*. In reality, the familial link can prove to be both a boon and a bane: If they succeed at putting the welfare of the company above their personal welfare or personal sensitivities and at organizing the management and development of the company in consensus, this will constitute a crucial factor for the stability and the growth of the company. If they do not succeed in this respect, drawn-out conflicts often lead to the disintegration of the company, to the (partial) sale of the company, or to bankruptcy. Here are a few figures that illustrate how influential family businesses are economically: 50% of total turnover in Germany comes from family businesses, which have an equity ratio of 50:60% of all jobs subject to social security requirements are in family-run companies; 9% personnel growth domestically from 2006 to 2010, 11% employment growth at the top 500 since 2006; 90% of family businesses are run by the owners themselves, and among German family businesses, ≈1200 are global leaders; finally, the 500 German family businesses with the highest turnover generate a total turnover of almost 900 billion euros (Stiftung Familienunternehmen (The Family Business Foundation) 2014).

Qualitatively, the German *Mittelstand* is known for its respectability in the design and conception of its products and services. Qualification levels are generally high. The German journeyman (Geselle) and masters in skilled trades (Meister) have a reputation for being knowledgeable, meticulous, and reliable. The German skilled trades are a brand unto themselves, and stand for challenging professional training with the corresponding examinations. Academic and/or technical professional training, entrepreneurship, independence, and a willingness to take risks are virtues that have also made German SMEs successful on a global scale. After the 2nd world war, most family businesses built their companies on technology and engineering.

Culturally, the *Mittelstand* is characterized by people who show a great willingness to take on responsibility, who have ideas, and who dare to realize these ideas. Passion and pragmatism are two driving forces that enable them to inspire others to follow their lead. In economically strong and healthy SMEs, founders and owners often have an exemplary role; they live what they preach, and they often have a strongly relationship-oriented management style. Their thinking is often generation-oriented, and long before the term "sustainability" became popular, they have greatly valued qualitative growth. Hence, even today, traditional values often determine their corporate culture: Continuity in management, regional rootedness, a stable workforce, cost-consciousness, brand management, commitment and finally hard work—just to name a few. Many successful SMEs adopt the latest findings and methods from personnel management and economic control concepts from modern conglomerates. But in many aspects, SMEs constantly differ from conglomerates (Classen and Happich 2013, p. 245 ff.). However, SMEs are increasingly on their way to professionalizing their companies, although they have just begun. This semi-professionalism can be compensated for in the interim by inventiveness, innovation, pragmatism, and risk-taking; however, over the long run SMEs will be successful if they take advantage of the best of both worlds: On the one hand modern management concepts and entrepreneurial flexibility, and on the other the advantages of creative freedoms and short decision-making routes, which are typical for the successful SME.

16.2 Professional Counseling "from Next Door"

Creative freedoms and short decision-making routes characterize small and medium-sized companies, which is why it makes sense that that there is a very close proximity between the coach and the coachee in SMEs. Metaphorically, this equates to regional/spatial proximity, contact via network partners, neighborhoods and friendly competitors, personal recommendations or mutual acquaintances from non-corporate spheres such as sports, culture, clubs, or politics. In SMEs, the coach seldom gets in touch with the coachee through "cold" acquisition. Often, this close proximity also means short travel times and low travel costs, little to no investment costs (e.g. advertising or similar measures); generally, it means being able to get in touch and meet up quickly—after all, the coach is "just next door". Among other things, the following real-life examples illustrate this close proximity, the quick availability, and the pragmatic manner in which their collaboration is organized—the proximity of "being next door". The diversity of the *Mittelstand* will be illustrated in the approach, and the coaching aspects specific to it emphasized in the main characteristics. We will not go into explanation of the coaching process itself, as it is assumed that the reader has the requisite knowledge of the professional and methodological procedures used in coaching.

16.2.1 Real-Life Example 1: A Small Architectural Firm on the Verge of Ruin

Initial situation

A small architectural firm established itself over the course of many years, and has been able to compensate for occasional fluctuations in the number of orders through vacation days and temporarily doing without freelance employees. This changed when a long-standing client changed its business policy and decided that in the future, it would only rent the premises it required, instead of building them. The architectural firm was located in a small town in Central Germany and had specialized in the construction of commercial property, but had worked primarily for that one client. It did have a handful of other regular customers, but they only commissioned small-scale renovations and extensions. The head of the architectural firm, the owner, was the sole managing director, and at that point in time had six permanent employees on the payroll. When the coach was contacted, the grave situation—the shortage of work—had already persisted for over ¾ of a year, and there was no foreseeable possibility that this would change.

Task identification

The coach had been contacted due to a private recommendation. The managing director expressed his desire to try coaching, saying that at that point in time, he no longer knew what else he could do to obtain more contracts and continue to "keep the ship from sinking". Personally, he was in a bad way, and complained of insomnia and had lost a few kilograms. The managing director and the coach agreed on three measures over the next 14 days: Comprehensive analysis of the acquisition strategy and the behavior of the managing director when communicating with clients, a ½-day workshop with all permanent employees for a brainstorming session, and an individual coaching session with the managing director.

The results of the measures were as follows: The behavioral analysis of the managing director expanded his sense of self in two aspects: On the one hand, his self-image was that of a construction engineer and conceptionally acknowledged architect who preferred to speak with the upper management of the clients awarding the contracts. In that respect, he felt that he saw eye-to-eye with the client with his rather professorial attitude. He came to realize that this attitude and implicit expectations made it difficult for clients who had more of a "hands-on" mentality to relate to him. On the other hand, it came to light that his behavior when communicating with clients was already very directed at an early point in time, without there having been sufficient discussion about a corresponding mutual goal. In times of economic crisis, both these characteristics had been reinforced. Up till then, he had believed that this would allow him to reach his goal faster.

These findings resulted from dialogical reflection with the coach, and did not immediately lead to concrete stimuli for change. The workshop with the employees took place with a rather somber atmosphere; they appeared to be at a loss, and some employees were afraid of being let go. There were almost no creative ideas. One employee volunteered to help acquire new projects. The managing director was rather surprised by this offer, as he had considered that job to be his alone, but accepted. The coach suggested that all employees consider reduced working hours to alleviate the financial situation and avoid having to let people go for the time being. The issue was discussed intensively, and at the end all the employees agreed to reduced hours. In the first coaching session with the managing director, the results of the workshop were reflected upon, and the results from his behavioral analysis were also discussed repeatedly. Consequently, he decided on the following measures: Visiting a three-day seminar on acquisition strategies, coaching sessions or telephone calls at short notice before and after communicating with new clients, implementing a three-month reduced working hour phase, "activating" previous satisfied clients and requesting that they recommend the firm to others.

Sustainability
Approximately six months later, the managing director gathered all the employees for a two-hour meeting to discuss and evaluate the changes. The session was moderated by the coach. Results: Two new clients were acquired, the reduced work hours phase had lasted a total of four months, until the banks were once again willing to grant the necessary pre-financing loans, and the managing director felt significantly more confident when communicating with new clients. For the future, he had the following plans: Assigning a second employee to focus on acquisitions, a conscious emphasis on a heterogeneous client portfolio, shifting from 1/3 permanent employees to freelance employees, and regionally expanding his acquisition efforts.

Typical for coaching in SMEs: Spontaneous crisis intervention within a tight time frame
The situational analysis in a small company like this one can be done quickly and without much technical effort. The owner has knowledge of all relevant information to give the coach an idea of the situation. In this case, the coach enjoys added trust, as he was recommended personally. The focusing on the issue of and issues related to the shortage of contracts is unambiguous and does not clash with other issues. This allows the managing director to act rapidly and in a targeted manner, something he is used to and which he experiences as being strongly implementation-oriented. The greatest attention was paid to increasing his negotiating competency when communicating with clients in order to conclude contracts. The participation of all employees in the problem-solving process in the workshop relieves him of pressure and motivates them, to the extent that one even volunteered to take over the acquisitions and related communications. The expert advice on cost management (reduced working hours) from the coach alleviates the financial situation and gives all involved parties some breathing room.

Conclusion
In this case, what is typical for an SME intervention in this real-life example is the "packaged" aspect: Arranging for closely-spaced yet irregular individual coaching sessions that accompany the owner in his daily working routine, expert stimuli for employee management and cost management, sales and negotiation

training from the coach, as well as team moderation and the organization of an external seminar for the coachee. For the coach, this means clearly separating the various roles, making the corresponding role behavior of his transparent, and continually adapting to the expectations of his interaction partners. The counseling architecture is transparent and seen in its entirety. Helpful concepts and methods in this project come from Transaction Analysis (Dehner and Dehner 2013), the Formats of Change Management (Seewald 2006), Non-directive Conversation Management (Rogers 1972), Systemic Organizational Development (Schmid 2014), and the expert advice on the issue of payment models.

16.2.2 Real-Life Example 2: Out of the Conglomerate and into Freedom: A Software Spin-off Searches for a Profile

Initial situation

Employees and management staff often lament the fact that conglomerate structures cripple creativity, or that creativity does not even develop in such structures. Symptomatic for such situations are slow development processes, difficult voting sessions, insufficient proximity to the market and clients, and high costs. A company in the mobile communications industry wanted to deal with this dilemma by creating a spin-off using a section of its software development. The development of market-ready applications within the group had failed to prove itself against the intensive competition on the market. With this distancing measure—a spin-off without crippling conglomerate structures—the parent company hoped to achieve faster product development and higher application quality. With this objective in mind, the parent company pre-financed the spin-off for two years. However, this "independence movement" had a handicap: All employees of the spin-off as well as the responsible managing director only had years of experience working for a conglomerate, but were now faced with the challenge of working in a small, agile start-up company. After a year, the managing director contacted a coach he knew from an earlier project, and requested that they both reflect on the development of the spin-off thus far. The economic situation was a precarious one, the atmosphere among the 25 employees gloomy, there was no success to speak of in sales, as before, various applications were released on the market too late, employees threatened to leave, and worst of all, it seemed that they would have no chance of receiving follow-up financing from the parent company. In reality, the performance results had not changed much compared to the original situation.

Task identification
The managing director and the coach met up for an exploratory discussion: Analysis of possible root causes, the managing director's point of view, imminent and threatening future scenarios. The result of this exploratory discussion was that a briefing be carried out together with all employees, and that it be moderated by the coach. The task required the briefing to be carried out at short notice. Subsequent steps are, if at all, to be agreed upon in sequential planning and commissioned.

Task 1: Moderating the entire team
The main result of the briefing was that all 25 employees now had the same information about the critical situation; two employees announced that they would be leaving the company—regardless of how things proceeded. This did not particularly surprise the rest. In order to firmly turn the attention of the parties involved towards the future, the coach posed a question to everyone with the request that they write the answer on a slip of paper to guarantee relative anonymity. The question was: "If this company belonged to you and the budget was exhausted, and you only had the option of implementing one single measure to improve the situation, what would you do?" This was in effect a bid to generate ideas—every man for himself, no holds barred, and daring to think the impossible. The most frequently mentioned measure was: better collaboration; the second most common one was to downsize; the third-most frequent one was to take out a bank loan to continue financing the company, and four slips of paper suggested replacing the managing director. The managing director was relatively surprised by this, as well as by the frequent mention of better collaboration.

Task 2: Organizational advice
Subsequently, the coach was asked to give suggestions on how collaboration could be improved. This took the form of carrying out a workshop with the working title: "As much standardization as necessary—as much freedom as possible". With respect to content, the focus was to be on comparing conglomerate and start-up structures, and subsequently update role models accordingly, express mutual expectations, and to agree on a few defined processes and rules of behavior. The suggestion was accepted and carried out. The coach provided stimuli for all issues and areas. The result was that the participants gained a clear understanding of their situation as a start-up company with the necessity that each employee to redefine his own role in interaction with the others, and to fairly distribute process responsibilities, as well as to take on these responsibilities.

Task 3: Conflict management

At this point in time, the managing director requested that the coach mediate in a conflict between two employees he considered difficult. This task took place in two phases: First of all, the coach carried out individual sessions with all three involved parties to clarify the conflict situation and motivations. This was then followed by a combined conflict clarification session, resulting in one of the two employees leaving the company, and the other being transferred from sales support to field staff at his own request. Subsequently, the managing director requested additional personal coaching sessions.

Task 4: Individual coaching

Four individual coaching sessions with the managing director followed, as he desired to further develop his management style. He felt that it was necessary for him to act in a less hierarchical manner, to develop more confidence in the competency of his employees, and to focus more strongly on activities that promoted sales.

Sustainability

One year after the last coaching session with the managing director, the coach called him and asked how things were going. The managing director was extremely satisfied with the coach's interventions, even in hindsight. He reported that the working climate between employees was now well-balanced. Two more had left the company, but he had hired five new employees. The product development processes were constantly being re-examined, the technical quality of the products had increased, but was not yet sufficiently high enough, and the sales figures were continually improving. He was of the opinion that, if things continued to develop as they had, the company would be able to finance itself in the foreseeable future. Any surplus would then be used to finance an appropriate sliding employee bonus. This had motivated a number of employees to continually contribute to the process of improvement.

Typical for coaching in SMEs: Coaching is a measure "ordered" in hindsight

In this project, the company took a detour before turning to coaching measures. What triggered the contact with the coach and the consultation were initially the rather unspecific performance and organizational problems caused by the spin-off. The managing director did not have a clear idea of what he expected from coaching, and if he wanted to use such services at all. He was unaware of a number of his own weaknesses in management, or at least did not mention them. In this situation, he also did not request a consultation process, but only individual measures. In addition, there were also financial bottlenecks, and no budget for external consultations. It was only when he learned of and understood the economic value of coaching and the coach agreed to the sequential assignments that the managing director became willing to finance a more comprehensive consultation process, thereby enabling continuous changes to be made to the organization. Over the course of this development, the managing director's willingness to carry out (self-) reflection increases, and he "discovers" the option of attending individual coaching sessions for himself.

Conclusion

A sequential string of assignments that sometimes takes place in extremely small steps allows a number of SMEs to pursue continuous organizational and personal development despite limited financial means and without taking too large a risk. The most important thing is to act and to not precede all interventions with drawn-out analyses, but to instead jump on urgent issues and to rapidly be able to have initial results to show for. Deeper and more advanced issues will then come up as trust in the coach increases and when additional means have been secured. For the coach, his ability to plan spontaneous sessions, often at short notice, is also a factor. A clear and explicit management of expectations is critical for success in sequential process planning: What is achievable with which module and what is not? How much time do processes of change require in order to mature? Success means setting realistic goals. The coach will need to continuously re-affirm them with the client and to ensure that progress is being made in the processes of change, even if only in small steps. Helpful concepts and methodological approaches in this real-life example come from constructive communication (Motschnig and Nykl 2009), adaptive coaching (Bacon and Spear 2003), systemic consultation (Königswieser and Exner 2001), communication psychology (Schulz von Thun 2000), scenario techniques (Seewald 2014), and the cost-benefit relationship of coaching (Filbert 2013).

16.2.3 Real-Life Example 3: Brothers! Role-Finding and Positioning in a Family of Managing Owners—A Tightrope Walk Between Rivalry and Cooperation

Initial situation

A third-generation family-run SME in the garment industry felt increasing pressure from low-cost Asian providers and wanted to develop a strategy for the future that would ensure success. Two brothers from the community of five heirs, who had the same number of shares, led the company with equal rights. The advisory board consisted of family members and non-family members and reliably carried out its controlling function. Within the family, there was a great deal of tension that consisted mainly of conflicts in personal relationships—arising from primary familial socialization—as well as from the difference of opinion regarding the further development of the company. Looming above them all was the spirit of the founding father, whose enterprising tact everyone swore upon. Various active family members also claimed to have this particular tact, which they used—at least argumentatively—to compensate for their own lack of professional competency, and to justify their intervention. In order to defuse the familial conflict at the relationship level, the ownership family had commissioned a team of advisors to carry out two-day family conferences at various dates during the year. In the third year of these consultations, various reasons resulted in the relationship between the two managing brothers worsening. Due to this, the family and the consultants decided to provide each of the brothers with an additional, external coach. The goal of the individual coaching sessions was to process the individual conflict, such that the interactions between the brothers would once again take on a professional tone. In the following, the coaching sessions with one of the two brothers will be illustrated.

Task identification

The individual objective of the coachee confirmed the goal set during the family conference, but expanded the target perspective with the following points: Firstly, the coachee wanted to strengthen his standing in the family, as he felt that he was not sufficiently accepted by various persons. The same applied to two of his management staff who used to work under his predecessor, who were older than him, used to a different management style, and showed little willingness to accept him as the new boss. Thirdly, he found it difficult to make entrepreneurial decisions when he was supposed to or had to do this alone within his own area of responsibility.

Coaching project

The coach and coachee agreed upon a coaching process for the next nine months, in which the coachee determined the sequence of his issues. Over the course of the process, he gained increased confidence in his decisions, and at a more rapid rate as well. This resulted in him letting one of his two "difficult" management staff go. In the relationship with his brother, which was previously characterized by rivalry, he focused a lot more on the exchange of information and opinions as colleagues, and learned to show more appreciation for his contributions to company management. His also put aside his own attitude of putting down other people, and instead carried out in-depth discussions with his interlocutors and business partners, and attempted to convince them for the long term.

Sustainability

Three months after finishing the coaching sessions, the coachee felt that he had made significant personal progress and was able to understand how roles within a family arise and how they could be modified. He admitted to having made mistakes and neglected to do certain things in the past, and also communicated this to other family members. He felt that he now had significantly more self-confidence, felt more confident in his management role, and avoided difficult persons less often. He said that he now saw significant slights and offenses from the past in a different light, and that he understood the psychological dynamics of his "fellow players" better. It had become particularly important for him to differentiate between professional and private relationships, and to behave accordingly. He had become more disciplined, controlled, and significantly less impulse-driven in the way he experienced himself.

Typical for coaching in SMEs: Management—both in and with the family

This example shows that it can often be useful to create an individual, professionally coached developmental space in addition to a regularly conducted family conference at work—or in another complex technical consultation context. The interwoven nature of family and the company and those who play a significant role in both is already a focus of research and being discussed in detail. It is often important that individual family members become independent in their roles within the company without damaging the familial link, or even entirely doing away with it altogether. The creation of individual developmental spaces, such as in individual coaching sessions, can efficiently support the more complex consultation process. This then gives the coachee a good chance of finding an internal psychological distance to other family members, and to assume a meta-perspective in order to see the working relationships as being dependent on the family dynamics, to understand them, to recognize patterns of transfer, and to clarify role-related conflicts.

Conclusion

From a systemic perspective, it is advisable to examine if and which partial systems require special developmental support in parallel in order to accelerate developmental processes. From this perspective, individual coaching can be an auxiliary parallel measure in a more complex consulting approach. This not only applies to situations in family businesses. However, in this case, their responsibility for may have a conflict-strengthening effect for protecting the company over the medium and long term, as everyone wants to do it correct and particularly well, and a conflict ensues for the relevant positions. It is particularly important to pay attention to ensuring that the consultant and the consulting approaches fit with each other. When we look at the most frequently occurring problems in family businesses that result from family conflicts, the transparency of general and specific measures plays an important role. The consulting architecture itself then serves as a good model of how a system with various problems and stakeholders can be further developed constructively. Such a consulting architecture provides various developmental spaces for different requirements. The primary methodological foundations of this project were relationship-oriented coaching (Seewald 2012), communications psychology (Schulz von Thun 2000), personnel selection (Ruppert 2001), emotional intelligence (Goleman 1996), family dynamics (Schreyögg 2005; Chap. 17 in this book; Simon 2002).

These three real-life coaching examples are only an arbitrary selection from the conflict situations and issues SMEs face, and are primarily meant to illustrate the breadth of such phenomena. If we now assume the coach's perspective, a good question is then: Which competency profile will he need in order to prevail in such a heterogeneous field in order to not only give the impression of semi-professionalism, or even to fall prey to it. Naturally, it is clear that each coach finds "his" clients, and that each client in return also finds "his" coach. Despite this, an attempt has been made to describe typical competency characteristics of a coach which are particularly pertinent in SMEs.

16.3 What Makes a Coach Successful in SMEs?

The competence profiles developed by the German Federal Association of Executive Coaching (DBVC 2012) for coaches and senior coaches specify the basic requirements for professional business coaching. The special fit between the coach and coachee in SMEs can tentatively be supplemented by the following characteristics.

Relatability
SMEs, which structurally and in their mentality are extremely heterogeneous, require coaches to be able to relate to their clients as well as the client's system to a great extent. Language, background, social similarities, behavior, bearing, and appearance which more or less correspond to the client's everyday reality are factors that promote a trusting relationship and increase the coaching client's degree of acceptance. If the coach succeeds in "finding his way" to the client emotionally and emphatically, there is great initial promise that an instrumental relationship will develop. Being able to "go along", signal unspoken understanding, and being able to quickly create common ground that resonates are all interactional qualities that the coach will require in order to appear as competent and reliable as possible to the coachee from the very first encounter. Consultation and decision-making processes in SMEs are often driven by a rapid dynamic, and not much time is spent on getting used to each other. Often, it is the first impression that decides whether an encounter will result in collaboration. Hence, in the heterogeneity of SMEs, the coach will need a particular knack to be able to recognize "his" clients, and conversely also be able to see himself self-critically when he is unable to provide this relatability, or only with great difficulty.

Seniority
For the coach, the often-encountered relationship-oriented culture in SME management styles implies that both professional *and* life experience is expected of his profile. Coaches are expected to themselves also have something to show for; to have achieved something, to have built something, shouldered a special responsibility, be a personality that one can experience, and to have special expertise. The client not only expects a partner who is on equal footing, but who is also in some way "more than…". He appreciates, in the most positive manner, an expert and/or human authority. This does not have to come from an advanced age, but seniority can be useful.

Directness

SME mentality and culture is often—in successful companies—characterized by rapid decisions, openness, and relationships that range from those characterized by a good understanding between colleagues to those resembling a friendship. Generally, people simply "understand each other". For the coach, this means having to act appropriately, quickly and without being asked, but at the same time with great respect and appreciation, in order to be accepted. This includes being able to acclimatize to the everyday culture of the client's system without any problems. He makes his acclimatization apparent via direct and quick feedback, the spontaneous willingness to react, recognizably giving personal opinions, and dealing with information in a transparent and goal-oriented manner. Efficiency in communications saves time, and the clear orientation towards the client's needs are crucial for the coach's success. There is generally little time for detours or unproductive encounters, for indulgent self-expression or elaborate presentations. Being able to get to the point quickly and deliver results are qualities that SMEs live by and on.

Flexibility of roles

Coaching in SMEs often means coaching both the owner and management, in close proximity to the decision-makers and resulting in more rapid assignment management. The check "Is the implementation working out?" takes place equally quickly and without frills. This proximity to implementation supports the rapid development dynamic, which in turn frequently brings secondary requirements to light, which then often results in auxiliary consultation and/or training appointments. In this regard, the coach is challenged in a variety of different roles: as an expert in specialized knowledge, e.g. in marketing, human resources management, financial controlling, stress management, press relations, complaint management, or elsewhere as someone who provides stimuli. Training modules such as employee evaluations, rhetoric, management fundamentals and similar components can also be a good complement to the coaching process. When the coach carries this out himself, he has the opportunity to network himself constructively in the client's system, and to integrate a wider technical competence. Trainer, moderator, supervisor, suggestion-giver, advisor, intermediator—coach: Differentiating between roles and incisively switching between them are what characterize the professional coach.

Economic attitudes

The transparent and often tightly-calculated cost-benefit relations in SMEs require the coach to have a keen consciousness for his own resource and price management as well. Economically utilizing time and money is not only in the interest of the SME, but also in its coach's. This includes transparency in products and services and costs on both sides, and a mutual evaluation of the work results. A demonstrated proximity to implementation and a meticulous use of all resources signals to the client that the coach is acting in his interest.

Benchmarking
In the *Mittelstand*, it is success that ultimately convinces; results count more than visions, strategies, assumed potential, or novel ideas. "What are the benefits of that?" is an often-posed and justified question when time and money are scarce. The coach would be prudent to have relevant results from other people for comparison, and be able to provide this information in a manner that can be clearly understood. "Not invented here" is not an SME problem. There is often enormous willingness to innovate in SMEs, but often it is the means and contact that are lacking to adapt innovative concepts and products or research results quickly enough. This is where the coach can act as a mediator by e.g. translating academic language for SMEs, by recommending interesting networks, associations and media to them, or even by referring them to his own customers.

16.4 Outlook

Successful coaching in SMEs concentrates on the personality and competency development of managing owners, influential managers and authoritative management staff. The four primary target categories are survival, disencumbering, professionalization, and growth—often in combination with each other. In doing so, the coach not only has each person with his own individual needs and wants in mind, but also thinks of the company at the same time. The current structural challenges in the SME macrocosm include lack of personnel, financing, competition from the Far East, and pressure to innovate: The lack of personnel happens when specialist labor is not trained in sufficiently large numbers, and because conglomerates at attractive locations are more appealing for the few budding talents out there; public financial programs often require complicated application procedures that regularly overwhelm SMEs; the financial strength and adaptability of Asian markets, particularly China, looms ever larger; the pressure that traditional brands and industries are feeling to innovate require greater investments in research and development in order to take on the competition (cf. Wirtschaftswoche dated 12/09/2013, p. 72 ff.). The successful business coach not only supports his clients within the microcosm of his company, but also pushes him to think outside the box, to identify overall economic contexts, recognize trends, and to evaluate them for his own company. He is mutually networked with his client actively and reactively, and also includes business partners from other consulting professions, such as headhunters, IT consultants, and marketing experts in order to push forward the SME's professionalization and provide the client's future-oriented development and his company with strong driving forces.

References

Bacon, T., & Spear, K. (2003). *Adaptive coaching*. Palo Alto: Davies Black Publishing.

Classen, M., & Happich, G. (2013). Coaching im Mittelstand – Wer ist der Mittelstand? *Organisationsberatung, Supervision, Coaching, 20*(3), 245–259.

Dehner, U., & Dehner, R. (2013). *Transaktionsanalyse im coaching*. Bonn: Manager Seminare.

DBVC – Deutscher Bundesverband Coaching e.V. (Hrsg.) (2012). *Leitlinien und Empfehlungen für die Entwicklung von Coaching als Profession. Kompendium mit den Professionalisierungsstandards des DBVC* (4., erw. Aufl.). Osnabrück: DBVC Geschäftsstelle; Engl. version under http://www.dbvc.de/publikationen.

Filbert, W. (2013). Rechnet sich coaching im mittelstand? *Organisationsberatung, Supervision, Coaching, 20*(3), 273–282.

Goleman, D. (1996). *Emotionale Intelligenz*. München: Hanser.

Königswieser, R., & Exner, A. (2001). *Systemische Interventionen. Architekturen und Designs für Berater und Veränderungsmanager*. Stuttgart: Klett-Cotta.

Motschnig, R., & Nykl, L. (2009). *Konstruktive Kommunikation*. Stuttgart: Klett-Cotta.

Rogers, C. R. (1972). *Die nicht-direktive Beratung*. München: Kindler.

Ruppert, F. (2001). *Berufliche Beziehungswelten. Das Aufstellen von Arbeitsbeziehungen in Theorie und Praxis*. Heidelberg: Carl-Auer.

Schmid, B. (2014). Der isb Ansatz zur Organisationsentwicklung. In B. Schmid (Hrsg.), *Systemische Organisationsentwicklung. Change und Organisationskultur gemeinsam gestalten* (S.7–23). Stuttgart: Schäffer-Poeschel.

Schreyögg, A. (2005). *Coaching von Doppelspitzen. Anleitung für den Coach*. Frankfurt: Campus.

Schulz von Thun, F., et al. (2000). *Miteinander Reden: Kommunikationspsychologie für Führungskräfte*. Reinbek: Rowohlt.

Seewald, C. (2006). *Sozial nachhaltiges Changemanagement*. München: Reinhardt.

Seewald, C. (2012). Im Auge des Zyklons. *Gesprächspsychotherapie und Personzentrierte Beratung, 43*(4), 205.

Seewald, C. (2014). 4 Zukünfte. In B. Schmid & O. König (Eds.), *Train the Coach* (pp. 255–262). Bonn: Manager Seminare.

Stiftung Familienunternehmen (2014). www.stiftungfamilienunternehmen.de.
Simon, F. B. (Ed.). (2002). *Die Familie des Familienunternehmens. Ein System zwischen Gefühl und Geschäft*. Heidelberg: Carl-Auer.
Simon, H. (1991). *Die heimlichen Gewinner*. Frankfurt/M.: Campus.

Author Biography

Dr. Cornelia Seewald has worked as an executive coach and change management consultant for reputed corporations and SMEs since 1996. Fields of focus: change management, leadership, strategy and communication. Previously, she worked as an academic researcher, organizational developer, and personnel manager in key roles at complex companies. Her book "Socially sustainable change management" was published in 2006.

Life Coaching: Family-of-Origin Dynamics

17

Astrid Schreyögg

Abstract

Recently, approaches in which coaching is expanded to include the client's entire life have become popular. A person's current or biographical relationships are also addressed under the label "life coaching". In particular, the individual biography of a person constantly influences a person's professional actions and decisions. Above all, a person's family of origin and its specific configuration appears to play a role here. This includes the parents, siblings etc.: For example, it makes a difference whether a person grew up as the oldest or the youngest child. Furthermore, it is also relevant for a person's future occupation whether the client only lived among brothers or only among sisters. Overall, the hypothesis is that all these phenomena, as early socialization experiences, also influence a person's future professional activities in one way or another.

17.1 Introduction: The Perspectives of Life Coaching

For some time now, people have called for coaching to focus less narrowly and not too exclusively on occupational issues. American authors (Feldman and Lankau 2005) had previously referred to a special type of coaching for which they used the term "life coaching". This form of coaching aims to address the "entire person" with

A. Schreyögg (✉)
Breisgauer Str. 29, 14129 Berlin, Germany
e-mail: info@schreyoegg.de
URL: http://www.Schreyoegg.de

A. Schreyögg and C. Schmidt-Lellek (eds.), *The Professionalization of Coaching*, DOI 10.1007/978-3-658-16805-6_17

his "ambivalences and options" (Martens-Schmid 2007). This means that even professional topics are to be seen in the light of the private world and addressed as such. Later on, in the year 2008, a book was published in the German-speaking world entitled "Life Coaching", and its authors Ferdinand Buer and Christoph Schmidt-Lellek gave it the following subtitle: "About meaning, happiness, and responsibility at work" (Buer and Schmidt-Lellek 2008). Three years later, they published another book with the title "Life coaching in practice. How coaches provide comprehensive consultations" (Schmidt-Lellek and Buer 2011).

The objectives of these readers was to achieve an unusually broad understanding of coaching. Already the target groups were defined more broadly than is generally the case. Contrary to "business coaching", which is aimed exclusively at businesspeople, life coaching is also used when providing consultations for persons from government agencies and social service systems. And unlike the usual "coaching for business" (e.g. Böning and Fritschle 2005), the roles of the working professional in his private life are also taken into consideration. What this means is that life coaching targets the entire social life environment of a person. Furthermore, life coaching is not only aimed at his intellect, but equally at his feelings and even at his corporality. This type of coaching also contains an existential dimension, in that it touches on issues such as: "My work appears increasingly meaningless and makes me unhappy: What can I do? I can no longer carry the responsibility: What can I do to help myself? I can no longer keep up with my work and life. How can I reconstruct my life?"

Hence, life coaching does not only aim to free people from current afflictions through the encounter with the coach. It also intends to open up encouraging perspectives. This means that positive experiences should be reinforced, and negative ones corrected. Ultimately, a central goal of life coaching is the promotion of a happy, successful life. It is oriented according to the following anthropological premises: Man is at once the product and the designer of his own life. He requires meaning in everything he does in life. He is a social creature from the very beginning, and lives in institutions which simultaneously secure *and* plague him. Man has a fundamental drive to surpass himself.

With this description, Buer and Schmidt-Lellek describe an exceedingly challenging program which requires a coach to have comprehensive competencies as a dialog partner. These include sociological, philosophical, and psychological aspects. However, the authors do emphasize that their concept does not require the "unlimited expansion of a coach's background knowledge". "Rather, the goal is to introduce coordinates which open up significant new dimensions behind the topics which have been brought to light and need to be addressed. The expansion of coaching topics takes place in two directions:

(1) *Horizontal expansion*: The work-related issues are not viewed in isolation, but in the context of a coaching client's entire living environment and life planning: In their "length", this includes the biographical perspectives in the span of life and the lifelong development of personality, as well in their "breadth", the various areas of life with their reciprocal effects.
(2) *Vertical expansion*: Life coaching targets the entire person in all his dimensions, with his body, soul, and mind; this means that the goal is not only success, effectiveness and work efficiency for the coaching client (external effects) but also how occupational work is experienced and processed emotionally (internal effects). One could also say that, in life coaching, *personnel development* (occupational roles within work-related organizations) and *personal development* (e.g. overarching life goals, finding meaning and happiness through work as well) are mutually related and their individual intentions addressed. This is because a person and his roles should be distinguished, but never separated completely. With this expanded perspective, life coaching can give any form of coaching an existential dimension" (Schmidt-Lellek and Buer 2011, p. 16).

A natural next step would be to examine the coaching client's familial situation in the past, which serves as significant coordinates (points of orientation) for life coaching for a horizontal and/or vertical expansion. After that, the focus is on what he has become in the context of his family of origin and its influence on his current professional life. And it is the significance of this influence for coaching which I wish to outline in the following.

17.2 The Significance of the Family Constellation in One's Family of Origin for Later Life

The family constellation which a client was part of in his family of origin is a biographical information which is not difficult to obtain in coaching. Particularly the position which a person had in the sibling constellation of his family is easy to determine and has a predictive function for his later role in his professional life that is not to be underestimated. I would like to illustrate this with the use of the "family constellations" concept by Toman (1961, 2002) and place it in the context of coaching.

17.2.1 Socialization in the Family

This approach is a psychoanalytical socialization concept. In this case, socialization is understood as the lifelong societal integration process of persons (Geulen 2001). However, it can be shown that there exist particularly sensitive phases over the course of a person's life. These are development stages which are of particular significance for further socialization and therefore the entire later life of a person.

This particularly applies to early childhood. The psychoanalysis of Sigmund Freud and his successors provided decisive figures for argumentation which explained why early experiences have such a profound effect. In this case, it is postulated that the personality of a person is shaped only when social processes takes place. A helpless infant which comes into this world, and which is far removed from any socialization, is initially regulated by his attachment figure only with regard to the satisfaction or non-satisfaction of his needs. It is only with increasing maturity that the child experiences his attachment figure as a unique person and forms more or less intensive bonds with him or her depending on his/her emotional satisfaction value, as Spitz (1976) and Bowlby (1951) were able to show.

This phenomenon was described by Freud (1936) as "sociabilization". This means that, from this stage on, at eight to twelve months, the child is ready to be imprinted socially by his caregivers. From now on, in the form of a "motherly identification" (ibid.), it shows an initial willingness to accept standards and norms. Over the course of further processes of maturity, when the child learns to perceive gender differences at four to five years of age, it begins to orientate itself according to its parent of the same gender and use him or her as a model in a specific manner. This process was described by Sigmund Freud (1909–1913) as "identification in the oedipal phase".

The norms and standards acquired from this stage on also contain gender-specific components. For example, Nancy Chodorow (1978, as cited in Geulen 2001) was able to show that small girls were already being socialized to take on a "mothering" role. Because of their greater proximity to the mother, they receive a different form of "role training" as the boys. Hence, psychoanalysis assumes that the first relationships serve as the model for further socialization processes and, to a certain extent, also represent the template for all later social relationships.

It is also these early relationship partners towards whom a person learns to orientate his actions and decisions, and it is in their eyes which he is able to see himself as a specific individual for the first time. Hence, in psychoanalysis the general assumption is that experiences from early contexts have a longer-lasting effect on the later life of a person than later ones. In classical psychoanalysis according to Freud (1905), who saw human development as being strongly linked to the infantile drive destiny of a person, this refers to the first five to six years of life. For later psychoanalytical authors, particularly for Erikson (1964, 1966), the existence of additional sensitive phases was assumed. For example, puberty was again of particular significance for the development of a person's identity, a stage lasting from twelve to fifteen years of age.

The family represents the first social context with which a child is confronted, and the family members are the first interaction partners according to which a child orientates his actions and decisions, and in the eyes of which it learns to perceive itself. Freud and the majority of his followers initially address only the interaction between children and their parents as being crucial for later social life. It was Adler (1933) who first reported on the importance of sibling relationships. From the 1920s onwards, a number of American authors examined age rank positions in series of siblings and their psychological effects as part of empirical studies, such as how the behavior of firstborn children differs from that of later siblings. In a number of these studies, the effects of loss were also addressed, such as how the death of the father or the mother affects the further development of a person (cf. Toman 2002, p. 235 ff.). As informative as all these studies are, they all have certain weaknesses, as they are based neither on a system for sibling relationships, nor on a system for losses within a family. Furthermore, their prognoses focused primarily on children and youths, and in exceptional cases on persons with psychopathological disorders. However, effects for "normal" adults were seldom studied.

17.2.2 Basic Aspects of the Theory of Family Constellations

Walter Toman, a Viennese psychoanalyst and professor for psychology, attempted to avoid all these weaknesses in his work "Family Constellations" (1961), which was first published in the USA. This work appeared to provide a relatively timeless diagnostic basis for human interaction and system phenomena—in 2002, the book appeared in its seventh revised edition in the German-speaking world.

The author kicks off the debate with statements that every person was born into a more or less intact family, that in 9 out of 10 cases the family remains together up till the child's adolescent phase, that in 5% of all cases the children experience a separation through divorce or death, which is the father in 8 out of 10 cases. From 1951 up till the 1980s, he and his colleagues investigated several thousand families. Even though the author repeatedly cautions that other conditions such as the living environment or the peer group have strongly modificatory effects on the family constellation, and that the statistically obtained results only apply in a limited fashion to individual cases, the goal of his research was to obtain a *prognostic map* for the later private and professional life of a person from the corresponding family constellation. His theory is divided into three areas which are concerned (1) with sibling constellations, (2) with personal losses and (3) with various relationship types.

17.2.2.1 Sibling Constellations

Toman distinguishes sibling constellations according to two aspects: according to rank and gender. Because one can only speak of "siblings" when there are at least two children in a family, the rules of combinatorics result in eight basic constellations, namely four female and four male types:

s (s) the older sister of a younger sister
(s) s the younger sister of an older sister
s (b) the older sister of a younger brother
(b) s the younger sister of an older brother

b (b) the older brother of a younger brother
(b) b the younger brother of an older brother
b (s) the older brother of a younger sister
(s) b the younger brother of an older sister

The notation I have presented here is the one suggested by Toman. According to this notation system, the person who is being spoken of lies outside of the brackets, and their siblings are indicated within the brackets. Hence, the older brother of two sisters and an even younger brother is indicated as such: b (ssb).

For the basic types, Toman came up with elaborate portraits. Similar to Richter (1969), he understands these types as roles. The parents, siblings and other family members unconsciously project specific personality characteristics onto the oldest and/or youngest siblings as the oldest or youngest, who then unconsciously accommodate their behavior according these projections. In this manner, the children form an identity as the oldest or youngest sibling. Through the daily interactions in the family, they then practice certain patterns for action, which they at least attempt to realize later on. Without going into too much detail here – for this, please refer to the original text (Toman 2002)—two basic hypotheses can be formulated for our purposes, namely for professional contexts:

- Oldest siblings, also called seniors, tend towards dominance, while younger siblings have generally learned to subordinate themselves. Hence, older siblings are more willing and able to take on positions of leadership than young ones later on.
- Siblings who grew up only among others of the same gender tend to also prefer colleagues of the same gender later on in their professional lives. However, in reverse, this means that e.g. an older brother of younger sisters will be able to cope better with managing women than an older brother of brothers. In turn, the latter will probably be a more successful manager in male-dominated spheres than a brother of sisters.

In addition to the basic types mentioned above, there are of course middle siblings, only children and twins. *Middle siblings* can often be subcategorized under one of the other corresponding basic constellations depending on the age difference to the other siblings. Hence, the middle sister of an older brother and a younger sister (b) s (s) is more likely to turn out as the younger sister of a brother when the age difference with the older brother is only two years, while the age difference with the younger sister is 10 years. After all, until that sister was born, she was the younger sister of a brother for 10 years of her life. More difficult to analyze are same-gender constellations with only a minimal age gap, such as (s) s (s). If the middle sister to two sisters only has an age difference of two years to both the older and younger sisters, she will probably experience difficulties with maintaining and defining her identity between the oldest and youngest sisters in her childhood. She may then be wary of being ignored later on. In a best-case scenario, she is particularly able to integrate herself into social systems where dominance vs. subordination plays a role. Particularly for prognoses for middle siblings, it is important to reconstruct the entire family constellation.

For *only children*, Toman assumes that from a young age, they are used to being at the focus of attention and being somehow important. Furthermore, they tend to assume the sibling constellation of the parent of the same gender. Hence, a female only child with a mother who was the oldest sister of a sister s (s) is also more likely to manifest as the older sister of sisters. However, if the mother herself was also an only child, Toman would assume that the characteristics of an only child would be particularly pronounced in this woman.

In the case of *twins*, a distinction needs to be made between identical and fraternal twins. Identical twins are not only born at the same time, but also have the same developmental status. Hence, they often have an extremely close relationship and find it hard to be separated even in later years. In the case of fraternal twins, the relationships are not quite as close, especially when it is a boy and a girl.

Generally, the children then tend to identify even more strongly with the parent of the same gender, and therefore assume personality characteristics from their sibling constellation.

17.2.2.2 Personal Losses

According to Toman, personal losses play a key role in the analysis of family constellations. Such losses include death, divorce, or other forms of separation. Due to the loss of an emotionally significant person, the one who suffers the loss also experiences a certain degree of uncertainty in his relationships with other persons in his environment. Here, Toman distinguishes between permanent and temporary losses. The author attempts to ascertain the psychological significance of losses according to a list of criteria (Toman 2002, p. 48). According to his findings, they are experienced more intensely

(a) the less time has passed,
(b) the earlier they occur in a person's life,
(c) the older the person lost (relative to the oldest family member),
(d) the longer a person lived with the person lost,
(e) the smaller the family,
(f) the greater the extent to which the balance of the sexes in the family is affected by the loss,
(g) the longer the remaining family members need in order to obtain a replacement for the person lost,
(h) the greater the number of losses and the severity of the losses that have already occurred.

Apart from (g), all criteria apply to both permanent and temporary losses. Criterion (c) indicates that the loss of a parent is significantly more severe than that of a sibling. In turn, the loss of an older sibling is more severe than that of a younger one. Overall, this means that the longer a person lived with another, the more pain the loss of that person causes. Particularly important for our context is also point (f). When, for example, in a family with three daughters which were born at intervals of two years to each other, the father dies shortly after the birth of the third daughter and the mother does not enter into a relationship with a new partner, this family remains purely a female household. For the socialization of the daughters, this represents a deficit, as (at least in their close family environment) they have no male family member and they could not experience a heterosexual relationship at close range. In their later interactions, they are then unable to fall back on familiar patterns when dealing with men. This may result in increased trepidation or an increased lack of distance awareness.

As Toman (2002, p. 45) pointed out, in 8 out of 10 cases, it is the father who leaves the family, either due to death or more frequently, due to a divorce. In case of death, the father's memory is often exaggerated in a positive manner, such that it is not rare for him to live on as a positive model in their imagination. On the other hand, in the period leading up to a divorce as well as in the subsequent family situation, the father is often assigned negative attributes, such that unpleasant and distorted ideas of him are formed. In the family constellation theory, this fact is of vital significance for the later professional lives of these "abandoned children": In most cases, persons in authority are assigned paternal attributes, even if they are female. If the subordinate employees had a well-balanced and satisfying relationship with their father, they generally tend to have a trusting attitude towards their superiors. In turn, their superior is very likely to also react in a positive manner. However, if the relationship with their father was a disappointment, this expectation is often transferred to the superior in the form of negative attributes. Such relationships end up as relationships of mistrust – although in most cases this takes place in a concealed manner. Conversely, a successful relationship with one's father often forms the basis for successful leadership positions. In many cases, a disappointing relationship with one's father is the underlying reason why taking over a position of leadership fails or turns out to be particularly difficult.

17.2.2.3 Relationships

Toman distinguishes between relationship phenomena in a manner similar to Watzlawik et al. (1969, p. 68 f) into "complementary" and "identification relationships".

Complementary relationships: According to what is called the "duplication theorem", Toman (2002, p. 81) was able to prove with the aid of various data sets that the more similar newly-formed relationships are to the earlier and earliest social experiences of those involved, the more successful and permanent they are. Above all, for partner relationships, this means that the greater the similarity of their new relationship to their respective sibling constellations from the past, the more lasting their relationship will be.

Hence, partner relationships of an older brother of a younger sister b (s) with a younger sister of an older brother (b) s prove to be exceedingly lasting, as both partners were already able to get used to living with a person of the other gender in their respective families. In the words of Toman (2002, p. 87 ff.), they have no "gender conflict". Furthermore, the older brother naturally exercises dominance later on, which is perfectly acceptable for the younger sister, who is junior in this case. Hence, they also do not have a "rank conflict".

Predictably, the most unfortunate partner relationship would then be one where the woman is the oldest sister of a sister s (s) and enters into a relationship with the older brother of a brother b (b). From their childhood, neither of the two is used to living together in a familial situation with persons of the same age of the opposite gender. Hence, they are unable to spontaneously put themselves in each other's shoes or deduce each other's secret desires. In the words of Toman, they have a "gender conflict". Furthermore, both are used to asserting dominance from an early age, which is why they will wrestle for dominance in the relationship. Hence, they also have a "rank conflict" according to Toman.

However, it should be mentioned that couples who live in such constellations permanently have generally developed a large number of common interests which then bind them together despite their sibling constellations. In a worst-case scenario, they may have children with severe disorders for which they have to care for in a united manner. In the family therapy approach by Selvini Palazzoli et al. (1985), it was even postulated that the pathological symptom of a child—such as anorexia—in its function as a partnership bracket for the parents is also maintained over the long term in the context of a "symptomatic benefit".

The things I have mentioned here for partner relationships also apply to professional relationships to a certain extent. For example, the younger brother of a sister (s) b will probably be more receptive to being managed by the older sister of a brother s (b) than an older sister of a sister s (s). It is also to be predicted that the older sister of a brother s (b) would be more understanding of the specific extravagances of a junior male employee than the older sister of a sister s (s). The latter is more used to "protecting small princesses than small princes".

Identification relationships: Toman calls the other relationship type "identification relationship". In this case, the relationship is not characterized by complementarity, but similarity. What takes place here is narcissistic selection: Each person falls in love with himself in the other person. This type is found primarily among people of the same gender. For example, it can be observed that older brothers of brothers b (b) often also seek out older brothers of brothers b (b) as confidants. Similarly, younger sisters of sisters (s) s often prefer other younger sisters of sisters (s) s as friends. In addition, Toman also shows that the relationships between father/son and mother/daughter are either positive or negative according to the degree of identification. Hence, a father who grew up as the younger brother of a sister (s) b will find it easier to accept a son who also grows up as the younger brother of a sister (s) b than a father who is the older brother to multiple brothers b (bb). His son may remain permanently distant to him as a "pampered baby".

We also encounter positive identification relationships in work relationships. For example, collaborations between two older brothers of brothers b (b) + b (b) may be extraordinarily fruitful in the pioneer stages (i.e. initial set-up stage) of organizations. Each finds in the other the dominance realized in oneself and affirms it in the other person. Similar phenomena are also observed repeatedly for older sisters of sisters s (b) + s (b). In this rather "robust" dominance, each of the two respects themselves in the other.

17.3 The Applicability of the Family Constellation Theory to Coaching

In coaching, I use Toman's approach primarily for two purposes: for the reconstruction and managing of conflicts and for prognoses and/or stimuli during career counseling.

17.3.1 Applications During Conflict Coaching

Many conflicts that are described as "problems of management" can be traced back to complications arising from familial socialization after performing an exact reconstruction.

17.3.1.1 Incompatibilities with Parents

Today, management problems are often observed that result from incompatibilities with parents. Among the generation of the 40–60 years old men, there exists a historically motivated ambivalence with regard to the assumption of managing positions. This ambivalence is aggravated even more when one's own father was experienced primarily as demanding and perhaps as punitive with sadistic tendencies. This is not at all rare when fathers who are younger brothers of brothers (bb) b are constantly locked in a rivalry with their oldest sons, who happen to be older brothers of brothers b (b). As part of a "sibling transference", the son is then made to pay for what he could never do to the real older brother, perhaps because the brother, unlike the much younger son, permanently remained in a position of superiority. In this manner, frustration from the past is unleashed upon the son.

In leadership personnel who have such relationships with their father, there usually exists the idea that, in definite contrast to their father, they generally need to approach their subordinate employees as friends or buddies. By doing so, they hope that these employees will then fulfill their duties optimally all the time. When this strategy does not work, something which happens much too often, such superiors are entirely helpless. In such cases, it is wise to make the context described experienceable to them and to practice it using concrete situations, so that they slowly acquire the ability to take on the role of a formally demanding superior who is also able to act in a constructive manner at the personal level. This should take place in the first few work sequences in a contrastive delineation to the own father. As the sessions progress, the coaching client generally realizes on his own that, in the eyes of his employees, he can only stand to gain respect by emphasizing his formal role as their superior.

17.3.1.2 Sibling Relationships

Many other leadership problems also stem from sibling relationships. Probably the most frequent conflicts between superiors and subordinate employees occur in the form of symmetric problems, i.e. as rivalry conflicts. This takes place often when both were senior in their family and now wrestle for the position of priority in their professional lives. In this case, after a reconstruction during coaching, it would be expedient to identify options for complementarity while also taking into consideration the formal constellation. When doing so, it may be a good idea for the superior to utilize his formal position of seniority to channel the dominance claims of the employee. By doing so, he will be able to explore the strengths of his employee in more detail and cede to him areas of specialty as a "stage of dominance" according to his expertise.

Relationships that were originally complementary may also pose a problem. It is not rare for an older superior who grew up as a younger brother in a long series of siblings (sbsb) b to hire a new employee who was an older brother in a series of siblings b (sbs). Initially, he may have a great understanding with this employee due to their complementarity. However, after a certain amount of time passes, when the complementarity deepens unnoticed, the superior experiences an increasing discomfort. In the reconstruction during coaching, it may then come to light that he has unconsciously been relegated to the role of the junior in interactions with the employee, a role that collides heavily with his formal position and his professional self-image. When this happens, the first step in coaching is then to uncover the current emotional constellation, and the second step would be to practice alternative patterns. In this case, it would be wise to reinforce the client in his formal role patterns without unnecessarily frustrating the employee. Here, it is particularly helpful to utilize imagined interaction sequences to try out new patterns of speech, and behavior with the employee such that the superior is slowly able to reacquire relationship forms that are more adequate professionally.

17.3.1.3 Early Losses

Some leadership problems result from early losses. For example, it came to light for a female manager from the human resources department of a company that, although she constantly planned to delegate more tasks to her employees, she still ended up doing too much herself. When a reconstruction was conducted which also included biographical information, it came to light that she had lost a three-year-old brother in an accident when she was seven years old. Although she was not present during the accident, in her dreams she was often tortured by the question of whether she had failed in some way, and if she should have accompanied her brother, whom she had often picked up from kindergarten, that time as well. This issue was also crucial for her weakness during delegation. She constantly had the fantasy that things could only be done "safely and with certainty" through her direct participation. After this reconstruction, she was able to delegate in a much more calm and serene manner.

17.3.2 Applications During Career Counseling

In career counseling, analyses with the help of the family constellation theory often provide stimuli and encouragement as to the direction in which the person involved could take.

17.3.2.1 Rank Among Siblings

Some of these issues had to do with the rank in the series of siblings. For example, a very experienced journalist who was preparing to change his job asked the coach which of two jobs he should take. The first job was a position as a CEO in a renowned association with above-average remuneration. However, there was a lot of infighting taking place at this organization, and it was expected that he would have to act in a very flexible and agile manner in future in order not to be caught in a bad position or take sides. The other position was a much less well-paid head position in a journalism firm with a number of friendly employees, but the professional requirements were rather one-sided. In the first case, which he actually preferred, he would need to be extremely flexible and tactful in order to move between super- and subordinate roles, while in the second he would be in an uncontested, but rather "boring" position of leadership, in his own words.

Over the course of the reconstruction of his professional life so far, he spoke about his position in the family and hence among his siblings. Growing up in a pastor's house, he was the middle brother of two older siblings, a sister and a brother, and three younger siblings, a brother and two sisters, and served as an intermediary between the older and younger siblings. His position is represented as follows: (sb) b (sbs). When he spoke of his "mediation work" in the family, he suddenly realized that there was a generational conflict in the association between a number of board members and most of the members. "Somehow, I feel that I am on familiar ground with such conflicts", he stated with satisfaction. "As the CEO, I am also positioned between the board and the members." After considering a number of other aspects, he decided to accept the position in the association. "I love being a part of such scuffles", he said, "and the fact that I'll be making good money is so much the better."

17.3.2.2 Gender Relations

Many other issues in career counseling concern themselves with gender relations. During career counseling or career planning, the issues dealt with are frequently concerned with how promising leadership positions can be for a man in women-dominated spheres, or for a woman in male-dominated spheres. As a rough orientation, it can be said that male leadership personnel who had older or younger sisters are more likely to be accepted by their colleagues in women-dominated spheres such as nursing or social pedagogy than if they only had brothers. A man who experienced how women deal with conflict or which actions result in particular feelings of offense in women as part of his socialization will intuitively consider and incorporate these phenomena in his actions and decisions as a leader.

The same applies for women who grew up among men. The older sister of brothers s (bb) is more likely to perform her leadership role in male-dominated spheres with a certain ease. And a younger sister of brothers (bb) s will probably be particularly popular and successful in male-dominated spheres, as she is able to cater to the needs of males in a particularly flexible manner.

It was precisely due to this that a young, hitherto extremely successful female economist with this sibling constellation who had to search for a new field of employment after her company declared bankruptcy was able to quickly become a highly valued employee in a typical male-dominated sphere. Through a "coincidence", she got to know an older man who headed a corporate consulting business for technology companies. After he experienced the considerable success with how she handled a "difficult" client, he decided the following: "Every time a consultation client gets cumbersome to deal with, we'll call on our young lady." In this manner, she received a large number of consulting contracts, which she successfully handled as expected, and from which she made more money than ever.

17.4 Final Remarks

Even though there are a large number of plausible examples in which the family constellation theory "works well", caution is advised. Toman himself points out that his findings are based on statistical data from a large number of persons. Hence, they only have a limited validity for applications in individual cases. When this "path" does not appear sufficiently evident to the client or the coach, they should simply follow another. Hence, this approach forms part of a pool of widely varying concepts which the coach can make use of as part of an integrative coaching concept (Schreyögg 2012).

References

Adler, A. (1974). *Praxis und Theorie der Individualpsychologie*. Frankfurt: Fischer. (Orig. 1933).

Böning, U., & Fritschle, B. (2005). *Coaching fürs Business*. Bonn: ManagerSeminare.

Bowlby, J. (1973). *Mütterliche Zuwendung und geistige Gesundheit*. München: Kindler. (Orig. 1951).

Buer, F., & Schmidt-Lellek, C. (2008). *Life-Coaching. Über Sinn, Glück und Verantwortung in der Arbeit*. Göttingen: Vandenhoeck & Ruprecht.

Erikson, E. (1973). *Identität und Lebenszyklus*. Frankfurt/M.: Suhrkamp. (Orig. 1966).

Erikson, E. (1992). *Einsicht und Verantwortung*. Frankfurt: Fischer. (Orig. 1964).

Feldman, D. C., & Lankau, M. J. (2005). Executive coaching: A review and agenda for future research. *Journal of Management, 31*(6), 829–848.

Freud, A. (1936). *Das Ich und die Abwehrmechanismen*. Wien: Int. Psychoanal. Verlag.

Freud, S. (1969). *Gesammelte Werke aus den Jahren 1909–1913*. Frankfurt/M.: Fischer.

Geulen, D. (2001). Sozialisation. In H. Joas (Hg.), *Lehrbuch der Soziologie*. Frankfurt/M.: Campus.

Martens-Schmid, K. (2007). Die „ganze Person" im Coaching – Ambivalenzen und Optionen. *OSC, 14*(1), 17–29.

Richter, H.-E. (1969). *Eltern, Kind, Neurose*. Reinbek: Rowohlt.

Schmidt-Lellek, C. (2011). Perspektiven des Lebensganzen. Die Lebensspanne und die Lebensbereiche im Coaching. In C. Schmidt-Lellek & F. Buer (Hg.), *Life-Coaching in der Praxis* (S. 27–49). Göttingen: Vandenhoeck & Ruprecht.

Schmidt-Lellek, C., & Buer, F. (Eds.). (2011). *Life-Coaching in der Praxis. Wie Coaches umfassend beraten*. Göttingen: Vandenhoeck & Ruprecht.

Schreyögg, A. (2012). *Coaching. Eine Einführung für Praxis und Ausbildung* (7., überarb. u. erw. Aufl.). Frankfurt/M.: Campus.

Selvini Palazzoli, M., Boscolo, J., Cecchin, G., & Prata, G. (1985). *Paradoxon und Gegenparadoxon* (4. Aufl.). Stuttgart: Klett-Cotta. (Orig. 1975).
Spitz, R. (1976). *Vom Dialog. Studien über den Ursprung der menschlichen Kommunikation und ihre Rolle in der Persönlichkeitsbildung*. Stuttgart: Klett-Cotta.
Toman, W. (1961). *Family constellations*. New York: Springer.
Toman, W. (2002). *Familienkonstellationen* (7., durchges. Aufl.). München: Beck.
Watzlawik, P., Beavin, J. H., & Jackson, D. D. (1969). *Menschliche Kommunikation*. Bern u. a.: Huber.

Author Biography

Dr. Phil. Astrid Schreyögg Dipl.-Psych., psychotherapist, supervisor, coach; head of research at the German Academy of Psychologists of the BDP for Supervision and Coaching; domestic and international fellow; trainer for supervision and coaching; textbook author; publisher of the journal "Organisationsberatung, Supervision, Coaching" (OSC).

18 Gender Coaching—A Critical Analysis

Gabriele Bollhöfer

Abstract

Gender-coaching or gender-competent coaching is being used to support cultural change in organizations. Therefore it should be offered equally to women as well as to men. The author criticizes a common practice that defines gender-coaching as a developmental tool for women only as this purely focuses on individual competencies. In doing so organizations miss the opportunity for cultural change towards gender diversity. A criteria for the expected impact of gender-coaching is the context of change processes it will be related to. A real-life coaching episode illustrating unconscious gender-related biases completes this chapter.

18.1 Introduction

Gender diversity has been a top priority for German companies for many years, with a whole range of strategies, processes and measures being implemented with the aim of ending the underrepresentation of women in management positions. Yet despite serious efforts, only minor progress has been made with regard to gender diversity at management levels in Germany. A glance at the figures for women in management positions clearly illustrates this: in the period from 2004 to 2010, the proportion of women in senior management at major companies actually *fell* from

G. Bollhöfer (✉)
Heinz-Mohnen-Platz 3, 50937 Cologne, Germany
e-mail: gabriele.bollhoefer@hoganlovells.com

A. Schreyögg and C. Schmidt-Lellek (eds.), *The Professionalization of Coaching*, DOI 10.1007/978-3-658-16805-6_18

6.8 to 5.9%, but increased slightly in middle management at major companies from 12.6 to 18.3% (Hoppenstedt 2010; Fraunhofer-Gesellschaft 2012). The situation at small and medium-sized enterprises looks slightly better. However, no meaningful successes were recorded anywhere as regards the significance for business and the investments made.

This chapter does not attempt to determine the social interrelationships—this has been capably done by others (Mühling and Schwarze 2011; Schreyögg 2013); instead, it describes an approach to coaching that is relevant in the context of gender diversity initiatives as well as in many other coaching processes.

18.2 Attempts to Explane the Situation

The situation described above occasionally leaves those responsible perplexed because this ostensibly achievable management task is proving to be a drawn-out process of cultural change. The figures alone suggest that rapid change is possible in view of the large number of highly qualified women who *say* they want a career *and* a family. In the case of career entrants, the distribution of men and women in most industries is comparatively good. There is also a broad commitment from politicians and companies to increase the proportion of women in management positions. However, it almost goes unnoticed when, in the course of their careers, women decide to quit, go part-time or postpone their next career step. As each individual decision appears logical and sensible, it is usually not questioned or even preventively addressed.

The result is that barely any progress is made with regard to the representation of women at management levels, and this is frustrating. It is understandable that those responsible for this issue within companies are somewhat perplexed because a variety of measures has been taken to ensure equal opportunities. In informal conversations, this very often leads to the following self-absolving statement: "Women must actually want and accept the many offers made." "They just don't want to." These are, incidentally, typical remarks from both women *and* men in management positions. The interpretations do not differ according to gender.

So what is the problem here? Firstly, it should be noted that it is difficult to force a change purely through gender diversity measures that come from management. From a purely objective point of view, companies have the best intentions and, for many years, have been committed to developing promotion processes and flexible working time models as well as specific ways to promote women. Needless to say, these projects are driven by tangible economic interests. At the same time, managers are willing to accept difficulties, e.g. managing teams in which 80% of staff are part-time. Nevertheless, there are no signs of success compared with the efforts made. That is why this issue is rarely dealt with in a level-headed manner. This applies to those responsible for ensuring the change as well as to women, who expect career opportunities to result from the change, and their male colleagues, who may feel exposed to greater competitive pressure.

As important as the organizational and methodological frameworks are for the development of gender balance, most of them nevertheless do not function reliably in the areas where unconscious preferences emerge: in the awarding of positions, involvement in the most exciting and prestigious projects, the exchange of informal information with bodies, the assessment of behaviour and performance, which can never be purely objective. I will address this in more detail in Sect. 18.4.

18.3 Classification of Gender Coaching

Gender coaching or gender-competent coaching (Abdul-Hussain 2012) is an offering that is included in diversity programmes. As illustrated in the introduction, the underrepresentation of women in management positions is linked in a complex manner to cultural, institutional and individual effects.

All attempts at classification logically always address several approaches with regard to effects and explanations. For example, Welpe (2014) from the LMU Munich divides the approaches to explaining the underrepresentation of women in management positions into the following three levels: (1) at the level of the *individual*, women are assumed to have too little self-confidence and not to be active enough in their career planning. (2) At the level of the *organization*, there is a lack of powerful role models and access to networks. (3) At the level of the *system*, role expectations and difficulties balancing work and family life have an effect. On the basis of this practical division, gender coaching begins at the level of the individual and is thus limited in terms of its institutional effect. Gender coaching has a greater effect at management levels as organizational power is involved here.

Gender coaching cannot be described without taking a look at the objectives, strategies and measures established by companies in their diversity initiatives. The diagram below shows the context in which gender coaching in companies can usually be placed (cf. Fig. 18.1). Gender coaching is an optional measure in change processes, and it cannot be assumed that, without being embedded in such a context, gender coaching will have an institutional effect in the form of changing the proportion of women represented.

According to the conclusions of the Fraunhofer-Gesellschaft study "Change corporate cultures—avoid career breaks" (2012), too, all levels must be addressed

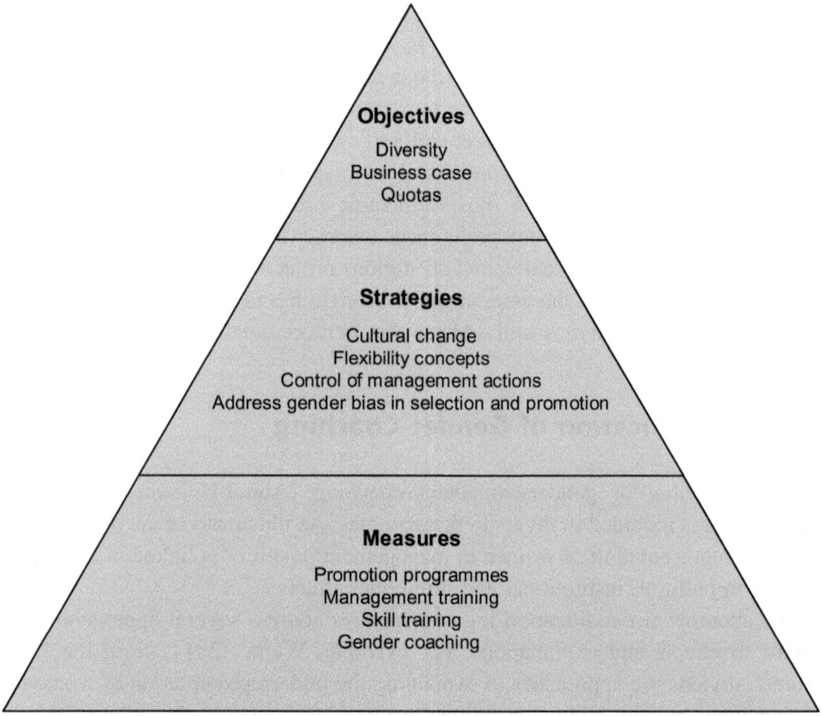

Fig. 18.1 The context of gender coaching

in a change process. With regard to the question of the institutional effectiveness of gender coaching, this means that such coaching should be used in a manner that is tailored to change objectives and change measures.

Gender coaching can certainly be viewed critically because, as an advisory product, it can run the risk of individualising a phenomenon determined by the culture—something which can certainly apply to many occasions where coaching takes place. In respect of gender coaching, however, the influence of cultural conditions that perpetuate unequal opportunities is particularly evident.

If the aim is to have an effect at institutional level, the individual approach is definitely inadequate because there is a lack of platforms, agreements and practical processes that promote women's careers and offer specific courses of action and levers. The objective is to systematically lower the threshold for the advancement of women and not to accommodate individuals who find individual paths that some people have always found.

It is therefore a quality criterion of gender coaching that it be used in a context-specific manner and that both the positive and negative conditions of the culture and the diversity initiatives be identified and incorporated.

18.4 What Is Gender Coaching and Who Is It Suitable for?

In an initial approach to the subject, I will define gender coaching as a coaching process that takes into account the effects of gender on the management and career decisions of all parties involved and relates this to the corresponding skills and knowledge from gender research. Gender coaching is therefore *not merely an offering of advice to women* who want to increase their opportunities, but also of course to *men* who wish to examine the effects of gender. It is aimed at men and women who deal with competing women, experience gender-specific effects in communication situations or manage women. When looking at the issue in this way, the term "*gender-competent coaching*" coined by Abdul-Hussain certainly seems appropriate, as it highlights the competence of the coach with regard to gender effects and thus prevents gender coaching from being understood solely as an advisory format for "promoting women". Conversely, this would mean that the lack of equality in the workplace is attributable to a kind of personal deficit on the part of women. It is therefore surprising that many companies still take precisely this view and provide women with a variety of "qualifications" as if unequal opportunities were due to a qualifications deficit. This seems absurd in view of the fact that women tend to have better academic qualifications and often demonstrate high social skills. Gender-competent coaching should not fall precisely into the same "*a training/coaching course for every problem*" trap, but should seriously incorporate the context of the gender debate and the organizational conditions.

Gender coaching with managers—whether male or female—who address the issue of their unconscious gender bias in their perception and promotion of their staff is especially effective. In this way, aspects of gender coaching always appear in both management and career coaching. So why do we need a new label? The answer is simple: any label allows a better understanding if the coachee defines the problem accordingly. At the same time, it is of course true that an initial "diagnosis" may change in the course of the coaching process; thus, whether a course called gender coaching will in fact contain gender coaching is not guaranteed, but is not particularly relevant either. Conversely, it is also possible that a substantial proportion of a management coaching course will turn into gender-competent coaching. However, the most important advantage seems to be that this differentiation allows companies to also offer an attractive range of measures at the individual level as part of diversity initiatives.

18.5 Unconscious Bias—A Relevant Concept When Advising on Gender Effects

Since the psychologist Kahneman (2012) who has been awarded with the Nobel Prize for Economics the idea that our actions, and of course the actions of management, as well as our decisions are significantly determined by unconscious prejudices and stereotypes has become socially acceptable. But reality tells a different story. In management training sessions that are intended to create awareness of these mechanisms, a typical reaction is that it is always the others who succumb to stereotypes. This should not surprise psychologists because no one ever promised that it would be easy to make people aware of unconscious or pre-conscious issues.

The mere idea of presenting the effects of unconscious bias in a training format for managers creates the expectation that the unconscious is manageable or can be "coached out" of people. This concept is clearly reflected in the title of the training: "Eliminating Unconscious Bias"—to which the only response can be: good luck!

Viewed without irony, it is indeed difficult to introduce this relevant concept—which offers very powerful explanations for business decisions—adequately in companies and to ensure that sufficient attention is given to it. The concept promises no direct practical benefits for management work, but increases the complexity of reality. This is usually the opposite of what managers find attractive. Nevertheless, such training courses are held, and those responsible for diversity in particular define such measures in their diversity business plans, which means that a certain proportion of managers encounter this concept. From a coach's point of view, workshops that generate attention are indeed helpful with regard to gender coaching. If the coachees have previously looked at the issue of unconscious bias, this makes it easier to understand the effect of individual values and preferences in the actions of management.

18.6 A Coaching Episode

A discussion with a (male) manager begins "harmlessly" as a review of the development of a female employee who attended coaching as agreed with the manager and has since left the company. The meeting therefore does not begin as a coaching discussion, but as a joint assessment—suggested by the coach—of the process. The manager had previously attended a workshop on unconscious bias.

The discussion starts with a massive complaint from the manager that he does not know how the objective of a quota for women at management level can be achieved at all. According to the manager, there are too few women in the pipeline and, as the current example shows, they leave without managers having any significant influence on the matter. The discussion focuses for a time on what actually influenced the ex-employee's decision and on how the issues of part-time work and her position in the team were handled; statements are made to the effect that such problems simply did not arise with the man on the team. The manager states that the woman did not have the courage to put herself forward and was not decisive enough in the way she presented herself and her work. He adds that she simply used the belt and braces approach too often, although her subject-area expertise was very good—in fact better than some of the others, who tended to be "pushy".

At one point, the coach asks about the team as a whole, which includes other women, and about the overall situation here. The manager responds first of all by emphasising the attitude of the only male team member in a positive light. The coach again asks specifically about the women on the team. The manager names one female team member who he says is *very good* at self-marketing (his tone of voice indicating that he finds this inappropriate and astonishing), which makes an "extremely good impression" with customers. This effect, too, is not connoted entirely positively, but described with very mixed feelings. The manager also states that she delegates everything that can be delegated, and uses the team very effectively for her purposes. It occurs to the coach that the manager is describing all the qualities looked for in a manager but has no idea he is doing so. On the contrary, in all respects it is clear that he is critical of the team member's behaviour.

The coach then asks the coachee's permission to look into his values as a manager, in order to begin changing the nature of the discussion. The manager's consent to this is coupled with a certain curiosity as to what might come next. The coach repeats the manager's statements and accompanying feelings with regard to the employee who has left and the employee whose pro-active approach he is critical of, and asks the manager whether the things for which he criticises the second employee are in fact those that he thinks were lacking in the first employee? There is a moment of surprise; the manager begins to go through the individual aspects and agrees that this is astonishingly coherent and that it is a problem if behaviour that is actually looked for is viewed as problematic. In order to try to identify his motives, we address his own career development and the values that were dominant in a conservative, performance-driven world. He begins experimentally reassessing the negative associations that he experiences with the employee and questioning his feelings. It appeared to be particularly striking that, at an emotional level, he rejects the rational criteria that he applies to women who want to advance their careers. This is both funny and interesting, and has an unburdening effect because he now has the feeling that he does not necessarily always have to get worked up all the time about his pro-active female colleague, but instead can see the whole thing as positive as well, and somehow he likes this. The coach takes the opportunity to mention the unconscious bias workshop in order to make it clear that such discoveries are valuable and that it is almost impossible for us to recognise such tendencies in ourselves. He suggests continuing to work on these issues.

This brief report of a discussion that turned into a coaching episode shows that workshops that create awareness of the effects of bias do not necessary lead to a change of behaviour in individuals, but on the other hand can reinforce the awareness achieved as well as the willingness and the ability to address effects and possibilities for change at an individual level.

18.7 Conclusion

Gender-competent coaching is in the process of gaining a place among the wide variety of diversity measures. The organizational and social frameworks as well as knowledge of gender effects and corresponding research findings are important for coaches in this field. It is no coincidence that gender coaching regularly appears on websites of specialist consultants and coaches in connection with advisory services relating to gender mainstreaming and cultural analysis. This is reassuring because it means that the subject of gender coaching appears to have been sensibly classified. Gender-competent coaching is an instrument for women and men as well as for managers and employees, because gender effects on attitudes, behaviour and thus also on management decisions occur at all hierarchy levels. We can expect to see further areas of activity relating to diversity being reflected in coaching. Examples of these are the megatrend of age diversity in companies or sexual orientation, cultural, ethnic and religious affiliation and others.

References

Abdul-Hussain, S. (2012). *Genderkompetenz in Supervision und Coaching*. Wiesbaden: Springer VS.

Fraunhofer-Gesellschaft (2012). Unternehmenskulturen verändern – Karrierebrüche vermeiden. http://www.fraunhofer.de/de/presse/presseinformationen/2012/oktober/karrierebrueche-von-frauen-vermeiden.html (called up on 15 August 2014).
Hoppenstedt (2010). Frauen in Führungspositionen. Unternehmenstypen im Vergleich. http://www.hoppenstedt.de/xist4c/web-/Frauen-im-Management_id_567_.htm (called up on 15 August 2014).
Kahneman, D. (2012). *Thinking, fast and slow*. New York: Farrah, Straus and Giroux.
Mühling, T., & Schwarze, J. (Eds.). (2011). *Was begünstigt die berufliche Ungleichheit von Frauen und Männern in Deutschland, Schweden und Frankreich. Ein Familienpolitischer Vergleich*. Leverkusen: Barbara Budrich.
Schreyögg, A. (2013). *Familie trotz Doppelkarriere*. Wiesbaden: Springer VS.
Welpe, I. (2014). *Wenn Gleiches unterschiedlich beurteilt wird. Die Wirkung unbewusster Vorurteile*. Speech entitled "Zukunft der Führung" ["Future of Management"] at the Munich Leadership Dialog held at the Bundeswehr University, 17 October 2014.

Author Biography

Gabriele Bollhöfer Dipl.-Psych., 10 years freelance counselor for personnel and organization development in co-operation with national and international consulting companies; today responsible for the strategic personnel development and coaching in a consulting company; furthermore freelance counselor and coach; publications and lectures on the practice and implementation of coaching.

Coaching Through Modern Media 19

Harald Geißler and Stella Kanatouri

Abstract

The growing need for coaching formats that combine an increased supplier or user flexibility with a favorable price-performance ratio, has made coaching increasingly open for the use of modern media in recent years. Modern media allow on the one hand, basic communication between coach and client independent of location and time, via telephone, video calling technologies and/or via electronically generated and transmitted texts. On the other hand, modern media enable the development of content-related problem-solving tools, which can also be used in face-to-face coaching settings. This chapter provides a comprehensive overview of the technical and conceptual features of the available approaches and offers.

19.1 Introduction

Coaching through modern media, in this case electronic media (Clutterbuck and Hussain 2010; Geißler 2008; Geißler and Metz 2012; Ghods and Boyce 2013) is an innovative alternative to face-to-face coaching with traditional media, i.e. not

H. Geißler (✉) · S. Kanatouri
Helmut-Schmidt-Universität, Holstenhofweg 85, 22043 Hamburg, Germany
e-mail: Harald.Geissler@hsu-hh.de
URL: http://www.virtuelles-coaching.com

S. Kanatouri
e-mail: kanatous@hsu-hh.de

A. Schreyögg and C. Schmidt-Lellek (eds.), *The Professionalization of Coaching*, DOI 10.1007/978-3-658-16805-6_19

virtualized media (Schreyögg 2012, p. 315). The driving force of this emerging innovation (Geißler 2013) is the growing demand for flexible and cost-effective coaching formats (Geißler and Stephan 2014).

Modern media can be used for coaching in two ways: The first option is the electronic transmission of communication material, which is created without electronic means ("naturally"). Examples include spoken language, facial expressions and gestures, the material objectivity of handwritten flipcharts and materials that are used for constellations. The electronic transmission of oral or visual cues in these communications media are enabled through telephone or video communication and enable coaching over distance in either a synchronous or asynchronous mode. The emerging new coaching formats will be referred to as e-coaching throughout this chapter. It should be noted however, that this term is currently not the prevalent term in use, but other terms such as online coaching (Koch 2012), virtual coaching (Clutterbuck and Hussain 2010) and distance coaching (Ghods 2009) are also used in literature.

The second option of using modern media is through electronically transmitted communications data, such as electronic texts, symbols, drawings, images, objects, figures or avatars in virtual worlds. This second possible use of modern media enables coaching over a distance, but it can also be used in face-to-face coaching. It is thus possible, and in some cases beneficial, not to use a constellation tool with physical objects but rather with virtual objects, where clients can slip into the figures and observe their environment through their own eyes (Grabow 2012). The use of modern media in face-to-face coaching will be referred to as blended coaching in this chapter.

19.2 Coaching and Clients' Practice as Constructionist Problem-Solving Media

From a constructionist perspective (Backhausen and Thommen 2003; König and Volmer 2002), the problems and challenges that coaching focuses on can be considered to be problem-generating conceptions, which clients have of themselves and the world and which they can work on and overcome through coaching. Thus, coaching is a problem-solving medium that takes into account that the ultimate medium for solving clients' problems is not coaching practice, but the clients' reality. This reality is created firstly by clients' relation to and involvement in multiple current and past social settings and secondly, through the continuous pressures to act or to make decisions and to take responsibility for these, even if they decide not to act or to make a decision (Fig. 19.1).

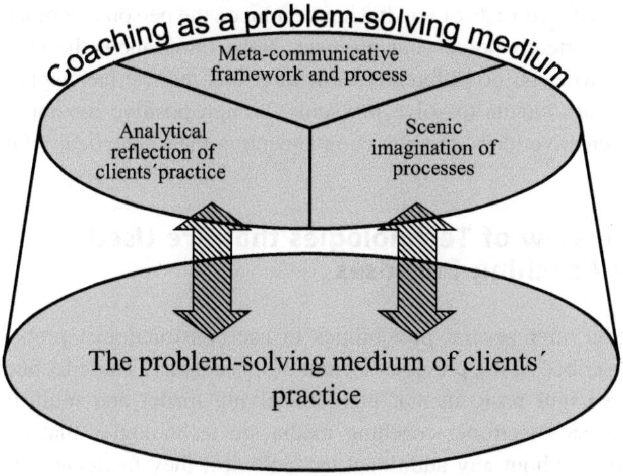

Fig. 19.1 The four constructionist problem-solving media of coaching

Coaching practice as a constructionist problem-solving medium (Geißler 2014, p. 148) is characterized by a working relationship that is agreed between coach and client. Through this coaching relationship, the structure and process of coaching is guided in a meta-communicative fashion.

From a constructionist perspective, this meta-communicative coaching framework and process can be considered a constructionist problem-solving medium. Empirical research (Geißler 2015) has demonstrated that the coaching process depends heavily upon this medium, as almost half of all communication exchanges between the coaching pair serve this function.

Two further constructionist problem-solving media are the analytical reflection of clients' practice and the scenic imagination of processes.

The idea of "analytical reflection of clients' practice" (Fig. 19.1) is that clients make their current, past and future reality relate to the objects they are attending to in a very particular way: firstly, they must adequately understand their current problem and secondly develop sustainable solutions to them. Through scenic imagination, clients retrospectively re-live experiences or sequences of experiences in their lives, much like a movie. The particular advantage of this "movie" is that it can be stopped at any time and it can run slower or faster. In addition, this movie generates imaginative events that never happened, but they can be imagined through the "miracle question" This question can be presented in different versions. Our favorite version is: "Dear client, please imagine that just now a miracle has taken place. The miracle consists of you having developed the personal competencies that allow you to perfectly solve your problem. Now, think about the next days and weeks: What will you do differently, now after this miracle has happened?" This approach enables clients to solve problems through positive memories, intuitive insights and creative ideas, thereby complementing their analytical reflection.

19.3 Overview of Technologies that Are Used for Coaching Purposes

Modern media offer several possibilities to use constructionist problem-solving media, as described in the previous section of this chapter. These technologies can be categorized into basic media, problem-solving media and multi-media platforms. The basic electronic coaching media are technologies that can be used independently, without any additional technologies; they facilitate the communication between coach and client, particularly with regard to the content and relational aspect. These include the telephone, video communication, synchronous text-based communication, asynchronous text-based communication, and virtual worlds with verbal or written communication.

These basic media can be used for implementing the three constructionist problem-solving media described previously. Yet the great flexibility of the basic media requires intensive guidance by the coach. Notably, basic media such as telephone, email, sms, Skype, Webex, Second Life, and TriCAT are not specifically designed for coaching purposes. In addition, there are basic media that are specifically designed for coaching, such as onlineCoaching.

On the other hand, electronic problem-solving tools are technologies that complement basic media and typically serve a particular coaching purpose, and thus refer to the "content aspect" of communication. These tools serve one specific coaching purpose and they focus either on analytical reflection, such as CoachMaster™ and Virtuelles Coaching, or they focus on the scenic imagination of positive resources, such as CoachSpaces and ProReal.

In addition, to the above mentioned tools, which are specific to coaching there are other problem-solving tools such as Youtube videos, SurveyMonkey for pre-/post session follow-ups, whiteboard tools such as IDroo and the drawing function in Google docs, or simulation tools such as Forio, that are not specific to coaching. It should be noted that such tools may require stronger guidance by the coach, in contrast to the previously mentioned coaching specific tools.

A further characteristic of coaching specific problem-solving tools is their emphasis on self-coaching. Some of these tools have been specifically developed for self-coaching, such as the eCoach System or the "Virtuelle Selbstcoaching" (Geißler et al. 2007). Self-coaching tools do not rely on a basic medium. They can be used for preparation and follow-up after face-to-face or distance coaching in combination to basic media. This supports two-way communication in coaching and particularly in the closing phase of a coaching program, in order to enhance sustainability (Geißler 2011). Under certain circumstances, for instance when dealing with less complex issues or with a target group with favourable conditions, it is possible to replace dialogical coaching fully through virtual self-coaching or to occasionally resort to dialogical formats (Geißler et al. 2007).

Multimedia platforms are electronic technologies that combine several problem-solving tools to enrich basic media, in some cases they integrate "management" functions such as documentation or appointment setting.

The technical features of electronic basic media, problem-solving tools and multi-media platforms can be distinguished based on ten dimensions:

- As described in the introduction of this chapter, modern media can be used for the electronic transmission and/or generation of communication data. Firstly, communication data can be generated through verbal or body language communication and it can be transmitted electronically, enabling coaching that is independent of location. Examples of this include telephone and video communication. Modern technologies may also be used to create electronic texts, objects, figures, avatars and virtual contexts.
- The three technologies, suitable for coaching purposes that were described in the beginning of this section serve three main functions: (1) they enable the communication between coach and client (2) they enable a goal-oriented structuring of the communication contents and (3) they enrich coaching through "management" functions such as scheduling sessions, sending reminders, documenting coaching outcomes and/or coaching processes, making notes and journal entries, facilitating personal correspondence or allowing the coach to create pre-determined coaching materials.
- A further criterion is complexity. This characteristic is rare in problem-solving tools, as they serve one main function, for instance making constellation work (Weber et al. 2013) (CoachingSpaces, LPScocoon® and ProReal), drawing or painting, or pre-prepared coaching questions (CoachMaster™ and Virtuelles Coaching). Multi-media platforms on the other hand, tend to have much higher complexity. Examples include Covocative, JournalEngine™, TheLearnScape, CoachingCloud®, CoachCampus, Life Coach Hub or CAI® Coaching World.
- Problem-solving tools have—as it will be discussed in the fourth section of this chapter—nine electronic and two non-electronic components.

- All electronic technologies that can be used for coaching may be distinguished between coaching-specific and non-specific to coaching media. Examples of non-specific media include telephone, Skype, Webex, email, instant messaging, Second Life, Youtube videos, Dropbox, IDroo, MS Word, Powerpoint, One-Note, Evernote or Google Docs. Coaching-specific technologies on the other hand, include onlineCoaching, CAI® Coaching World, CoachAccountable, CoachCampus, CoachingCloud®, CoachingSpaces, CoachMaster™, Covocative, Jigsawbox™, JournalEngine™, LPScocoon®, ProReal, The LearnScape or Virtuelles Coaching (VC) and other coaching applications such as, the Breeth App, Beyond Expectations App und The Coaching App™.
- Data can be transmitted through technological media in a synchronous or asynchronous mode. Media that enable synchronous communication are the telephone, video communication (Skype, Webex), instant messaging and avatar-based communication (ProReal, Second Life, TriCat, vComm AULA). Media that enable asynchronous communication are email and web applications such as The eCoach System, The Coaching Tools Company, Jigsawbox™, CoachAccountable, JounalEngine™, Covocative, Life Coach Hub, TheLearnScape, The Coaching App™, Beyond Expectations App, Breeth App. CoachMaster™, CoachCampus, Virtuelles Coaching (VC), LPScocoon®, CoachingCloud® and CAI® Coaching World offer the possibility of synchronous and asynchronous communication.
- Communication in coaching can take place through a variety of modalities, such as (1) auditory data, for instance verbal communication, music, sounds etc., (2) written data, (3) visual-static data, for instance photographs, symbols/icons, graphics etc., (4) visual-dynamic data, for instance silent films, drawing and painting synchronously or spatial positioning and movement of objects, figures, symbols/icons, or avatars (e.g. CAI® Coaching World, CoachingSpaces, LPScocoon®, Second Life® or TriCat), and (5) audio-visual data, for instance films/videos and video communication. These modalities can be combined with one another. For instance, the dynamic nature of avatars can be combined with written or verbal communication. An audio-visual communication medium is a rich medium, whereas a text-based communication medium is a lean medium.
- The contents of communication can be pre-determined or user-generated. Pre-determined text and/or visual contents can be found in The Coaching Tool Company, Virtual Coaching (VC), LPScocoon®, ProReal, The eCoach System, CoachingSpaces, Breeth App, The Coaching App™, Beyond Expectations App and Second Life®. This feature is apparent in text-based technologies. Examples include, Jigsawbox™, CoachAccountable, JournalEngine™,

CoachingCloud®, Life Coach Hub and CoachCampus. Examples of applications with both, pre-determined and user-generated possibilities are CoachMaster™, Covocative, CAI® Coaching World and TheLearnScape.

- A further criterion is the extent to which media are user-friendly, determined by the accessibility—for example, access to some technologies is blocked through firewalls—or the compatibility of the application, and through its complexity and ease of use.
- Finally, technologies can be distinguished based on the extent to which they can be customized. Two important aspects of this include, how precisely these technologies can be tailored to meet the clients' coaching needs and how flexible the client can use the application. The extent to which technologies can be customized may depend for example, on how many objects and figures are available to the client for virtual constellations and how much clients can change their size and their appearance.

19.4 The Basic Media of Coaching

Coaching consists of non-electronic and electronic basic media. The electronic basic media used in coaching have the same characteristics as the non-electronic basic media.

19.4.1 Non-electronic Communication

According to Watzlawick's systems communication theory communication exists of words and paralinguistic phenomena, such as voice tone, the speed of speech, pauses, smiles and sighs, posture, physical expression (body language) etc., within a specific context; "every type of behavior" (Watzlawick et al. 1969, p. 51). So there are four different communication data: linguistic, paralinguistic, non-verbal and contextual data, where the linguistic material is the most important.

Taking into account that every communication has a content and a relational aspect (Watzlawick et al. 1969, p. 53ff.), it becomes apparent that the linguistic part of communication has two components: a content and a relation component. Verbal propositions or expressions lie at the center of the first component (Geißler 2009, p. 97). These expressions can be combined with body based emotional expressions, for example eye contact, vocal training, facial expressions, gestures or posture that provide clues as to how the actor experiences emotions. In addition, vocal propositions can be enriched through deictic expressions, which can be expressed through words like: "this", "that" or "there", or through non-verbal body movements. Also for the communication elements that constitute the relationship there are numerous possibilities. On one hand these can be expressed through verbal illocutionary inquiry, reply, asking, contradicting etc. (Geißler 2009, p. 97) and on the other hand, through non-verbal body expressions that indicate the relationship of the actor to his co-actor, for instance whether to be welcoming or to be afraid of him.

It can be concluded that body and verbal language are highly significant for human communication and coaching processes. It is noteworthy that non-verbal communication has an archaic character, indeed it is much older than evolutionarily verbal communication. We shall leave this feature of non-verbal communication is positive or negative for coaching open for now.

19.4.2 Coaching Through Telephone, Audio-Visual and Text-Based Communication

As presented in Table 19.1, there are significant differences between non-electronically and electronically generated and transmitted basic media.

These differences have consequences for the intensity of using electronic basic media for coaching. Interestingly, video communication is not number one, but rather telephone is the preferred option, presumably due to its user-friendliness. Empirical studies have also demonstrated that telephone coaching is an equal alternative to face-to-face communication (Berry 2005; Ghods 2009) or it is even partially superior (McLaughlin 2013) and that the lack of visual cues in telephone coaching can be overcome if the coach is skilled (Charbonneau 2002; Frazee 2008). Ralf Borlinghaus pays particular emphasis to this last aspect with his ambitious thesis that with adequate training coaches can use all media in telephone coaching that are also used in face-to-face coaching. However, this requires modifications in the coaching process. The coach using the telephone for coaching can only make an appropriate picture of the client when the client has shared in detail with the coach which objects he is currently holding or where and how he is positioning them.

In contrast to telephone and video coaching, in asynchronous text-based coaching and synchronous text-chat coaching, communication data is not naturally, but rather electronically generated through the medium of the written word. The important areas for face-to-face communication, being paralinguistic, non-verbal and contextual communication data cannot be transmitted in this way. Video

Table 19.1 The various options of implementing communication data through video communication, telephone and text-based communication

		Face-to-face communication	Audio-visual communication	Telephone	Text-based communication
Linguistic communication data	Content based data	Propositions of verbal communication	Transmittable	Transmittable	Transmittable
	Relationship data	Illocutions of verbal communication	Transmittable	Transmittable	Transmittable
Paralinguistic communication data		The pitch of the voice, tone of voice, speed of speech, pauses, smiles, sighs etc.	Transmittable	Transmittable	Transmittable
Non-verbal communication data		Non-verbal bodily expressions, such as facial expressions, gestures, posture, body movement, and spatial positioning	Transmittable	Transmittable	Transmittable
		Physical appearance, clothing, environment	Transmittable	Transmittable	Transmittable
Contextual communication data		Visibility of the context through the observer's view	Only partially transmittable	Not transmittable	Not transmittable

Table 19.2 Advantages and disadvantages of asynchronous text-based coaching compared to face-to-face coaching (Clutterbuck 2010, p. 16 f.)

Asynchronous text-based coaching	
Advantages	Weaknesses
Need of the client can be met within a very short time	Clients need to be open for using electronic media and to have sufficient technical skills
Writing enables a reflection need	Face-to-face relationships facilitate the initial connection with the coach
Absolute independence of time and location	The coach cannot observe the client's behavior when he gives him tasks
High flexibility with regard to the coaching sessions' duration	Higher risk of misunderstandings
Better possibilities for building a network	Slower development of the relationship between coach and client
The lack of visual stimuli reduce the risk of stereotyping	The lack of stereotypes desensitizes the coach for potential diversity problems the client might have
The social barriers for the client to give feedback to the coach are minor	Lower commitment of the client
Introverted, shy and insecure individuals find it easier to express themselves	Risk of paying less attention to communication contents and appointments

communication also does not completely fulfill the same conditions as face-to-face communication, because the setting of the camera determines what the partner can see Table 19.2.

A particular characteristic of text-based communication is that it is connected with the need for careful reflection or self-reflection in coaching (Clutterbuck 2010; Koch 2012; Reindl et al. 2012). As Poepsel's (2011) empirical study demonstrated, asynchronous text-based coaching can increase the levels of goal attainment and clients' subjective satisfaction significantly.

On the other hand, it should be taken into account that text-based communication media is the furthest from face-to-face communication and that this, in connection to the effort to express one's thoughts and ideas in written form can create considerable acceptance barriers. Synchronous and asynchronous text-based coaching has therefore been used relatively little in practice.

19.4.3 Avatar Based Basic Communication in Coaching

An avatar is an electronically created presence that moves in an electronically generated world and can resemble a real person. The following possibilities are available (Bredl et al. 2012):

- Avatars can either be modeled as concrete people, distinguishing men from women and providing clues about the age, ethnic background, culture or social status based on skin colour, face and clothing (as for example in Second Life, CAI® Coaching World or TriCat), or they can be abstract figures with no face or clothing (as for example in ProReal).
- Coach and client can both enter a virtual world as avatars and act in space and time, or only the client enters as an avatar in a virtual world and acts in space and time.
- The virtual world is partly created, so that client and coach have for example, the possibility to create objects, symbols, human figures or animals and to position them in the virtual world (as for example in CAI® World and ProReal) or also to write captions. An alternative is that the virtual world is pre-determined, as for example when Second Life is used for coaching purposes.
- Coach and client can communicate with one another through auditory or written chat.

Depending on which of these alternatives are chosen, avatar-based communication may function as a basic medium and/or a problem solving tool. Thus, avatar-based communication can only be considered as a basic medium for coaching,

- when coach and client both appear as avatars
- and when they can identify with the avatars emotionally
  - based on the avatar's appearance,
  - and based on the virtual world's possibilities, allowing clients to move flexibly or position themselves, to hold a posture and to control their facial expressions and gestures.

Furthermore, it becomes apparent that avatar-based communication as a basic medium is a hybrid, as it connects electronically created and transmitted visual signals with telephone or with synchronous text-chat (Fig. 19.2).

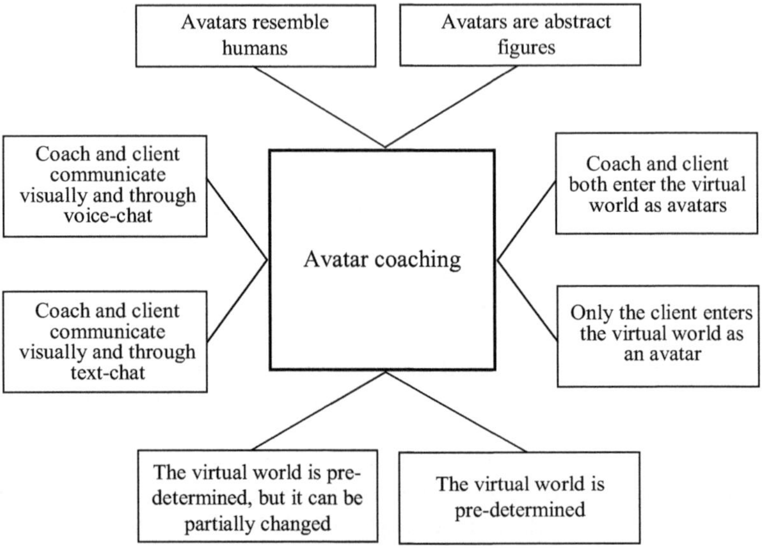

Fig. 19.2 The variety of avatar-based coaching forms

19.5 The Problem-Solving Tools that Support Basic Media in Coaching

As mentioned in prior, it is possible to distinguish seven different basic coaching media (face-to-face-coaching, video-coaching, telefon-coaching, synchronous and asynchronous text-based coaching, audio-based avatar coaching and text-based avatar-coaching). These basic coaching media can be combined with various coaching problem-solving tools that can be clustered in the following eleven groups (cf. Fig. 19.3):

1. Physical objects or materials that are not already pre-structured, such as modelling clay for representing visions or emotions (Schreyögg 2012, p. 315ff.).
2. Partially open and partially pre-structured physical objects or materials such as wooden figures or stones for constellation work (ibid.).
3. Electronically recorded and transmitted data about the clients' reality (Rock et al. 2011) through photographs or videos for instance.

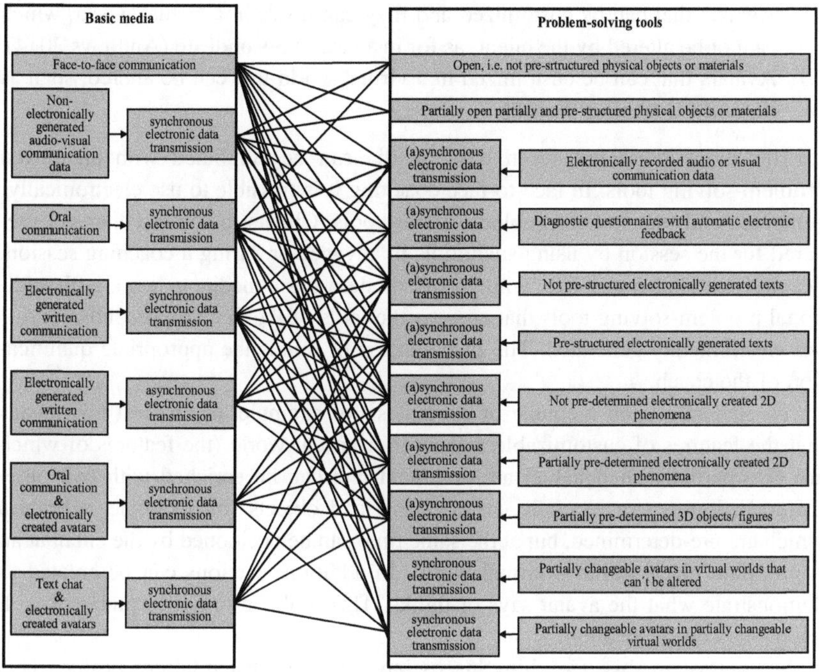

Fig. 19.3 Coaching basic media and problem-solving media

4. Electronically created multiple-choice diagnostic questionnaires, where the client can select an answer and receive an automatic feedback, such as for instance the platform Theratalk, which targets couples with relationship difficulties (Zezula and Beer 2012).
5. Electronically generated pre-prepared texts (Ribbers and Warringa 2015).
6. Pre-structured text data, such as coaching questions that are available in electronic form, for example those in CAI® Coaching World, Virtual Coaching (Geißler 2011, 2012) or CoachMaster™.
7. Electronically generated 2D phenomena, such as painting and drawing that are not pre-structured like in CAI® Coaching World.
8. Partially pre-determined electronic 2D phenomena, such as index cards, figures or symbols.
9. Partially pre-determined electronic 3D phenomena, such as those included in CoachingSpaces or LPScocoon (Grabow 2012).

10. Avatars that can be customized and they can move in a virtual world, which cannot be altered by the client, as for instance in SecondLife (Andrews 2014).
11. Avatars that can be customized in a virtual world that can be altered, such as in CAI® Coaching World.

The above presented seven basic media can be combined with all eleven problem-solving tools. In face-to-face coaching it is possible to use electronically-generated and transmitted problem-solving tools. Clients therefore either get prepared for the session by using such tools in advance or during a coaching session. Secondly, it is also possible, while using modern basic media, to work with additional problem-solving tools that are—as the tools of the first and second group—not electronically-generated. The precondition of this is the appropriate qualification of the coach.

To elaborate upon a couple of examples: for example, in ProReal this means that the features of customizable avatars in a virtual world (the features of which are also partially changeable) are dominant and can be enriched with two other features: figures (for example, an elephant) and objects (for example, a bridge) which are pre-determined, but at the same time can be positioned by the client at an appropriate place within a virtual world. In addition, captions can be created to demonstrate what the avatar says or thinks. This tool can only be combined with telephone communication.

In contrast to this, CoachingSpaces have a somewhat different profile. This includes pre-structured 3D objects or figures. Similar to ProReal, texts can be created to name the objects or figures, and to demonstrate what they say or think. In contrast to ProReal however, this tool can be combined with telephone, but also with video communication.

A different tool, Virtual Coaching (VC), can only be combined with telephone communciation. Its main feature is the pre-set electronically written coaching questions, which clients answer in written (Geißler 2012) form.

19.6 Outlook

Coaching through modern media—e-coaching and blended coaching—is in an early phase of development. Empirical investigations within the realm of coaching through modern media are also at an early phase, as they focus mainly on telephone coaching and less on text-based coaching communication. Although there are some exceptions, such as the studies by Geißler et al. (2012, 2013, 2014), empirical research has focused only on distance coaching, without additional support through problem-solving tools.

Taking into account state-of-the-art coaching through modern media and with a view towards a positive further development of coaching practice, we believe that it would be useful to carry out a systematic comparison of the potential and limitations of telephone, audio-visual, synchronous and asynchronous text-based, avatar-based and face-to-face coaching communication media and the various options to support coaching through problem-solving tools. When carrying out such comparisons, four aspects deserve attention. First, thoroughly examining the coach's and the client's situations, analyzing the characteristics of the selected coaching technology or technologies and exploring their effectiveness in-depth and examining the implications for creating a theoretical basis. We believe that such investigations offer important insights into the factors affecting the effectiveness or the perceived value of face-to-face coaching, e-coaching, and blended coaching.

Second, clients' affinity to technology, third the qualifications and attitudes of the coach in relation to the special characteristics of coaching by modern media, and fourth, the specific clients' coaching needs.

On the basis of such differentiated access, it appears helpful to systematically explore how various formats, such as telephone, video and avatar coaching, as well as synchronous and asynchronous text-based coaching differ in their effectiveness from one another. Such an exploration could be based on two hypotheses: the first suggests that communication partners in face-to-face settings—also because of their intensely stimulated projections—use much of their concentration and energy on the "here and now", particularly in regards to their emotional relationship management, and therefore less on content based work in relation to their actual coaching issues. Correspondingly it would have to be clarified, if there are, in e-coaching and blended coaching, particular approaches that offer a more productive concentration and energy management of the client. A first hint in regard to this hypothesis offers the study of Chen et al. (2013) since it shows that mutual eye-contact has negative impacts when one tries to change the opinion of a communication partner. Further tests and developments of this hypothesis could support the estimation of Wastian (2014) that the so far discussed "success factors" would have to be expanded by the factor of writing down relevant results by the client during either before or during coaching sessions, as has been indicated by certain e-coaching approaches, such as the Virtual Coaching (VC) (Geißler 2012).

Our second hypothesis refers to our experience that modern problem solving media in which 3D figures or avatars are created electronically facilitate an emotional immersion of the client in this virtual world, and furthermore offer an impressive variety of possibilities for changing the client's perspective and activities. In order to explore this potential fully, we first of all need didactic models guiding us on how to use those modern problem solving media effectively.

Finally, it would be useful to further clarify whether the various e-coaching and blended coaching formats are conceptually neutral or whether some formats emphasize or distance themselves from particular coaching concepts or schools of thought. We presume for example, that Virtual Coaching (VC) is based on solution-oriented theoretical models (Grant 2006) and that ProReal is more focused on a psychoanalytical approach to coaching (Diamond 2013).

We believe that future research focusing on these issues would contribute to filling in the gaps in knowledge and experience, and it would overcome the current scepticism of coaching through modern media, which our previous research findings demonstrates still exists (Geißler et al. 2013, p. 134 ff., 2014).

We predict an increasing need for innovative, highly effective and flexible coaching formats that enable a favorable cost-benefit ratio and which are suitable for creating target groups, for instance through avatar communication, that have been until now neglected due to the perceived proximity to psychotherapy (Geißler and Stephan 2014).

References

Backhausen, W., & Thommen, J.-P. (2003). *Coaching*. Wiesbaden: Gabler.

Berry, M. R. (2005). *A comparison of face-to-face and distance coaching practices: The role of the working alliance in problem resolution*. Unpublished doctoral dissertation, Georgia State University, Atlanta, Georgia.

Borlinghaus, R. (Ed.) (no year). *Coaching 2.0*. Kreuzlingen: Bora Text.

Bredl, K., Bräutigum, B., & Herz, D. (2012). Avatarbasierte beratung und coaching in 3D. In H. Geißler & M. Metz (Eds.), *E-Coaching und online-beratung* (pp. 121–136). Wiesbaden: Springer.

Charbonneau, A. M. (2002). *Participant self-perception about the cause of behavior change from a program of executive coaching*. Unpublished doctoral dissertation, Alliant International University, Los Angeles, CA.

Chen, F. S., Minson, J. A., Schöne, M., & Heinrichs, M. (2013). In the eye of the beholder: Eye contact increases resistance to persuasion. *Psychological Science, 24*(11), 2254–2261.

Clutterbuck, D. (2010). Welcome to the World of Virtual Coaching and Mentoring. In D. Clutterbuck & Z. Hussain (Eds.), *Virtual coach, virtual mentor* (pp. 31–52). Charlotte: Information Age Publishing.

Clutterbuck, D., & Hussain, Z. (Eds.). (2010). *Virtual coach, virtual mentor*. Charlotte: Information Age Publishing.

Diamond, M. A. (2013). Psychodynamic approach. In J. Passmore, D. B., Peterson & T. Freire (Eds.), *The Wiley-Blackwell Handbook of Psychology of Coaching and Mentoring* (S. 365–384). Oxford: Wiley-Blackwell.

Frazee, V. R. (2008). *E-coaching in organizations. A study of features, practices, and determinants of use.* Unpublished doctoral dissertation, San Diego University, USA.

Geißler, H. (2008). *E-Coaching—eine konzeptionelle Grundlegung.* Baltmannsweiler: Schneider Hohengehren.

Geißler, H. (2009). Die inhaltsanalytische „Vermessung" von Coaching. In B. Birgmeier (Ed.), *Coachingwissen* (pp. 93–125). Wiesbaden: VS Verlag.

Geißler, H. (2011). Coaching meets Training – zur Lösung des Transferproblems durch „Virtuelles Transfercoaching (VTC)". In R. Wegener, A. Fritze, & M. Loebbert (Eds.), *Coaching entwickeln* (pp. 123–134). Wiesbaden: Springer VS.

Geißler, H. (2012). Virtuelles Coaching—programmgeleitetes Telefoncoaching mit Internet-Support. In H. Geißler & M. Metz (Eds.), *E-Coaching und Online-Beratung* (pp. 137–164). Wiesbaden: Springer.

Geißler, H. (2013). Produktdiversifizierung und Erschließung neuer Marktsegmente. In R Wegener, A. Fritze & M. Loebbert (Hrsg.), *Coaching-Praxisfelder. Forschung und Praxis im Dialog* (Online-Teil, S. 260–272). Wiesbaden: Springer VS; www.springer.com.

Geißler, H. (2014). Traditionelle und moderne Medien im Coaching. In R. Wegener, M. Loebbert, & A. Fritze (Eds.), *Coaching-Praxisfelder* (pp. 135–158). Wiesbaden: Springer VS.

Geißler, H. (2015). *Die Grammatik des Coachens - eine entscheidungstheoretisch-empirische Rekonstruktion.* (in prep.).

Geißler, H., Hasenbein, M., & Wegener, R. (2013). E-Coaching: Prozess- und Ergebnisevaluation des Virtuellen Zielerreichungscoachings. *OSC, 20*(2), 125–142.

Geißler, H., Hasenbein, M., Kanatouri, S., & Wegener, R. (2014). E-coaching: Concept and empirical findings of a virtual coaching programme. *International Journal for Evidence Based Coaching and Mentoring, 12*(2), 165–187.

Geißler, H., Helm, M., & Nolze, A. (2007). Virtuelles Selbstcoaching – Konzept und erste Erfahrungen. *OSC, 14*(1), 81–93.

Geißler, H., Kurzmann, Ch., & Metz, M. (2012). Coaching und Beratung mit und ohne moderne Meiden—ein empirischer Vergleich. In H. Geißler & M. Metz (Eds.), *E-Coaching und Online-Beratung* (pp. 359–380). Wiesbaden: Springer VS.

Geißler, H., & Metz, M. (Eds.). (2012). *E-Coaching und Online-Beratung.* Wiesbaden: Springer VS.

Geißler, H., & Stephan, M. (2014). Das medientechnische Innovationsdefizit von Coaching und eine Möglichkeit, es zu überwinden. In S. M. Weber, M. Göhlich, A. Schröer, & J. Schwarz (Eds.), *Organisation und das Neue* (pp. 351–361). Wiesbaden: Springer VS.

Ghods, N. (2009). *Distance coaching: The relationship between coach-client relationship, client satisfaction, and coaching outcomes.* Unpublished doctoral dissertation, San Diego University, USA.

Ghods, N., & Boyce, C. (2013). Virtual Coaching and Mentoring. In J. Passmore, D. B. Peterson, & T. Freire (Eds.), *The Wiley-Blackwell handbook of psychology of coaching and mentoring* (pp. 501–523). Oxford: Wiley-Blackwell.

Grabow, C. (2012). Virtuelle Strategie-Simulation im Telefoncoaching mit LPScocoon. In H. Geißler & M. Metz (Eds.), *E-Coaching und Online-Beratung* (pp. 103–120). Wiesbaden: Springer VS.
Grant, A. M. (2006). An integrated goal-focused approach to executive coaching. In R. D. Stober & A. M. Grant (Eds.), *Evidence Based Coaching* (pp. 153–192). Hoboken: Wiley.
Koch, B. (2012). 'onlineCoaching': ein geschriebener Dialog unabhängig von Zeit und Raum. In H. Geißler & M. Metz (Eds.), *E-Coaching und Online-Beratung* (pp. 87–102). Wiesbaden: Springer VS.
König, E., & Volmer, G. (2002). *Systemisches Coaching*. Weinheim, Basel: Beltz.
McLaughlin, M. (2013). Less is more: The executive coach's experience of working on the telephone. *International Journal of Evidence Based Coaching and Mentoring, 7,* 1–13.
Poepsel, M. (2011). *The impact of an online evidence-based coaching program on goal striving, subjective well-being, and level of hope*. Doctoral dissertation, Capella University.
Reindl, R., Hergenreider, M., & Hünniger, J. (2012). Schriftlichkeit in virtuellen Beratungssettings. In H. Geißler & M. Metz (Eds.), *E-Coaching und Online-Beratung* (pp. 339–357). Wiesbaden: Springer VS.
Rock, L. M., Zigmond, P. N., Gregg, M., & Gable, A. R. (2011). The power of virtual coaching. *Educational Leadership., 69*(2), 42–48.
Schreyögg, A. (2012). *Coaching*. Eine Einführung für Praxis und Ausbildung (7., überarb. u. erw. Aufl.). Frankfurt/M.: Campus.
Wastian, M., (2014). Wirkfaktoren auch im E-Coaching nutzen: Was passiert in der Blackbox des virtuellen Coaching-Prozesses? In H. Geißler & R. Wegener (Hrsg.), *Coachingprozesse bewerten. Eine erste Bilanz*. Wiesbaden: Springer VS.
Watzlawick, P., Beavin, J. H., & Jackson, D. D. (1969). *Menschliche Kommunikation*. Stuttgart, Wien: Huber.
Weber, G., Schmidt, G., & Simon, F. B. (2013). *Aufstellungsarbeit revisited ... nach Hellinger?*. Hweidewlberg: Carl-Auer.
Zezula, P., & Beer, R. (2012). Theratalk: Ein Online-Portal für Paar und Partnerschaft. In H. Geißler & M. Metz (Eds.), *E-Coaching und Online-Beratung* (pp. 87–102). Wiesbaden: Springer VS.

Websites

Breeth App: https://play.google.com/store/apps/details?id=com.thegoodcoach
Beyond Expectations App: https://play.google.com/store/apps/details?id=com.smallpackageapps.beyondexpectations&hl=en
CAI® Coaching World: www.cai-world.com
CoachAccountable: http://www.coachaccountable.com
CoachingCloud®: www.coachingcloud.com
CoachingSpaces: http://coachingspaces.com
CoachMaster™: https://coachmaster.co.uk/
Covocative: www.covocative.com

Das Online Coaching: http://das-onlinecoaching.com
CoachCampus: https://www.coachcampus.nl/
Jigsawbox™: http://www.jigsawbox.com
JournalEngine™: http://www.journalengine.com/
Life Coach Hub: https://www.lifecoachhub.com
LPSCocoon®: http://www.lpscocoon.de/
ProReal: http://www.proreal.co.uk/
SecondLife®: http://secondlife.com/
The Coaching App™: http://www.thecoachingapp.com/
The LearnScape:http://thelearnscape.com/
TriCat: http://www.tricat.net/
vComm AULA: http://www.vcomm.ch/
Virtual Coaching: https://www.virtual-coaching.net/

Author Biographies

Prof. Dr. Harald Geißler professor of pedagogy specializing in occupational pedagogy and in-company education and training at the Helmut-Schmidt University of Hamburg, where he heads the Competence Center Coaching at the Management Development Center, focusing on coaching evaluations and virtual coaching. Research focus: Organizational learning and coaching.

Stella Kanatouri research fellow at the Helmut-Schmidt University/Bundeswehr University in Hamburg (institute for general pedagogy, specializes in occupational pedagogy and in-company education and training), field of focus: coaching with modern media.

MIX
Papier aus verantwortungsvollen Quellen
Paper from responsible sources
FSC® C105338
www.fsc.org

If you have any concerns about our products,
you can contact us on
ProductSafety@springernature.com

In case Publisher is established outside the EU,
the EU authorized representative is:
Springer Nature Customer Service Center GmbH
Europaplatz 3, 69115 Heidelberg, Germany

Printed by Libri Plureos GmbH
in Hamburg, Germany